STUDIES IN HISTORY, ECONOMICS AND PUBLIC LAW

Edited by the

FACULTY OF POLITICAL SCIENCE
OF COLUMBIA UNIVERSITY

NUMBER 422

THE CAPE-TO-CAIRO DREAM

A STUDY IN BRITISH IMPERIALISM

BY

LOIS A. C. RAPHAEL

CECIL JOHN RHODES
Drawing by the Duchess of Rutland, reproduced with the
permission of The Rhodes Trustees

THE CAPE-TO-CAIRO DREAM

A STUDY IN BRITISH IMPERIALISM

BY

LOIS A. C. RAPHAEL

OCTAGON BOOKS

A DIVISION OF FARRAR, STRAUS AND GIROUX

New York   1973

Reprinted 1973
by special arrangement with Columbia University Press

OCTAGON BOOKS
A Division of Farrar, Straus & Giroux, Inc.
19 Union Square West
New York, N. Y. 10003

Library of Congress Cataloging in Publication Data

Raphael, Lois Alward (Childs) 1900-
    The Cape-to-Cairo dream.

    Reprint of the ed. published by Columbia University Press, New York, which was issued as no. 422 of Studies in history, economics, and public law.

    Originally presented as the author's thesis, Columbia University.

    Bibliography: p.
    1. Great Britain—Colonies—Africa.   2. Railroads—Africa.
    3. British in Africa.   4. Great Britain—Foreign relations—
    1837-1901.   I. Title.   II. Series: Columbia studies in the social sciences, no. 422.

DT32.R3   1973   325'.342'096   73-9550
ISBN 0-374-96714-8

Manufactured by Braun-Brumfield, Inc.
Ann Arbor, Michigan

Printed in the United States of America

To

THE MEMORY OF

PARKER THOMAS MOON

"What was attempted by Alexander, Cambyses, and Napoleon we practical people are going to finish."

CECIL RHODES.

PREFACE

In 1815, British interest in Africa aside from some settlements on the West Coast, centered around Cape Colony in the south and Egypt in the north. Between these two extremes stretched some four thousand six hundred miles of country unoccupied and largely unexplored by white men. By 1900, however, except for a block of German territory between the southern end of Lake Tanganyika and the first parallel of south latitude, British influence was paramount from Cape Town to Alexandria.

An essential feature of this expansion through the Dark Continent was the development of lines of communication. Distances in Africa are enormous. Roads, railways and the telegraph are of primary importance in opening up the country to commerce, trade and civilization. It is not surprising, therefore, that in the last quarter of the nineteenth century, people in England and in Africa began to talk about a transcontinental telegraph and a Cape-to-Cairo railway. Furthermore, clustering about the plans for the telegraph and the railway, there grew up more ambitious schemes. The promoters saw trading centers along the route developing into colonies and, finally, the colonies merging into a British empire from the Cape to Cairo.

It is the purpose of this study not only to trace the development of transcontinental telegraph and railway schemes but also the influence of the Cape-to-Cairo idea upon British expansion in Africa.

My attention has focussed upon the great diplomatic struggles over the partition of Africa in the last quarter of the nineteenth century. I have, however, attempted in the epilogue to round out the story and to sketch in lightly the

9

history of recent developments along the Cape-to-Cairo route.

The political map of Africa changed rapidly during the last quarter of the nineteenth century. The history of the period is complicated and crowded with events. In fact, so much was compressed into this short span of years and so much was happening simultaneously, that I have felt it would be confusing to follow a strictly chronological order. I have, therefore, treated the subject topically and geographically.

The history of British expansion along the Cape-to-Cairo route is so recent that many aspects of the story are controversial. It is still difficult to write an impartial and dispassionate history of that expansion. At this time, the most that can be done is to break paths for future work. Since I was primarily interested in British expansion, I have turned largely to British sources for my material and have approached the subject from that angle. My readers may not agree with my conclusions. I only hope that my errors in judgment and my shortcomings in respect of information may be of some value in provoking others to rectify and round out my narrative.

There is now an abundance of material available on British expansion in Africa and international rivalry along the Cape-to-Cairo route. The problem of selection is becoming increasingly difficult. Nevertheless, although the material is so abundant, there are still important gaps some of which may be filled eventually by the further opening up of the archives in England, Italy, France and Germany. Furthermore, there is great need for more extensive and impartial biographies about outstanding leaders in the political and financial world of the day.

For the history of the early development of transcontinental railway and telegraph projects, I have turned chiefly to unpublished Colonial Dispatches kept in the Public Record

Office in London, to the published records of the Cape Legislature and to the files of South African newspapers in the British Museum. I have also found valuable pamphlet material in the libraries of the Royal Colonial Institute and the Royal Geographical Society.

The history of international rivalry along the Cape-to-Cairo route I have based upon *Die Grosse Politik,* the French Foreign Office *Documents Diplomatiques,* popularly styled " Yellow Books " and the collections of British documents contained in *Parliamentary Sessional Papers* and *British Documents on the Origins of the World War.*

A considerable number of memoirs and biographies threw light on various aspects of my subject. Of these, I found Dr. Leo Weinthal's four volume compilation on *The Story of the Cape to Cairo Railway and River Route, 1887-1922,* especially valuable because it contains short sketches by men who were actually engaged in the work of building the Cape-to-Cairo line. I have used Hansard's *Parliamentary Debates,* British newspapers and periodicals in an attempt to evaluate the influence of the Cape-to-Cairo idea upon public opinion.

I am grateful for the kind assistance and cooperation of friends both in England and America and for the excellent facilities afforded me for study in the Public Record Office, the British Museum, the Royal Colonial Institute, the Royal Geographical Society, the British Museum and the Institute of Historical Research in London and in the Columbia University Library, the New York Public Library and the Library of Congress in America. Everywhere I have met with unfailing courtesy and helpfulness.

While in London, I was especially fortunate in having the advice and wise guidance of Professor Arthur Percival Newton, then Professor of Imperial History at Kings College and now Rhodes Professor of Imperial History at the University of London. I am greatly indebted to him for his counsel at the time and for his continued interest in my work.

I am indebted to Dr. F. G. Spurdle, History Master of Consett Secondary School, Durham for his painstaking and scholarly research on the subject of the Overland Telegraph.

Dr. R. I. Lovell of Harvard University kindly let me read his unpublished doctoral thesis, *The Anglo-German Estrangement, 1894-1896.*

To Professor Robert Livingston Schuyler, Professor of British Imperial History at Columbia University, I owe my first interest in British Imperialism. I am particularly pleased, therefore, that he has read my manuscript and offered many helpful suggestions.

Professor Barnouw, Queen Wilhelmina Professor of the Language and Literature of the Netherlands at Columbia University has also read the manuscript and I am grateful for his much needed and helpful criticisms.

Professor Parker Thomas Moon's book *Imperialism and World Politics* first aroused my interest in Cecil Rhodes and the Cape-to-Cairo idea. It provoked questions in my mind which led me on a search for answers into the history of British expansion in Africa. Professor Moon not only stimulated my interest in this subject but he has followed my work throughout. I owe much to his judicious guidance, and his comprehensive and masterly grasp of my subject. His searching comments constantly challenged me to greater efforts. I find it difficult to express my appreciation adequately for his helpfulness. For his sake, I wish this were a better book.

I owe much to the patience and helpful interest of my husband. Without his encouragement and continued cooperation, this book would never have been finished.

Lois A. C. Raphael

Washington, D. C.
June, 1936.

TABLE OF CONTENTS

13

CHAPTER VIII
Painting Central Africa Red

CHAPTER IX
The Raid and Its Consequences

CHAPTER X
The Final Struggle For South Africa

CHAPTER XI
Into the Heart of the Dark Continent

CHAPTER XVI

The Surrender of the Cape-to-Cairo Corridor

CHAPTER XVII

Plots Laid In Ethiopia

CHAPTER XVIII

The Reconquest of the Sudan

CHAPTER XIX

The Fashoda Crisis

CHAPTER XX

THE EPILOGUE

MAPS

All the maps were drafted by Mr. F. I. Burnham of Georgetown University. I am grateful for his assistance and careful work.

The map on " European Expansion in Africa, 1820 to 1936 " was drawn on a eumorphic equal area projection with the kind permission of Mr. S. W. Boggs of the State Department, Washington, D. C.

ILLUSTRATIONS

A drawing by the Duchess of Rutland, reproduced with the kind permission of the Rhodes Trustees, Rhodes House, Oxford, England.

Photograph reproduced with the kind permission of the Legation of the Union of South Africa, Washington, D. C.

Photograph reproduced with the kind permission of the South African Railways and Harbours Administration.

Photograph reproduced from Coates, F. C., *Life of Lord Rosebery*, vol. ii, with the kind permission of E. P. Dutton & Co., Inc., New York.

Photograph reproduced from Weinthal, Leo, *The Story of the Cape to Cairo Railway and River Route, 1887-1922*, vol. i, with the kind permission of the Pioneer Publishing Company, Ltd., London.

CHAPTER I

Paths Into Africa

In the brief caption, " from the Cape to Cairo," we find an epitome of an important chapter in the history of British expansion in Africa and in the story of international rivalry on the Dark Continent. This graphic little phrase, probably coined by Sir Edwin Arnold,[1] had a peculiar fascination for British empire builders of the last quarter of the nineteenth century. British interests were then already strongly entrenched in the south and north: in Cape Colony and Egypt. It was, therefore, natural that they should look with longing eyes at the tempting territory which lay between these two extremes. The Cape-to-Cairo idea in turn exercised a potent influence also in shaping the policies of the other nations engaged in the scramble for Africa. Indeed, the fear that a vast British empire might someday span the continent from the south to the north played a significant rôle in stimulating the activity and in arousing the watchfulness of rival colonizing Powers.

The long strip between Cape Colony and Egypt, offered great attractions to a people who felt the need for new colonies and markets overseas. From the mountains which rise above the Cape of Good Hope to the great lake district in the heart of Africa, there stretches a high tableland which is healthy and suitable for white settlement. It is, furthermore, rich in minerals and, except for certain barren and arid stretches in Bechuanaland, possesses fertile soil. This tableland, the backbone of Africa, terminates around a chain of great lakes. The lake district, likewise, possesses fertile soil and high regions suitable for white settlement. Its chief importance, however, lies in its strategic position. The lakes feed all the great water systems of Africa. The Congo and White Nile rivers rise here, while from Lake Nyasa issues the Shire, an important tributary to the Zambezi river. So important are the Nile, the Congo and the Zambezi for the life and commerce of the rest of Africa that it is hardly an exaggeration to say that whoever secured this lake district held the key to the Dark Continent.[2]

Beyond the lake region lies the Sudan, the hinterland of Egypt. Through the Sudan, flows the Nile River which feeds, waters and gives life to Egypt. In brief, whatever nation secured the long strip from the Cape to Cairo, possessed the best part of Africa and a large share of the regions which are adapted to permanent settlement by the white race.

It would be going too far to say that Great Britain followed a consistent Cape-to-Cairo policy and that the British people set out upon any preconceived and comprehensive plan to make this desirable strip their own. It is true, however, that some British statesmen and politicians talked about building a line of communication from the south to the north of Africa and that this idea played a part in shaping policies. The magic phrase, " from the Cape to Cairo ", caught and inflamed the imagination. It inspired articles in the press and it added considerable heat to the debates in Parliament. It was undoubtedly a factor to be considered in the history of British penetration into the interior.

The Cape-to-Cairo dream took concrete form for most Britishers in plans to span the continent by rail and telegraph. Englishmen imagined a line of communication stretching some five thousand miles from the south to the north of Africa. They saw this line tapping the gold and diamond fields of the south and then running north through a land of promise, the possibilities of which were just unfolding. Finally, they saw it binding together firmly British interests in both the south and north.

To the bolder imperial dreamers, this line would be colored a good British red on the map, i. e., it would be an all-British route running entirely through British territory.[3] Some visionaries even pictured an all-British Africa with the Cape-to-Cairo railway as the ridgepole. They felt that, with British interests secured on the Niger, Zambezi and the Nile and along the Cape-to-Cairo route, an all-British Africa was the logical outcome. From these regions, English influence would gradually pervade the whole continent.[4]

This dream of an all-British line of communication from the Cape to Cairo was shattered by the Anglo-German treaty of 1890 which made German East Africa conterminus with the Belgian Congo and completely blocked the British path to the north. The story of that agreement will be taken up in a later chapter. It is sufficient, here, to note how firmly rooted the Cape-to-Cairo idea had become by 1890 in British minds and how tenaciously the English people clung to their dream. There was, in fact, serious opposition to the Anglo-German treaty from a group of Cape-to-Cairo enthusiasts.[5] Although the treaty was adopted in spite of this opposition, the idea of a through line of communications was so strong that in 1894 one great English statesman tried to repair the damage done by leasing a railway strip through the Congo.[6]

Although this attempt was unsuccessful and the road to the north remained closed, the Cape-to-Cairo vision still persisted in a modified form. Now its exponents talked of a south-to-north railway, built by British capital and under British control, running through country which, although not entirely British, was for the most part under the paramount influence of Britain. "It was absurd", said one optimist, "to suppose that a few miles of territory far from the coast, at the farthest end of the German possessions could stand in the way of a great work of civilization." [7]   It was still possible to establish a British hegemony from the Cape-to-Cairo.   Even if a strictly all-red route were impossible of attainment, still a railway opening up the heart of Africa to trade and commerce would benefit English markets, would be a powerful weapon in fighting the slave trade and would be an entering wedge for British influence.

These Cape-to-Cairo dreams are closely bound with both economic needs and imperial aspirations.   It is this relationship between gigantic economic undertakings and the shaping of imperial policies which makes the story of the influence of Cape-to-Cairo ideas on British expansion such a significant chapter in the history of British imperialism.

Cape-to-Cairo projects grew and flourished best in the fertile imperial soil of the last quarter of the nineteenth century, because they required the support of both British capitalists and British political leaders.   In the period from 1886 to 1900, British commercial magnates were looking eagerly for markets overseas and English statesmen were busy pegging out claims for the future in the undeveloped regions of the world.   To be sure, the ground was broken and prepared for imperial undertakings before this period but not until the eighties and nineties were conditions really favorable for the development of extensive imperial enterprises in Africa.   Indeed, schemes for building a chain of communication from the south to the north of the Dark Continent could only mature at a time when the British people were fully awake to the potentialities of Africa.

Prior to 1886, British attention was focussed primarily on domestic and European affairs rather than on oversea interests.   As the leader in the new machine age, Great Britain was fully a generation ahead of the United States and Western Europe in industrial development and the English people had in their possession far greater productive resources and capital for investment than the other countries.[8] Great Britain's markets, whether at home, in the British colonies, in America or in Europe were still adequate for the absorption of British manufactures. The English people had not yet felt the pressure of competition with other countries for raw materials. They could afford for a while to be complacent about increasing overseas responsibilities and there was a general feeling that the British government should decrease rather than increase its imperial burdens.[9]

Partly because of this trend of the times, the English people were more or less indifferent before 1850 to Africa as a field for imperial enterprise. To be sure, Great Britain had already scattered possessions and circles of influence in the Dark Continent: at Cape Town, on the Gold Coast, at Zanzibar and elsewhere,[10] but few men dreamed as yet of building up a vast British empire in Africa. The Dark Continent had scarcely any intrinsic value for the "Little Englanders" of the day.[11] Indeed, from 1795 when the British occupied Cape Town to 1884 when a new era of imperialism set in, "the Little Englanders" regarded Africa as "the Dark Continent" and their possessions there more as burdens than assets.

Nevertheless, barren as this period is in aspirations to embark on large-scale imperial adventures in Africa, still it cannot be wholly neglected in a complete story of the growth of Cape-to-Cairo dreams and projects. A survey of this era is important because, during this time, British interests spread gradually here and there and the foundations were laid upon which a new generation of empire builders could construct more ambitious schemes. In fact, with little thought of establishing an African empire, the British entered the Southern Continent and circles of British influence spread along the south to north route. These British circles were destined later to become important links in the Cape-to-Cairo chain.

Although the English, themselves, were unaware of the fact that they were forging the links of this great transcontinental chain, their movements were watched with some apprehension by outsiders. As early as 1798, Dr. Lacerda, a Brazilian explorer and scientist, warned the Portuguese Minister of State that " the new possessors of Table Bay require watching or our want of energy will enable them to extend themselves northward." Dr. Lacerda did not stop with this warning; he took active measures to prevent the northward march of the British. On July 3, 1798, he set forth upon an ill-fated journey up the Zambezi with the avowed objects of securing communications from the east to the west coast of Africa and of placing an obstacle in the path of British progress to the north.[12]

Dr. Lacerda's warning is significant. He prophetically foresaw the danger to Portuguese imperial ambitions in the momentous power of expansion of the nation which had just secured a foothold at Cape Town. He also accurately predicted the direction in which British influence was to spread from South Africa. In short, Lacerda's fears and premonitions foreshadowed the Cape-to-Cairo movement. It is significant that a foreigner should be the one to foresee this great expansion to the north and to realize that some day the hinterland between the Portuguese possessions of Mozambique and Angola was bound to become a bone of contention between the two nations. This is perhaps the first appearance of the Cape-to-Cairo bogey who was later on to haunt the minds and influence the policies of rival European Powers in Africa. It is noticeable that throughout the whole history of British expansion in Africa outsiders were inclined to attribute a conscious consistency of imperialistic policy which indeed might not exist in the minds of the British themselves.

In 1798, however, Lacerda's fears seemed groundless. The British in fact, occupied Table Bay from 1795 to 1802 in the name of the Prince of Orange.[13]   By the treaty of Amiens in 1802, they handed the settlement back to Holland. It was not until 1806, that the English came into final possession.   Any thought that this outpost of Cape Town would become the terminus of a great transcontinental line of communications probably never entered the heads of the practical Englishmen who occupied the station.   The British simply wanted a harbor, half-way on the route to India, where their ships could repair for fresh provisions.   In order, however, to supply the seamen with fresh fruits and vegetables and other necessities, farms were scattered here and there back of Cape Town and a small colony struggled into existence.[14]

Without any encouragement from the Home Government, the Cape colonists pushed their way gradually into the interior until the colony extended as far as the Orange River. Dutch farmers trekked even farther north and founded the semi-independent Orange Free State.[15] In Cape Colony, itself, a little railway was pushing north, back of Cape Town; first, to tap the corn and wine districts around Stellenbosch and then to reach the diamond fields at Kimberley.   This railway was sometimes called "the main trunk line to the North", but the local politicians who wrangled in the Cape Parliament over its construction never dreamed that they were sanctioning the building of the first southern section of the Cape-to-Cairo line.[16]

While the colonists, on their own initiative, were slowly spreading British influence northwards, the Home Government continued to talk about retrenchment and curtailing expenses in South Africa.   Nevertheless, the imperial authorities were forced occasionally to come to the defense of the Cape Colonists against the natives and even to bring new territory under imperial control to form a buffer state on the colonial frontier. Thus the ground was unconsciously prepared for one section of the Cape-to-Cairo railway to run over a strip of all red-country from Cape Town to the Orange River.

Following the map still farther north, British influence was strongly entrenched in Zanzibar off the East Coast of Africa because of the expansion of the Indian trade. Zanzibar was at one time a dependency of Muscat, an important post on the road to India. British commerce spread from Muscat across the water to the east coast of Africa and the island of Zanzibar thus became another outpost in the Indian trade. In 1861-1862, the Sultan of Zanzibar shook off his dependence upon Muscat and asked for British protection. H. M. Government agreed to recognize the independence of Zanzibar and concluded a treaty with France by which both France and England bound themselves to respect the independence of Zanzibar and Muscat. Great Britain, however, refused formally to take the kingdom under her protection. The chief concerns of H. M. Government at the time in the island of Zanzibar were the protection of British commercial interests and the maintenance of the " status quo, the independence of the twin Arab sovereignties over Muscat and Zanzibar ". At various times after 1874, the Sultan of Zanzibar showed his willingness to place his dominions under British protection but H. M. Government, hampered by the Anglo-French agreement of 1862, was prevented from establishing an actual protectorate here until 1890. British relations, however, were very close with Zanzibar. In fact, H. M. Government kept an astute agent and advisor to the Sultan in the country, Sir John Kirk, who exercised a profound influence over His Highness Sayyid Barghash.[17]

Sir John was an ardent imperialist and keenly interested in schemes for opening up the interior of East Africa to British influence. His vision, however, extended beyond the limits of this vast region. Indeed, he played with Cape-to-Cairo ideas. In 1878, as will be seen in the next chapter, he gravely considered and gave advice upon the construction of an Overland Telegraph from Egypt to Cape Colony. In 1884, he discussed plans for opening up the interior with Sir Harry Johnston who was at the time keenly interested in a program of building a British Empire from the Cape-to-Cairo. There is every reason to suppose that Kirk was in sympathy with Sir Harry's imperial schemes. At any rate, he worked hand in hand with him in spreading British influence into the heart of the Dark Continent and ranks with Johnston as a Cape-to-Cairo pioneer.

At first glance, the Island of Zanzibar, off the East Coast of Africa, seems far removed from the Cape-to-Cairo route which runs north, many miles inland, through the lake region. In reality, however, the Sultan's kingdom was of vital importance in the development of Cape-to-Cairo projects. In fact, it was the friendly cooperation of the Sultan with Sir John Kirk which made Zanzibar an important base for exploration into the interior. Furthermore, Sir John Kirk was instrumental in persuading the Sultan to grant extensive concessions to British commercial corporations which might bring much-needed capital into East Africa. His first schemes, to be sure, were unsuccessful. Some concessions were accepted but soon dropped and the early adventurers sent home discouraging reports. Indeed, as will be seen later, it was not until the Germans, in the middle of the eighties, discovered the natural wealth of East Africa and began commercial operations there that Englishmen were finally aroused. Nevertheless, fruitless as were these first attempts at spreading British influence into the interior, Sir John broke the ground for further advances.[18]

In the far north, the British had been for over a century actively interested in the destinies of Egypt. It was not, however, the intrinsic possibilities of that fertile region and the desire to exploit them which first fastened British attention upon the Nile country. It was Egypt's strategic position in command of one of the main approaches to India which primarily concerned H. M. Government. In fact, ever since the treaty of Paris of 1763 gave the British a firm foothold in India, Englishmen were on the alert to guard the approaches to their new empire. Over the Isthmus of Suez and down the Red Sea lay the short road to the Far East. The master of Lower Egypt could easily control this route and seriously menace British power.

To be sure, British trade with the Far East before the middle of the nineteenth century did not follow this short cut. It went the longer way around the Cape of Good Hope. Until the rapid development of commercial and imperial interests after the Industrial Revolution, the Cape passage was adequate to meet British commercial needs. Furthermore, the British were in control of this route and had no particular interest in developing a new channel for their Indian and Far Eastern trade. They were, therefore, not anxious to possess the shorter route via Suez for their own commercial advantage but they were anxious, for imperial reasons, that it should not fall into rival hands. They could not afford to have a potential enemy strongly entrenched in Lower Egypt and prepared to use the Isthmus of Suez and the Red Sea for the development of rival interests in the East. " Egypt," said Lord George Hamilton, " is the natural resting-place, the natural stepping-stone between England and India." [19] It was because of British interests in India, for example, that the English compelled the army left by Napoleon in Egypt to evacuate the country and later on, steadily opposed all the French proposals for digging a canal across the isthmus.[20]

In the early part of the nineteenth century a change set in and the British began to take a new interest in the Red Sea route itself. By 1838, regular steam navigation had been established between India and Suez. In 1840, a British steamship company, the Peninsular and Oriental, was organized to operate over this route. Between 1839 and 1848, the British acquired Aden and Perrin on the Red Sea. It was becoming increasingly necessary to find a shorter passage than that by the Cape for the transmission of dispatches to India. The French had been talking for years about digging a canal across the isthmus. One or two Englishmen championed the idea of a Suez Canal but for the most part, the British people were opposed to the canal proposals. They saw another way out of their difficulties by constructing a railway between Alexandria and Suez. In 1834, an English engineer, Galloway Bey, was commissioned by the Khedive, Mehemet Ali, to survey a prospective railway route from Alexandria to Suez. Galloway even went so far as to order ties and other equipment for the line. H. M. Government, however, was not yet ready to support the railway proposal and refused to sanction Galloway's work because of strained relations then existing between the Porte and the Khedive. The project was abandoned and the rails left to rust.

Railway plans, however, were revived a few years later only to meet again with the cold disapproval of H. M. Government. Conditions in the Near East at the time were too unsettled for the British Government to enter into any railway ventures in Egypt. H. M. Government, nevertheless, were becoming increasingly interested in the proposition and, finally, in 1847, Palmerston recommended that Mehemet Ali undertake the construction of a line from Alexandria to Suez. This time, Mehemet Ali turned down the proposal. The French were strenuously opposed to the railway scheme. They were afraid that it would strengthen British influence in Egypt and be a menace to their own canal project. Mehemet Ali discreetly decided not to take sides and to oppose both the British railway proposal and the French Suez canal project.

Mehemet Ali's successor, Abbas Pasha I, was also opposed to a railway proposal made to him, March 1849, by Sir John Pirie, former Lord Mayor of London, and several directors of the Peninsular and Oriental Company. Later on, however, he began to regard the scheme for a line between Alexandria and Suez with greater favor. By October, 1850, he was ready to discuss the subject with Stephenson, a British engineer. He, finally, agreed to the construction of the railway on condition that it be laid in two sections in order to mollify French opposition. The first line was to run from Alexandria to Cairo; the second from Cairo to Suez. Construction was at last started. The line was carried as far as Cairo by 1854 and reached Suez in 1858.[21]

Suez was of course the objective of the line. No one probably realized at the time that Abbas Pasha I, in authorizing the construction of a railway from Alexandria to Cairo, was likewise sanctioning the building of the first northern section, through Egypt, of the Cape-to-Cairo railway. Nevertheless, Abbas Pasha I and the British railway promoters were, all unwittingly, laying that first section in the north of this great transcontinental line.

Ismail Pasha was the next Khedive to take an active interest in railway construction. He was more farseeing, or perhaps merely more grandiosely extravagant, than his predecessors. At any rate, he launched a scheme of building a railway through the Sudan south of Wadi Halfa. The route of this railway, as originally projected, was to follow the valley of the Nile as far as the foot of the great bend of the river at Debba, and then to strike southwards into the Bayuda desert towards Omdurman, with a branch to El Obeid.[22] Ismail Pasha, however, was thinking in continents. When consulted regarding the gauge to be used on the line, he ordered the same as that used in South Africa because, he remarked, " it would save trouble in the end ".[23] Not much came of this magnificent scheme of Ismail's. Because of lack of funds, only thirty miles of tract were laid between Wadi Halfa and the village of Sarras. Here the railhead remained until the arrival of the Gordon Relief Expedition of 1885.

Thus, British interests gradually obtained footholds in northern, eastern and southern Africa and railways were started in the south and in the north; not indeed as parts of a transcontinental system but with more immediate objectives in view. Nevertheless, the foundations were actually laid for later Cape-to-Cairo imperial and commercial projects. Compared with the imperialistic period of the late eighties and the nineties, the rate of penetration before 1884 was exceedingly slow. Here and there were glimmerings of a Cape-to-Cairo idea. A few adventurous persons like Arnold, Johnston and Sir John Kirk were talking about a transcontinental line of communication but to most people these ideas were still wild and extravagant fantasies. The British government had no thought of building up a vast new empire along the Cape-to-Cairo route in the Dark Continent. The British followed no definite policy of expansion in Africa. Still, in the history of the Cape-to-Cairo movement, the ever-widening red circles in the south, east and north were important. Some day, future empire-builders would set seriously to work to connect these scattered spheres of British influence; but before that day came, it was necessary for the British to drop their feeling of indifference towards their overseas possessions in general and towards Africa in particular.

A radical change in the general attitude towards colonial ventures in Africa, however, took place during the decades of the seventies and eighties. There were many factors involved in the change but chief among them was a gradually awakening interest in the southern continent. Towards the middle of the century, Africa began to acquire a new significance. Missionaries and traders were commencing to penetrate into the interior. They brought back glowing reports of high tablelands suitable for white colonization, of fertile country where cotton and grain could be profitably cultivated and of evidences of latent mineral wealth.[24]

They also roused public sympathy and indignation with pitiful stories of the atrocities of the slave trade. The British public was genuinely shocked by tales of the brutal treatment of the Negro by Portuguese and Arab slave-traders and by horrible descriptions of slave wars which were waged between the black men themselves to supply the slave traders on the coast. Opposition to the traffic in black men was the banner under which much popular support was enlisted for the British advance into Central Africa. Part of the enthusiasm for railway construction in the late eighties and indeed much of the popular support for the Cape-to-Cairo railway itself was due to the prevalent belief that opening up the interior of the Dark Continent to European and, particularly British civilization and commerce, meant death to the traffic in black men.[25] It was with real sincerity that H. M. Government subscribed to the declaration of the Brussels Conference of 1890 " that the construction of roads and especially of railways linking the outposts to the coast and allowing speedy access to the interior waters

. . . with the object of substituting economical and rapid methods of transport for the actual portage by human beings " would be an effective means of stopping the slave traffic.[26] In short, the history of the organized effort to abolish slavery and the slave trade is closely bound up with the story of British penetration into Africa.

Time would fail to tell of Cameron, of Baker, Speke and Grant. The list of travellers and explorers who helped to awaken a new consciousness of Africa in England and in Europe is a long one. The stores of their adventures are so arresting that they must have captured the imagination of many from the schoolboy up to the politician and statesman. There is, unfortunately, too little space here to go into this history of exploration into the heart of Africa although much of this pioneer work was along what later became the Cape-to-Cairo route.[27] Two men in particular, however, deserve a brief mention: David Livingstone and Henry Morton Stanley.

Livingstone was a noteworthy forerunner of the Cape-to-Cairo movement because he did so much to inflame popular indignaton against slavery, to arouse wide-spread interest in Central Africa and to break a path for British expansion to the north over ground which was later to become a section of the Cape-to-Cairo route.

In 1841, David Livingstone made his first missionary journey into Africa. In 1856, he returned to England and published a book on his travels. The book made a deep impression. " Ten thousand " [copies], wrote Livingstone, " were taken by the London trade alone. Thirteen thousand eight hundred have been ordered from an edition of twelve thousand, so the printers are again at work to supply the demand." [28]

British Government officials recognized the abilities of this missionary, scientist and explorer and decided to make use of his talents. In 1858, Livingstone returned to Africa in government service, with consular authority. From 1858 to 1864, he was engaged in exploring the Zambezi on an expedition "which settled the position of England for a long time in those parts and brought English power home to the mind, to the eyes, and to the feelings of the wild tribes ". Upon his return, he published a second book which again aroused great enthusiasm in England and led to the founding of the Universities Mission in the Island of Zanzibar and the establishment of five mission stations on Lake Nyasa by the Free Church of Scotland.[29]

In his writings and his speeches, Livingstone constantly challenged the English people to join in the crusade against the slave trade. Furthermore, he was both a zealous missionary and a scientist of no mean ability. He contributed much to the growing knowledge of Africa. He always kept careful records of his journeys and faithfully described everything which might be of scientific interest. He was anxious to awaken a popular enthusiasm in the development of British trade and commerce in the interior because he believed firmly that one of the most effective ways of combating the iniquitous slave traffic was to open commercial routes into the heart of the continent and to fight the greed of the slave trader with a new traffic in British manufactures and the products of British civilization.

Livingstone's popularity indeed was enormous. He was welcomed everywhere not only by missionary organizations but by scientific societies and Chambers of Commerce. Doctors, merchants, explorers, scientists, missionaries were eager to hear him. The Royal Geographical Society took a deep interest in his work. The Manchester Chamber of Commerce listened attentively and sympathetically to his gospel of carrying the benefits of British civilization, commerce and Christianity to the black men of Africa. Honors were heaped upon him. Livingstone became a national hero and his influence was deep and far-reaching.[30]

One other figure stands out among the numerous African explorers and travellers as conspicuous for his service in rousing a popular interest in Africa: Henry Morton Stanley. In 1871, he started on a hazardous expedition from East Africa into the interior to find Livingstone. He met Livingstone, November 10, 1871, at Ujiji on the eastern shore of Lake Tanganyika and then returned to the coast in 1872.[31] In 1874, Stanley set out once more for the heart of Africa to complete Livingstone's explorations: to navigate Lakes Tanganyika and Albert and to trace the course of the Lualaba River. He, again, entered Africa from the East Coast, proceeded into the Lake region. He traversed the Victoria Nyanza, was graciously received by Mtesa, Monarch of Uganda and crossed Lake Tanganyika. He made the important discovery that the Lualaba river was part of the Congo and then followed the course of the Congo to its mouth, arriving at Boma, August 9, 1877.[32] Stanley's work did not end here. In a few years time he was back again in Africa. In a later chapter, his further activities in the Congo region will be discussed in greater detail.[33] It is sufficient here to note that in the years 1871 to 1889, he accomplished much. He crossed the continent twice. He traced the course of the great Congo river and he played a major rôle in opening the Congo region to European civilization and commerce. The very magnitude of his achievements was enough to focus European attention on his work.

Stanley, however, was not only an intrepid explorer but also a journalist of recognized ability. He was, therefore, a master of the art of popularizing his ideas. He wrote copious letters to newspapers, especially the *Daily Telegraph,* and articles and books upon his travels. His major theme was much the same as that of his great predecessor,

Livingstone. He, like Livingstone, challenged his countrymen to open up the interior of Africa, especially the Congo
region to the beneficent influences of European commerce,
civilization and Christianity. Stanley, however, laid greater
emphasis upon the imperialistic aspects of his message. He
appealed first to England and then to King Leopold to seize
the Land of Promise and to plant colonies and settlements
there.

. . . It was Stanley's wonderful Trans African journey, in
1875-1877 [writes Sir Harry Johnston], notably his letters home
from Uganda to the *Daily Telegraph* in 1876, that first gave
some definite impulse to British minds to establish an uninterrupted British control over South, Central, East and North
Africa which might link up Egypt with Cape Colony in a series
of peaceful, prosperous, well-governed states.[34]

Livingstone and Stanley were two conspicuous leaders in
this age of explorers but they were not the only men in the
field. Other writers were telling their African experiences.
African subjects began to occupy greater space in newspapers, magazines and scientific journals. There were more
and more books about African travels.

Interest in the Dark Continent was thus growing gradually but steadily when certain events occurred which centered the attention not only of Englishmen but also of Europeans on South Africa. In 1866, the first South African
diamond, the O'Reilly, was discovered. It was picked up
by a Dutch youth, Erasmus Stephanus Jacobs, on the Dekalk
farm in the district of Hope Town. A little later, in 1868,
a bushman witch doctor traded " the Star of South Africa "
to a Boer, Schalk Van Niekerk, " for 500 sheep, ten head of
cattle and one horse! " [35] Then in 1871, came the discovery
of the Kimberley Mine, at that time known as Colesberg
Kopje or New Rush Mine.

Furthermore, during the years 1865 to 1886, important discoveries of gold deposits were made in Mashonaland, Matabeleland and the Transvaal. In 1865, Henry Hartley, a hunter, discovered ancient gold workings in Mashonaland. In 1867, Carl Mauch, a German geologist, reported gold in Mashonaland and at Tati on the southern border of Matabeleland. People had known, also, for some time, that there was mineral wealth in the Transvaal but, says Professor Walker, " transport difficulties and, to a certain extent, popular prejudice against miners stood in the way of any mineral developments." [36] Nevertheless, the pressure from fortune seekers was too great to be held back. Gold was found in the eastern Transvaal and a mine opened up at Eersteling. A small gold rush began in 1872 to the alluvial fields of Lydenburg. In 1882, another rush set in for these fields and the next year gold-bearing quartz was discovered in the De Kaap district in the vicinity of the present Barberton. Ever since 1883, prospectors had been experimenting with gold findings along the Witwatersrand reef in the Transvaal. In 1886, however, the main reef of the famous Banket conglomerate was traced all along the Rand and pegged off for more than twenty miles. This new discovery eclipsed the former gold findings. A rush set in from all over South Africa for the Banket reef. A new city called Johannesburg sprang up in the vicinity of Langlaagte.

These gold and diamond discoveries revolutionized the whole course of South Africa history. From poor and struggling agricultural colonies, the Cape and Natal grew in wealth and importance. A new industrial element was introduced into the country; for not only diamond digging itself soon developed into a regular industry, but it stimulated others required to supply the needs of the diggers.[37] Capital flowed into the land and enabled the colonists to embark on new enterprises hitherto far beyond their capacities.[38]

An indication of this fresh vitality and prosperity was the comparatively rapid growth of railway systems. For example, the privately owned railroad back of Cape Town, after ten years of tedious haggling, crawled at a snail's pace as far as Wellington in 1862 (just 57¾ miles beyond Cape Town). After the Diamond discoveries, however, it took a new lease of life. It was purchased by the Colonial Government in 1872. Under Government management, and with the diamond fields acting like a magnet, it reached Kimberley in 1886.

Furthermore, in 1874, bills for railway construction covering nearly eight hundred miles were introduced into the Cape Parliament and " a scheme which but a few years ago would have been deemed extravagant and visionary . . . received the unanimous support of all parties." [39] Three trunk systems grew up in the colony as a result of this railway boom; the Western line which had already started on its way north from Cape Town, the Midland line commencing at Port Elizabeth and running north towards Colesberg, and the Eastern line from East London to Queenstown. In 1873, Natal colonists talked of joining their railway with a Cape line. In 1880, they asked for an imperial government loan to construct a railway from Durban to the border of the Transvaal. Between 1878 and 1882, negotiations were started with the President of the Orange Free State to connect the Cape line with that of the Free State. By this time, the race between Cape Colony and Natal for the first railway to reach the gold reef had begun in full earnest. [40]

The railway boom was not, however, the only indication of the increasing prosperity ushered in by the diamond and gold discoveries. There was a new vitality in the southern colonies, an impulse towards expansion, a reaching-out especially in the northward direction. The diamond fields were, naturally, the first objective. They lay just North of Cape Colony in land whose ownership was a subject of dispute. The Griqua Chief, Waterboer, claimed the territory but his claims were disputed by the two Boer Republics; the Transvaal and the Orange Free State. It is not necessary to unravel here the complicated story of these claims. It is sufficient to point out that, after the diamond discoveries, H. M. Government took an active interest in the contest. H. M. Officials stepped into the dispute on the side of the Griqua Chief who was friendly to British interests. The result was that the High Commissioner recognized the rights of Waterboer and thereby barred out the Boers as claimants. The Griqua Chief, shortly thereafter, very obligingly surrendered his sovereignty to the British Crown. In 1877, the new territory was annexed to Cape Colony under the name of Griqualand West.[41]

This step forward is significant in the history of British expansion along the south-to-north route because by occupying this strip, Great Britain limited the extension of the rival Boer States to the West and opened the way for British expansion to the north. Robert Southey, Colonial Secretary at the Cape, deserves great credit in this dispute for keeping the country to the north open to the British advance. In fact, he was largely instrumental in agitating the questions of the acquisition of Griqualand West. He was, Williams claims, " the first, perhaps, of his generation to realize the importance of securing the territory north of the Orange River and west of the two republics as a corridor for Great Britain into the interior of Africa ".[42]

The occupation of Griqualand West marked the commencement of a new era of imperialism in Africa. It was the beginning of the race for the North. Before 1880, the boundary lines of European possessions, on the political map of Africa, changed very little. After this period, they shifted rapidly and usually in the direction of the interior.

Before 1880, Africa was truly a Dark Continent, with only scattered groups of European settlements along the coast and in the north and south. By 1906, a British survey committee reported " . . . there are now no 'hinterlands' in British Africa, the partition of the continent is complete, and the boundaries are, with few exceptions, well defined." [43]

Other people, moreover, besides the British were aroused by the gold and diamond discoveries to an interest in the country north of Cape Colony. There was a motley rush of prospectors of various nationalities into the Transvaal and Natal. Fortune seekers, also, wandered north of Cape Colony into Bechuanaland. The Portuguese from their colonies on the west and east coasts turned longing eyes towards the interior. They began to trump up claims to the hinterland between Angola and Mozambique and to dream of a transcontinental empire stretching from the Atlantic to the Indian Ocean. In 1877, the Portuguese explorer, Serpa Pinto, went on an expedition from St. Paul de Loanda to the Zambezi, then through the Barotse country to the Kalahari Desert and, finally, to the Transvaal. Two Portuguese, Capello and Ivens traced the Upper Zambezi to its source and then descended the river to the Indian Ocean.[44]

The Boers in the Transvaal and the Orange Free State were ready to assert claims in Bechuanaland.[45] Behind the Boer ambitions there was a lurking suspicion of German machinations. As will be noted later, the Germans were awake to the colonial and commercial potentialities of the coastal region in southwest and southeast Africa. The British were watching the movements of both Boers and Germans with some apprehension and a lurking fear that the Boers might join hands with their German kinsmen to establish a Boer-German state across the continent.

Just at the time of this newly awakened interest in Africa, economic conditions at home were forcing Englishmen to

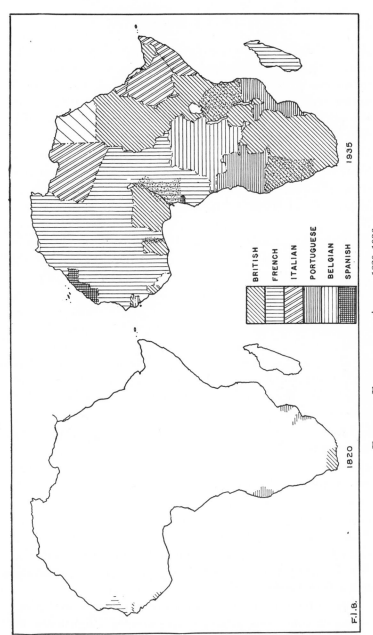

BRITISH
FRENCH
ITALIAN
PORTUGUESE
BELGIAN
SPANISH

1935

1820

F.I.B.

EUROPEAN EXPANSION IN AFRICA, 1820–1936

direct their attention abroad, especially towards countries not yet exploited by other European powers. The British were fast losing their position as leaders in the industrial world. It was not that the English people were manufacturing less or producing less. In fact, there was an actual increase in the volume of British trade in the seventies and early eighties. It was rather that industrial development in England was not keeping pace with the rapid rate of industrial progress in Europe and the United States. Competition was keener and profits were smaller.

During the decade of the fifties, British capital flowed towards Europe and North America to aid in their industrialization and chiefly to help in railway construction. During the seventies, however, Germany became a strong unified state. The new nation displayed a decided adaptibility to trade. Indeed, the German people exhibited a shrewd " knowledge of the markets of the world " and " a desire to accomodate themselves to local tastes or idiosyncrasies ", a determination likewise to obtain a footing wherever they could and " a tenacity in maintaining it ".[46] During this period, the United States was well on the road to recovery after the Civil War. Especially in the cotton trade, the Americans were becoming keen competitors of the British.[47] In 1880, the French began to apply a bounty system to their mercantile marine, thus hitting at the British carrying trade, the foundation of British commercial supremacy. In Germany, France and the United States, tariff walls restricted the British market for textiles.

The tendency was growing for the nations in Europe to supply their own wants and to send their surplus products to neutral markets. British goods were not only being driven out of the European markets, but competition was becoming keen even in the neutral markets: in colonies and dependencies. It is no wonder, therefore, that British trade failed to bring in the sizable profits it formerly enjoyed. Around 1873, a period of depression set in which reached its climax in 1879. Recovery was slow. Finally, a royal commission was appointed to investigate the causes of this alarming state of affairs and in 1886, they made a voluminous report in which they recommended further expansion of trade as the chief remedy for the disturbing situation. They urged greater activity in the search for new markets and greater readiness to accommodate British productions to local tastes and peculiarities.[48]

In this search for new markets and a wider field of enterprise, the English people turned naturally to remote regions not already exploited by Europeans. Africa presented a particularly inviting field for new commercial ventures. Its vast stretches of undeveloped country, its latent wealth were tempting. Its hordes of natives who supposedly coveted the gay cotton, the arms and ammunition of the Europeans [49] offered a promising market for British manufacturers. In Egypt, the English were already greatly interested in the cultivation of cotton. The growing of cotton was proving a lucrative investment and the Egyptian plant was of a fine quality well adapted to competition with the rival American products.[50] In South Africa, diamond and gold industries were booming. In the interior, the possibilities of fresh mineral discoveries lured the prospector.

In short, Englishmen were fully awake by 1886 to opportunities for trade and commerce in Africa. Distances, however, between stations and new fields of enterprise were enormous and transportation was difficult. Only the most valuable and least bulky goods could be profitably exported from the interior regions. Transportation still depended largely upon caravans of black men.[51] If the British wished to make the best use of their commercial opportunities in the Dark Continent, if they were sincerely in earnest in fighting the slave traffic and abolishing portage on the backs of Negroes, they must enter into large-scale undertakings to improve transport facilities; to build railways and roads into the interior and to place steamers on the lakes. In the words of Sir Rutherford Alcock, President of the Royal Geographical Society, 1877:

Whether the giant strides made in the last few years by geographical discovery, . . . is to be followed by equally vast and rapid changes in the condition of Central Africa, and the whole continent stretching from Egypt to the Cape of Good Hope, must depend . . . upon the means which individuals or governments may bring to bear. It is mainly a question of money and the employment of capital. All other means will fail without this *primum mobile*; and with it, nothing in the existing physical and moral condition of the African Continent or people can offer any serious obstacles. I can only express a hope, in which I feel confident all who are present will heartily join, that Great Britain, so long in the foremost rank, will not be the last on the muster roll of those countries which are destined to bring the African race and the inexhaustible wealth of their fertile soil, their mineral products, and free labour, within the circle of modern civilization, and under the safeguard of public law and humanizing influence.

Making practicable roads [he remarked further] . . . is undoubtedly the first and indispensable condition of all progress in Africa. The bullock wagon and the steamboat will do the rest until the time comes, and it cannot be far distant after these have possession for *the rail and the telegraph to complete the work.*[52]

Great Britain's European rivals were already conscious of the need for better communications in Africa. The French had begun a railway in Senegal and were harboring ambitious schemes for a Transsaharan line. The Portuguese were considering plans for railway construction both in their colony of Angola on the west coast and in Mozambique on the east. They had designs for a railway from Loanda to Embaca in Angola and they were listening to proposals for a railway from Lourenço Marques in Mozambique to the Transvaal border.[53]

The British must not lag behind in the effort to improve communications if they wished to maintain their commercial preeminence and retrieve the losses in their European markets. They must be on their guard to forestall competition in Africa. The conditions of the time pointed to large-scale construction of roads, railways and telegraphs. It was natural, therefore, in the last quarter of the nineteenth century, for them to conceive the project of connecting South Africa and Egypt with lines of railway and telegraph. It was an age of imperialistic scheming and dreaming. While the French were discussing plans for a transcontinental line to run across the desert and link together their possessions in North and West Africa, a group of British Empire builders and entrepreneurs had their dreams, likewise, of an all-red line of communications stretching the whole length of the African continent from the Cape to Cairo.

CHAPTER II

Wires Across Africa

THE first embryonic Cape-to-Cairo project grew directly out of the movements and tendencies discussed in the last chapter. It took the shape of proposals for a transcontinental telegraph from the Cape to Alexandria. These proposals did not materialize and the scheme has long since been forgotten. Nevertheless, it is important in a well-rounded study of the Cape-to-Cairo movement to turn back once more to the neglected records of this premature project because these records tell the story of the genesis of the Cape-to-Cairo idea.

The " Overland Telegraph " proposals developed specifically in answer to two major needs. In the first place, the conception of a transcontinental line arose out of the growing demand in the seventies for better communication between England, Europe and the South African Colonies. As trade expanded after the diamond discoveries and capital began to flow more rapidly into this once remote corner of the empire, it became more and more necessary to keep in closer touch with the mother country. The slow journey of from one to two months by ship to the Cape was too tedious to meet the impatient demands of the new business interests.[1]

In the second place, this first inchoate Cape-to-Cairo scheme was a product of a growing and wide-spread interest in Central Africa. Better communication was the primary essential for penetrating into the heart of the Dark Continent. Missionaries, travellers, philanthropists and traders were clamoring for easier and safer access into this land of

47

promise and the Overland Telegraph scheme was one of the first tentative attempts to meet these needs.

The scheme was in its nature a genuine Cape-to-Cairo project. To be sure, the actual name " Cape-to-Cairo " telegraph was not applied to it. Nevertheless, it was in its essential features at the beginning of the movement to connect the south and the north and it foreshadowed in many respects later Cape-to-Cairo plans. Like them, it centered around the construction of a line of communication from the Cape to the Mediterranean. Like them, furthermore, the proposal did not stop here. It was a plan of broader significance than the mere erection of a line of poles across the continent. Its promoters intended not only to bring England into closer touch with British possessions and settlements in Africa but also to open up the interior to trade, commerce, civilization and eventually colonization. Colonel Grant, for example, called the proposal " an idea of civilizing Africa." [2]

Extravagant hopes, in fact, were woven around the project by its early sponsors. Nicholls, for instance, anticipated that the telegraph line would develop into a " highroad of communication through Africa which would check and finally abolish the inhuman traffic in slaves." [3] " To the African ", another promoter wrote glowingly, " the influence of the telegraph would be an inconceivable boon. It would direct his ideas and pursuits. It would substitute industry and commerce for slavery: it would educate and elevate him, and form a band of friendship between him and the foreigners." [4] One other enthusiast went so far as to anticipate the day when the grateful natives would regard " the thin wire suspended a few feet above their heads . . . as the dawn of a new era of enlightenment and prosperity." [5]

Europeans, as well as the natives and the British, were to benefit from the construction of the line and the potentially wealthy Southern continent was thus to be opened to European commerce and trade. In the optimistic words of Nicholls:

[The telegraph could be relied upon] to bring a message from every vessel which rounds the Cape of Good Hope. . . . It would certainly be carried across to India, by Madagascar and Mauritius, thus opening up an alternative line to the East; while branches would be very soon taken to Zanzibar and the West Coast settlements. It would be hailed with equal satisfaction by the Colonial Office, the Viceroy of Egypt, and the British Colonists at the south of Africa. . . . Merchants would make use of the line; governments would subsidise it; colonies would form in groups within easy distance of or by the line.[6]

Because of these benefits to all concerned, the promoters anticipated international cooperation. The line, they claimed, should be constructed by a European staff and supported by subsidies from the Egyptian, Cape, Portuguese, Zanzibar and European Governments.[7]

In short, the new telegraph would be an answer to Livingstone's humanitarian call to open up the Dark Continent to the light of European civilization, commerce and Christianity. It would substitute legitimate trade for the commerce in black men and thus help to crush slavery. It would also be an answer to the demand of the Manchester cotton merchants and other manufacturers for new markets and finally, it would facilitate communication with the Far East.

Since the Overland Telegraph proposal is the first concrete expression of the Cape-to-Cairo idea, it is well to know something about its early sponsors, the fathers of the movement. There is still some question as to who was the first man to envisage an overland telegraph from Cape Colony to Egypt. It may have been Sir James Sivewright, a telegraph engineer by profession, who served for some years as telegraph man-

ager at the Cape.[8] It may have been, as Sir Harry Johnston suggests, Sir Edwin Arnold, leader-writer to the *Daily
Telegraph* and a warm sponsor of the Cape-to-Cairo idea.[9]

It may have been, on the other hand, some quite obscure
person who has left very little impression on the history of
the day. A certain H. B. T. Strangway, for example,
claimed that he suggested the construction of the Overland
Telegraph as early as 1875, in a series of articles published
in the *Colonies and India* and in the *English Mechanic*. He
also brought the subject before the Royal Geographical
Society during the discussion on a paper presented by Lieutenant Cameron, June 18, 1876. Strangway, in fact,
boasted that Kerry Nicholls, a leader in the movement in
England, derived all his information on the subject of the
telegraph from him.[10]

Another possible candidate for the honor of being the
author of the first Cape-to-Cairo project is Thomas Watson,
an active Cape politician. Sir Bartle Frere calls him " a
prominent South African." [11] Certainly, his name appears
frequently in the Cape legislative records in connection with
railroad schemes.[12] Thomas Watson, also, took an early
interest in the telegraph project. Indeed, he claimed that
" the novel idea of an overland telegraph was first mentioned
to Mr. Nicholls by myself while in England two years ago ",
[i. e., 1875]. He adds further, " I have kept up a correspondence with him and found him a most enthusiastic
colleague." [13]

Dr. Atherstone, a Grahamstown physician and distinguished geologist was also interested in the project at an
early date. In 1875, while in London, the doctor was seriously considering the scheme and had even gone so far as
to investigate the subject of the proper coating for an under-
ground wire to be used in parts where the line might be
" liable to injury by fire, animals or natives ".[14]

Anyone of the men just mentioned, Sivewright, Arnold, Strangway, Watson or Atherstone may have been the author of the Overland Telegraph project or possibly the scheme originated in the mind of some person who has left no record at all of his plans. Whoever was the author, the fact remains that the subject was mooted about 1875 and that it found able sponsors both in England and in South Africa.

In England, three men in particular stand out as leaders. They did more than anyone else to popularize the idea and to push the project forward. They were Sir Edwin Arnold, Colonel J. A. Grant and Kerry Nicholls. These three men undoubtedly rank as the chief promoters, if not the authors, of the embryonic Cape-to-Cairo project.

The two most notable figures in this trio were the newspaper editor, journalist and poet, Sir Edwin Arnold and the well-known and well-liked [15] African explorer Lieutenant-Colonel J. A. Grant.

Arnold was, from 1861 to 1873, a leader-writer for the *Daily-Telegraph*. In 1873, he became chief editor of the newspaper and maintained this position for twenty-eight years. He was deeply interested in the opening up of the Dark Continent. With the proprietors, he took an active part in dispatching several important missions into the heart of Africa.[16] In 1874, for example, H. M. Stanley was sent out by the proprietors of the *Daily Telegraph* and by Gordon Bennett of the *New York Herald* to complete the explorations of Livingstone. The far-reaching influence of that famous mission has already been discussed in the previous chapter and likewise the importance of Stanley's letters to the *Daily Telegraph* in arousing a new imperialistic interest in the Dark Continent.[17] In fact, according to Sir Sidney Low, the expedition " did more to open up the heart of the continent and to elucidate its geography than any other before or since." [18]

Arnold and the proprietors of the *Daily Telegraph* were also instrumental, in conjunction with the Royal Society and the British Association in sending Harry Johnston into the Kilimanjaro district in 1884 on the expedition which, as will be seen later on, laid the foundations for the work of the Imperial British East Africa Company. Johnston's experiences like Stanley's were faithfully recorded in the *Daily Telegraph*. Johnston was an exponent of the Cape-to-Cairo idea. He undoubtedly did much to popularize the dream of a vast British empire spreading over Central Africa and joining the British spheres in both the south and north.[19]

Later on, in the decade of the nineties, the proprietors of the *Daily Telegraph* dispatched another African traveller, Lionel Decle, to the Southern Continent. Decle subsequently wrote a series of articles for the newspaper mainly on " the potentialities of Rhodesia and British Central Africa ". His reports did much to promote settlement in these regions.[20]

Sir Edwin Arnold, as chief editor of this enterprising newspaper, not only took an active interest in these expeditions, but he seems also to have challenged his readers to a new imperialism. In fact, he was an able spokesman for British imperialism and a staunch advocate of the spread of British power from the Cape to Cairo. He it was, in fact, who first indoctrinated Harry Johnston with the idea and, Johnston claims, that Arnold was one of the first interpreters of the Cape-to-Cairo dream.[21] When Arnold, therefore, lent his support to the Overland Telegraph project that scheme became something more than a mere proposal to improve communications between England and South Africa. It became, in fact, a project for carrying out Sir Edwin Arnold's imperialistic dreams.

Lieutenant-Colonel J. A. Grant, although perhaps he is not so widely known today, was a prominent figure in the circle of African explorers of the sixties and seventies. He travelled with Speke on a famous journey through East Africa, the lake district and the Sudan.[22] He was awarded medals for his accomplishments both by the Royal Geographical Society and by Pope Pius IX. He was granted the order of C. B. for his services on the expedition with Speke. Besides achieving so much, he possessed a pleasing personality. He must, in the first place, have been a striking figure because he was " of remarkably fine physique, six feet two inches in height and broad in proportion ". He was, furthermore, a kindly person and is remembered for his unselfishness, his extreme modesty and peculiar quality of winning the friendship of African natives.[23] People must have listened with pleasure to this kindly giant. They must also have trusted his words because he was so unassuming and because he could speak with the authority born of experience about the prospects of an Overland Telegraph through North Africa. Although his arguments for a transcontinental line now sound visionary and over-enthusiastic, they must have carried considerable weight in the minds of his contemporaries.

Kerry Nicholls has left less of a mark on the history of the day than Arnold or Grant although he seems to have been an intrepid and adventurous explorer. In 1882, for example, he volunteered to go through the dangerous Maiori country in the North Island of New Zealand and the following year he set out upon a six-hundred-mile journey through this land where the natives were particularly hostile to Europeans.[24] Whether he had had any personal experience with travelling in Africa does not appear. He was, however, keenly interested in African exploration. He had had some experience, furthermore, in telegraph laying and was much interested in telegraph projects in different parts of the world.[25] His arguments for the Overland Telegraph line were based largely on the beneficial effects which had resulted from the erection of great transcontinental lines in other countries. Other countries had successfully constructed telegraph lines over vast stretches of country and against great odds. The British in carrying a telegraph line from Cape Colony to Egypt, should find no more insuperable obstacles than had been encountered elsewhere.[26]

Nicholls, Arnold and Grant as chief promoters of the scheme gave their views in a pamphlet published in 1876, about the feasibility and the advantages inherent in the erection of the Overland Telegraph. All three men emphasized the fact that there were already lines in existence in South Africa and in Egypt and that the intervening distance could be spanned without too great difficulty. Arnold called the idea of a telegraph from the south to the north of Africa " perhaps startling " but " at once practical, natural, necessary " and he predicted, " profitable ".[27]

With such rosy hopes floating before them, the three Englishmen deemed their project to be " of such vast importance to Africa " and to Europe that they ventured to present their proposal before the International Conference invited by His Majesty the King of the Belgians to meet at Brussels, September 12, 1876.

The plan was presented but it never found its way into the minutes of the conference.[28] The illustrious delegates were, indeed, intent upon the problem of how best to open up the heart of Africa to exploration. They even considered a south-to-north route to some extent, but their plans centered around a trunk road between the eastern and western coasts through the lake region south of the Equator rather than on the telegraph scheme. The English, French and Italian sections suggested subsidiary lines through the lake region which would connect the trunk road with the Nile basin and the lower course of the Congo to the north and with the Zambezi country to the south and would debouch at convenient points to the seacoast. The British thus, indicated that they were already considering connecting lines between the Nile Basin and South Africa. The telegraph scheme, however, was not mentioned. Probably the European delegates did not consider it practical enough to warrant their attention. The fact that opening a south-to-north route to exploration was considered and advocated by the British, nevertheless, is significant. In conclusion, the minutes read: " the conference expresses the desire above all that a line of communications as continuous as possible be established from one ocean to the other following approximately the route of Commander Cameron. The conference likewise expresses the " wish that following this, lines of operation be established in the north-south direction." [29]

In Great Britain the Overland Telegraph proposal sponsored by Nicholls, Arnold and Grant met with a warmer reception. The Royal Geographical Society took particular interest in the project. In fact, Sir Rutherford Alcock, president of the Society, was enthusiastically in favor of the proposal. He believed firmly in the probable success of the undertaking and called the plan " No speculative dream, but a sober reality lying straight before them." [30] Africa, he predicted, would " in a short period ", be opened from one end to the other.[31]

The idea of preparing the way for an overland telegraph crept into the plans for expeditions which the Society was about to send out. Keith Johnson, for example, was dispatched, in 1879 on an ill-fated journey to explore the region between Dar-es-Salaam on the East Coast and the Northern end of Lake Nyasa. He was especially instructed " to observe and note the routes best adapted for future more ex-

tensive communication" and "the practicability of constructing and maintaining a line of telegraph from north to
south ".[32]

A committee was appointed by the Society to inquire into
the feasibility of the telegraph scheme and to gather information on the subject.[33] A mine of information was collected by the committee from men well acquainted with
African affairs. In fact, it is remarkable that so many men
prominent in the African world took a serious interest in
the project. The list included such well-known figures as
Commander V. Lovett Cameron, famous for his journey
from the east to the west coast of Africa; Henry Morton
Stanley; Sir Samuel Baker, noted explorer of the Nile
region; Sir John Kirk, the astute adviser to the Sultan of
Zanzibar; C. Giegler, director of the Sudan and Red Sea
Coasts Telegraphs; Sir James Sivewright, telegraph manager at the Cape and Sir Bartle Frere, the Cape Governor.
To be sure, the opinions of these experienced travellers and
Government agents were "singularly contradictory"[34] in
regard to the telegraph proposal. C. Giegler, for instance,
was enthusiastic over the idea of a transcontinental line and
rashly asserted that the Egyptian Government would heartily
support the undertaking. He stated further that he was sure
of the cooperation of Colonel Gordon, the Governor General
of the Sudan.[35]

Commander V. Lovett Cameron was also enthusiastic
about the proposition. In fact, he could see no difficulties
in the way of constructing a telegraph through Africa and
thought that such a proceeding would be an immense step in
opening up the country.[36]

Sir John Kirk was in favor of a land line at some future
date but felt that the section from Zanzibar to Gondokoro
was not immediately practical. "In the present state of
Africa", he admitted, "it would be an enormous risk".

The impecunious Sultan of Zanzibar was, however, ready to grant any assistance short of money.[37]

H. M. Stanley opposed such a vast undertaking at the beginning. Later on, he modified his objections somewhat. Although " bitten by the scheme ",[38] he still saw a great obstacle in the unhealthiness of the climate and predicted that ten men would die yearly from sickness or violence out of a force of fifty-two workers on the telegraph.[39]

Sir Samuel Baker was perhaps " the greatest opponent of any inland line ".[40] In many places, he pointed out, there was no wood suitable for poles and the tribes along the White Nile had no metals. " I do not think ", Baker wrote, " any police supervision would protect a wire of gold from London to Inverness, and I think it would be equally impossible to protect a wire of iron through the tribes I have mentioned." [41]

On the whole, the evidence collected by the Royal Geographical Society seems hardly encouraging for an immediate construction of an Overland telegraph from Cape Colony to Egypt. Although most of the experts were in favor of such a telegraph from a general point of view, they were dubious about the difficulties to be met with along certain sections of the line and, especially, about the sections which they knew best.

In spite of this discouraging evidence, the committee of the Royal Geographical Society passed " with amendation ", a report recommending the construction of a line from Cape Colony to Egypt through the heart of Central Africa. The committee optimistically estimated that the total cost of construction of such a line would be only £500,000. They expected subsidies totalling £20,000 a year from the Cape and Natal and £10,000 a year from the British and Transvaal Governments. They anticipated returns of £30,000 to £40,000 per year from the operation of the line.[42]

Finally, with the blessing of the Geographical Society, the report was sent to the Colonial Office. The officials of the office had for some time taken an interest in the scheme. As early as October, 1878, they applied to the Society for information as to the feasibility of constructing a telegraph between Pretoria and Gondokoro.[43] Sir Michael Hicks Beach, the Colonial Secretary, in particular, was anxious for whatever information could be gathered on the subject.[44] He asked the Royal Geographical Society from time to time " to communicate to him . . . the results of the explorations " then being carried on in Africa " observing that, while it may perhaps be necessary for the present to have recourse to an ocean cable, it is very desirable to acquire all possible information as to the nature of the country over which any land line which may hereafter be erected could be carried with least difficulty and the greatest commercial advantage." [45]

There was no doubt, after the annexation of the Transvaal in 1877, that there was urgent need of better communications between the authorities at home and British colonists in South Africa. In fact, the only question before the Imperial Government was how to improve communications most effectively and economically. As will be noted later in this chapter,[46] the British officials were, at the time, considering two specific schemes. One was the Overland Telegraph proposal sponsored by the Geographical Society and the other was a plan for laying a submarine cable.

The opinions of the colonial officials in regard to the prospects of the Overland Telegraph line were divided. Some called the scheme for the present visionary and impracticable. Others were more optimistic about the Overland line. The latter group believed that the maintenance of a land line would prove easier than that of an ocean cable. Some of the officials thought that if the whole line could not be erected, it would be immediately feasible and profitable to construct certain sections. One man advocated, for example, a connection between Zanzibar and the Cape although he felt that, north of Zanzibar, a submarine cable was preferable.[47]

Even at this early date, the idea of an all-red line is faintly foreshadowed by one or two of the annotators of Colonial dispatches who wanted the Overland Telegraph to be wholly British in character and to have the work undertaken by the Imperial Government with the colony contributing some of the cost.

I have not suggested [writes one man], any contributions from foreign sources because any contributions would in any case be very small and it would be far better to keep the line under our own control. Egypt is now so much under British influence that it would not signify our being dependent on Egypt, and at Zanzibar we should have practical command of the line, though it may hereafter be desirable to acquire either the island of Zanzibar or some settlement on the coast.[48]

The need for better communications, however, was pressing. H. M. Government was willing to cooperate to some extent with the Cape Government to construct either a cable or an overland line. The time element was very important and H. M. Government finally decided that a submarine cable could be laid more expeditiously. Furthermore, they did not find the final report of the special committee of the Royal Geographical Society wholly in favor of a land line. " The Geographers ", they complained, " look at this question from their special standpoint of developing the interior of Africa for commercial, missionary and scientific purposes . . . we must look to economy of construction and security ".[49] The general opinion of the colonial office is ably summarized by one of its prominent officials, F. R. Round, in a minute dated January 29, 1879.

I have [he writes], been very carefully through these papers [the report of the committee of the Royal Geographical Society], and can come to no other conclusion than that however desirable a land line may be with a view to opening up the dark continent, the scheme is hopelessly impracticable with a view to establishing direct communications between South Africa and this country at an early date and a reasonable price, and therefore it would be unwarrantable that it should receive any financial support from Her Majesty's Government.[50]

While the question of the overland telegraph was receiving so much attention in England, there was also considerable agitation for a land line in South Africa.

The colonists had been interested, previous to 1878, in the subject of a cable to England or to Aden. They had even entered into a contract with Hooper's to lay a submarine cable from England to the Cape on payment of a subsidy. The company, however, backed out of the contract "and for some time afterwards there was nothing but talk about a cable without any practicable step whatever being taken." [51]

The chief promoter of the Overland Telegraph proposal in South Africa was Sir James Sivewright. He was a telegraph engineer by profession and held the post of General Manager of South African Telegraphs, 1877-1885. In 1896 he became commissioner of Crown Lands and Public Works and held this post until 1898. He was active in politics and a Minister in Cecil Rhodes' first cabinet.[52] Rhodes put great confidence in Sivewright, "the brain-carrier of the administration as Hofmeyr called him " [53] and he was Rhodes' right-hand man in certain railway transactions with Kruger. There is a great probability that, sometime during the long period of their intimacy, Sivewright discussed with Rhodes his early schemes for an Overland Telegraph from the south to the north of Africa. There is, therefore, probably a direct connection between the project of a transcontinental telegraph which Rhodes began sponsoring in 1892 and Sivewright's early proposal for an Overland Telegraph in 1878. Indeed, the relationship between the two men became strained over this very question. Sivewright felt that he was the first man to advocate the idea of an overland telegraph through the continent. Rhodes, on the other hand, behaved as though the transcontinetal telegraph project was purely his own creation and never invited Sivewright to participate in his plans.[54]

Sivewright advocated a telegraph line either from Pretoria in the Transvaal or Kimberley in Cape Colony to Zanzibar and from there to Gondokoro. This route, he claimed, was first suggested to him by Merriman of Cape Town. He anticipated little difficulty in erecting the first 1600 miles to Zanzibar. The weakest link in the chain, Sivewright acknowledged, was the stretch from Zanzibar to Gondokoro. If this line proved impracticable, however, the telegraph might be taken along the coast to a point opposite Aden or, " striking in from Zanzibar along the well beaten caravan track to Ujiji," it might be carried then by Lakes Tanganyika and Victoria Nyanza to the Soudan.

The word could be carried on if necessary by the " salted and acclimatized half-caste " if the climate proved too unhealthy for white men. Native tribes near the wire could look after ordinary repairs such as clearing the undergrowth raming poles and the like.[55]

Sivewright had investigated the prospects as thoroughly as he could. He had travelled " on foot or on horseback from King William's Town to Pretoria " and discussed " the project with almost every man in the country whose experience would give his opinions any weight ".

[He was convinced] that the scheme of an overland telegraph through Africa [was] no wild visionary dream [but] a practical proposal which to the civilizing Anglo-Saxon race wears a look of grim earnestness about it. [Furthermore, he knew of] no undertaking which could appeal for support more strongly to all classes of that race from the philanthropist downwards, than this, for, setting commercial considerations aside altogether [he could think of] none that would strike a surer blow at that " inhumanity of man to man" which at this moment in the " weird " continent more than in any other quarter of the globe, is still making " countless thousands mourn ".[56]

Sivewright found an able colleague in Merriman who was commissioner of Crown Lands and Public Works in 1878. Michell describes Merriman " as the most interesting Cape figure of his generation ". He was like Sivewright, an active politician and was called, " the spoilt child of the House of Assembly ".[57]

On March 30, 1878, Sivewright delivered a lecture before the Philosophical Society at the Cape in which he weighed the respective merits of land and cable lines and found a preponderance in favor of the former. The idea of the telegraph " took root " and an influential provisional committee was formed with Merriman acting as honorary secretary. The Committee decided to bring their proposal before the Cape Parliament. There was a bill already pending before the legislature to grant a subsidy to improve communications between South Africa and England. The promoters of the Overland Telegraph planned to introduce a clause into this measure which would make the subsidy equally applicable to either an overland or a submarine line.[58]

Sir Bartle Frere, the governor of Cape Colony, himself, showed great sympathy for an overland line. He was primarily anxious, to be sure, from a practical point of view, to secure better communication between England and the colony and other British spheres of influence as quickly as possible, be it by land or water and he finally lent the weight of his support to the cable project because it gave greater promise of speedy completion. He wrote, however, to the Secretary of State:

I have no doubt a land line might easily be devised which would [next word indecipherable, probably "supply"] all the wants of South Africa, of the Portuguese possessions, or the coast of Zanzibar and be connected with the European system through the Egyptian line. I have also little doubt but that such a line might be made to pay and it would be unquestionably a great advantage in every way in facilitating the civilisation of all the countries through which it passed and be of the greatest possible advantage in the event of any temporary interruption of the submarine line . . . but it will take some time to complete it and [it] will always be liable to interruptions of inconvenient length.

I would therefore not delay connecting East Africa with the Indo-European system by means of a submarine cable.[59]

In spite of this decision to support the cable proposal, Sir Bartle Frere was at heart very much interested in the idea and disposed to adopt a land line if shown to be at all practicable.[60] He cherished the idea that even if the Overland Telegraph was not an immediately feasible proposition, still it might become desirable and practical in the future. He felt that a submarine line, if laid, would not "militate against an overland line" but rather "have a contrary effect by accustoming merchants trading with the interior to use the telegraph; and feel it to be a necessity of commerce". He pointed out that the colony would support the cable plan simply as the "quickest mode offering for getting what they wanted: otherwise there was a great feeling in favour of giving what the colony can afford . . . to an overland line."[61]

There was undoubtedly an influential group at the Cape who were agitating for the land line. The promoters of the cable project, however, were just as energetic. The Eastern Telegraph Company Ltd., offered to lay a submarine cable between Aden and Natal. John Pender, chairman of the company, sent his own son, James, out in 1878 to commence negotiations with Cape Colony, Natal, Delagoa Bay, Mozambique, Mauritius, Bourbon and Zanzibar and to arrange for subsidies from these governments. Most of the governments were willing to grant a subsidy for twenty years.[62] Even Sivewright, chief spokesman for the Overland project, fell in with Pender's plans. " For what we want ", he said, " is a telegraph to England primarily, no matter how; and if for £15,000 a year the Cape gets its cable, I for one think that the Cape has not the worst of the bargain." [63]

The Cape Government, finally, agreed to a satisfactory subsidy. The upshot of the matter was that, by the middle of 1879, contracts were at last concluded to lay a cable between Aden and Durban. By the close of 1879, the cable was completed between these two points and the line was ready for traffic.[64] The South African colonists were satisfied. At that time, they felt they were in no position to pursue a quixotic adventure of opening up Central Africa to civilization and commerce. The Cape-to-Cairo dream had not yet kindled their imagination. The Overland Telegraph proposal was allowed to slumber until a more auspicious period, about thirteen years later, when it was revived by Cecil Rhodes.

The Overland Telegraph project was abortive. In the light of the subsequent struggle, during the nineties, to stretch a telegraph wire across the continent, the glowing optimism of the sponsors of this early proposal seems wildly extravagant. Very little was known about the vast regions in the Lake district and the Sudan through which the line must pass. Some control, furthermore, must be exercised over the myriad native tribes along this great south-to-north route. Either an international control or a British hegemony must be established here before overland telegraph promoters could hope to succeed in such a tremendous undertaking.

Nevertheless, in spite of its inevitable failure, the Overland Telegraph project was not a mere bubble. It was a proposal which, as has been seen, was sufficiently important to attract the serious attention and provoke the earnest interest and support of influential groups both in England and South Africa. It appealed to men of practical administrative experience in Africa like Sir Bartle Frere, Sivewright, Sir John Kirk and C. Giegler. Famous travellers, like Cameron and Grant were in favor of such a line. Even officials of the colonial office, although they rejected the proposal, displayed a real interest in the project. As Sivewright pointed out, " the subject when once mooted " had " a strangely enticing interest which almost chains one to it ".[65]

The proposal led to considerable study and investigation and the collection of a valuable store of information about the south-to-north route. Finally, it occupied an important place in the history of the development of the Cape-to-Cairo movement. It was a clear indication that in the latter part of the seventies, men were beginning to speculate upon the possibilities of spanning the entire continent. In short, in the Overland Telegraph proposal is found the birth of the Cape-to-Cairo idea.

CHAPTER III

The Red Paint Brush

WHILE Sivewright and Merriman were attempting to launch their Overland Telegraph proposal, another Cape Colonist was dreaming of an even more ambitious program. In 1877, Cecil Rhodes, (then a young man of twenty-four years), drew his first will. This will, Williams calls a "pathetically naive" instrument.[1] In temper it may suggest the work of an impulsive and overenthusiastic school boy but it is an indication of Rhodes' boundless ambition. All his prospective wealth he left to a Secret Society to extend British rule throughout the world. The Society was directed to promote:

The colonisation by British subjects of all lands where the means of livelihood are attainable by energy, labour and enterprise, and especially the occupation by British settlers of the entire continent of Africa, the Holy Land, the Valley of the Euphrates, the islands of Cyprus and Candia, the whole of South America, the islands of the Pacific not heretofore possessed by Great Britain, the whole of the Malay Archipelago, the seaboard of China and Japan, and the ultimate recovery of the United States of America as an integral part of the British Empire, . . . colonial representation in the Imperial Parliament, which may tend to weld together the disjointed members of the Empire, and finally, the foundation of so great a Power as to hereafter render wars impossible and promote the best interests of humanity.[2]

Cecil John Rhodes was already beginning to think in continents. Later on, Lobengula described this dreamer as "the Big Brother who eats up countries for his breakfast".[3]

66

This will is an expression of the *leit motif* which ran throughout Rhodes' life. He regarded himself as a second Loyola, as the apostle of British imperialism. His mission was to bring as much of the world as he could, within his short span of life, into the British fold. He believed firmly in salvation under the British flag. There was, he reasoned, at least "a fifty per cent chance" that there was "a God Almighty". If there was a God Almighty, he must have a plan for his universe. That plan, Rhodes concluded, was "the perfection of the species attained by the elimination of the unfit . . . the conferring upon the perfected species or race the title-deeds of the future." Rhodes set up the standard of this perfection as the power to control the destinies of the world for the benefit of everybody, "not for an elect few in a corner." Applying this standard to the peoples of the world, he decided that the white race, and particularly the Anglo-Saxon, was indisputably the nearest perfection. It was the race, he claimed, most likely to universalize certain broad general principles—justice, fair play to all, liberty and peace.[4]

Therefore [he concluded in his "curious way"], if there be a God, I think that what He would like me to do is to paint as much of the map of Africa British red as possible and to do what I can elsewhere to promote the unity and extend the influence of the English-speaking race.[5]

Rhodes believed in this creed of British imperialism with "apostolic fervor." Indeed, he turned to his mission with such well directed zeal and energy that he did more, perhaps, than any other one man to establish British power over vast stretches of the dark continent.

Rhodes has been criticized for the simplicity of his arguments, for his obvious and possibly tiresome repetition "of a few large thoughts vibrating through his brain." He has been dubbed childish, sophomoric.[6] Perhaps, however, it was the very simplicity of his thoughts and of his creed which gave him such a tremendous driving force. He was able in a rough, homely manner to give expression to the growing imperialism of his day. Men liked "the remarkable frankness and bonhomie of his disposition." [7] Furthermore, he was able to furnish the men of his generation with a new faith. He took the sordid, commercial side of nineteenth century imperialism and gave it fresh idealism. He infused into the desire to acquire wealth and power overseas, the patriotic fervor of a great movement to increase the beneficent influence of the British Empire.

. . . Most people [Sydney Low claims], even those who have been immersed in the petty worries of party politics and the sordid cares of amassing wealth, have their idealistic side; and Rhodes appealed to it. There are shrewd financiers, keen men of action, life-long worshipers of money and material success, to whom a belief in Cecil Rhodes became a substitute for religion. Minds of more subtlety and more accurate intelligence than his own yielded to his sway.[8]

It is not intended here to add to either the eulogies or the critical character sketches of Cecil Rhodes which are so numerous today. Indeed, there seems to be nothing new to contribute to what has already been written, time and again, about the man. His influence, however, was so far-reaching in the history of British expansion in Africa and particularly in the development of the Cape-to-Cairo movement that it is essential to inquire into Cecil Rhodes' plans and projects and to find out what resources he had at hand for accomplishing his work.

When he wrote his first will, just noted, the young dreamer saw the whole world gradually permeated by British influence. The world, however, was too large a field to engage the efforts of even this South African Caesar.[9] He confined his attention chiefly to Africa and especially to that highly desirable portion of Africa which stretched from Cape Colony to Egypt. " All this is to be painted red; that is my dream ", Cecil Rhodes remarked, running his fingers over a map of Africa from the Cape to the great Lakes and, again, placing his hand on Africa, " That is my dream, all English." [10] He wanted all of Africa under British influence. He was, however, a practical dreamer. He realized that he must seize the keys of the continent first. " From a youngster," he declared, he cherished a plan to have Cape Colony " as the basis for the development of Africa." From Cape Colony, he saw British influence spreading northward through the center of Africa to the lakes. He believed that the nation which controlled this " backbone " of the continent would hold the position of dominance in Africa. " Give me the center," he said, " and let who will have the swamps which skirt the coast." The first step, therefore, in the realization of his dream was to build a chain of British settlements along this central ridge. The next step was to join the British sphere of influence in the south with that in the north. With the British firmly esconced along this south-to-north route, " the conquest of Africa by the English nation," would become " a practical question." " You must deal," he told his fellow countrymen, " with the whole world and here is a chance of your getting another continent." [11]

The chief instruments which Rhodes planned to use in this conquest of a continent were railway and telegraph. A Cape-to-Cairo telegraph would open the heart of Africa to British commerce and influence. It would bind the various settlements together and unite the country in a way nothing else could do. Once British interests were linked together by this chain of communication, it would be almost impossible for H. M. Government to leave the country. " If this telegraph is made," he insisted " it will also give us the keys to the continent." " We shall," he predicted confidently, " get through to Egypt with the telegraph, and subsequently with the railway . . . we shall not relax our efforts, until by our civilization and the efforts of our people we reach the shores of the Mediterranean." If Rhodes' words are any criterion of his intentions, there is no question that his railway and telegraph were closely bound up with his imperial objectives. They were merely the tangible outward expression of the realization of his dreams.[12]

This magnificent dream was never realized in Cecil Rhodes' lifetime. It is not fulfilled today. Rhodes was destined to meet with many failures and disappointments. He was compelled to modify some of his earlier and more expansive projects. He had to cut his cloth to meet the requirements and exigencies of the time. As he was dying, Sir Lewis Michell heard him murmur: " So little done, so much to do ".[13]

Nevertheless, as will be seen in the following chapters, Rhodes did accomplish a great deal. At the time of his death in 1902, the map of South Africa was painted a good British red from Cape Town to the Great Lakes. In other words, Rhodes, through his untiring energy, added about 291,000 square miles to the British empire overseas, or an area larger than that of France, Belgium, The Netherlands and Switzerland combined. The railway to the north was at Buluwayo and the telegraph almost at Ujiji on Lake Tanganyika. All this had been done largely under his own auspices. Indirectly, he cooperated in the establishment of British hegemony from the south to the north of Africa. Finally, he inspired others to work for the fulfillment of the Cape-to-Cairo dream after his death.[14] This was a remarkable achievement for one young empire builder.[15]

This large measure of success is due partly to Rhodes' undaunted energy, the breadth of his vision and his persuasive powers in enlisting the support of others for his work.

It was also undoubtedly due to his business acumen. Rhodes was living in a commercial age in which money was a powerful weapon. He realized fully its power and determined to use wealth in building up a British empire in Africa. " It is no use," he insisted, " having big ideas if you have not the cash to carry them out." Then again: " Pure philanthropy is all very well in its way but philanthropy plus 5 per cent is a good deal better." [16]

Rhodes, therefore, set to work to provide financial support for his gigantic imperial undertakings.[17] He came as an observant boy of seventeen to South Africa just at a time when the course of history was rapidly changing for that country. He landed in Natal in 1870, about the time of the famous diamond discoveries. He stayed one year on his brother Herbert's cotton farm but he was soon seized by the diamond fever and joined the rush of diggers at Kimberley. There, on the fields, he proved that he was more than an ordinary young fortune seeker. In the midst of the scramble and the sharp competition between diamond speculators, he bought and sold claims with remarkable success. Finally, he joined forces with Alfred Beit, another notably successful diamond dealer from Hamburg. Both men were out " to control the whole diamond output ". Gradually through the amalgamation of conflicting interests, the two men built up a powerful company, the De Beers Ltd., and amassed a fortune. At the age of thirty, Rhodes could boast that he was the head of one of the largest financial corporations in the world.[18]

Rhodes, however, saw beyond the control of the world diamond market. In forming De Beers Ltd., he took the first step towards laying the foundations of a new British Empire in Africa. He insisted that the profits of the diamond company be available for use in promoting his own imperial schemes. The story of his all-night struggle with

Barney Barnato, who thought the profits should be used only in enlarging the diamond industry, is a dramatic and familiar one.[19]   Rhodes, finally, succeeded in making De Beers a tool in his imperial schemes.   " You have a fancy for building an empire in the north," his opponent admitted, " and I suppose you must have your way."   Rhodes obtained for De Beers Ltd. a trust deed which was, to say the least, an astonishing instrument, granting him all the freedom he desired.   By this trust deed, De Beers Ltd., was transformed from a mere business concern for mining and marketing diamonds into a great trading corporation resembling the old East India Company.   In fact, Sir Henry de Villiers pointed out: " Diamond mining " formed " an insignificant portion of the powers " which might be exercised by the company.[20] The whole tone of this remarkable trust deed sounds very much like the work of the young dreamer, who in 1877, left all his prospective wealth to extending British influence throughout the world.

Rhodes was instrumental, likewise, in founding the Gold Fields of South Africa, Ltd. in 1887.   He was not quite as successful at the Johannesburg gold reef as he was on the Kimberley diamond fields.   He was a little late in entering into the gold rush.   He could not obtain a monopoly of the gold production.   Nevertheless, the Gold Fields of South Africa was a wealthy company.   Its capital increased " by a million and a quarter " in six years.   By 1895, it paid a dividend of no less than fifty per cent; Rhodes himself for several years drew from the company an income of between £300,000 and £400,000.[21]

The profits from his companies Rhodes devoted, to a considerable extent, to painting the map of Africa red.   In fact, says Edmund Garrett of the *Cape Times,* much of Rhodes' finance may be described as " making De Beers and the Goldfields bleed freely for ' the north ' when required;

then making it up later when the see-saw of the market allowed." [22] He used not only the profits of the companies but he gave unsparingly of his own private wealth to the cause of expansion. The expenses of the transcontinental telegraph line were borne at the beginning almost entirely out of Rhodes' " private purse." [23] During the closing years of his life, he threw much of his fortune into the Cape-to-Cairo project. When he was negotiating for the capitalization of his interest as director of De Beers, he exclaimed, " I am quite poor. I want money badly, not for myself, but for my railway and telegraph." [24]

Rhodes realized not only the power of wealth in promoting his schemes but he also appreciated the value of political influence. Here again he used his political achievements, as he had his financial successes, largely in his plans of empire building. He entered the Cape Parliament with the thought, " if possible to use my political power to obtain the balance of unclaimed country for the British Empire." [25] He left no stone unturned in securing a hold on politics both in South Africa and in England. He was elected to the Cape Parliament in 1880 as a member from Barkly West and " he held the seat against all comers till his death " in 1902. In 1890, he became Prime Minister of Cape Colony and kept this office during two Ministries; one from 1890 to 1893 and the other from 1893 to 1896. In Parliament, he soon became a leader in the movement towards northern expansion. He was active in 1882 in overthrowing the Sprigg ministry because of its failure to bring the railway north to Kimberley. As will be noted in the following chapters, he was constantly fighting to keep the route open to the north.[26]

Rhodes was not a greater orator in the Cape House. He did not speak often. His speeches are rambling, disjointed, badly organized and full of repetition. Rhodes, himself, perhaps believed too firmly that " if you reiterate your ideas

often enough, you will carry conviction in the end." [27]   The
House members, however, listened to him attentively, especially after his reputation as "the great amalgamator" and
expansionist began to grow.[28]   They were very proud of
him, says Williams, and were "flattered . . . by the glory
reflected on the Colony from the deference paid at home to
their leading statesman."   Possibly, the very informality
of Rhodes' talks was flattering.   He seemed to be taking
the whole House into his confidence.   He was literally
thinking aloud and allowing the House a glimpse of his
own mental processes as he laboriously hammered out his
thoughts.[29]

Although Rhodes usually spoke to an attentive and
friendly audience, he preferred to settle most controversies
in the lobby or outside of Parliament.   He knew the art of
fraternizing with the people.   During his early years in
the House he made many friends, particularly among the
Dutch.   He was popular, writes Michell, "with the officials
of the House, down to the humblest messenger."   He
chatted with the clerks.   He visited the Dutch farmers in
their homesteads.[30]

Furthermore, Rhodes let his money do a great deal of
talking.   Every man, according to Rhodes, had his price [31]
and he insisted, "I have not found in life any one I could
not deal with."   The price was not always money.   Sometimes it was entrance into a club, a seat in the House, or a
coveted position on some committee.   Quite frequently,
however, it was a judicious distribution of chartered shares,
or some offer of financial assistance.[32]   Rhodes was frank
about the matter himself.   He believed that money possessed
power and that most men could be moved by appealing to
their mercenary instincts.

Undoubtedly Rhodes was not too nice in his methods.
It is, however, unnecessary to pass judgment upon the ethics

of Rhodes' work. The important point is what this "lust for power," or, as his admirers preferred to call it, this "unquenchable idealism" accomplished. Whether from grossly selfish motives or from a highly altruistic sense of public duty, Rhodes was essentially an imperialist and his ideas had a potent influence over his contemporaries.

Rhodes was well aware of the value of the press in winning popular support for his gigantic task of painting Africa red. He was chief proprietor of the *Cape Times*. He was not, however, wholly able to control the policies of this paper. Edmund Garrett, its editor, was an admirer of Cecil Rhodes but he was not blind to Rhodes' weakness. The newspaper did not become a Rhodes mouthpiece although it undoubtedly did come under the Rhodes spell at times.[33] Cecil Rhodes once remarked to Garrett, "I have never inspired an article in your paper or requested that a given line should be taken, but you might at least be careful about facts."[34]

He was careful to secure a share in the *Cape Argus* and that leading South African newspaper did its part in giving publicity to Rhodes' operations.[35] He had connections also with a considerable group of other South African newspapers. "Not," says Williams, "that he dictated their policy, but he was at any rate secure of their general support."[36].

Rhodes also, had his press friends in England. Chief among his journalistic allies was the fiery reformer, W. T. Stead. Stead, it will be recalled, was editor of the *Pall Mall Gazette* from 1883 to 1889. In 1890, he founded and edited the *English Review of Reviews*. He was a conspicuous figure in the newspaper and journalistic world of this period. He had the reputation of being a fearless, albeit somewhat insolent and dogmatic, crusader. "Great statesmen," writes Wemyss Reid, "though they might hate Mr. Stead personally, accepted his newspaper as though it were the organ of Fate itself." [37]   Stead's reputation has distinctly faded since the early nineties but his contemporaries were apparently greatly impressed by his resounding voice and his thundering campaigns to right the wrongs of his fellow-creatures.

At first, Stead directed his bolts against Cecil Rhodes, especially in regard to the dispute between Rhodes and the missionary Mackenzie in 1884 over the Bechuanaland Protectorate.   The story of this quarrel will be discussed in greater detail in the next chapter.   Mackenzie was deeply interested in the welfare of the native.   He felt that native interests were far safer in the hands of Her Majesty than at the mercy of a great soulless trading corporation like the chartered company of Rhodes.   Stead, the philanthropist, therefore, took the part of the negrophil Mackenzie and attacked the Rhodes policy.[38]

In spite of Stead's campaign against him, Cecil Rhodes was very much interested in the aggressive editor of the *Pall Mall Gazette.*   Perhaps he realized that it would be more politic to have this reformer for his friend rather than his opponent.   Perhaps, too, he saw in the impulsive editor a potential agent for propagating the Rhodes brand of philanthropy.   At any rate, he determined to talk to him.   Stead was sentenced in 1885 to two months' imprisonment for the indiscreet part he had just taken in a reform campaign. Rhodes tried to see him in jail but was unsuccessful.   It was not until 1889, that Rhodes was able to arrange for a meeting at a dinner at the Cape Agency in London.   Stead, still slightly prejudiced against the South African, went to the dinner somewhat unwillingly.   In the conversation which ensued, however, Rhodes took his opponent completely by storm and converted him into an ardent supporter of his policy in South Africa.

The two men had much in common. They were in particular agreed upon " federation, expansion and consolidation of the Empire." Rhodes confided " a secret scheme "
to Stead in which his paper was to play an important role.
The *Pall Mall Gazette* was at the time in financial difficulties.
Rhodes offered Stead as a " free gift " £20,000 to buy a
share in the paper. He promised to do more in the future.
He even talked about bequeathing his fortune to the scheme
of which the paper was to be an integral part. Stead entered
enthusiastically into his plans. In fact, he was carried off
his feet by Rhodes' generosity. " It seems like a fairy
dream," he wrote to his wife.[39]

Thereupon, Rhodes and his new convert struck up an
intimate friendship which lasted without a quaver until the
outbreak of the South African War in 1899, when their
mutual respect was broken. Stead was as bitterly opposed
to war against the Boers as Rhodes was ardent in supporting it. This sharp difference of opinion, although it did
not destroy the friendship between the two men, destroyed
Rhodes' confidence in Stead's judgment.

During the period of their greatest intimacy, however,
nearly all their plans and hopes centered around " the grandiose idea of a world-wide English-speaking confederation."
Rhodes, in 1891, was still dreaming and talking to Stead
about that curious secret society for anglicizing the world
which, as has been seen, bulked so large in his first will and
which was probably the " secret scheme " discussed at their
first meeting in 1889. In fact, the " secret society " was
beginning to take definite shape. Rhodes had, also, confided his plan to Lord Rothschild and Sir Harry Johnston.
Stead, Johnston and Rothschild formed the nucleus around
which the organization was to grow. In 1891, Rhodes drew
up his third will in which he appointed Stead and Lord
Rothschild as trustees of his fortune.[40]

It will be noted in a later chapter what valuable service the "leaders" in the *Pall Mall Gazette* performed for Rhodes at the time of the creation of the British South Africa Company. The *Review of Reviews,* likewise, loyally cooperated with his schemes.

Rhodes was successful, as well, in winning the support of other influential men in the journalistic circle of his day. He converted Sir Sidney Low of the *St. James Gazette* from open hostility to a friendly attitude. He also gained the friendship of Moberly Bell, the manager of the *Times.* Furthermore, he took Miss Flora Shaw, "one of the most brilliant and accomplished members" of the *Times* staff, into his confidence. That influential newspaper changed its skeptical and slightly disparaging tone towards his activities into a whole-hearted support for his plans.[41]

Rhodes seems to have been on friendly terms with the Reverend John Verschoyle, the sub-editor of the *Fortnightly Review.* At any rate, he is found at a dinner in Verschoyle's home in 1889.[42] Then, later on in 1900 Verschoyle conducted a spirited but biased defense of Rhodes' South African policies in his book entitled *Cecil Rhodes. His Political Life and Speeches.*

There may be some question as to just how responsible the press is in shaping and expressing that elusive something called "public opinion." At any rate, Rhodes had faith in its efficacy. He was very sensitive to praise or blame as reflected in the newspapers. He wanted to feel that he had the people at his back and he took great care to reach the people, as far as he could, through the press.[43]

Cecil Rhodes was in touch with political and financial leaders as well as with the journalistic world. As already noted, he placed great confidence in Lord Rothschild. Indeed the House of Rothschild took an active interest in the development of the country both in the south and north of

Africa. The story of Disraeli's purchase of the Suez Canal shares through Messrs. N. M. Rothschild & Sons is well known. The story of Rothschild's work in the south, however, is not so well known. Yet it was this great banking house which supplied the means which made possible the first northward push of Cecil Rhodes. It was, in fact, largely through the financial assistance of Lord Rothschild that Rhodes was able to effect the consolidation of various diamond mining companies into De Beers Ltd., the cornerstone of his African empire. Later on, the House took part, though in a minor degree, in the development of Rhodesia.[44]

Largely through the cooperation of Alfred Beit of Wernher Beit & Co. and through Baron Émile Beaumont D'Erlanger of the Banking House of Erlanger, Rhodes was able to build up and operate the whole system of railways in Rhodesia. Baron D'Erlanger, in fact, became a director of the British South Africa Company and of the Rhodesia Railways Trust, Ltd.[45]

Baron de Worms of the firm of G. & A. de Worms in London, fought hard for the grant of a charter for the British South Africa Company.[46] There is some evidence that this firm was involved financially in Rhodes' schemes.

In other words, says Baron D'Erlanger, Rhodes " fired the imagination of that most conservative class of human beings, the British investor, by christening his route the Cape to Cairo." [47] As will be seen in the later chapters, these financial leaders and these hard-headed British investors stood by Rhodes through many adversities. They contributed, for example, to his railway line even when H. M. Government failed to give a guarantee. They supported him loyally even after his reputation was tarnished by the Jameson fiasco. In the shareholders of his British South Africa Company, for instance, Rhodes could always rely on solid support and could feel that he had " a compact body of English public opinion behind him." [48]

Rhodes could count among his friends such powerful leaders as Lord Rosebery, Rothschild's son-in-law; Kitchener, Colonel Charles Gordon, Sir Hercules Robinson, Jan Hofmeyr and Lord Milner. He had, at times, the much-needed support of Lord Salisbury. Salisbury, to be sure, looked with some skepticism at this bold empire builder. He was willing to cooperate, however, in Sir Harry Johnston's and Rhodes' extensive plans for a British Empire in Central Africa and he gave a reluctant consent to the grant of a royal charter to the British South Africa Company. Joseph Chamberlain, although he criticized Rhodes severely at one time, was genuinely in sympathy with much of Rhodes' work. Later chapters deal in greater detail with the development of Rhodes' plans and the influence of his work on British expansion. These politicians, military leaders and statesmen will be met once more and their relations with Rhodes viewed in the proper setting. It is sufficient here to note that Rhodes had many supporters in various circles both in England and South Africa.

The direct influence of Cecil Rhodes upon British expansion in Africa was great but his indirect influence upon the imperial thoughts, aspirations and activities of his fellow countrymen was, also, far-reaching. He played a leading rôle on the South African stage but he was, likewise, a wire-puller behind the scenes. As the history of British penetration into Africa develops, traces of that influence will be found along the whole Cape-to-Cairo route, in British Central Africa, in Uganda and in the Sudan.

CHAPTER IV

Cape Colony as the Base of Operations

The first step before Rhodes in the realization of his ambitious program was to bring the territory from Cape Colony up to the Zambezi River under the British flag.

He turned in the beginning to the men on the spot to help him in his work of expansion. It was his cherished dream, in fact, to make the Cape " the basis for the development of Africa ".

I have faith [he boasted], that, remote as our starting point is, the development of Africa will occur through the Cape Colony; that, exempt from the risks of the unhealthiness of the East and West Coasts, we shall be able to obtain the dominant position throughout the interior, starting from the Cape Colony, passing through Bechuanaland, adopting the Matabele arrangement, and so on to the Zambesi, and I have confidence that the people of the Cape have the will, and the pluck and the energy to adopt this as their inheritance.[1]

Out of this movement of northward expansion from the Cape, he hoped a great confederation of all the South African States would grow. He could then build his African empire upon a firm and substantial foundation of good will. In fact, he believed that he could submerge all provincialism, all racial prejudices in this great drive for the North.[2]

This United States of South Africa, as he called the confederation, would be an autonomous unit within the British Empire. In this respect, Rhodes followed the most progressive colonial policy of his generation. He believed ardently in imperial federation and also in home rule for the separate states within the imperial union.[3]   He considered too much interference on the part of the home government as meddlesome, mischievous, and unnecessary and even talked indiscreetly about eliminating the " Imperial Factor " in the work of winning the hinterland for Cape Colony.[4]

Rhodes' extreme views about home rule and his annoyance at " Grandmamma ", as he called H. M. Government, led to a grave misunderstanding of his motives in England. He was looked upon with suspicion as an Afrikander, as an anti-imperialist ready to " cut the painter " which bound the colony to the Mother Country.   His loyalty to the Empire was severely questioned.   There was, however, very little real foundation for this distrust.   In his estimation, the new confederation should have " the most perfect self government internally ", whilst retaining at the same time " the obligation of mutual defense against the outside world ".[5]   When asked by Borckenhagen, an editor of a Dutch paper at Bloomfontein, to join in the movement for a completely independent South Africa, he replied sternly:

You take me either for a rogue or a fool.   I would be a rogue to forfeit all my history and my traditions, and I would be a fool, because I would be hated by my own countrymen and mistrusted by yours. . . . The only chance of union is the overshadowing protection of a supreme power.   Any German, Frenchman, or Russian would tell you that the best and most liberal Power in the world is that over which Her Majesty reigns.[6]

There were two elements fighting for supremacy at the Cape: the English and the Dutch.   The Dutch, however, " outnumbered the British by three to two ".   In any plan of a federal union, in any scheme of expansion to the North with the cooperation of the colonists, therefore, Rhodes must take this larger group into consideration.   Furthermore, the Dutch possessed a compact and powerful political machine called the Afrikander Bond.[7]

The Bond was founded by Rev. S. J. du Toit. Du Toit was a Dutch Reform Minister and at the same time editor of a paper called *The Patriot*. He was an ardent nationalist. He mistrusted the British rule in Cape Colony and used his paper " to fan into a flame the smouldering discontent of the Dutch " against British control. In 1879, he suggested the formation of an association for the dissemination of Dutch culture all over the colony. The ultimate aim of the society was a free and independent United South Africa. " Africa for the Africanders " was the watchword of the new organization.

The Afrikander Bond grew slowly but steadily. At the end of 1880, there were only twenty branches in the Colony. By 1881, the number had increased to thirty-one and in 1882, fifty-two new branches were added. The influence of the Bond spread north into the Free State where it was supported by F. W. Reitz, chief justice, later President. It also secured the cooperation here of another editor, the young German, Borckenhagen. It had roots, likewise, in the Transvaal, where Du Toit was called as superintendent of education.

Fortunately for Rhodes' plans, the leadership in the Bond in 1883 passed to Jan Hendrik Hofmeyr. Hofmeyr was an Afrikander who followed a middle course and who endeavored to hold the extremists of his party in check. In fact, he " had joined the Bond in order to wean it from its anti-English views ". At heart, Hofmeyr, possibly, was full in sympathy with the ultimate goal of his compatriots; an independent South Africa under its own flag. He was, however, a practical and astute politician. He realized that conditions in South Africa were not ripe for complete independence. South Africa was too much at the mercy of other powers to break away from British protection and he was particularly apprehensive of German machinations.[8] Although Hofmeyr had no great love for the English, he feared the Germans.[9] It was too early, therefore, he thought, to talk about casting off the protecting British yoke and he was opposed to what he considered mischievous anti-British propaganda.

Cecil Rhodes, the realist, recognized in the new leader of the Afrikander Bond a man whom it would be better to have as a friend than as a foe. In fact, he considered Hofmeyr as "the most capable politician in South Africa".[10] Furthermore, it was plain that he needed the Dutch vote in order to carry out his schemes and Hofmeyr was the virtual dictator of the Bond. Rhodes, therefore, set to work to enlist him and, with him, the cooperation of the Bond, in his program of expansion to the North.

The Dutch were chiefly farmers and wine-growers. Hofmeyr wished to promote these agricultural interests of his constituents by protective tariffs. Rhodes was, also, genuinely in favor of agricultural protection. On this basis of common interest, he finally concluded a bargain with the leader of the Bond. Rhodes promised to defend the Cape Protective system. Hofmeyr, in turn, "pledged himself in the name of the Bond not to throw any obstacles in the way of northern expansion". Thenceforth, the Bond leader loyally kept his pledge even at the risk of losing the support of the more intransigeant Boers who wanted the North exclusively for the Dutch.

For a while, Rhodes almost succeeded in his plan of co-operation with the Cape Boers. He liked the Dutch farmers "and always got on well with them individually". He used to visit them in their homes. He was, likewise, truly interested in the agricultural development of the colony and did everything in his power to improve conditions. He created a ministry of Agriculture. He advocated a railway program for connecting the central farming districts with their markets. He saved the pest-ridden orange groves by introducing the American ladybird. He brought over California fruit experts to improve fruit culture. He imported Arab horses to improve the breed of Cape horses. He introduced Angora goats. He tried to persuade Harcourt to give a preference to colonial wines.[11]

While he was intent on improving conditions within the colony, he was also talking in glowing terms about gold in the north, about farms in the hinterland for the growing families of the Cape colonists and about seizing the trade of the interior for the Cape. In short, he offered the colonists the key to the interior and, finally, a dominant position in a federated South Africa.[12]

The more moderate members of the Bond were willing, for a time, to listen to the seductive arguments of Cecil Rhodes. They were ready to postpone the question of complete independence to some more auspicious period. They were interested in the satisfaction of more immediate and practical needs. They gave their votes to the leader who protected their interests at home and there was even a general belief that his policy of northward expansion was right.[13] In short, the Dutch farmers at the Cape seemed to like Rhodes. Certainly, he was sent to Parliament by a Dutch constituency and he kept his seat even after the disastrous Raid. As prime minister, he was maintained in power largely by the Dutch vote. In fact, he refused to accept the office of prime minister in 1890 until he was assured of the favorable attitude of the Afrikander Bond. Even the republican du Toit became finally " a devoted adherent of Rhodes." During the period from 1881, when Rhodes first entered the Cape House, to 1895 when the Raid destroyed his hopes, his popularity with the Dutch element was strong enough to encourage his belief that he could work with and through the Cape Boers.[14]

Rhodes was, however, only partially successful even during this period when his hopes ran high. His policy of expansion to the north through the cooperation of both Cape Boers and Englishmen was the plan of a statesman but it entangled him in a complicated political web. He never could count with perfect assurance on the continued support of the Cape Colonists. The English Party, Rhodes considered, "hopelessly divided and individually incapable. And it had no policy beyond that of securing office." [15] Although he could rely much oftener on the support of the Dutch moderates, the Cape Boers were drawn in two directions. They were both Cape Colonists and at the same time Boer nationalists. Rhodes could appeal to their self-interest as colonists but he steadily refused, as has been already noted, to join in the movement for a South Africa under its own flag. In other words, he was opposed to the primary principle upon which the Bond was founded.

As Boer nationalists, the Cape Dutch were drawn towards their freedom-loving kinsmen in the Transvaal. The Transvaal Boers cared for no dealings with the English beyond what the necessities of the moment required. They were interested in Northward expansion but they wanted the North exclusively for the Boers. In fact, they considered the country to the North and west of the Boer republics as their natural heritage and the English as meddlesome intruders. In their dreams, the Transvaal, not Cape Colony, would play the dominant rôle there. The Transvaal presidents from Pretorius to Kruger aimed at "the formation of a great independent republic north of the Orange." They set to work, therefore, to enlarge their country's boundaries on the west and northeast and to seek for outlets on the coast which would make them less dependent on the Cape ports. [16]

A survey of the Transvaal Boer attempts to secure both commercial and political independence is essential to an un-

PRESIDENT PAUL KRUGER
Reproduced with the permission of the Legation of the Union
of South Africa, Washington, D.C.

derstanding of the development of the ever-widening cleavage between Cecil Rhodes and the northern Boers. The story is a tangled one of conflicting imperial and economic ambitions but it is so important in the study of the development of the Rhodes program that it is well here to try to undo some of the knots.

Along the western borders of the two Boer Republics of the Orange Free State and the Transvaal, ran a great trade route to the interior called the " English " or " Missionaries' road ".[17] There were other roads to the north but this was the main route. The other roads to the westward were less direct for purposes of trade and were so deficient in permanent water that they could not be used at all times. Furthermore, along the frontier of the Boer Republics, between them and the Kalahari desert, lay fertile country, suitable for pasturing cattle. Further westward the sandy and arid soil of the so-called desert was less inviting. The Boers, naturally, wanted this fertile strip beyond their western boundary and the route to the north which ran through it. Indeed, both Boers and Britons realized that whoever controlled this road could command the trade of the interior.[18]

Moreover, in 1868, as noted before, gold was reported at Tati along the Missionaries' road a little northwest of the Transvaal. With this discovery, " The Great North Road," writes Professor Walker, " sprang at once into first class importance." [19] President Pretorius, thereupon, attempted to annex the gold fields at Tati but withdrew from this debatable ground at the protest of Great Britain and Portugal.

The Boers were also keenly interested in securing a port on the Indian Ocean. They had to have some outlet for sending their produce to European markets and the distance from the Transvaal to sea towns on the east coast was much less than to the harbors in Cape Colony and Natal. In fact, there were two possible ports within comparatively easy reach of the Transvaal; one in St. Lucia Bay in Zululand and the other, Lourenço Marques in Delagoa Bay.

The coast from Natal to Delagoa Bay was independent native land before 1884. In 1867, President Pretorius attempted to annex "a thin strip of territory running down to Delagoa Bay." Great Britain and Portugal protested and Pretorius retracted the annexation.[20]

The Boers next turned their attention to Zululand, the corridor to St. Lucia Bay. Native disturbances which broke out in 1884 furnished them with an opportunity to step in and establish a small Boer Republic in Zululand on the border of the Transvaal.

On October 26, the New Republic proclaimed a protectorate over two-thirds of Zululand, including St. Lucia Bay. H. M. Government thereupon protested. Perhaps the chief reason for British disapproval was fear of German intrigue with the Boers. Indeed, there was some grounds for this fear in the fact that a German in the service of the Transvaal did acquire a large concession on the Bay from Dinizulu, the native chief, and then sold his concession to Herr Lüderitz. Herr Lüderitz, as will be noted later on in this chapter, was a German merchant with imperial ambitions. He was at this time busy establishing a German trading post on the southwest coast in Namaqualand as a nucleus for a colony. When the German agent for the Transvaal, therefore, turned over his concession in St. Lucia Bay to Lüderitz, the British felt that the Boers were going too far. H. M. S. *Goshawk* was forthwith dispatched to the Bay and on December 18, 1884, the British hoisted their flag over the harbor. The Bay and its hinterland were then declared to be British on the basis of "a somewhat questionable agreement" with a former native chief. Pretoria and Berlin protested. On May 7, 1885, Germany agreed, however, to "withdraw her protest against the hoisting of the British flag at Santa Lucia Bay, and to refrain from making acquisitions of territory or establishing protectorates on the coast between the colony of Natal and Delagoa Bay." [21] The Boers were not prepared to take effective action. Thus, the British secured St. Lucia, "The only serviceable harbor between Durban and Lourenço Marques." [22] Great Britain then proceeded to annex the rest of Zululand, excluding the New Republic which they had previously recognized, and to place it under the government of Natal. Finally, in May, 1895, the British Government annexed Amatongaland and its appurtenances up to the Portuguese border. The Transvaal was thereby made a completely land-locked country. Its schemes, therefore, for securing a port of its own on the Indian Ocean were shattered. [23]

There was still a possibility, however, of securing a shorter railway route to the sea than the lines coming up from Cape Colony and Natal, i. e., that from the Portuguese harbor of Lourenço Marques in Delagoa Bay. The Transvaal presidents from Burgers to Kruger looked eagerly towards Delogoa Bay as a harbor " free from the trammels of British ports and influence." [24] They all played with schemes for a railway line from Lourenço Marques to Pretoria. [25]

In 1881, as is well known, the Transvaal Boers defeated the British forces at Majuba and secured autonomy for their country in the subsequent Pretoria Convention of August 3, 1881. British prestige was considerably lowered in the eyes of the victorious Boers. They were in no meek and submissive mood. Hopes of an independent Boer State with enlarged boundaries on the west, north and southeast were given new life and, with them, schemes developed for the railway from Delagoa Bay to Pretoria.

The leader of the Republican Dutch farmers at this time was Oom Paul Kruger. He successfully carried through the negotiations over the Pretoria Convention and was the hero of the hour. In 1882, he was elected to the presidency by a large majority. Indeed, he exercised a profound influence over Dutch nationalists both in the Transvaal and all over South Africa. His election, however, boded ill for all Rhodes' plans of cooperation with the Dutch and for his schemes of expansion to the Zambezi. Kruger would have nothing more to do with the English than he could help and he mistrusted the Bond for its unholy alliance with the British.[26] The South African Republic, however, was still economically dependent on the Cape and would probably continue to be until a Delagoa Bay railway was complete. The Transvaal Boers must have some outlet to the sea for their interior trade. Thus, for a time, there seemed to be some ground for cooperation between the Cape and the Transvaal. To be sure, Kruger was making a vigorous effort to promote a Delagoa Bay railway line and in 1884 there were prospects that such a railway would be constructed. Nevertheless, the railway negotiations were involved and tedious and the Transvaal must continue to look south to the Cape and Natal Ports for some time.

In December, 1883, the Portuguese Government granted a concession to Colonel Edward McMurdo, an American railway promoter to construct a railway from Lourenço Marques to the Transvaal border. Instead of asking for a cash subvention, McMurdo agreed to build the line without pecuniary assistance provided the Portuguese Government " would allow no line of railway to be built in competition " and that the company " should have absolute and uncontrolled right to fix tariff rates." [27]

Towards the close of 1883, Kruger set forth with a Boer deputation to England primarily to negotiate for an agreement to replace the Pretoria Convention of 1881. Besides this major objective, however, Kruger was anxious to push forward with the Delagoa Bay railway plans. After the commission left England, they journeyed to Holland. Here, Kruger tried to raise a loan for the railway. Although the commissioners were received " with the greatest heartiness and enthusiasm ", the Dutch burghers were not impressed by the railway proposal.[28] Kruger was able, however, to form a committee of private financiers who undertook to organize a company to construct the Transvaal section of the line on the condition that they could also obtain the concession to construct and exploit the Portuguese section.[29]

From Holland, the Boer Commission went via Belgium and France to Portugal. In Portugal, they found more interest in a Delagoa Bay railway than elsewhere but they also discovered that the Portuguese Government had granted the McMurdo concession. The exclusive rights given to McMurdo were not compatible with the desire of the Dutch financial group who wanted to control the Portuguese as well as the Transvaal section of the line. The McMurdo concession, however, was a *fait accompli*. The Portuguese Government refused to retract it. Both the Portuguese and Boers were anxious to have communication between Lourenço Marques and Pretoria. The Portuguese badly needed the help of the Dutch company. The section through the Transvaal was much the hardest, longest and most costly to construct. Finally, the Transvaal delegates suggested a possible solution to the dilemma. They asked for a tramway or light railway [30] between Delagoa Bay and the Transvaal for transporting railway material to the Transvaal in case McMurdo's Company did not complete its section rapidly enough to allow work to commence on their end. This arrangement was accepted by the Portuguese Government and embodied in a secret agreement between that Government and the Transvaal.[31]

On the strength of this secret agreement, the Boer delegation succeeded in enlisting the help of a few Dutch financiers to lay the foundations of a railway company. To this group Kruger granted a concession " giving them the sole right to construct and work railways in the South African Republic (the rights of the Government itself only excepted)". By article XXII of the concession, the Government of the South African Republic was to have control of the railway in time of war or when there was danger of war or in case of internal disorder. The concessionaires formed a nucleus for the Netherlands South Africa Railway Company which was formally constituted three years later, i. e., in 1887. The new company was nominally a Dutch company located at Amsterdam but it was virtually a department of the Transvaal Government. In fact, the Government of the Transvaal retained a right to 85 per cent of the surplus profits.[32] The Germans, also, had large interests in the company. The greater portion of its funds was obtained from German sources. 6,836 shares out of a total of 14,000 were held by Germans and Austrians. It had on its working staff 197 Germans to 115 British; 1,777 Hollanders to 777 Afrikanders.[33]

McMurdo, meanwhile, was having difficulty in finding capital to finance his Portuguese railway company. News of the secret agreement between the Portuguese Government and the Transvaal delegation leaked out and, McMurdo claimed, prevented him from obtaining the advances which had been promised in Germany and Holland. He was equally unsuccessful at Brussels. Finally, in 1887, he succeeded in forming a British company to help him in his undertaking. Technically his " Delagoa Bay and East African Railway Company " continued to exist as a Portuguese concern but actually many of the shares were held by the British company and McMurdo, himself, retained a controlling interest.[34]

Thus, plans for building the railway from Lourenço Marques to Pretoria were launched under inauspicious circumstances. Two rival companies were engaged in the construction; one Dutch in which German nationals had large interests, the other nominally Portuguese but financed by a British company and controlled by an American. The ill-feeling between the two companies continued to grow and the complications arising from this rivalry played an important part in shaping the future policies of both Kruger and Rhodes and in widening the breach between the two leaders.

All these difficulties delayed railway construction. For a time, McMurdo's railway appeared to have " foundered . . . in the mud-flats behind Delagoa Bay " and the prospective Netherlands Railway Company showed no signs of activity. In 1883, as was already noted, gold-bearing quartz was found in the De Kaap district of the Transvaal. Quartz required heavy machinery for transportation. Some cheap, speedy and Tsetse-proof means of transport to the sea was imperative and a definite railway policy was forced on the Transvaal. Kruger had to utilize a railway running north from the Cape or Natal to the Transvaal since he could not secure his Delagoa line immediately. Furthermore, Kruger was not opposed to railway extension to the North. In fact, " in his attitude towards railways," writes Metcalfe, " the old President showed himself far more progressive than most of the people in Cape Colony." [35] He realized, as well as Rhodes, that railway construction was essential to the development of the interior trade. He was primarily interested, however, in securing communications with some port on the coast. For these reasons in January 1886, Oom Paul sent an agent south to take soundings at Cape Town. He then came forward with a proposal for a customs agreement and permission to extend the Kimberley railway into the Transvaal.[36]

Rhodes had been anxiously watching the progress of Kruger's negotiations for a railway from Delagoa Bay to the Transvaal. He saw in the prospective Delagoa line a menace to Cape Commerce and to the eventual union of the states of South Africa under the dominance of Cape Colony. He was, moreover, apprehensive about a new tariff which the Portuguese were preparing in 1883 to put into effect at Delagoa Bay in favor of the Transvaal. If the Delagoa Bay line was completed to Pretoria before a colonial line to the Transvaal and the new tariff went into effect, the trade with the interior would be diverted from the southern ports to Delagoa Bay. Rhodes insisted that " the development of the interior was the birthright " of Cape Colony. With this trade in the Transvaal's hands, the Cape Colonists would either lose all desire for the future union of South Africa or else would have to beg to come into a union dominated by the Transvaal and at the Transvaal's own price.[37] Rhodes, therefore, welcomed Kruger's attempt in the early part of 1886 to cooperate with the Cape because he saw in the Boer President's offer a means of putting a stop to the Delagoa Bay Railway and of drawing the Cape and the Transvaal closer together. He urged the House to act at once in conjunction with Kruger.[38]

In spite of Rhodes' ardent support, however, the Cape Ministry rejected Oom Paul's offer. Rhodes' warning proved true. Kruger never again asked for Cape cooperation in his railway plans. He turned his attention thenceforth to promoting the Delagoa Bay railway project and the importance of connecting the Transvaal with a sea port on the east coast outweighed his interest in the development of the North. From this time on, he was anxious to have the Delagoa Bay Railway reach Pretoria before the Cape or Natal lines crossed the Transvaal border. In an interview with Charles Metcalfe in 1888, over the prospects of a Bechuanaland Railway, " Kruger gave a grunt, and then said, ' I must have first my Delagoa Bay Railway.' " To be sure, he was not opposed to the railway to the north *per se*. In fact, four years later, he asked Metcalfe whether he would make the northern railway through his country past Pretoria.[39] He did not, however, want any interference with the Delagoa Bay line. In fact, the completion of that railway was of primary importance in his estimation. " Every railway," he said, " that approaches me I look upon as an enemy on whatever side it comes. I must have my Delagoa line first, and then other lines may come." [40]

Furthermore, with the influx of gold diggers to the Witwatersrand in 1886, the Transvaal received a new importance. Its treasury was no longer bankrupt. At the same time, McMurdo's railway began advancing from Delagoa Bay. Kruger felt strong enough to shake off economic dependence upon the south. In 1888, he refused to join in a conference between the Cape, Natal and the Orange Free State over a customs union and railway extension. In the same year, as will be seen later, he opposed the extension northwards of the Cape and Natal railway systems.[41] He carried his obstructionist policies so far at one time that Sir Hercules Robinson, governor at the Cape, wrote home: " It was felt by many, Dutch as well as English, that the Cape should not any longer be at the mercy of the Republics in the matter of northern railway extension." There was, he continued,

a general belief among both Dutch and English in Cape Colony that . . . the true policy to pursue would be the gradual expansion of the Cape Colony towards the Zambesi, the Imperial Government preparing the way, and the eventual extension of the railway to the interior through either colonial territory, or through territories under British protection or influence.[42]

This growing independence both economically and politically of the Transvaal was a decisive factor in the development of Rhodes' program of northward expansion. For a time, to be sure, he refused to acknowledge defeat in his policy of cooperation with the Boers. He persisted in thinking that he could join hands even with the freedom-loving and determined president of the Transvaal. In fact, as late as the summer of 1888, he still tried to cooperate with Kruger's railway schemes. He discouraged the extension of a Cape line north of Kimberley because Kruger opposed such a line. Indeed, Rhodes was actually voting against the construction of a section which later became an important link in his Cape-to-Cairo railway.[43]

In conformance with his desire to cooperate with the Transvaal Boers, Rhodes also adopted a new policy in regard to the Delagoa Bay Railway. In 1888, McMurdo's company and the Netherlands South African Railway were at loggersheads over the question of tariff rates to be levied on their respective sections. Furthermore, the Netherlands Company was in financial straits. The Portuguese Government, at the same time, was apparently in connivance with the Dutch Company. The Portuguese officials claimed that McMurdo's company was not completing its end of the line within the specified time and threatened to create difficulties unless the latter company agreed to the rates asked for by the Dutch group.[44]

Cecil Rhodes saw in this troubled state of railway affairs and in the financial weakness of the Netherlands Company an opportunity for the Cape Colonists to step in " and settle their differences by offering a scheme of extension from Bloemfontein to Delagoa Bay, or from the Vaal River to Delagoa Bay ". If the Dutch concessionaires were weak, it might even be expedient for the Cape Colonists to take some share in the reflotation of their company. In other words, in true Rhodes fashion, he wished to go ahead on the basis of amalgamating conflicting interests.[45]

This was Rhodes' railway extension policy in the summer of 1888; and a full understanding of this policy is essential to a comprehension of the gradual development of Rhodes' future plans. It was perfectly consistent with his general plan of cooperation with the Dutch. It fits neatly into his picture of a United South Africa bound closely together by a network of railways and by a customs union. It was an essential feature of his South African confederation. Upon the formation of this confederation, as noted, he based his plans for the spread of British and Dutch influence to the north. In this sense, therefore, his railway scheme was consistent with his ideas of expansion.

Although his railway policies were thus in harmony with his general plan of procedure, railway extension was not, however, in the summer of 1888, an integral part of his scheme for securing the hinterland from the Orange River to the Zambezi. He was already dreaming of an Africa painted a good British red but the specific steps by which he was to realize this dream developed gradually.[46] He was more intent on seizing the land to the north than he was in building a railway into a still largely unknown country. In fact, it is doubtful whether railway projects played any direct and definite rôle, at this date, in his ambitious imperial program. To be sure they would play such a rôle a few years hence. Rhodes seems to have developed his plans for a Cape-to-Cairo railway first in connection with the formation of the British South Africa Company. He had undoubtedly heard of Sivewright's Overland Telegraph. Possibly by this time, he was already turning over in his mind inchoate plans for a Cape-to-Cairo line of communication.

There is no doubt, however, that by 1882, Rhodes was "seeing red". Expansion was a cardinal principle in his political creed. Africa was the ultimate goal. The immediate objective was the Zambezi River. He might dicker and bargain about railway proposals which, as yet, had no direct bearing on this plan but when the Transvaal Boers tried to block his route to the north, he fought them with as much stubbornness as their own stalwart leader, Oom Paul.

The race for the North had already commenced when Rhodes took up the cudgels in parliament for his ambitious scheme of seizing the interior for his countrymen. The bone of contention was Bechuanaland lying just north of Cape Colony. Boer ambitions in Burgers' day for the goldfields which lay along the Missionaries' Road have been noted on a previous page.[47]   It has been pointed out likewise that, aside from the well watered pasture lands to the west of the Boer States, the major part of Bechuanaland was arid and uninviting for colonization and settlement. There was, to be sure, a valuable gold deposit at Tati and people were still hopeful that gold or other minerals might be discovered elsewhere in the territory.[48]   The chief importance of Bechuanaland, however, lay in its strategic position along the route to the north.[49]   It was, furthermore, the wedge between three rival powers. On the west, the Germans were shortly to plant a colony in Damaraland and Namaqualand. On the east were the Boers and, on the south, the Cape Colonists. Three conflicting dreams of empire were forming above this corridor to the North. One was that of an independent Dutch confederation spreading through South Africa. The second was a vague vision of a German colonial empire stretching from the west to the east coast and then north through Bechuanaland and the Transvaal into Central Africa. The third was the still inchoate ambition of British imperialists to advance north from Table Mountain to the Nile.[50]   Stretching like a swollen neck up into the north between the territory of these rival powers, Bechuanaland threatened to become the Macedonia of South Africa.

In the early eighties, Dutch farmers spread across the Transvaal frontier into the good pastures of eastern Bechuanaland. In 1882, J. G. Van Niekerk set up the Republic of Stellaland and Van Pittius, another Boer frontiersman, founded the Republic of Goschen. Natives were already settled in these regions and, as might be expected, disturbances broke out between them and the newcomers. Two of the chiefs, Montsoia and Mankoroane, appealed to the Cape for protection while two others, Massouw and Moshette, turned to the Transvaal.[51] There is no need here, however, to go into the whole troubled and complicated story of the difficulties on the Transvaal border except to point out that the disturbances precipitated the struggle for the north between the Boers and the British.

Paul Kruger decided that the best way to stop the quarrels in the neighboring territory was to incorporate a large slice of the disturbed area, including the Missionaries' Road, within the Transvaal. Partly with this idea in view, he set out, as already noted, in 1883 with a Boer deputation for London. One of the primary requests of the Boer delegates, upon their arrival, was for a rectification of the southwest boundary line of the Transvaal. They suggested a line which enclosed about 90 miles of the direct trade route from the Cape to the interior of the continent. H. M. Government, however, had no intention of giving up this vital artery to the interior. Lord Derby, secretary of state for the colonies, insisted firmly " . . . Her Majesty's Government cannot consent to any portion of the existing trade road being placed within the Transvaal ".[52] H. M. Government, further, insisted that the boundary question was of such primary importance that it must be settled before any of the other issues which the Boers wished to discuss. The Boer deputation had other irons in the fire [53] and they, finally, yielded to Lord Derby's persistence. They consented to a southwest boundary line which entirely excluded the northern trade road from the Transvaal.[54]

The Convention of London of February 27, 1884, which terminated these negotiations settled the burning question of the trade route to the north. It also redefined the boundaries of the Transvaal or South African Republic as it is called in the convention. Furthermore, Article IV stipulated that the Republic could not conclude any " Treaty or engagement with . . . any native tribe to the eastward and westward of the Republic, until the same has been approved by Her Majesty the Queen ".[55] Nothing was said, however, about the tribes to the north. Thereby, the question of northward expansion was left open. As will be seen in the next chapter, this omission caused serious complications. It is sufficient here to note that Great Britain, by implication at least, was given a free hand in the coveted Bechuanaland territory to the west of the Boer Republics.

Behind Derby's firm stand on the issue of the trade route was the pressure of public opinion and a considerable amount of agitation over the Bechuanaland issue. This pressure from outside marks a growing interest in the interior. It shows the momentum which the movement for northward expansion was gaining. There was a considerable number of people both in England and South Africa who were ready to support the British march forward into Central Africa. Lord Derby, without this support, might have pursued a different policy. He was well disposed towards the Transvaal Boers and inclined to be neutral on the subject of the Bechuanaland difficulties.[56] He yielded, however, to the growing determination to keep the way open to the north.

Mingled with this popular desire to seize the key to the interior, with all its possibilities for trade and development, was a genuinely humanitarian interest in the African natives and a feeling that their welfare was secure only under imperial protection.

Three men were outstanding leaders in the campaign for Bechuanaland and were largely responsible for arousing the public to the importance of the territory.   They were John Mackenzie, a missionary; Sir Hercules Robinson, High Commissioner at the Cape and Cecil Rhodes, the rising political leader in the Cape House.

John Mackenzie was keenly interested in the African natives.   He was also an ardent imperialist and believed that Great Britain was the best guardian of native rights.   As early as 1871, he urged the British government to extend its control over Bechuanaland.   He now entered with all his energy into the campaign for this vital strip of territory. His addresses at public meetings, his articles in the press did much to win the support of the Aborigines Protection Society, of philanthropists and of men interested in the African native.   Unfortunately, his tactless hostility to the Dutch was later to lead him into difficulties.   As an enemy to the Boers, he was a severe critic of Rhodes' policies.   He wanted expansion, as much as Rhodes, but he wanted it under imperial and not Cape auspices.[57]   Although, later, he tangled the whole Bechuanaland question in a bitter race conflict, he performed a real service, at this time, to the cause of northern expansion by arousing men in England and South Africa to the great value of Bechuanaland to England and to Cape Colony as the key to the interior.[58]

Sir Hercules Robinson was an ardent expansionist but of a less imperialistic tinge than Mackenzie.   He looked at the Bechuanaland question from the point of view of a Cape Colonist.   Like Rhodes, he wanted to see the authority of the Colony extend to the Zambezi.[59]   It was better for colonial interests that this strategic strip fall into British rather than Boer hands.   Robinson fought hard, therefore, for this channel to the interior.   It was, in fact, largely through his efforts that Lord Derby was nerved to take a vigorous stand on the question of the Missionaries' road.[60]   Robinson was called to England to advise the Colonial Office on the best policy to be pursued and his advice was to hold the trade route securely in British hands.   "It seems to me," he urged, "that it would be a serious injury to British commerce, and to the interests of the British communities in South Africa, if the great highway from the Cape to the interior of the continent were given over to the Transvaal government." [61]

Sir Hercules Robinson's unwavering insistence upon British control of Bechuanaland helped, also, to throw the support of Thomas Scanlen, prime minister of the Cape, into the scales on the side of retaining Bechuanaland.   The Scanlen ministry was in an insecure position and Scanlen was fearful of losing the support of the Cape Dutch.   He was watching anxiously the course of the discussion in London and at the same time keeping his finger on the pulse of public opinion at the Cape.   The firmness of Sir Hercules Robinson did much to veer his vacillating opinion toward securing the coveted land to the north.   The British Government wanted the cooperation of Cape Colony in the matter of the maintenance of the new territory.   Scanlen, finally, intimated cautiously that if the Transvaal Volksraad agreed to a British protectorate over Bechuanaland, Cape Colony "would be prepared to undertake a joint share in the responsibility of maintaining a protectorate over these territories and to keep open the northern trade route." [62]   In short, it was Robinson's steady championship of the northern trade-route question and Scanlen's timorous promise which stiffened Derby's policy in regard to Bechuanaland and, finally, led H. M. Government to exclude this territory from the Transvaal's sphere of activity. Rhodes, although he was a well-known figure in the Cape parliament, was not well known in England, and can scarcely have had, at this time, any appreciable influence over the deliberations of H. M. officials at home.[63]

While the negotiations were going on in London, however, Rhodes was doing his part in South Africa where his influence was stronger. He had already been sent up to Bechuanaland on a boundary commission in 1883. On this expedition, he pursued a general policy of conciliation and agreement and triumphantly returned to the Cape with an offer from Mankoroane of his kingdom for annexation and a petition for annexation from a considerable group of the people of Stellaland. The Cape Parliament, however, repudiated Mankoroane's offer although Rhodes used all his persuasive powers with Scanlen. They, further, refused to grant Rhodes' request that the Colonial Government should be represented when the Boer deputation entered into their negotiations in London.[64]

When the deputation returned from London, Rhodes found his stiffest fight ahead of him to make the occupation of the new territory effective. Politically, the Bechuanaland question seemed to be settled by the Anglo-Boer convention of 1884, but Great Britain soon found that even conventions were not enough to give undisputed possession. Disturbances still continued along the Transvaal border. In April, 1884, the Imperial Government dispatched the arch-imperialist, John Mackenzie, as British deputy commissioner to the new Protectorate. Mackenzie, by his tactless behavior and by his uncompromising hostility to the Boers, made matters worse. Both the Transvaal and the Cape ministry protested. He was recalled and Rhodes sent up in his place.

Rhodes, still trusting in his ability to win the cooperation of the Dutch, patched up a peace with Van Niekerk to Stellaland but he was unable to come to terms with Van Pittius in Goschen. In fact, Van Pittius actually attacked the native chief, Montsoia, while Rhodes was there and the attack was made in spite of Rhodes' protests. It was successful. Montsoia was forced to sign a treaty giving up his land to the Republic of Goschen.

Kruger took this opportunity to reassert his authority. In the interests of preserving peace on the Transvaal border but in violation of the spirit and implications of the recently concluded London Convention, he proclaimed a protectorate over the disputed area. Protests came from Lord Derby and from all over Cape Colony. Kruger, thereupon, promptly retracted the offending proclamation.[65]

Clearly, however, something must be done to put fear and respect for the British flag into the hearts of the people of Bechuanaland and their Boer neighbors. Rhodes' dispatches from Bechuanaland, the conduct of Van Pittius and Kruger's boldness all indicated that more stringent measures should be taken. The London Convention did not adequately safeguard the territory from Boer encroachment.

Furthermore, behind the Boer issue, there was a lurking fear that the Germans might be prepared to reap some colonial advantage from the troubled conditions in South Africa. In fact, just at this time, the British were watching with some anxiety German operations on the West Coast. In August 1883, Lüderitz, mentioned previously in connection with the St. Lucia Bay controversy,[66] hoisted the German flag on a newly founded trading post at Angra Pequeña on the Southwest Coast of Africa in Namaqualand. Bismarck, although formerly uninterested in overseas colonies, was willing in 1883 to extend German protection to the new trading factory. A year later, August

7, 1884, he grew bolder and declared a German protectorate over Damaraland and Namaqualand, thus laying the foundations of German Southwest Africa. In September of the same year, the British duly recognized the German protectorate but they were determined not to let matters go further. There was some anxiety lest the new colony might wish to expand into Bechuanaland.[67] There were, furthermore, vague newspaper rumors afloat that the Germans were planning to join hands with their Boer kinsmen in the Transvaal to set up a great German African empire from the east to the west coast and thus completely block British expansion northwards. There was certainly considerable talk among German commercial circles about establishing colonies in the Dark Continent. For example, as early as 1875, Ernst Von Weber returned from a journey in South Africa full of imperial dreams and plans. In 1876, Von Weber and Lüderitz, supported by a group of Bremen merchants, approached Bismark with a proposal to found a colony among the Boers. Bismarck received them courteously enough but turned down their proposal as premature. Nothing practical could be done, he believed, for nine or ten years.[68] Meanwhile, however, missionaries, explorers and commercial interests were agitating for a new imperialism. Books and pamphlets urging the German people to build up their overseas empire poured into the market. Furthermore, trade was steadily growing with Africa on the west and east coasts.[69]

In 1878, Ernest Von Weber published a book on his experience, *Vier Jahre in Afrika, 1871-1875*. In this work, he particularly urged Germany to purchase Delagoa Bay and thus to seize the key to Central Africa. With this harbor as a starting point, he foresaw the growth of a Germanized South Africa spreading along the healthy and fertile highland from the Orange River to the Equator and from the Drakensburg Mountains to the Congo.[70] Again, in November 1879, he published another spirited appeal in the Berlin *Geographische Nachrichten* which excited considerable interest in German commercial and political circles and awoke some anxiety in Cape Colony. The article was, likewise, a plea for German colonies and settlements in South Africa as nuclei for a new vast German empire, " more valuable and more brilliant than even the Indian Empire " of Great Britain. In building up this new dominion overseas, he relied upon the support and friendship of the Boers, especially the Transvaal Boers. They were the kinsmen and brothers of the Germans. They had suffered intolerable grievances at the hands of the English and were eager, he claimed, to come under the protection of Germany whom " they properly regard as their parent and mother ". The Transvaal, moreover, afforded easy access to the immensely rich tracts of country which lie between the Limpopo, the Central African Lakes and the Congo. Germany ought at any price to get possession of some points on the East as well as the West coast of Africa and establish a chain of German trading stations on the Zambezi and from these settlements, with the friendship of the Boers behind them, build up their new African empire. This would be Germany's answer to the challenge of British hotspurs : " *Africa shall be English from Table Mountain to the Nile.*" [71]

In 1882, the Kolonialverein was founded by a group of journalists, explorers, merchants and travellers and by 1885 the verein had more than ten thousand members. In 1884, Dr. Carl Peters established the Gesellschaft für deutsche Kolonisation with the object of raising funds for establishing colonies in East Africa.[72]

The British regarded the new German colonial activities with anxiety. The fear of Boer-German cooperation in South Africa may have been without foundation but it served its purpose in arousing them to action.

In 1880, for example, Sir Bartle Frere called Kimberley's attention to Von Weber's article in the Berlin *Geographische Nachrichten*. Frere noted also that the Germans and Dutch Republicans were drawing closer together in Cape Colony. It is doubtful that much credence was given by H. M. Government to rumors about such a grandiose scheme. It seems somewhat significant, however, that Sir Bartle Frere's dispatch of July, 1880, enclosing Von Weber's article was included in the collection of papers concerning Angra Pequeña published in 1884. Quite obviously, also, Lord Granville was at least vaguely worried about any further extension of German activities to the east of the new protectorate in Damaraland and Namaqualand. Furthermore, some such suspicion may have been a factor in the previously mentioned British annexation of Zululand.[73] Probably, however, the decision of H. M. Government to set bounds to Germany's colonial activities was due more to a determination to ward off the encroachment of any rival power in the south than to a definite fear that the Germans were contemplating the establishment of a transcontinental empire in Africa.[74]

This idea, however, played an important rôle in arousing popular support for keeping the route to the north open through Bechuanaland. Rhodes made good use of the German bogey. He did not fear, to be sure, an alliance, such as Von Weber suggested, between the Boers and the Germans. His experience with the Bond led him to believe that the freedom-loving Dutchmen would not tolerate a German yoke. In fact, as noted before, Jan Hofmeyr, the Bond dictator, was no lover of the Germans. This talk of Von Weber about kinship and brotherhood between the two peoples was sheer sentimental nonsense in Rhodes' estimation. Rhodes did fear, however, that the weakness of the Transvaal would tempt the Germans to step in and absorb the country.

Do you think [he warned the House, June 30, 1885] that if the Transvaal had Bechuanaland it would be allowed to keep it? Would not Bismarck have some quarrel with the Transvaal; and without resources, without men, what could they do? Germany would come across from her settlement at Angra Pequeña. There would be some excuse to pick a quarrel—some question of brandy or guns, or something, and then Germany would stretch from Angra Pequeña to Delagoa Bay. . . . What was the bar in Germany's way? Bechuanaland. What was the use to her of a few sand-heaps at Angra Pequeña, and what was the use of the arid deserts between Angra Pequeña and the interior, with this English and colonial bar between her and the Transvaal? If we were to stop at Griqualand West, the ambitious objects of Germany would be attained. There is then good ground for England's interference in this country.[75]

This Bechuanaland territory, therefore, was, according to Rhodes, not only " the Suez Canal of the trade of this country, the key of its road to the interior " but also a buffer state against German aggression. The road to the north must be kept open. If the Cape Colonists were unwilling to shoulder the burden, H. M. Government must step in. Rhodes was, in fact, among the first to urge intervention and to call in the " imperial factor." [76]

H. M. Government was by this time awake to the dangers inherent in the Bechuanaland difficulties. In December 1884, therefore, Sir Charles Warren was dispatched with four thousand troops to quell the disturbances and to instill a salutary respect for British authority. Warren took his mission seriously. He brought law and order to Bechuanaland but at the price of repudiating the more conciliatory measures advocated by Rhodes. Warren was recalled in August 1885 and Rhodes' suggestions finally adopted. There is no need here to enter into the bitter controversy which arose over the policies of Warren and Rhodes save to point out that the Warren expedition did much to alienate the Boer's affection and to make Rhodes' program of co-operation with the Boers more difficult.[77]

The great question who should be master in Bechuana-land, however, was at last definitely settled.[78] Bechuana-land was twice rescued by " Grandmamma "; once, in the diplomatic field at the time of the London Convention and now, by the actual intervention of British troops. Whether or not Rhodes himself was thinking specifically in Cape-to-Cairo terms at this date, he was sincerely glad that H. M. Government secured the key to the interior, this indispensable corridor on the road to the north.

He saw, in other words, one part of his program fulfilled. South Africa, to be sure, was not united but Bechuanaland was safely under the British flag and the territory to the north was open for colonial expansion. Triumphant but not wholly satisfied, he laid his plans for still greater expansion. He was growing tired of wrangles with the Cape Parliament. He was impatient with the meddling policy of the home government. He turned next to the time-honored method of British penetration into new countries, the building up of a gigantic trading and colonizing corporation, his own British South Africa Company.[79]

CHAPTER V

The Trunk Line from Cape Town to Cairo

The story of railway construction in South Africa is an integral part of the history of British expansion northward. In fact, the progress of the railways towards the north was a good thermometer of the desire and capacity to advance into the interior. It has already been noted in the first chapter how the little railroad back of Cape Town was drawn north to Kimberley by the diamond discoveries and how three trunk systems developed in the colony as a result of the new prosperity ushered in by the mining boom.[1]

It is significant of the close relationship between railway extension and colonial expansion northwards that the colonists talked from the very beginning of railway discussions in 1845 about tapping the trade of the interior.[2] The short line from Cape Town to Wellington from its inception was regarded as " the main trunk route of our Interior Trade." [3] From 1862 to 1868, there was considerable discussion as to the direction of future railway extension. The crux of the question was whether the new line was to be merely a local railway to supply local needs or " the main trunk route to the interior ". The colonists, finally, decided that the Cape Town railroad was a main trunk line and that it should be built with the long range prospect of a growing trade with the north.[4] Cecil Rhodes understood this fundamental principle behind colonial railway expansion and used his knowledge to arouse popular support in his Bechuanaland Campaign in 1884. " The colony ", he urged, " had built its railways for the sake of trade, and were they going to allow them-

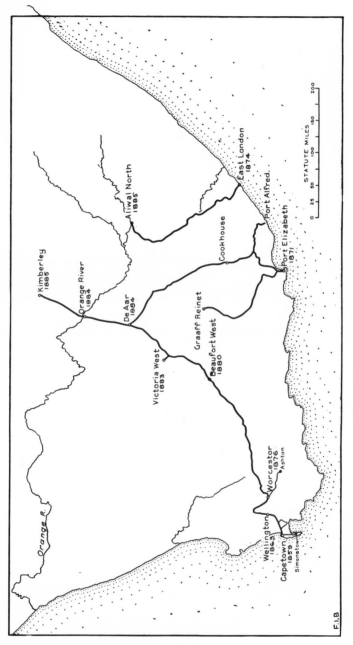

TRUNK LINES IN CAPE COLONY, 1888

Kimberley
1885

Orange River
1884

De Aar
1884

Aliwal North
1885

East London
1874

Port Alfred

Cookhouse

Port Elizabeth
1871

Victoria West
1883

Graaff Reinet

Beaufort West
1880

Orange R.

Worcester
1876
Ashton

Wellington
1863

Capetown
1859
Simonstown

STATUTE MILES

0 25 50 100 150 200

F.I.B

selves to be shut out from the future trade of the interior? " " Hear, hear ", replied the House.[5]

In the early part of 1888, it was an open question as to which one of the Cape trunk lines would become the main artery to the north and whether further extension should be through the Transvaal or British Bechuanaland or both.[6] It is customary today to consider the railway through Bechuanaland as the main line to the north and it is easy to forget that the colonists could have chosen an alternative route.   In fact, Sir Hercules Robinson, an ardent advocate of the spread of colonial influence up to the Zambezi River, admitted the possibility of a railway to the north through the Transvaal.   If Rhodes' plans of cooperation with the Boers had been successful, the Cape-to-Cairo line might now run through the Boer States.   In 1888, at any rate, there was an urgent and growing cry to extend the Cape lines to the north but there was a great divergence of opinion as to which direction the new line or lines should take.[7]

The future development of Bechuanaland and trade with the far north attracted one group of colonists.   To be sure, the existence of mineral wealth in Bechuanaland was still doubtful but then there were the Tati goldfields on the southwest border of Matabeleland and prospectors were pushing still further into Matabeleland as far as Buluwayo, the Kraal of Lobengula, paramount chief of the Matabele tribe.   On February 11, 1888, J. S. Moffat, assistant commissioner of Bechuanaland, concluded a treaty with Lobengula.   This treaty will be referred to later on.[8]   It is sufficient here to note that it gave H. M. Government " a kind of option " over the vast dominions of the native chief.   It looked as though Matabeleland and its tributary kingdom Mashonaland would one day fall like a ripe plum into the lap of Great Britain.   Furthermore, the colonists were confident

that H. M. Government intended to hand British Bechuanaland, then a Crown Colony,[9] over to the Cape as soon as
the latter was ready to annex it on fair terms.   In fact, the
Home Government had twice before, once in 1883 and again
in 1885, suggested that the Cape annex this territory.   If
British Bechuanaland were incorporated in the colony and
British influence secured in the north, it might be a sensible
plan to bring the railway north towards the Zambezi
" through either colonial territory, or through territories
under British protection or influence " but free from Boer
interference; i. e., through Bechuanaland rather than through
the Orange Free State and the Transvaal.[10]

On the other hand, the lure of the Transvaal Gold Fields
held another group at the Cape.   In March, a conference
was held at Cape Town on the questions of Customs Union
and Railway Extension.   The conference was attended by
delegates from the Orange Free State and the colonies of
the Cape of Good Hope and Natal.   There were no delegates, however, from the Transvaal partly for reasons discussed in the preceding chapter.[11]   The members of the Conference recommended the extension of the Cape line from
Colesberg to the Orange River, rather than through the Free
State via Bloemfontein to the border of the Transvaal.
This was, they considered, the shortest route from the Cape
to the Johannesburg gold fields.   The Cape and Free State
delegates promised to recommend this proposal to their respective legislatures and governments.   Accordingly, on
May first, 1888, an announcement was made in the Cape
House that a bill would be introduced to carry out this ex-
tension from Colesberg to the Orange River.

In the Transvaal, however, President Kruger, in line with
his policy of delaying extension from the South until his
Delagoa Bay line reached completion, was resolutely opposed
to the recommendation of the conference.   The recommend-

ation was, also, opposed by a large section of the Free State burghers. When the question was brought before the Free State Volksraad, that body approved only by the casting vote of the chairman of a *survey* of the prospective railway from the Orange River to Bloemfontein. They left the subject of the construction of such a line for further consideration.[12]

The railway extension bill which finally came before the Cape Parliament provided for two northward extensions: one from Colesberg to the Orange River and one from Kimberley to a point on the north bank of the Vaal River about three miles from the Transvaal border, and twelve miles from the British Bechuanaland boundary. There was no disagreement over the Colesberg extension but considerable controversy over that from Kimberley. Finally, in the summer of 1888, as already noted in the previous chapter, the majority in the House, irritated by the obstructionist policies of the Transvaal and anxious to shake off Boer interference, voted for the Kimberley extension. The railway question seemed to be settled. The measure was carried by a majority of forty-one to twenty-five. Apparently the colonists were ready to set to work on two northern lines. One was a prolongation of the Midland railway to join the prospective Free State line and thus reach the gold fields. The other was a purely colonial railway which was the prolongation of the Western trunk line from Cape Town to Kimberley. At a later date, this Kimberley extension might be carried into the Transvaal or might go north through the newly acquired Bechuanaland to tap the wealth of the far interior.[13]

The railway issue, however, was not as definitely settled as the action of the Cape Parliament indicated. In reality, the railway question was bound up with that of the final disposition of British Bechuanaland. So sure were the colonists that British Bechuanaland would be handed over to the Cape that Sir Gordon Sprigg, then Premier, made an indiscreet speech at East London advocating annexation. The speech met with a most unfavorable reception in England. There was a strong feeling at home that the Cape Parliament was dominated by the republican Boer element whose loyalty to the British Empire was mistrusted. Furthermore, British philanthropists were roused by tales of Boer mistreatment of the natives. They believed with the Reverend John Mackenzie that Bechuanaland should remain under direct supervision of H. M. Government. English newspapers published such tactless statements as " the Cape has no genius for ruling natives ".[14]   Bechuanaland would be valuable to England in the event of the defection of the African Colonies.[15]   Cape Colony, quite naturally, received the decision of H. M. Government against annexation " as an unfriendly act, and a slap in the face to the colony." [16]

At the same time, Président Kruger became alarmed. He was opposed, as has been seen, to colonial railway extension until the Delagoa line neared completion but he was even more opposed to a line beyond Kimberley towards the Bechuanaland territory if that territory remained permanently under the direct control of the Imperial Government. He decided, therefore, to put a stop to the Kimberley extension even at the cost of throwing some weight in favor of the Colesberg line. He requested the Cape Parliament to delay construction on the Kimberley-Vaal River railway until the January session of the Volksraad. In return, he promised to induce the Volksraad to undertake the construction of the Colesberg extension right through the Free State.[17] The Cape Parliament, smarting from the blow it had just received, listened to Kruger, and pushed on rapidly with the Colesberg railway while they deemed it inexpedient to pro-

ceed with the construction of the other northern extension
from Kimberley to the Vaal River.[18]

With such fluctuating policies in the Cape Parliament and
such reversal of plans, the prospects looked dark for railway construction north to the Zambezi. Sir Hercules Robinson wrote home in despair:

this new departure on the part of President Kruger taken in
conjunction with the refusal of Her Majesty's government to
part with British Bechuanaland will effectually stop any possible
railway extension to or through the territory. . . . The importance of Bechuanaland as the road to the interior will cease.
The Cape Colony will then no longer care to be burdened with
that territory; and the result will be an expensive, valueless, in-
accessible inland Crown colony will be left indefinitely on the
hands of the imperial Government.[19]

So important was the railway issue in the development of
the North that the High Commissioner felt that the failure
to carry through the Kimberley extension was a fatal blow.
He felt that his hard-fought battle for Bechuanaland had
brought only a barren victory. The railway to the Zambezi
could alone bring life to Bechuanaland and colonial trade to
the north.[20]

Sir Hercules Robinson, however, was looking at expansion
to the north only from the colonial point of view. The
situation was not so hopeless as he feared. The movement
towards the countries near the Zambezi was too strong to
be checked by the wavering policies of the Cape Parliament.
The railway, indeed, was an essential part of the development of Bechuanaland and the northern countries but the
Cape politicians were not the only men to realize its importance. Two English corporations, founded in 1888, were
ready to take the northern railway problem out of the hands
of the Cape politicians. They were the Bechuanaland Ex-

ploration Company and the Exploring Company; two allied corporations principally under the direction of George Cawston and Lord Gifford.[21]

As early as May 4, 1888, Cawston asked for the support of H. M. Government, " to negotiate with Lobengula for a treaty for trading, mining and general purposes." Lord Knutsford, Secretary of State for the Colonies, however, refused to entangle the British Government in private concerns over mining grants. Undaunted by this rather discouraging reception of his proposal, Cawston proceeded to organize the Exploring Company for the purpose of acquiring and working the mining wealth of Mashonaland.[22]

The development of the country to the north was the main objective of the Bechuanaland Exploration and the Exploring companies. Contributory to this end, however, was the construction of a railway north through Bechuanaland.

The Bechuanaland Exploration Company commenced negotiations in 1888 for a concession to build a railway from the Southern border of British Bechuanaland to the Zambezi. As a first step, they proposed to bring the line from the Colonial frontier through British Bechuanaland via Taungs and Vryburg to the neighborhood of Mafeking. R. V. Murray was dispatched to South Africa by the Bechuanaland Exploration Company to make arrangements for the project with the Cape Government. At the same time, Sir Charles Metcalfe and John Blue, two engineers, were sent out by the Exploring Company to undertake a survey of the line from Kimberley to Vryburg.[23]

These new companies were about to change the whole character of the railway beyond Kimberley as well as to rescue the line from the tangle of Cape politics. Sir Charles Metcalfe, when he accepted his appointment from the Exploring Company was looking far beyond even the Zambezi

River. He was already dreaming of a railway from the
" Cape to Cairo." It was with the hope that the Kimberley-
Vryburg strip might be the first section on that great transcontinental line that he set out for South Africa.[24] Now
for the first time, the railway to the north was linked to the
Cape-to-Cairo idea. From this time on, it became, prospec-
tively, not only the " trunk line to the interior " but the trunk
line from Cape Town to Cairo.

Fortunately, the negotiators for the new railway line were
favorably regarded by the Imperial authorities at home.
Lord Knutsford had already given the company the promise
" that no offer from any other party for a Railway Company in British Bechuanaland should be entertained during
the period required for making a survey of the route and
for the consideration of their proposals." H. M. Government further promised to exercise their influence fairly
to induce the native chiefs to agree to reasonable arrangements with the company.[25] The project, although not
actually an imperial undertaking, was certainly strongly
backed by H. M. Government.

Murray, Metcalfe and Blue, however, were not warmly
received at Cape Town. They arrived at a time when the
Cape Parliament was still looking forward to the annexation
of British Bechuanaland.[26] The Cape colonists were still
expecting the development of the country to the north under
colonial, not imperial, auspices. In fact, Robinson, the
High Commissioner himself, was eager to see the Cape take
the lead in Bechuanaland and was inclined to look askance
at imperial intermeddling.[27] Both the Cape colonists and
the High Commissioner were suspicious of the imperial
color of the new proposals and not at all " disposed to welcome the project ".[28] Since the question of the fate of
British Bechuanaland was, for the moment, hanging in the
balance, Sir Hercules Robinson felt that, from the point

of view of both Cape and Imperial interests the time was not
propitious for plunging into such an enterprise. The railway scheme might " interpose many obstacles in the acceptance by the Cape of the Crown colony."[29]

Sir Sidney Shippard, administrator of British Bechuanaland, gave a grudging and half-hearted assent to the prose-
cution of the railway scheme. He considered the company's
terms extravagant and said that he would prefer to have
the railway constructed by the government. Nevertheless,
the need for railway extension was great. It was an object
of such primary importance that he was willing to agree even
to " the exorbitant terms " of the company in regard to
mineral concessions.[30]

The railway promoters found a more sympathetic listener
in Cecil Rhodes. Metcalfe, an old Oxford acquaintance,
met Rhodes at Kimberley soon after the cool reception of
the railway group at Cape Town. As already noted, Rhodes
was opposed to extension of the Cape colonial line northward because such a procedure interfered with his cherished
policy of cooperation with the Boers.[31] He was, however,
keenly interested in the opening up of the interior. He saw
in the new railway scheme proposed by Metcalfe a way to
circumvent Cape politics, and to secure a railway to the
north. Whether Metcalfe at this meeting fired Rhodes' imagination with his plans for a transcontinental railway is
doubtful. Rhodes, for some time, was inclined to look at
Metcalfe's expansive program as impractical. He was,
however, impressed by the immediate prospect of a railway
into Bechuanaland and offered to join forces with the new
group. Metcalfe and Murray advised the Companies at
home to accept Rhodes' offer but the Bechuanaland Exploration and the Exploring Companies were not at all anxious,
at this time, to cooperate with Rhodes. In fact, they were
direct rivals of Rhodes' own company, the Goldfields of

South Africa in a race to secure Matabeleland.[32] That rivalry led directly towards the formation of the British South Africa Company and will be discussed in greater detail in the following chapter.

It is sufficient to note here that in the summer of 1888 plans for northward extension were at a deadlock in the Cape Parliament. There were prospects, however, that the line would be carried forward by outside English companies. The lure of the north was pulling the railway forward like a magnet. The little "railroad back of Cape Town" was growing fast. Plans were already made to carry it to the Zambezi River and Metcalfe was dreaming that it might one day become a great transcontinental trunk line from the Cape to Cairo.

CHAPTER VI

THE CAMPAIGN FOR THE CHARTER

THE next step forward in Rhodes' scheme of expansion was to occupy the reputedly rich country of the Matabeles, north of Bechuanaland. British influence was already entrenched in this region. As early as 1836, Sir Benjamin D'Urban, Governor of Cape Colony, concluded a treaty of friendship with the Matabele at the request of the father of the famous Lobengula.[1] In 1870, a British company was formed by Sir John Swinburne to work the Tati gold field in the southwest of Matabeleland. In the same year, Thomas Bain obtained a concession from Lobengula to prospect and dig for gold. By 1884, English trading stations were springing up in the territory. When the Warren Expedition was in Bechuanaland, 1885, Sir Charles sent some of his men further north into Lobengula's country. Their reports of the wealth of Matabeleland were quoted by the *Times* and roused considerable commercial interest in Matabeleland. By 1888, concession hunters were invading Lobengula's Kraal in uncomfortable numbers and already disputes over grants had begun to disturb that monarch's peace of mind.[2]

Rhodes saw in the rush of prospectors and concessionaires into the north country an opportunity to step in and to apply his favorite tactics of amalgamating, negotiating, bargaining and agreeing. Matabeleland and Mashonaland were, however, at that time under the protection of no European power. His first move, therefore, was an attempt to persuade Sir

Hercules Robinson to obtain a British protectorate over Lobengula's territory. Sir Hercules, however, felt sure that the Colonial Office would not consent to such a measure but he was willing to do all that he could to help Rhodes. Rhodes then suggested a clever solution to the dilemma. He proposed an agreement with the chief which would not involve Great Britain in any responsibility, but at the same time, would give that country an option to a protectorate over the native chief's dominions. Sir Hercules Robinson agreed and Moffat was dispatched post haste to Matabeleland.[3]   In the words of the treaty.

The chief Lobengula, ruler of the tribe known as the Amandebele,[4] together with the Mashona and Makalaka, tributaries of the same [agreed to] refrain from entering into any correspondence or treaty with any foreign State or Power, to sell, alienate, or cede, . . . any part of the said Amandebele country under his chieftainship, or upon any other subject, without the previous knowledge and sanction of Her Majesty's High Commissioner in South Africa.[5]

Rhodes had, then, done all he could through the Cape Government but he was not content with this accomplishment.   He set to work to make the occupation of Mashonaland definitely effective through his own private company, the Goldfields of South Africa.   The company sent up Charles Dunell Rudd, Rochfort Maguire and Francis Thompson to negotiate with Lobengula for a mining concession.   They were wholly successful.   The Matabele King granted them not only the complete and exclusive charge over all metals and minerals in his dominions but also the right to exclude from his kingdom all persons " seeking land, metals, minerals or mining rights therein ".   Lobengula, furthermore, promised to render them such needful assistance as they might from time to time require for the exclusion of such persons and also to grant no concessions of land or mining rights from and after this date without their consent and concurrence.[6]

The next concern of Cecil Rhodes was to make this concession watertight. Native chiefs were notoriously fickle and Lobengula was likely at any time to deny that he had made the agreement. Rudd was instructed to carry away the precious document as soon as possible. He managed to get away with the original paper but on the way back, he found all the water holes dried up. Almost perishing with thirst, he hid the concession in an ant-bear hole from which it was safely recovered and brought at last to Rhodes.[7]

Furthermore, Rhodes deemed it wise to keep friendly agents at Lobengula's kraal. He had Thompson and Maguire stay behind to keep the mistrusted Lobengula true to his promises.

Events proved that Rhodes' fears about the changing policies of the Matabele King were well founded. Thompson and Maguire were able to ward off the agents of the Austral Africa Company from asking for a concession but they were not able to forestall those of the Exploring Company. In the early part of 1888, E. A. Maund, formerly one of Sir Charles Warren's commissioners to Matabeleland, and then in the service of the Exploring Company, was dispatched to Lobengula's Kraal. Maund claims that Lobengula never fully understood the previously granted Rudd concession. The bewildered monarch, he insisted, " thought he gave the Rudd people leave to dig for gold in a deep hole like Kimberley Diamond Mine." However that may be, Lobengula very obligingly proceeded to bestow upon the newcomer " ' the Mazoe District ', i. e., all the country drained by that river and its tributaries " or, a large slice of Mashonaland. He, also, promised to make Maund Induna of the District. Maund, in return, engaged to take two of Lobengula's Indunas to England " to see whether the Great White Queen really existed, and if so, why she allowed white men, who claimed her as Queen, to ' duba ' or annoy, him ".[8]

Thereupon a race ensued between Rhodes and Maund to make their respective concessions effective. Rhodes tried hard, but in vain, to stop Maund and the Indunas from embarking for England. He did, however, succeed in placing some doubts in Maund's mind as to the ultimate success of the Exploring Company's operations. Rhodes insisted " that if it came to a fight, money would be no object " but, he hinted " there might be means of accommodation ". As a result of this talk, Williams maintains, Maund thought it prudent for the time being to withhold certain important letters and documents in his possession.[9]

Rhodes was aided right along by his faithful colleague, Sir Hercules Robinson. Sir Hercules tried first by telegraph to stop Maund and the Indunas before they reached Cape Town. When in spite of his efforts they arrived there, he interviewed them at Government House. He questioned the status of the Indunas and accused Maund of picking up natives on the veldt. He made every effort to prevent their embarkation and, when all his " brow-beating " failed, offered to send one of his own officers with them. Robinson was wholly unsuccessful. Maund sailed on the *Moor* but without any colonial officer to interfere with his plans.[10]

The Home government was, apparently, inclined to look with greater favor upon Rhodes' undertaking than upon that of the Exploring Company. Lord Knutsford placed every obstacle in the way of the reception of Maund and his Indunas at court. " There was no precedent for a subject bringing a foreign mission ", etc., etc. " The Queen was going to Cannes and could not see the Indunas ". The persistent Maund, nevertheless, did secure an audience with the

Queen for his native emissaries. The audience, however, was of no avail as far as Maund's schemes were concerned. Lord Knutsford told the Exploring Company that he refused to entangle H. M. Government in private concerns over mining concessions.[11]

Rhodes was busy, meanwhile, amalgamating other conflicting concessions. He bought claims right and left [12] and, finally, he scored his biggest victory in the game of merging divergent interests by persuading his most serious rivals, the Bechuanaland Exploration and the Exploring Companies, to come in with him and to ask for a charter for the British South Africa Company. The directors of the Exploring Company at last consented and cabled Metcalfe at the end of 1888, " Join hands with Rhodes." [13] Murray and Metcalfe left Cape Town that evening and went to Kimberley. There they enlisted Dr. Jameson's cooperation in their schemes. Then Murray left for England to make a report to the Bechuanaland Exploration and the Exploring Companies and to advocate the opening up of the country, which is now Southern Rhodesia, through the instrumentality of a powerful corporation.[14]

As early as January 3, 1889, Lord Gifford of the Bechuanaland Exploration Company wrote to the Colonial Office inquiring whether, in the event of the amalgamation of existing British enterprises in the Bechuanaland Protectorate, an application for a charter would be favourably received by Her Majesty's Government.[15] Lord Knutsford replied that " Her Majesty's Government " did " not feel able to entertain such a proposal without full consideration of its possible effect, financial and political, upon the present position and future prospects of British Bechuanaland and without the recommendation of the High Commissioner and Governor." [16] Sir Hercules Robinson, the High Commissioner, was, as noted, a warm friend of Rhodes and an ardent expansionist. He was, therefore, decidedly in favor of granting a royal charter to a large corporation which would amalgamate the conflicting interests in Matabeleland and, in this vein, replied to Lord Knutsford, Secretary of State for the Colonies, March 18, 1889.[17]

In the meantime Rhodes arrived in England towards the end of March to take up the cudgels at home for the formation of his new company.[18]

On April 30, Lord Gifford of the Exploring Company wrote to Lord Knutsford submitting the outlines of the scheme for the new corporation. He emphasized, in his letter, the imperial aspects of the prospective concern. It had for its ultimate object the development of the Bechuanaland Protectorate and the countries lying to the north. More specifically, the company aimed:

1. To extend northwards the railway and telegraph systems in the direction of the Zambezi.
2. To encourage emigration and colonization.
3. To promote trade and commerce.
4. To develop and work mineral and other concessions under the management of one powerful organization, thereby obviating conflicts and complications between the various interests that have been acquired within those regions and securing to the native chiefs and their subjects the rights reserved to them under the several concessions.

The Exploring Company, then, promised to proceed at once with the construction of the first section of the railway and the extension of the telegraph system from Mafeking to Shoshong.

For the accomplishment of its purposes, the company proposed to petition for a charter, asked for the " sanction and moral support of Her Majesty's Government and the recognition of such rights and interests as were legally acquired in the territory." [19]

At the same time, Rhodes' company, the Gold Fields of South Africa Ltd., signified to Lord Knutsford their willingness to cooperate with Lord Gifford's Exploring Company.[20] The campaign for a royal charter was thus definitely launched.

The Government's attitude towards the undertaking was, in large measure, determined by the international scramble for South Africa. Indeed, the rivalry over the next section of the route from the Cape to Cairo furnished some of the most compelling arguments for the establishment of a gigantic colonizing company and for the construction of an independent line of communication into Central Africa.[21]

Once more the British encountered Boer opposition to their march northwards. The sturdy Afrikanders by no means gave up their struggle for the north when the Bechuanaland territory was wrested from them. They claimed that Matabeleland was a free and open field for their expansion. They pointed to Article IV of the London Convention [22] and contended that, since this article expressly excluded the Kafir races to the north of the Republic from the stipulations that treaties with native chiefs be subject to H. M. Government, therefore, gave them, by implication, freedom to carry on their operations in the north.[23] Furthermore, they protested that they had treaties of their own with the Matabele chief. They pointed to two treaties made in 1853 and a recent treaty concluded July 30, 1887, between Lobengula and the South African Republic. The latter was one of peace and friendship, confirming the former treaties and promising to give protection to a Boer resident consul.[24] The Transvaal acted promptly and appointed Piet Groblaar as consul for Matabeleland. To be sure, Groblaar never reached his post [25] but obviously the Boers intended to make good their claim " that the territory to the north of the Republic and through it the road to the north, should remain for them ".[26]   In fact, it was because of the seriousness of the Boer purpose that Moffat was told to hurry on his mission to Matabeleland.[27]   It was most desirable that Lobengula should have good British advice.   When Moffat returned home with his treaty, the Boers refused to recognize its validity.   They produced a report from Albertus Groblaar, made before the Justice of the Peace for the South African Republic, October 8, 1888, in which Albertus Groblaar maintained that Lobengula flatly denied signing such a treaty.[28]

H. M. Ministers were no more willing in 1888 than they had been a few years before in the Bechuanaland dispute to let the north pass out of their hands.   They insisted that Matabeleland was under British influence.   That, as far as the London Convention of 1884 was concerned, the chief purpose of the British negotiations was to secure the trade routes to the north and that among these routes the most important lay to and through Matabeleland and Mashonaland.[29]   They pointed out, on their side, that the northern limit of the Republic as well as its other boundaries had been definitely fixed by the convention.   They denied that the ambiguous clause in regard to the northern tribes precluded a British sphere of influence north of the Republic.

There is no need here to enter into the merits of the controversy.   H. M. Government stood its ground firmly. Finally, the South African Republic accepted a compromise. The British Government promised to withdraw from Swaziland and the territory of Zambane and Umbegesa to the southeast of the South African Republic, if that Republic would withdraw all claims to the north and would use its influence to support British expansion in Bechuanaland and Matabeleland.[30]

Thus, the British Government snatched from the Boer grasp one more great stretch of territory on the route north from the Cape to Cairo. It was faced, however, with an expensive problem of administering this newly acquired area and of maintaining some semblance of order in a country which was harassed by the quarrels of rival concessionaires and by troubles between the white men and the natives. Great Britain must also watch the movements of neighboring powers who were looking with covetous eyes at the Zambezia country.

The Boers were not the only people to object to the British advance into Matabeleland and the north. The Portuguese, roused by the colonial activities of the other European Powers, were beginning to take a fresh interest in their African possessions and to refurbish claims to extensive stretches of territory which dated back to the sixteenth and seventeenth centuries. Indeed, they could boast that at one time they were the paramount European power in Africa and possessed footholds in both southwest and southeast Africa. They claimed, for example, special interests in the ancient dominion. of the native chief Monomotapa which coincided very nearly with the later kingdom of Lobengula and in the ancient gold mines of Manica. In 1607, they maintained the Emperor of Monomotapa " ceded to the Portuguese all the mining rights of his territories." In 1630, he concluded another treaty with them which, later in 1875, became the basis of the MacMahon award of Delagoa Bay to the Portuguese.[31]   Both Monomotapa treaties were considered genuinely authentic; and says Keltie, " we fear, it must be admitted, that had Portugal been a strong power like Germany or France, the treaties would have had much more weight with the British Government in adjusting claims to Mashonaland." [32]

During the seventeenth century, however, Portuguese power in Africa rapidly declined. The Portuguese Government of the Monomotapa was abolished as quickly as it had been erected. In the east, they continued to occupy a few fortified places between Delagoa Bay and Mozambique but had to abandon all the coast further north.[33]

There were undoubtedly here and there isolated stations in the interior still belonging to Portuguese half-castes and Gazaland was placed by Portuguese soldiers in the hands of Gungunhana. One or two sporadic expeditions were sent into the interior, such as the ill-fated journey of Lacerda to the land of Cazembe in 1798 already mentioned in the first chapter. Half castes and natives with Portuguese names and titles may even have crossed the continent but there was no evidence of effective occupation anywhere except in the provinces of Angola and Mozambique.[34]

As early as 1877, a change was evident. The Portuguese took a renewed interest in South Africa. Explorers, as already noted, penetrated into the interior. Serpa Pinto travelled from St. Paul de Loanda across the continent to the Zambezi River and then into the Barotse country. Finally, he came via the Kalahari Desert to the Transvaal. Capello and Ivens travelled through the upper part of Angola and the basin of the Kwanga. Later, they traced the upper Zambezi to its source and then followed the river down to the Indian Ocean.[35] In 1888, Antonio Cardoso set out to explore the western shore of Lake Nyasa and the following year Serpa Pinto was dispatched to the same region on a relief expedition. In 1889, Colonel Paiva d'Andrade and Lieutenant Cordon proceeded to explore the valleys of the Mazoe and other tributaries of the Zambezi River. About this time, a royal decree established and endowed a Roman Catholic mission in the south shore of Lake Nyasa. Portuguese officials, also, tried unsuccessfully to induce various native chiefs in the neighborhood of Lake Nyasa to declare themselves vassals of Portugal.[36]

In 1878, Colonel d'Andrade obtained what was known as the Piava d'Andrade concession to exploit the resources and particularly the gold of the Manica region. In 1888, he formed the Mozambique Company, which resembled, in the scope of its operations, the future British South Africa Company. Agents were sent out by the new organization to find and work the gold which was reported to abound in the interior of Manica, along the eastern slopes of what was generally regarded as the Mashonaland Plateau.

The Government made an attempt to establish some kind of order in the interior by granting large areas as crown farms to persons, " mainly halfcastes,—most of whom ", says Keltie, " were independent of the government, and differed little from slave-holding, slave-trading native chiefs." The most powerful of these half-caste chiefs in Manica was Gouveia. With Gouveia's native irregulars, Portugal had been carrying on military operations along the Zambezi River and in the Manica district within the western border of Mashonaland. In short, in 1888 and 1889, the Portuguese were exhibiting an alarming activity in these regions.[37] They protested in no uncertain terms against the portions of the Moffat-Lobengula Treaty which claimed the Mashuna and Maka Kala tribes as tributaries of Lobengula.[38] These tribes, they insisted, belonged formerly to their ancient province of Sofala. Not only did the Portuguese protest against the treaty but during this period, they were importing ammunition to the mouth of the Pungwe River which afforded access to the interior of Manica land and to the Mashonaland plateau. Apparently, they were preparing to make good their claims to Mashonaland.[39]

Lord Salisbury insisted that " while admitting his readiness to adjust boundaries at a suitable time . . . Mashonaland was subject to Lobengula, and, therefore, within the British sphere of influence." [40] The British case, however, rested on the insecure foundation of the Moffat treaty with a somewhat capricious native chief. If Portugal succeeded in establishing an effective occupation of the country, Great Britain's paper claim would have little effect. The Portuguese activities, therefore, presented a strong argument for the British occupation of the disputed area either by direct imperial intervention or through the agency of a royal chartered company. As the opponents of Rhodes' prospective company maliciously suggested,

there must be some power responsible for this district. Portugal has already claimed the sovereignity of it, and if the sovereignty does not belong to us we have no right whatever to deny it to Portugal. But as a matter of fact, we have already denied [it] to Portugal. . . . It therefore does belong to us, and we have not only every right but it is our plain duty to interfere.[41]

The Portuguese were also causing the British considerable anxiety north of the Zambezi. Cardoso's expedition in 1888 to the Shire River and the west shore of Lake Nyasa has already been mentioned as well as the expedition which set out the following year under Serpa Pinto.[42] The Portuguese like the British evidently had their eye on a fertile coffee-growing district along the Lake Nyasa. Furthermore, the approach to the Nyasaland district and the Shire Highlands lay through Mozambique via the Zambezi and Shire Rivers. Portugal controlled the mouth of the Zambezi and was, therefore, in a strategic position to help or hinder the development of the British mission stations and coffee-plantations in the lake district.

In short, the British were not altogether comfortable about the presence of the Portuguese on the lower Zambezi.

In 1889, they were beginning to talk about a new route to the Shire Highlands through British territory, i. e., from Cape Colony, through British Bechuanaland up to the Zambezi and from there north into Nyasaland. Indeed, they were commencing to discuss the subject of constructing a railway, free from Portuguese interference, from the Cape to Nyasaland.[43] Conditions in this region, therefore, played, as will be noted further on, an important rôle in arousing popular support for Rhodes' operations in the Zambezi region and particularly for the railway which the promoters of the prospective chartered company promised to construct.[44]

The affairs of Nyasaland were indeed in a parlous state at this time. In 1887, a quarrel broke out between the Arabs and the natives in the lake district which led to a war involving the British settlers on the side of the natives. The latter appealed for help from the Shire Highlands. Adventurers like Lugard and Sharpe answered the call and, finally, a truce was brought about in the beginning of 1889. The Portuguese, who had large plantations on the coast and depended on slave labor for much of the work, were inclined to favor the side of the Arab slave traders. Without taking an active part in the conflict, they did all they could to prevent shipment of arms and ammunition to the English via the Zambezi River.[45]

The Nyasaland situation aroused great interest among people of influence, especially in Scotland. In June, 1887, Lugard returned to England and commenced an ardent campaign with pen and speeches in behalf of his suffering compatriots in Nyasaland. He found " a deep and strong feeling in response to his efforts." There was a growing demand that H. M. Government step in and establish a protectorate over the troubled area.[46]

Lord Salisbury was keenly interested in this region. He

could be counted upon to lend a sympathetic ear to suggestions for relieving the disturbances. There was also quite a group of men influential in government affairs who, ever since rival European Powers had entered the field, were ready to support the advance of British political and commercial power in Africa. These men included Lord Salisbury, Lord Rosebery, Sir Charles Dilke, Sir Henry Austin Lee, Lord Fitzmaurice, Sir Villiers Lister and Sir Henry Percy Anderson.[47] Goschen, Chancellor of the Exchequer, however, was one of the " most resolute Little Englanders " and, consequently, opposed to squandering public funds on wild adventures in East Central Africa.[48]

. H. M. Government, although anxious about the Nyasaland situation, was not ready yet to take a decisive forward step. It refused to send a military expedition into the troubled region or to establish a protectorate over the district. On the other hand, it insisted that " the Zambezi must be a route open to all and not confined to one." All that the Government could do on the sea coast, all that it could do diplomatically it did, short of becoming entangled in actual hostilities.[49]

Lord Salisbury was already contemplating plans for extending the British sphere of influence north of the Zambezi and for safeguarding British interests in Nyasaland. For some of this work, he chose Sir Harry Johnston, as his agent. In the summer of 1888, Johnston had several important conversations with Lord Salisbury over African questions, notably one at Hatfield House in June.[50] " It was in these and subsequent conversations ", Johnston writes, " that the phrase ' the Cape to Cairo ' was used, if not by Lord Salisbury himself, at any rate in his presence and with smiling acquiescence on his part." [51] The general plan was to make treaties with the native chiefs by which each one would promise not to cede his territories, or any special control over his territories, without the prior consent of the British Government. This, said Johnston, implied " a vague kind of British protectorate ". Its chief object was to ward off attempts of other foreign nations to establish control in these areas.[52] Following the talk at Hatfield House, Johnston published an article in the *Times* of August 22, 1888, on " Great Britain's Policy in Africa " by an African Explorer.[53]

In November 1888, Sir Harry Johnston was given the appointment of consul to Mozambique but in March of the following year, Lord Salisbury suddenly decided to send him to Lisbon instead. Johnston was told to come to an understanding which would keep the Portuguese out of the Shire Highlands and Central Zambezia. He was very nearly successful in his mission. Indeed, he had almost arrived at a settlement with the Portuguese which would have delimited the respective spheres of influence much as they are today. His plans, however, were upset by the intervention of Señor Luis de Soveral who had recently been the First Secretary of the Portuguese Legation in London. Soveral managed to have an amendment inserted in the agreement which would have admitted the Portuguese to the east bank of the Upper Shire and made the entire Shire River the Anglo-Portuguese frontier. This arrangement would have given the Portuguese the small but important region of the Shire Highlands on which the British missionary and coffee growing colonies had been for ten or twelve years established. Johnston was impressed by the smallness of the concession and consented to the amendment. Lord Salisbury, on the other hand, rejected the proposed arrangement because he placed a high value on this region in the Highlands.[54]

Johnston was next directed to proceed to East Africa " to report on local conditions, get through to Lake Nyasa, and, if possible, bring the Arab war to an end by negotiations." The Treasury, however, refused to sanction the funds necessary for the expedition. In fact, Goschen was opposed to any imperial adventures north of the Zambezi.[55] Lord Salisbury, although keenly interested in the Nyasaland situation, could not saddle the government with Central African responsibilities with no allotted funds to carry out the undertaking. He was unwilling, also, to provoke a cabinet crisis over the issue. It looked, at the time, as though Salisbury's and Johnston's schemes were doomed to failure because of financial difficulties.[56]

Just at this critical juncture, Cecil Rhodes came to the rescue. Rhodes was at this time in London, as already noted,[57] trying to obtain a charter for his new company. In late April or early May 1889, Johnston and Rhodes met for the first time at a dinner given by the Rev. John Verschoyle, sub-editor of the *Fortnightly Review*. The two men discussed their African schemes together until daylight. Johnston told Rhodes " of the Cape to Cairo scheme, of Lord Salisbury's sympathy with it," of the Nyasaland situation and of his financial troubles. The result of this all-night seance was that Rhodes volunteered to supply the money for Johnston's undertaking. " You are to see Lord Salisbury, at once," said Rhodes, " tell him who I am, give Lord Rothschild as my reference . . . Say that if money is the only hindrance to our striking north from the Zambezi to the headwaters of the Nile, I will find the money." Thereupon, he wrote a check for £2,000 for Johnston's initial expenses and promised H. M. Government ten thousand pounds a year for the administration of the district *on condition that he be granted his coveted charter*. Shortly thereafter, Lord Salisbury interviewed Rhodes himself and decided to accept his offer.[58]

Undoubtedly, Rhodes was genuinely interested in Johnston's plans for securing British influence in the country north of the Zambezi but he, also, had his attention focused at this time, on his prospective chartered company. The condition upon which he made his offer, therefore, was important. Furthermore, Rhodes realized that it would be wise to have Johnson and Salisbury as friends at court. In fact, Salisbury's acquiescence in Rhodes' plans was essential to the obtaining of the charter.

Johnston, soon, had an opportunity to help Rhodes at home. Joseph Chamberlain was inclined to look askance at Rhodes and his proposals for the new company. There was a rumor at the Foreign Office that Chamberlain " was going to put an awkward question in the House of Commons relative to Mr. Rhodes and his application for a Charter." Johnston saw Chamberlain, however, and persuaded him to suspend any further action.[59]

The result of the agreement between Rhodes and Johnston was that the latter started for Africa in the second week in May, confident that one more strip of territory would be colored a good British red. Furthermore, the arrangements in regard to Nyasaland and the country north of the Zambezi smoothed the way for the formation of the British South Africa Company. In fact, the Nyasaland difficulties demonstrated how advantageous it would be for H. M. Government to have some great imperial trading corporations in the field to shoulder the expenses and responsibilities which the government could not carry. Furthermore, they showed a pressing need of a railway north to the Zambezi so that aid and succour could be brought to the British settlers in the Lake region without Portuguese interference.

One other international rival was destined to play an important although less direct rôle than Portugal in the establishment of the chartered company. The British and the Germans were watching each other's movements in South Africa with a great deal of suspicion. The British, as already discussed in some detail in the fourth chapter,[60] were afraid of German intrigue with the Transvaal Boers. The German Government in its turn showed great jealousy and suspicion of Great Britain in connection with the Portuguese Colonies in Africa. They suspected the English of having designs if those colonies were broken up of making them British territory.[61]

The Germans were also causing the British some alarm in another quarter to the north. In 1886, an international commission, as will be noted in greater detail later, determined the spheres of influence of England and Germany along the coast in East Africa but did not settle the question of the interior. Germany, however, at this time, was just about to lay claims to all the region between the Congo and her sphere of influence on the coast.[62] The final settlement of Germany's claims and pretensions, to be sure, was not to come until 1890 but already in 1888, Rhodes had wind of a proposal to " cede to Germany a strip of territory extending from the east to the west right across the continent north of the Zambezi ".[63]   Rhodes asked Metcalfe to write home to protest against this proposal. " It will come better from you," he said, " as I am looked on with some distrust at home." [64]

At the Exploring Company's request, Metcalfe in collaboration with Major F. I. Ricarde-Seaver wrote an article for the March number of the *Fortnightly Review* in which he argued that Great Britain should keep open the path into the interior of South Africa and the way free for " the passage of the iron track that must ultimately join the Cape with Cairo, and carry civilization through the heart of the dark continent." He stressed the danger of the German east-to-west empire and international rivalry over the interior and asserted:

> . . . We must recognize the fact that there is positively a race for the interior, and that nothing but a firm policy will maintain British interests and keep open the way for development of British trade in Africa. . . .
>
> Perhaps the best way of effecting what we are bound to do, would be by granting a charter to some powerful company or corporation, which might include the countries shown within the sphere of British influence. . . . And thus, without expense or outlay on the part of the Imperial Government, . . . [such a company] would effect without an army a peaceful conquest fraught with the most advantageous results alike for the natives and for England and her people; . . . [65]

Out of this international rivalry between Boers, Germans, Portuguese and English over the Zambezi region, out of the growing clamor for better communications to develop this country and out of the demand for a railway to the north free from Boer or Portuguese interference, Rhodes drew considerable support for his British South Africa Company. In short, the new corporation was an answer to the urgent cry for a forward policy in Africa.

Although the countries just north and south of the Zambezi River were the immediate objectives, an even more expansive program crept into the discussions of plans for the new company. People were beginning to talk about a railway which was to push its way northward not only to the Zambezi River and to Nyasaland but ultimately as far as Cairo. This railway, furthermore, was to run through territory either British or under British paramount influence. In fact, the articles in the press, at this time, indicate clearly that the Cape-to-Cairo idea was already rooted in the popular imagination.

On May 16, 1889, the Colonial Office wrote to Lord Gifford requesting him to submit a draft charter to Lord Knutsford. Lord Knutsford was evidently seriously interested in the scheme for the chartered company. He was careful, however, to state that " much would depend on the *personnel* of the directorate " and that H. M. Government must be satisfied that the rights and interests of Europeans and natives were secured. Also, perhaps, Lobengula's interests should be considered.[66]   In submitting Lord Gifford's proposal to the Foreign office, Lord Knutsford pointed out that the new organization, like the Imperial East African Company, would probably " to some considerable extent relieve Her Majesty's Government from diplomatic difficulties and heavy expenditures ". He even ventured to say that, in his opinion, such a company as that proposed for the Bechuanaland Protectorate, if well conducted, would render still more valuable assistance to Her Majesty's Government in South Africa.[67]   Apparently, Rhodes and Lord Gifford had a friend in the Secretary of State for the colonies.

Lord Salisbury's attitude was somewhat more uncertain. He was inclined to look with disfavor upon the proposal to grant extensive powers to the new body.[68]   Nevertheless, imperial burdens and responsibilities in Zambezia and Nyasaland weighed heavily on his mind.[69]

In the meantime, a public campaign was under way for a great chartered company as a panacea for all Great Britain's troubles in Central Africa.   General Strachey, president of the Royal Geographical Society, for example, at the annual meeting of the society, May 27, recommended commercial associations as the best agents for bringing civilization to Central Africa.[70]   On May 29, the *Times* published a leader entitled " British Interests in the Central Zambezi " which heralded " the formation of a new company of British capitalists and philanthropists . . . which will seek to obtain and there is little doubt will receive, a charter for the opening up to trade and civilization certain territory lying to the north and south of the central Zambezi." The enthusiastic writer even foresaw the new company merging with the African Lakes Company and administering the whole region between the Lake district Bechuanaland, the Portuguese Colonies and the Congo. Further, ". . . by bringing it under British influence communications could be established from the *Cape to the Nile*".[71] All this could be accomplished with no additional burdens on H. M. Government.[72]

Another writer in the *Times* of the same date, traces a " distinct and significant connection " between the recommendation of General Strachey in regard to commercial associations, the reply of Salisbury to the Nyasaland deputation, the debate in the House of Lords over the position of British missionaries in East Africa and the article just quoted above concerning " British Interests in the Central Zambezi." This writer even talked about

those who dream in the future of the gradual extension of the sphere of British influence from Egypt and the Soudan in the north and the South African colonies in the south until they meet somewhere in the neighbourhood of the Victoria Nyanza. [i. e., a red empire from Cairo to the Cape].[73]

The *Pall Mall Gazette* of May 29 also spoke enthusiastically about " the great scheme of a gigantic amalgamated company " composed of the African Lakes, Lord Gifford's and Cecil Rhodes' companies. The task before this colossal concern was to color all that was " left of unappropriated Central Africa British red " and ultimately to link the Cape with the Nile. This corporation, it declared, was fostered by the " public spirit of patriotic millionaires who may be ready to subsidize an Empire rather than to allow the backbone of Africa to slip out of our hands." [74]

The Birmingham Post echoed the same story and talked about the establishment of a new company with a field of activity extending from British Bechuanaland to the parent waters of the Nile. It boasted:

With British authority predominant in Egypt, it would then only need the pacification of the Soudan . . . to give us the free run of Central Africa from north to south, including the whole of the high mountainous backbone of the dark continent, which is most suitable for European traders and explorers, and the greater part of the late system . . . [75]

These excerpts from the press indicate clearly that the Cape-to-Cairo idea was beginning to take root and to become a popular slogan as early as the spring of 1889.

Rhodes decided to support his campaign with further substantial promises. On June first, he offered, on behalf of the new company, " to pay for the immediate construction of a telegraph from Mafeking through the Protectorate . . . to Tati and also [to] give a contribution to Her Majesty's Government which would be sufficient to cover all the expenses of the supervision of Matabeleland " i. e., £30,000 for the telegraph construction and £4,000 per annum for the maintenance of a British officer in the country.[76] These promises bore fruit. Rhodes was subsequently informed, June 14, that Her Majesty's Government were disposed to give favorable consideration to his proposals of June first relating to the appointment of a resident in Matabeleland and the construction of the telegraph.[77]

Various articles in the press continued to comment favorably upon the scheme for a new company. The new sovereign company, said the *Spectator* for June first, would fulfill Sir Bartle Frere's old dream of stretching the British Empire up to the Zambezi. The Foreign Office could not govern this area directly. It had no agency for this work at its disposal. The Colonial Office had too much of Africa on its hands already. The chartered company was the solution to the problem. The administration of this area should be left, therefore, to the good British middle-class adventurous young men.[78]

The *Scotsman* was confident that the new company together with the British East Africa Company might prove the best way to combat the slave trade by substituting organized legitimate trade developed by European capital.[79]

The *Pall Mall Gazette* of June 11 noted that the proposal for a chartered company to administer the territory between Bechuanaland and Lake Tanganyika caused uneasiness at Berlin and Lisbon. Both the Germans and Portuguese were preparing to prevent encroachment on their spheres. "That which has ruffled the equanimity of these Powers", said *The Gazette*, " was the curious phrase used by the *Times* in speaking of establishing an English empire in Africa that would be another link between the Cape and the Nile ". "There was ", the writer insisted, " a through road from Bechuanaland to the north end of Lake Tanganyika which lies entirely outside both Portuguese and German possessions." [80]

On July 5, Lord Salisbury, finally, gave his consent to the project.[81] At heart, Lord Salisbury believed that " such far-reaching objects fell properly within the province of the government " rather than within that of a private corporation. He was, however, convinced that the House of Commons would not vote the money needed for government operations in the territories and, therefore, reluctantly consented to the grant of the charter.[82] Possibly, he was influenced by Rhodes' practical offers of financial assistance for the administration of Nyasaland and of Matabeleland.

With Lord Salisbury's hesitation and doubts overruled, Rhodes and Lord Gifford made a great advance forward in their campaign for the charter. They could now count on the support of H. M. Ministers. They still had, however, considerable opposition to face in Parliament and throughout England and South Africa.

There was a decided and organized opposition to the granting of the charter.[83] It came partly from aggrieved concessionaires,[84] partly from men who feared the consequences of granting such vast powers to a private corporation, and partly from a group led by Rhodes' former enemy, the Reverend John Mackenzie, who were particularly interested in the welfare of the African natives. Mackenzie was supported by such influential people as J. D. Hepburn of the London Missionary Society and by the Bishop of Bloemfontein. He, also, had the backing of the Aborigines Protection Society, the London Chamber of Commerce and the South African Committee. This last mentioned committee was composed of certain well known members of Parliament and others, such as Sir T. Fowell Buxton, Baronet; Albert Grey (afterwards Earl Grey), the Duke of Fife, Evelyn Ashley, Arnold Forster and Joseph Chamberlain.[85] Many of these men were like Mackenzie staunch imperialists. They disliked, however, entrusting such weighty imperial responsibilities to a private corporation.[86]

Mackenzie was importunate in his attacks. He submitted long memoranda to the Colonial Office deprecating the proposal to place the development of Matabeleland and Mashonaland in the hands of a chartered company. In season and out of season, he argued that all Bechuanaland from the Cape to the Zambezi should be directly under the sovereignty of the Queen. The government would draw on itself the opprobrium of shirking responsibilities if it gave up this region and placed it in the hands of a private corporation. Its prestige would be lowered if, at this critical time, it handed over its duties and responsibilities as the supreme power in the country to a commercial company. The difficulty in opening up the country was not one of money but of diplomacy and administration.[87]

Chief enemy to the chartered company among the disgruntled concessionaires was Sir John Swinburne, who was the founder of a company for working the Tati region in the southwest of Matabeleland.[88] He carried his grievances into the British Parliament, where he and Sir George Campbell fought the new company bitterly during the latter part of August. Swinburne attacked the progress of the charter in the legislature as a "hole-and-corner" affair. The measure had not, in his estimation, been sufficiently advertised and it was then being railroaded through Parliament at an outrageous speed.[89] He asked that H. M. Government abstain from advising the grant of a charter until the whole policy of granting such a monopoly could be discussed in more leisurely fashion in the next session of Parliament.[90] He objected on principle to granting such vast powers to the company. "The Fact is," said he, "this charter will give to a syndicate of private adventurers as much power as the Old East India Company possessed . . . the whole pith of the charter is, really to confer all these powers on one person, Mr. Cecil Rhodes." [91] Swinburne's arguments were decidedly weakened by the fact that he was well known to be an "interested party". Baron de Worms pointed out maliciously that without Swinburne's personal interest in the matter, [i. e., his Tati concessions], "the transaction would never have been heard of." [92] The Baron's words were greeted by laughter from the house. Although Swinburne was unsuccessful in postponing the grant of the charter, he did succeed in having his own concession, the Tati Gold fields excluded from the field of operations of the company.[93]

Sir George Campbell called the charter " a most objectionable concession ". He, also, protested against the secrecy of procedure in discussing the question. He pointed to the fact that the matter had not been brought up for discussion until most of the members of the House had left London. A speculator, he was sure, was at the bottom of the concession.[94]

Baron Henry De Worms, Secretary of State for the Colonies, however, defended the proposed charter valiantly against all assaults. " Her Majesty's Government," he maintained, " are satisfied that the establishment of a powerful company of this kind affords the best prospect of peaceably opening up and developing the resources of these territories, and of securing British interests concurrently with the advance of trade and civilization." The ultimate authority of H. M. Government was safeguarded by the charter. On public grounds, it was most important to grant the charter without delay. The members of Parliament had been given opportunity to consider the measure. In fact, the charter was advertised in the *London Gazette*, July 23.[95]

Whatever were the merits of the case, the charter was, finally, carried successfully through Parliament in spite of some awkward questions by freelances like Bradlaugh and Labouchere and attacks by Campbell and Swinburne.[96]

Rhodes was undoubtedly pulling many wires behind the scenes during the campaign. It was on April 4 that the meeting took place between Stead, the editor of the powerful *Pall Mall Gazette* and Rhodes. The results of that meeting and how Rhodes converted Stead have already been noted.[97] How Johnston did Rhodes a good turn by persuading Joseph Chamberlain not to ask a peculiarly delicate question in Parliament has been pointed out also.[98] Rhodes, also, obtained an introduction to Sir Charles Dilke, an influential figure in the Foreign Office. Dilke, says Williams, " was . . . impressed by the young statesman's broad-minded views on South African and Imperial politics." [99] Lord Rothschild gave him steady support in his financial undertaking. [100] He could count on a favorable reception of his measures by the Irish party in the House of Commons. He had already paved the way for their support the year before by a generous check of £10,000. [101]

Perhaps the most potent considerations, however, which led to the grant of the charter were the practical promises which have already been mentioned, i. e., Lord Gifford's pledge on behalf of the new company to extend the railway and telegraph systems in the direction of the Zambezi and Rhodes' offer of financial assistance in the immediate construction of a telegraph from Mafeking to Tati. [102] Furthermore, in a letter to Sir Gordon Sprigg dated October 24, 1889, Rhodes promised to secure the extension of the Cape railway system northwards if a charter were granted. " It was on the strength of this pledge," Rhodes himself maintained, " that my application was favourably regarded by Her Majesty's Government, and that the British South Africa Company has been granted a Charter for the development of the countries north of British Bechuanaland and the Transvaal." [103] Lord Gifford stated in his letter of April 30 that a sum of £700,000 had already been privately subscribed for the construction of the railway. [104] The new company, as will be recalled, likewise, undertook to unite most if not all the existing British interests in the Protectorate and the countries to the northwards and thus to end the disturbing wars between rival concessionaires. [105]

These were all practical and substantial offers to relieve H. M. Government of many of the financial burdens attendant upon the development of the British protectorate, and the British sphere of influence up to the Zambezi. The new company meant business. H. M. Government and the

British people were glad to shift the financial weight of British interests in the Zambezia region on to the shoulders of the British South Africa Company.

On October 14, 1889, the Committee of the Privy Council reported in favor of the project and the Queen affixed her seal to the royal charter the next day.[106]

The charter was "framed in accordance with the precedents, so far as they are applicable of the British North Borneo Company's, the Royal Niger Company's and the British Imperial East African Company's charters,"[107] i. e., the new company was distinctly an imperial undertaking. It was a huge colonizing corporation with avowedly imperial objectives.[108]   Its field of operation was, thanks to Rhodes' efforts, left undefined in the north.   Article I of the charter defined the principal field of operations as lying immediately north of British Bechuanaland and to the north and west of the South African Republic and to the west of the Portuguese dominions.[109]   "One of the difficulties which Rhodes had to overcome," writes Vindex, "was the wish of the government to limit the charter to the territories south of the Zambezi."[110]   In the royal charter this difficulty was successfully surmounted.   Rhodes was free, therefore, to spread British influence straight through to the Nile.   In obtaining the sanction of H. M. Government for the British South Africa Company he secured in a sense the blessing of the imperial government upon one of his schemes for painting Africa red.

The powers of the new company were expansive.   It could maintain a police force.   It could even hoist its own flag in the territories and on its vessels.   It could establish banking companies and companies or associations of every description for purposes consistent with the provisions of the charter.   It could make and maintain roads, railways, telegraphs, harbours, and any other works which may tend to the development or improvement of the territories of the company. It could hold concessions, agreements, grants and make treaties " necessary for the purpose of government and the preservation of public order." [111]

Rhodes sagaciously chose for the first board of directors, former leaders in rival companies and men prominent in political and social circles.[112] The press heralded this choice with great satisfaction. The names at the head of the company should " command public confidence that its terms will be honestly adhered to ", one writer maintained. They commanded " social position, even a flavour of Royalty—business capacity, broad-minded enterprise and ample means." [113] Imperial interests would be safe in the hands of such a board while philanthropic and patriotic ends " would be secure with the Duke of Fife and the Duke of Abercorn at the helm." [114] The affixing of the Great Seal of the United Kingdom to the charter of the British South Africa Company, the *Pall Mall Gazette* called " . . . an outward and visible sign of the colonizing genius of the Anglo-Saxon race. . . ." [115]

The news of the granting of the charter brought great satisfaction to the public throughout South Africa and there was especial rejoicing in Bechuanaland over the railway project.[116] As already emphasized before,[117] the chief value of Bechuanaland lay in its function as a trade route to the interior. To make this route effective, a railway was required. " Only by means of a great trunk line of railway," wrote Sidney Shippard, administrator of British Bechuanaland, " can the advantages of that route be secured to Cape Colony. Everything points to the necessity for ultimate railway extension to the Zambezi valley, and both the commercial and administrative centre must from time to time necessarily be shifted further and further north." [118]

The new company, in conformance with its charter, immediately took up the question of extending the railway from

Kimberley to Vryburg. To make this extension, the co-operation of the imperial government of British Bechuana-land and the colonial government of Cape Colony was essential. In accordance with the Exploring Company's sugges-tions, the British South Africa Company was, when con-stituted, substituted for the Exploring Company, as the Association with which the Government of British Bech-uanaland would thenceforth deal in respect of this railway. Negotiations were renewed. The British South Africa Company expressed its willingness to accept, in substitution for some of the fiscal and mining privileges which the Ex-ploring Company had previously desired to receive, a grant of 6,000 square miles of vacant Crown land, with the min-eral rights thereon, in respect of the construction of the line to Vryburg. A similar grant of an additional 6,000 square miles was anticipated if the line was extended to Mafeking.[119]

Meanwhile Rhodes was carrying on negotiations with the Cape Government. An agreement was, finally, entered into by which the Cape Government "undertook to give the British South Africa Company all facilities for making the line up to the Colonial border, and undertook to work the whole line at the rates in force in the colony, if so required by the company." [120]

The earthworks on the Kimberley-Vryburg section were commenced four days after the grant of the charter and by December 1890 the line was completed to Vryburg. As a result, British Bechuanaland entered on a new lease of life and "enormous strides" were taken in opening up and developing the country.[121]

Within less than ten years, therefore, i. e., 1885 to 1890, the country from Cape Colony to the Zambezi was colored a good British red. The road into the interior of Central Africa, as far as that great river, was securely in British hands. Rhodes had established an imperial trading company to occupy effectively this vast stretch of territory. The company, furthermore, possessed unlimited powers of expansion to the north. The first section of the Cape-to-Cairo railway was completed to Vryburg. There was evidence in the enthusiasm for the new chartered company that the Cape-to-Cairo idea had already taken root and was firing the ambition of men interested in African affairs. In fact, with the establishment of the British South Africa Company, the Cape-to-Cairo railway project first began to assume definite shape and form.

CHAPTER VII

"The Forward Policy" in South Africa

THE decade which began soon after the launching of the British South Africa Company was a period peculiarly adapted to the growth of a Cape-to-Cairo movement. It was the heyday of imperialism and Great Britain was as busy as the neighboring countries in "pegging out claims for the future." [1] Conservative and Liberal ministers alike were dyed with the new imperialism. Even Gladstone who at heart was opposed to any further extension of the empire, yielded to the strong current and in 1892 chose Lord Rosebery, an arch-imperialist, as his Secretary of State for Foreign Affairs.

There was, to be sure, a small but vociferous body of die-hards among the Liberals who still clung to the traditional "Little England" policies of that party and stubbornly opposed all overseas expansion. Labouchere and Sir William Harcourt talked at length and often in the House of Commons about the deplorable expense and responsibility of Great Britain's expanding empire overseas. On the other hand, whenever a vote was taken which involved the question of expansion, the result was almost invariably and overwhelmingly in favor of the British forward march through Africa. [2] Rhodes was right when he told his Cape Town audience:

My people have changed. I speak of the English people, with their marvellous common sense, coupled with their powers of imagination—all thoughts of a little England are over. They are tumbling over each other, Liberal and Conservatives, to show

151

which side are the greatest and most enthusiastic Imperialists
. . . the people have found out that England is small, and her
trade is large, and they have also found out that other people
are taking their share of the world, and enforcing hostile tariffs.
The people of England are finding out that "trade follows the
flag," and they have become Imperialist.[3]

It was natural that in this period, Cecil Rhodes' imperial
schemes and projects should mature rapidly. It is, to be
sure, necessary to remember that there was an evolution in
the practical working out of his ideas. In the earlier part
of the period, for example, between 1890 and 1895, he
seems to have been primarily intent upon building up a
solid foundation for northward expansion in South Africa
and in securing footholds farther north rather than in a
specific Cape-to-Cairo railway project. He was, as already
noted, in sympathy with the Cape-to-Cairo schemes of Sir
Harry Johnston of building up a British Central Africa as
a connecting link between the British spheres in the south
and north.[4] Furthermore, as will be observed in a later
chapter, he fought hard at the time of the Uganda crisis in
1893-1894 to keep the corridor to the north in British hands.[5]
There is no doubt " that, speaking georaphically, Rhodes'
' saw red.' " [6]

Moreover, he was certainly playing with the idea of a
Cape-to-Cairo line of communication although his plans were
not fully developed. In 1892, he launched the Transcontinental Telegraph Company. In a speech at the second
annual meeting of the British South Africa Company, November 24, 1892, he presented a proposal to the shareholders
to subscribe to the erection of the line as far as Uganda.
The line, however, was not to stop there.

From a commercial point of view [he boasted], I feel perfectly clear that when I get to Uganda I shall get through to
Wady Halfa. . . . I am perfectly clear that if I get the money

to make the line to Uganda I shall get the money with which to extend the line to Egypt.[7]

The imperial character of this telegraph was uppermost in Rhodes' mind. In fact, this imperialistic tinge is evident from the inception of the project. He had been considering the proposition of a telegraph to Egypt, he claimed, ever since "the charter was commenced" but his plans grew rapidly in 1892 because there was some question at the time about the retention of Uganda. The Uganda question will be taken up later on.[8] It is sufficient here to note that Rhodes felt that the erection of a telegraph line to Uganda might be of great service in holding this key position on the route north. "If I extend the telegraph to Uganda," he contended, "we shall certainly not hear any more about the abandonment of that place."[9] It was then with this distinctly imperial objective in view, that Rhodes hastened to present his proposal to H. M. Government. Furthermore, "The telegraph," he added "will be an end to the slave-trade, and it will also give us the keys to the continent."[10] Finally, it was to be the forerunner of the Cape-to-Cairo railway. Like the railway it would be an instrument in his plan of spreading British influence from one end of the Dark Continent to the other. In short, his whole contention for the line was based upon a practical imperialism.

In 1890, as will be noted in a later chapter, by the Anglo-German treaty, Germany had thrust a wedge of territory between the British spheres of activity in the south and in the north. By this treaty, German East Africa was made conterminus with the Congo State. In order, therefore, to carry the telegraph north, Rhodes must make arrangements to run the line for some distance through either Congolese or German territory. As a matter of fact, he attempted to carry lines through both countries. He was engaged in the period before 1895, however, in vainly trying to obtain wayleaves from the German Government for running the line through German East Africa. When, as discussed in a previous chapter,[11] the Germans planted their colony of southwest Africa in Damaraland and Namaqualand, they left the harbor of Walfisch Bay in British hands. Walfisch Bay, therefore, formed a British enclave within the German Colony. It was, however, Germany's most convenient part for the outlet for its trade. The Cape waived collection of duties here, partly as a matter of international courtesy and partly for the sake of creating a favorable attitude towards Rhodes' negotiations for way-leave for the transcontinental telegraph. Rhodes hoped that by this cooperation he could in turn carry the telegraph through East Africa. Contrary to his expectations, the Germans refused to grant him the desired permission. Rhodes was indignant:

> Without putting on these duties at Walfisch Bay [he told the House], I have been refused to let the telegraph go through their territory to civilize Africa. . . . For two years . . . they have refused to allow the telegraph to go through their East African possessions. They have refused over and over again, so that they are not entitled to the slightest consideration.[12]

This failure to cooperate with him in his telegraph schemes added greatly to Rhodes' animosity towards the Germans and it led to some heated remarks about their colonies especially in southwest Africa. There was, likewise, considerable anger in Berlin over Rhodes' offensive words. Even the British ambassador, Sir E. Malet, characterized them as " intolerably galling." [13]

The telegraph, then, formed an important feature of Rhodes' imperial schemes before 1895. Whether, on the other hand, the transcontinental railway was considered by him as an immediately feasible part of his program is doubtful. He was far more interested in establishing the chartered company in Zambezia and in building a solid foundation for northward expansion in South Africa than he was in pushing the south to north railway into regions which had not yet proved capable of supporting such a trunk line. This does not mean that Rhodes was not dreaming of a Cape-to-Cairo railway. It simply means that Rhodes was a practical man as well as a dreamer. His expansive railway schemes could wait until the ground was prepared for them. He was to be sure, ready to fulfill the first part of the promise made by the promoters of the British South Africa Company [14] and to carry the line from Kimberley to Vryburg but beyond that point he was not willing to go at that time. " Having," writes Metcalfe, " carried out the line to Vryburg, as demanded in the Charter, Rhodes was not inclined to go further . . . Finance, no doubt was difficult but if Rhodes had resolved to carry on the railway he could have done it." [15]

Sir Charles Metcalfe apparently was much more interested, at this date, in the immediate promotion of the Cape-to-Cairo railway than Rhodes. Metcalfe wished the Bechuanaland Railway called " the African Trunk Line." Rhodes, however, insisted on a more local title. Moreover, it was at Metcalfe's instigation that the line was finally built by Messrs. Pauling Brothers from Vryburg to Mafeking and opened to traffic at the end of 1892. The line, much to Rhodes' surprise, paid well from the start but even then he could not be induced to go further.[16]

Rhodes had other more immediate interests. He was intent upon developing the country to the north of Cape Colony and upon consolidating the gains already made in this direction. He was particularly interested in the vast and vaguely defined region which had been assigned to his new chartered company as their sphere of activity. Economically, it was more important for the work of the new

British South Africa Company to secure communications with its field of operations in Mashonaland and Matabeleland via a lateral line to the east coast than over the much longer route up from Cape Town in the south.[17] In fact in 1891, Robert Williams reported, after an expedition into Rhodesia, that a short railway to the coast was necessary for the mineral development of the country.[18] Rhodes, therefore, turned his attention to securing this lateral line. By the Anglo-Portuguese agreement of 1891, the Portuguese consented to construct a railway between Pungwe and the British sphere or to give the construction of the railway to a company to be designated by a neutral Power selected by the two Governments.[19] A concession for the building of the line from Beira on Pungwe Bay to the eastern border of Mashonaland was granted by the Portuguese Government to a man by the name of Van Laun. Rhodes was already discussing plans with the Pauling Brothers for opening up Rhodesia by railway. In conjunction with Van Laun, the Beira Railway Company, promoted by Rhodes' British South Africa Company, was formed in 1892 and a contract given to Messrs. Pauling for the construction of a narrow gauge line to the eastern border of Rhodesia.[20] The line was commenced in September, 1892 and completed in February 1898.[21]

As part of his program of laying a solid base in the south for future colonial expansion, Rhodes, as noted before, desired to build up a United States of South Africa under the hegemony of Cape Colony. He was interested at this period in strengthening the economic links between the Cape and the Boer states to the north and in expanding Cape trade. In this connection, as already seen in chapter IV, he took a great interest in the Delagoa Bay Railway. New schemes were already forming in his mind. They included not only an attempt to secure control of the railway but also to purchase the port itself and even the province of Mozambique. Rhodes' plans developed out of troubled conditions in Portuguese Southeast Africa. As noted in a previous chapter, the two companies engaged in constructing the railway between Lourenço Marques and Pretoria were engaged in a rate war. The railway difficulties were, furthermore, of far-reaching significance because they involved delicate relations between the nationals of five powers: The Transvaal, Germany, Portugal, Great Britain and the United States. As noted before, both Germans and Transvaal Boers had strong interests in the Netherlands Railway Company which was to construct the line from the Transvaal border to Pretoria.[22] The line from Delagoa Bay to the Transvaal was in the hands of McMurdo's Company. McMurdo himself was an American. His company while nominally Portuguese was controlled largely by British financiers. Because of these complications, the question of the ultimate control of the railway from Delagoa Bay to Pretoria was destined to play an important rôle in the diplomatic struggle for supremacy in South Africa and was an important and integral part of the future development of Rhodes' program.

It is not necessary, however, to follow in detail the whole story of the quarrels and difficulties between the Netherlands South Africa and McMurdo's Company. Affairs reached such an impasse that in June, 1889, the Portuguese Government stepped in and proceeded to take the construction of the line between Delagoa Bay and the Transvaal border under its control. Under this new arrangement the entire line from Lourenço Marques to Pretoria was finished by the end of 1894 and formally opened for traffic in June 1895.[23] At the state opening, Germany was represented by two naval officers. The British, in turn, sent a squadron to Delagoa Bay under Admiral Rawson.[24]

In the meantime, directly after the seizure of the railway by the Portuguese Government in 1889, McMurdo's widow and the shareholders in the Delagoa Bay Railway Company protested against the proceeding and put in claims for damages. The shareholders of the Railway company were largely British. The claims of McMurdo's company were, in turn, supported by Lord Salisbury. Both the United States Government, on behalf of McMurdo's widow and the British Government on behalf of the British shareholders put in complaints which were referred in 1890 to arbitration. The arbitration proceedings dragged out over the entire decade of the nineties. In fact, the award, commonly referred to as the Berne Award, was not rendered until 1900. According to this award, the Portuguese Government was justified in seizing the railway but condemned to pay 15,-314,000 francs by way of compensation to the concessionaires.[25] This book is less concerned, however, in the decision of the arbitrators than in the fact that it was so long delayed. The delay, as will be seen in tracing the history of events during the nineties, caused considerable uncertainty and was an important factor in the diplomatic situation during this period.[26] The Portuguese Government was in great financial difficulty during the nineties. The danger, therefore, of a possibly adverse decision by the arbitrators aggravated their embarrassment.

With this background in mind, the policy of Cecil Rhodes between 1890 and 1895 can be better understood. He was, during this period, considering various schemes for the purchase of Delagoa Bay and the railway. In 1890, in line with his general program of cooperation with the Boers, he went so far as to suggest to Kruger that the Transvaal take Delagoa Bay as a seaport by force if necessary. The sturdy

Boer President, however, spurned the suggestion. " I can't take away other people's property ", he replied, " . . . If the Portuguese won't sell the harbor, I wouldn't take it, even if you gave it to me; for ill-gotten goods are accursed." [27]

As early as 1891, Rhodes conceived the ambitious idea of helping the Portuguese out of their financial distress by buying up the whole province of Lourenço Marques on behalf of the Cape. He began a series of negotiations largely through Rochfort Maguire, Sir James Sivewright, Merriman and other agents which lasted until the close of 1894. In fact, he sent his first agent in 1891 to Lisbon to negotiate for the purchase of the province but the national sentiment was opposed to parting with any territory. [28]

Lord Rothschild was also making advances in concert with the Cape Government, and probably with Rhodes, for the purchase of the entire possessions of Portugal in Africa, south of the Zambesi. [29] The Cape Government seems to have been in sympathy with these ambitious schemes of Rhodes and Rothschild. On January 22, 1892, Merriman, the Cape Treasurer who was then in London, wrote to Rhodes that he had, per request, interviewed a " well-known international financier." The financier had advised the purchase of all the south-east African possessions of Portugal as a solution of the South African problem. " Transaction," he claimed, " was not beyond the limits of probability, as Portugal was in sore straits for money." [30]

In February, 1892, Rhodes began negotiations at Lisbon. There is no need here to discuss these transactions in detail which extended throughout 1892 and 1893. It is important to note, however, that twice success seemed imminent; once in 1892 and again in the summer of 1893. The first pourparlers were frustrated, however, by a change of ministry in Portugal in the spring of 1893. In the second series of negotiations, Rhodes was finally outbid by another competitor, probably the Transvaal Government supported by Germany.[31]   Rhodes claimed that the United States, also, placed a serious obstacle in his path and that American intervention on behalf of McMurdo's relatives at a time when success seemed assured was fatal to his plans. According to Erich Brandenburg's account, Germany acting with the United States frustrated his efforts.[32]   At any rate, it is likely that the part played by the Transvaal and Germany at this time increased Rhodes' growing impatience with the Transvaal Boers and the Germans.

In the spring of the following year, 1894, Rhodes received word from the High Commissioner that the Portuguese Government, although it was not willing to sell, might be persuaded to lease Delagoa Bay for 100 years. He suggested that the Cape Government stipulate minimum concessions and perhaps offer to pay the amount of the anticipated Berne award. Portugal, however, refused to do anything until after the Berne award was rendered. Negotiations continued during June and July. In September, a native insurrection broke out at Lourenço Marques of which Gungunhana was the ringleader. Gungunhana was well-known to be a chief friendly to Rhodes. Rhodes, for his part offered to subdue the uprising but there was strong suspicion at Berlin and at Lisbon that the outbreak was due to Rhodes' intrigues. Furthermore, the British consul, without consulting the Portuguese authorities, " ordered twenty blue-jackets to land for the protection of the Consulate." The Portuguese protested and H. M. Government, thereupon, reprimanded the Consul. The British Government, in its turn, protested successfully against the enrollment of volunteers from the Transvaal. The German Government, nevertheless, sent two warships to Delagoa Bay to safeguard, according to Baron von Marschall, " the large German interests involved, both on the coast and in the Transvaal." [33]

The crisis blew over and for the time being nothing more was done about the question of purchasing either the railway or the Portuguese possessions. Nevertheless, as will be seen in a later chapter, the question of the future ownership of Portuguese territory continued to cause discussion and considerable irritation between the interested Powers.

Rhodes was also faced with difficulties in the Transvaal itself. His repeated efforts to cooperate with the Boers, especially the Transvaal Boers, have already been noted.[34] He failed, however, to win the cooperation of Kruger. In fact, Oom Paul and his policies stood directly in the way of his plans for a United South Africa under a British flag and in the way of his program of northward expansion. Rhodes, undoubtedly, preferred the method of bargaining and dickering with Kruger or, in his own words, of " squaring " the Boer President but if this method failed, he was prepared to employ other tactics.

As his chances of cooperation with the Transvaal Boers became less, Rhodes grew receptive to more aggressive plans. Trouble had been brewing for some time in the Transvaal between the Boers and the Uitlanders or foreigners who had been attracted to the country by the lure of the gold fields. The numbers of the newcomers increased so rapidly that the Boers were afraid that they would be submerged by the new elements and that their country might even some day become absorbed by the Cape. They did not, therefore, welcome the Uitlanders into the political life of the community. The Uitlanders, for their part, complained of economic and political grievances. As early as 1892, a body called the Transvaal National Union was formed to secure Uitlander representation and other reforms by constitutional agitation. As time went on the list of grievances of the Uitlanders grew longer. In 1894, there were vague rumors of an insurrection on foot. Loch, the High Commissioner, even went so far as to concentrate Imperial Bechuanaland Police on the Transvaal border ready for intervention if necessary. As a matter of fact, just about this time, a conspiracy was forming to right the wrongs of the Uitlanders. Rhodes as director on the board of the Goldfields of South Africa took an active interest in the difficulties of his compatriots. In November 1894, therefore he lent a sympathetic ear to the plans of the conspirators. In fact, he went further. Together with Jameson, he arranged to have the chartered forces made as efficient as possible in order to be prepared for eventualities, so that if a revolt did occur in Johannesburg and help were required, he could use them at his own discretion.[35]

He also used his influence to obtain land on the border of the Transvaal on which to concentrate the chartered troops and supplies in case of trouble at Johannesburg. In the last chapter it was noted that the Imperial Government gave the British South Africa Company certain land grants in British Bechuanaland for the extension of the railway from Kimberley to Mafeking.[36] H. M. Government, furthermore, in 1894 agreed to the grant of a £20,000 subsidy from the annual revenue of the British Bechuanaland Protectorate for ten years for the extension of the railway to Palapye in the north of the Protectorate. The Government also gave the company certain exclusive rights of railway construction through the Bechuanaland Protectorate. It also promised the good offices of its officials in the Protectorate towards gaining the consent of the native chiefs to land grants in behalf of the railway as well as to the grant of mineral concessions, agricultural lands and town sites.[37] Clearly, H. M. officials were supporting the railway operations of the Chartered Company.

In 1895, the British Government made good its promise and persuaded the native chiefs along the Transvaal border to give an administrative strip to the railway company. Not only was this strip to be used for railway purposes but it was to form the frontier against the independent Boer state. The Chartered Company was charged with the responsibility of maintaining this frontier.[38] "It is absolutely necessary that the railway to Matabeleland should be proceeded with as quickly as possible," the Colonial Office wrote in no uncertain tone, "and that it should run through the eastern part of the Bechuanaland Protectorate . . . it will be necessary that each of the chiefs, Bathoen, Sebele and Khama give up a strip of country along the Transvaal border." [39] Khama had long been the friend of H. M. Government. He had loyally assisted the advance to the north.[40] He was, however, worried at the intrusion of this great commercial company into his territory. He, Sebele and Bathoen wrote to the High Commissioner:

We fear the company because we think they will take our land and sell it to others . . . we see that they are a people without gratitude; if Khama had not helped them they could not have established themselves in Mashonaland . . . and yet they try to take Khama's country secretly . . . we hear the words of the Makalaka and Matabele, who live under the company, and we see that these people do not like their rulers. . . . The government is great and good; it will not give us away without asking what we think about it.[41]

The chiefs, indeed, travelled all the way to England to plead their cause before the Great White Queen. The British Government, however, was firm and Chamberlain, the Colonial Secretary, finally, persuaded the natives to give up their land.

Ostensibly, the land was placed under the administration of the British South Africa Company to facilitate the extension of the railway to the North. Actually, the Government was unwittingly promoting the less worthy scheme of

Cecil Rhodes to prepare a "jumping-off ground" for chartered troops to be used in case of an insurrection in the Transvaal.[42] After some manoeuvring, then, Rhodes obtained his coveted strip along the Transvaal frontier and also the right to police the strip. "But," says Williams, "there is not a title of evidence that either Chamberlain or the Colonial Officials really understood, still less approved of Rhodes' schemes." The land was granted to Rhodes in all good faith simply to serve the purpose of constructing the railway to the North.[43]

As noted in the foregoing chapter, there was much popular enthusiasm for this railway and the extension of the line had been a large factor in persuading the Government to grant a charter. Already people were associating these iron rails with a project for communication from the Cape to the Nile. There was a considerable group who were talking about "a solid right of way" clear through to the North and that along that route the most effective method of civilization would be by railway communication.[44]

There is no indication, to be sure, in the correspondence between H. M. Government and the British South Africa Company that the British Government had this comprehensive program in mind when they agreed to support the railway by land grants, subsidies and the good offices of their officials.[45] In fact, the Government regarded the extension of the line from Kimberley to Palapye from the practical standpoint that the line would be of great service in the administration of the Bechuanaland Protectorate and would bring about real economy in government expenditure.[46] Nevertheless, the fact remains that H. M. Government did materially and substantially assist Rhodes' railway company in building this important section of the Cape-to-Cairo line through British Bechuanaland and the Bechuanaland Protectorate.

Not only did the Government cooperate with Rhodes in his railway project but it gave him valuable support in securing and effectively occupying the vast stretch of territory between Bechuanaland and Lake Tanganyika.

The first step forward in the occupation of the country to the North was to secure a firm hold over the extensive dominion of the Matabele King which lay between the Bechuanaland Protectorate, Portuguese East Africa and the Zambezi River. The Chartered Company held in their hands the Rudd Concession granting them mining rights throughout this area but they had no genuine land ownership there.[47]   Furthermore, the Rudd Concession was granted by Lobengula, a native ruler, who was notorious for changing his mind.   Already, Lobengula was attempting to deny the validity of the concession.   He wrote pathetically to the Great White Queen, April 23, 1889:

Sometime ago, a party of men came into my country, the principal one appearing to be a man named Rudd.   They asked me for a place to dig for gold, and said they would give me certain things for the right to do so.   I told them to bring what they would give and I would then show them what I would give.

A document was written and presented to me for signature. I asked what it contained and was told that in it were my words and the words of those men.

I put my hand to it.

About three months afterwards I heard from sources that I had given by that document the right to all minerals in my country.

I called a meeting of my Indunas and also of the white men, and demanded a copy of the document.   It was proved to me that I had signed away the mineral rights of my whole country to Rudd and his friends.

I have since had a meeting of my Indunas, and they will not recognize the paper as it contains neither my words nor the words of those who got it.

After the meeting I demanded that the original document be returned to me. It has not come yet, although it is two months since, and they promised to bring it back soon.

I write to you that you may know the truth about this thing and may not be deceived.[48]

To this letter, Lobengula's mark was affixed and this signature witnessed by G. A. Phillips, Moss Cohen and James Fairbairn. Fairbairn was a trader resident at Lobengula's Kraal. He was, also, an especially privileged person to whom was intrusted the King's " great elephant seal, without which treaties and concessions had no validity." Phillips was another concession hunter at the Kraal. The witnesses were rivals of the Rudd interests and the letter might easily have been a manufactured piece of propaganda against the Rudd Concession.[49] In fact, Moffat, British Commissioner to Lobengula insisted that the letter was irregular and hinted that there were " powerful interests desirous of working minerals in this country." There was strong and respectable evidence, he maintained, that Lobengula knew what he was doing when he signed the Rudd Concession and that this repudiation of it was an after-thought.

The Imperial Government decided to take the side of the Chartered Company and to approve the Concession. The Queen sent an imposing deputation consisting of " a military band and the three tallest of her Life Guards " to the native King, with a message sanctioning the Rudd Concession and informing Lobengula that a Royal Charter had been granted to the British South Africa Company. The message, also, told the King that Moffat was appointed as British resident in the King's Kraal.[50] Moffat, as noted before, was in sympathy with Rhodes and had already performed some valuable services which had prepared the way for his work.[51]

Lobengula's dominions were divided into two sections: Matabeleland to the West and Mashonaland to the East.

Matabeleland was inhabited by the chief's own warlike tribes and the King's Kraal was at Buluwayo in this territory. Mashonaland was inhabited, on the other hand, by a tribe of more peaceful nature. The Mashonas were tributaries of Lobengula but they were none too friendly with the Matabeles. Mashonaland although tributary to Lobengula was less directly under his control than Matabeleland. For this reason and because of the peaceful disposition of the Mashonas, the Chartered Company chose Mashonaland for their first field of operations. They had, however, to obtain permission first from Lobengula to enter the country. The native King, alarmed by the pending encroachment of these meddlesome white men into his kingdom, refused them the road. Rhodes dispatched Jameson to Lobengula's Kraal and, fortunately for him, Jameson arrived there simultaneously with Queen Victoria's deputation. The native chief, impressed by the importance of the missions, yielded and granted the required permission to enter Mashonaland.[52]

The Matabele King, however, was not the only danger to be faced on the road into the north country. As early as September 1889, Rhodes had wind of a contemplated Boer trek into the coveted Mashonaland. Once more Rhodes had need of the good offices of the Imperial Government and once more H. M. Government came to his assistance. Rhodes appealed to the Imperial Secretary for help. Sir Henry Loch, British Commissioner, thereupon, sent a protest to Kruger against the anticipated trek. Finally, at a conference at Blignaut's Point, March, 1890, between the High Commissioner, Rhodes and Kruger, the latter agreed, in return for some concessions in regard to Swaziland, to discourage the trek. Under pressure from Rhodes, the Afrikander Bond and the British High Commissioner, Kruger was persuaded to issue a proclamation to stop the expedition. The Queen, then, further reenforced the position of the Chartered Company by proclaiming a protectorate over Lobengula's dominions and warning off trespassers.[53]

In spite of warnings and proclamations, some of the trekkers continued with their plans. Nevertheless, it was a much reduced number of Boers who finally set out for Mashonaland in 1891. They were met at the Limpopo opposite Tuli by Jameson and a force of Bechuanaland police. Jameson persuaded part of them to turn back. Others decided to settle peacefully in the new country under the Chartered Company.[54] Thus ended the last Boer effort to win the North.

The way was ready for a hardy band of Chartered Company settlers called "the Pioneers." The story of their expeditions into Mashonaland in 1890 and the dangers and suffering which they endured while establishing themselves there during the next few years, is a tale full of interest but it has been well told often before. The occupation of Mashonaland was entirely the work of the British South Africa Company. It was, thus, through the efforts of Rhodes' "young men" that one more important territory was brought securely under British influence.

One grave danger to the new settlements in Mashonaland was that of hostile raids from their fierce Matabele neighbors. Twice in 1892, Lobengula sent raiders among the Mashonas and it was clear that sooner or later a clash must come between the Matabele forces and the newcomers in Mashonaland.[55] War finally broke out in the summer of 1893 and resulted in complete success for the forces of the Chartered Company. In this struggle, again, Rhodes received moral support and substantial aid from the Home Government. The Imperial Bechuanaland Police was reenforced and sent by Sir Henry Loch to threaten the Matabele from the West.[56] Rhodes, although he liked to boast that the greater part of the work was accomplished without help from home, acknowledged that the conquest of Matabeleland was effected by the Mashonaland settlers " with the cooperation of the Bechuanaland Border Police." In his own words:

There is one pleasurable thing to remember, and that is, that a combination of colonists and Imperial police has effected the destruction of ruthless barbarism south of the Zambesi, and established a further extension of the British Empire. . . . [57]

With the settlement of Mashonaland and the conquest of Matabeleland, Rhodes had attained another objective in his ambitious program. He had wrested the hinterland behind Cape Colony and up to the Zambezi from the grasp of Germans, Portuguese, Boers and natives. He had, largely through his own initiative and energy, colored the map red from Cape Colony to the Zambezi.[58] Behind Rhodes, however, stood H. M. Government with its approval, its moral support and at times its active cooperation. The British South Africa Company was, after all, the creation of H. M. Government and H. M. Government was ultimately responsible for the actions of that company. Furthermore, H. M. Government put no obstacle in the progress of the Chartered Company northwards but aided and abetted that advance. The Imperial Government was, to be sure, not willing to follow Rhodes unquestioningly in his entire program but, so far, it had given him staunch support. In other words, Rhodes was leading a willing government, not dragging a reluctant people into the heart of Africa.

CHAPTER VIII

Painting Central Africa Red

Rhodes was looking far beyond the Zambezi. As early as 1892, as already noted, he was talking about a telegraph to Uganda and then to Egypt.[1] Before he reached Uganda, however, there was one more vast stretch of country, from the Zambezi to Lake Tanganyika, which must be brought under the flag of the British South Africa Company. Other people, besides Rhodes, were interested in this section of Central Africa. Travellers and adventurers knew the country. F. C. Selous, a famous hunter and the guide to the " Pioneers " of the Chartered Company, had penetrated far into the region. Herbert Rhodes, Cecil's brother, died in Nyasaland in 1877.[2] Scottish missionaries already had roots in Nyasaland, the country bordering on Lake Nyasa. They planted stations here in the seventies and the African Lakes Trading Company was actively at work there. Its steamship was on Lake Nyasa and by 1891, its stations stretched as far north as Lake Tanganyika. The company had been authorized, as early as 1885, by British officials to secure treaties from friendly chiefs. Indeed, the company already had treaties with chiefs in the Shire Highlands, on Lake Nyasa and far to the West.[3]

Sir Harry Johnston was also keenly interested in Central Africa. How he joined hands with Rhodes and obtained the sanction and approval of Lord Salisbury to his scheme has already been noted in a previous chapter.[4] Johnston was like Rhodes, a Cape-to-Cairo dreamer, and his intention was definitely to make this Central African strip a connecting link between the British Protectorate on the Upper Nile and her Empire south of the Zambezi.[5]

Salisbury, himself, was probably skeptical, at the time, about the feasibility of Johnston's ultimate ambition.[6] He was, however keenly interested in the suppression of the slave trade and the potential value of the country.[7] H. M. Government knew, as well as Rhodes, that the earth's surface was limited, that "the largest tracts of unoccupied land" were "in Africa, which should be kept open for British colonisation and commerce."[8]

With the cautious sympathy, therefore, of the home government, Rhodes and Johnston set seriously to work to paint British Central Africa red. In the summer of 1889, Johnston started up the Chinde River for Nyasaland. He was soon to meet with the first indication of trouble. Below the confluence of the Ruo and Shire rivers, he encountered Serpa Pinto at the head of a Portuguese expedition consisting of over seven hundred Zulu soldiers. The expedition was apparently bound for the Makololo country and the Shire Highlands. Serpa Pinto, soothingly, assured him that he was only on a scientific mission. Johnston, in turn, warned Serpa Pinto, politely, that he must not take "any political action north of the Ruo River," that if Pinto disregarded this request, Johnston would be obliged to "protect the interests of Her Majesty's Government."[9] Johnston then proceeded on his way.

There was another slight cloud on the horizon. At Katunga, Johnston met a trader, a British subject but of German origin. This trader had previously concluded treaties with native chiefs in which the natives granted to him personally their sovereign rights and he was, in consequence, violently opposed to Johnston's program of securing treaties of friendship with the Makololo and Yao chiefs on behalf of H. M. Government. Johnston was suspicious of this gentleman's movements and previous German origin. Without openly accusing the trader of any unpatriotic designs, he admitted that the encounter " rather precipitated our political action." [10]

The Portuguese " scientific " expedition which Johnston had met at the confluence of the Ruo and Shire rivers, had, meanwhile, advanced up the Shire River. They had had a successful encounter with the Makololo and then they had boldly crossed the dead line set by Johnston, the Ruo River. Thence they marched northward until they menaced Blantyre. H. M. Government, however, were keeping watch over the Portuguese operations along the Shire. Lord Salisbury promptly responded to the Portuguese advance by sending an ultimatum to Portugal. Portugal immediately withdrew the offending expedition to the Portuguese side of the Ruo. Thenceforth, Portugal allowed the British to carry on their work in the Nyasaland region without molestation.[11]

Johnston's plan was to cover as much of Central Africa as he could and to gain a foothold everywhere by concluding treaties with the native chiefs. He enlisted in his service the well-known African traveller, Alfred Sharpe. To Sharpe, he assigned as a field of operation, the Central Zambezi, the Luangwa River as far north as Lake Mweru and Lake Tanganyika. Joseph Thomson carried on Sharpe's work later in the Central region.[12] Johnston, himself, travelled along Lake Nyasa and north to Lake Tanganyika. He made treaties with all the chiefs at the south end of the lake and with the chiefs of Itawa, in the direction of Lake Mweru. Then he reluctantly turned back. In his own words, " . . . It was a great disappointment for me to turn back at this juncture, as I desired to go to the North end of Tanganyika . . . I reluctantly postponed the completion of a scheme which was as I hoped to give us continuous communication between Cape Town and Cairo, either over international waterways or along British territory." [13] He did, however, send Swann to complete his work. Swann succeeded in concluding more treaties and in planting the British flag at the extreme northern end of the lake, but too late for his arrangements to be considered at the conclusion of the Anglo-German agreement of 1890.[14]

On September 21, 1889, John Buchanan, Johnston's representative, proclaimed a protectorate over Nyasaland after the news of the first conflict between the Portuguese and the Makololo.[15] This was not, to be sure, what H. M. Government intended to do when Johnston was first sent out to Central Africa. The British in the beginning, merely, wished to guard against the encroachments of either Germany or Portugal into the territory and to keep the country " open to British traders, planters and missionaries without let or hindrance." [16] The keen international competition for this desirable region, however, compelled H. M. Government to take more positive measures to secure British interest and influence there. In short, Portuguese aggressiveness forced the administration to proclaim a protectorate.

In the formation and administration of the Nyasaland Protectorate, as already noted,[17] Cecil Rhodes was working in close cooperation with Johnson. The Chartered Company kept its pledge and contributed £10,000 a year for the unkeep of the protectorate.[18] For some time, Rhodes had been negotiating with the African Lakes Company for a share in its business. Finally in 1893, he arrived at a satisfactory arrangement. He acquired control of the Lakes Company by exchanging Lake shares for those of the B. S. A. Co. at par. A new company was formed, called the African Lakes Corporation, with all the assets of the old company excepting mineral rights and most of its land which were transferred to the Chartered Company.[19] Johnston was allowed free use of the boats and steamers of the new company in his work as British Commissioner and Consul General of the protectorate.[20] In 1895, the British South Africa Company took over the direct administration of the districts previously owned by the Lakes Company " and made very large profits by the trading business acquired from the African Lakes Company." [21] The little Nyasaland protectorate had assumed an important place in Rhodes' scheme of northward expansion and the arrangements for its administration indicated how closely Rhodes was working with H. M. Government.

The acquisition of the Nyasaland Protectorate for Great Britain, however, was only a part of the ambitious program of Rhodes and Johnston for bringing all Central Africa from the Zambezi River to the Lake District under the British flag. In fact, the Nysaland Protectorate was only a comparatively narrow strip extending along the lake. Outside the Protectorate was a vast ill-defined stretch of country including roughly Barotseland, Manicaland and the district between the lakes Mweru and Tanganyika and Nyasaland. As early as 1891, the Imperial Government permitted the British South Africa Company to extend its operations over territory, exclusive of Nyasaland, under British influence north of the Zambezi and south of the territories of the Congo Free State and of the German sphere.[22] Sir Harry Johnston, as was just pointed out,[23] had already been active in this region and one of his agents pushed as far north as the northern end of Lake Tanganyika. After the Chartered Company took over the sphere, Johnston was assigned the dual rôle of British Commissioner and Consul-General to the Protectorate and administrator for the British South Africa Company in their field north of the Zambezi.[24] In other words, Johnston, representative of H. M. Government, and Cecil Rhodes were in close alliance and were striding arm in arm across Central Africa.

The country assigned exclusively to the Chartered Company presented many problems for the company to solve. It was an extensive stretch of territory not as yet effectively occupied by a European power but various sections were coveted by four rival colonial nations. Portugal possessed vague claims to land both on the west and east in Barotseland and Manicaland.[25] The Germans claimed territory in the Northeast between Lake Tanganyika and Lake Nyasa.[26] The Congo Independent State considered as its own the Katanga district in the Northwest.[27] Cecil Rhodes and Sir Harry Johnston, for their part, regarded the whole country between the Zambezi and Lake Tanganyika as an essential link between Great Britain's sphere of influence in the North and the ever-expanding British empire in the South.[28] By 1891, indeed, Rhodes could boast that the charter extended from Mafeking to Tanganyika.[29]

These chartered rights, however, were only paper rights. The next step was to assert them against rival claimants. In an earlier chapter Portugal's ambitious claims have been touched upon, particularly in regard to Manicaland and Mashonaland.[30] Roving bands under the half-caste Capitaõs Mors tried to forestall Rhodes' activity farther north. They wandered into Manicaland, Gazaland and on the outskirts of Mashonaland. They distributed Portuguese flags to the natives and one adventurer was bold enough to found a semi-independent native state to the east of the Manicaland.

England, however, was carrying on negotiations with Portugal in 1890 and soon after Rhodes' " Pioneers " reached Salisbury in Mashonaland, a convention was signed, August 20, 1890, delimiting the British and Portuguese spheres of influence.[31]

Rhodes was indignant with its provisions because the treaty ceded most of Barotseland and the whole of Manicaland to Portugal. "He wrote," says Williams, "angry letters to everybody whom he held responsible for it, bidding them 'drop this wretched treaty.'"[32]   He even spoke to the Foreign Office in peremptory tones. According to Lovell, Rhodes went to the point of " forcing Salisbury by the threat of leading a South African secession from the Empire, to press the Portuguese harder than he or the Queen wished."[33] Lovell bases his conclusion largely on the version of Baron de Staal, at that time Russian Ambassador in London. This, of course, is a serious charge to make against Rhodes' loyalty and lends color to the suspicions of his fellow-countrymen which have already been noted in the preceding chapters.[34]   So serious, in fact, is the charge that it may be well to examine De Staal's account further. The Russian Ambassador was apparently suspicious of Rhodes in the first place because of his support of Irish Home rule and the gift which has already been mentioned, of £10,000 to Parnell.[35] Furthermore, De Staal notes that Rhodes was a man of considerable influence in South Africa and even in England. The recent aggressive action of the British South Africa Company in Manicaland and elsewhere was approved by public opinion. Rhodes was the heart and soul of the Chartered Company. All these considerations, he said, carried weight with the British ministers but the argument which was most potent with the Foreign Office was the fear of secession.[36]

This point of view seems to be strengthened by the vague hint of Basil Williams " that Rhodes, concentrating all his attention on his own views, was apt to pay too little heed to views relevant to other parts of the Empire."[37]   Furthermore, there is evidence to be found in the *Grosse Politik* that H. M. Government had some reason to distrust Rhodes.

At the time of the Jameson Raid, Sir Frank Lascelles, British Ambassador at Berlin, hinted confidentially that H. M. Government adopted a mild policy in regard to the Raid because there was a fear that Cape Colony would declare its independence if too severe measures were adopted against Cecil Rhodes. Threats of this nature, Lascelles asserted *had been made repeatedly.* He did not, however, place much faith in them because Cecil Rhodes owed what he had accomplished up to this time to the connection of Cape Colony with England, especially to the power and prestige of the British fleet. Rhodes' future plans would be ruined if independence was too rashly declared.[38]

These various remarks do point to threats and menaces on the part of Cecil Rhodes and his followers. The evidence, however, hardly supports the conclusion that Cecil Rhodes was an anti-imperialist, nor does there appear to be any direct proof that he was actually threatening a secession of the South African colonies in 1890 and that H. M. Government was seriously alarmed by such a threat. To be sure, Rhodes certainly did not like the abortive Anglo-Portuguese treaty of 1890. He undoubtedly, also, used all the pressure he could to have it dropped and Lord Salisbury was perhaps swayed by his influence and by the work of the Chartered Company to take a firmer stand than he ordinarily would have assumed towards Portugal.[39]

It is interesting to note, however, that the Queen in her Journal, February 24, 1891 mentions that " . . . Sir H. Loch . . . told me a great deal about Mr. Rhodes, who he says is a very remarkable, honest, loyal man, and entirely anti-Republican, a tremendously strong man." [40]   Rhodes, himself, assured the Queen that " Great Britain was the only country fit to colonise, no other nation succeeded." He hoped in time to see the English rule extend from the Cape to

Egypt. He thought everything would be arranged and the difficulties got ever.[41]

Fortunately for Rhodes' plans, Portugal failed to ratify the agreement of 1890. On November 18, 1890, however, the two governments agreed to a *modus vivendi* based on the former convention. They consented to recognize the territorial limits indicated in the treaty of August, 1890, in so far that "neither Power would make Treaties, accept Protectorates, or exercise any act of sovereignty within the spheres of influence assigned to the other Party by the said Convention." The *modus vivendi* was to remain in force for a period of six months after its signature, i. e., from November 14, 1890 to May 14, 1891.[42]

While these negotiations were taking place, a race was in progress for Manicaland. The contestants were the agents of two rival companies. As was mentioned before the Mozambique Company was formed by D'Andrade to operate in Manicaland.[43] The British South Africa Company had its eye on the same territory. The agents of the British Chartered Company arrived first. Dr. Jameson, Colquhon and Selous set out for Manicaland before "the Pioneers" reached Salisbury in 1890. They found that the paramount native chief there, Umtassa, did not recognize the Portuguese claims and was willing to conclude a treaty giving the British company all the minerals of the country. The Portuguese reached Manicaland two months too late and proceeded to occupy Umtassa's Kraal. The British South Africa Company's police, thereupon, disarmed the Portuguese force and took some of the leaders prisoners.[44]

This bold and high-handed action did not escape criticism at home. In Parliament the Chartered Company was accused of conducting a filibustering expedition. H. M. Government, however, was apparently willing to defend the work of these adventurers in Africa. In fact, Sir J. Ferguson, Under Secretary of State for Foreign Affairs, took up the cudgels for the company. He pointed out that the collision between the British South Africa Company's police and the Portuguese occurred before the *modus vivendi* was known to the Chartered Company. The Company, furthermore, did not actually exercise any powers of sovereignty in Umtassa's country but it was simply, at Umtasa's request, keeping order there.[45]

The British South Africa Company, also, tried to secure a foothold in Gazaland and sent a deputation to Gungunhana, the chief. They succeeded in obtaining from Gungunhana a treaty in the form of a lease granting the Chartered Company certain mineral and territorial rights. The Portuguese, however, were awake to the danger. They protested against this encroachment and proceeded to seize one of the Chartered Company's ships which had been sent up the coast to meet the expedition and to bring arms to Gungunhana.[46] H. M. Government at first appeared willing to come to the Company's aid. Sir J. Ferguson was again the Government's spokesman in Parliament and asserted that there was nothing contrary to the *modus vivendi* in the action of the crew of the Company's ship.[47] The claims of Portugal, however, were too strong in this region and the territory of Gazaland was, finally, acknowledged by Lord Salisbury to lie within the Portuguese sphere of influence.[18]

In the west, Rhodes gained a foothold for the Chartered Company in Barotseland. In 1889, Lewanika, titular chief of Barotseland, asked to come under the British Queen's protection. His application was refused but in the following year, he gave to a trader, Ware by name, a comprehensive grant over his dominions. Rhodes bought up this and other concessions.

Finally, Great Britain and Portugal reached an agreement, July 3, 1891, by which Great Britain gained, as its sphere of influence, the Barotse Kingdom, Nyasaland and most of Manicaland leaving the greater part of Gazaland to the Portuguese.[49] The Portuguese also agreed, as noted before, to construct a railway between Pungwe Bay and the British sphere.[50] Furthermore, the British Government gained by Article VII an important stake in the future partitioning of the Portuguese colonies in South Africa. By this provision, the two Powers agreed to a mutual right of preemption over the territories south of the Zambezi assigned to their respective spheres of influence.[51] H. M. Government by ratifying this convention made possible the realization of the Rhodes and Johnston dream of a British Central Africa. It gave to Great Britain large stretches of territory which could be " worked and occupied by white men " while the more unhealthy coastal area was left to Portugal.[52] Thus, Great Britain took one more gigantic stride forward along the central ridge from Cape Town to Cairo.

Rhodes was busy also farther north. In the northeast, Germany claimed the whole country between Lakes Nyasa and Tanganyika as far as Lake Bangweolo, including the famous Missionaries' road, the Stevenson road, between Nyasa and Tanganyika. The road had some sentimental attachment for the English people because Livingstone had travelled over it and because the great missionary had died under a tree along it near Bangweolo.[53] Before the question of ownership was settled, the Chartered Company proceeded to erect two forts along the famous road. Rhodes astutely christened them Fort Fife and Fort Abercorn, after two prominent Englishmen of the day. The controversy was finally settled in Great Britain's favor by the Anglo-German Treaty of 1890. The Stevenson road was left within the British sphere.[54] " Oh," said Rhodes with a chuckle, rubbing his hands together, " I knew they could not give up a fort named after a member of the royal family." [55]

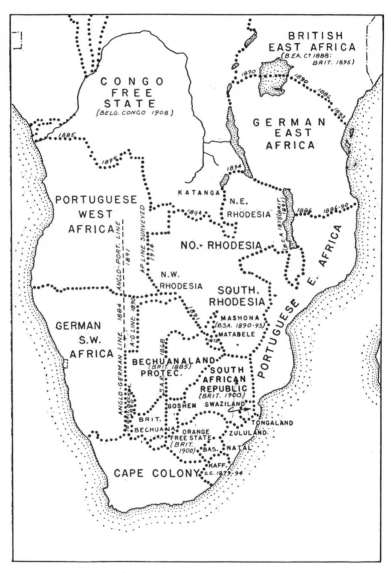

EUROPEAN EXPANSION IN AFRICA, SOUTH OF THE CONGO, 1866–1914

Rhodes was interested, likewise, in the rumored mineral wealth of the Katanga belt, about which he had received encouraging reports from Arnot, a missionary in that region. The country lay within the area, to be sure, assigned by treaties to King Leopold's administration. Nevertheless, the King had done nothing so far to effectively occupy the area. Rhodes boldly, therefore, dispatched Alfred Sharpe to make treaties with Myanwezi, paramount chief of the Katanga district. He was too late, however. In 1890, the Katanga Company was formed in Brussels. Although a large number of its subscribers were English, the company was a Belgian concern. As such, it secured from King Leopold a ninety-nine years concession of mineral rights over a third part of the Katanga region. Then, it sent out two expeditions in 1891 to explore the country. One group under Captain Stairs travelled in from the east coast. The other under Bia and Francqui made their way in via the Lower Congo. In short, on the basis of former treaties and the expeditions sent out by the Katanga Company, King Leopold was able to establish claims to the region.[56]

In spite of this setback, however, Rhodes could well be satisfied with the work of the British South Africa Company. That company, with the cooperation of H. M. Government, had now secured the whole strip from Mafeking to Tanganyika. Rhodes and Johnston had created a British Central Africa. So satisfactory did H. M. Government find the work that in 1895 Rhodes was made a Privy Councillor. He also received the great honor of having the Company's sphere of influence named after him, Rhodesia.[57]

In 1895, Rhodes was at the peak of his success. The territory from Bechuanaland to Tanganyika was securely under the flag of the British South Africa Company. The work of the Chartered Company in settling the country south of the Zambezi was flourishing. H. M. Government had given repeated evidence of its approval of the accomplishments of the British South Africa Company and of its willingness to defend the operations of the Company. At the Cape, Rhodes had been Prime Minister since 1890 and he felt that he had the people behind him. Cape Boers and British, alike, were willing to cooperate in his work of settling and developing Rhodesia.[58]

CHAPTER IX

THE RAID AND ITS CONSEQUENCES

JUST at the height of his power when he seemed about to strike across Africa, Rhodes, as noted, was growing impatient. He was beginning to drop his old tactics of bargaining, and cooperating with the Boers. He was turning to more violent methods of attaining his objectives of a United South Africa under Cape hegemony and expansion to the north. It will be remembered that there was considerable suspicion that Rhodes was behind the Lourenço Marques insurrection of September, 1894.[1] His indignation at Germany's repeated refusal to allow his telegraph line to run through German East Africa will also be recalled.[2] Furthermore, Rhodes was definitely aiding and abetting the Uitlander conspiracy for reforms in the Transvaal.[3]

The difficulties between the Transvaal Boers and the Uitlanders continued to grow. A railway rate war over goods transported into the South African Republic reached its climax in the late summer and fall of 1895. In order to avoid the high rates charged on the Transvaal lines, traders with the Boer Republic carried their goods from the Free State border to Johannesburg, in bullock-wagons. Kruger retaliated by declaring closed the Vaal drifts over which the wagons must cross. All parties at the Cape united in protest against this action and even the Bond members supported Rhodes in an appeal to Chamberlain against what the Cape Attorney-General declared to be a breach of the London Convention of 1884. Chamberlain, in turn, sent a " strong remonstrance " to Kruger which was tantamount to an ultimatum. The remonstrance was delivered November 4. The Boer President promptly reopened the drifts the next day.[4]

There seems to have been plenty of provocation on both sides and there are at least two versions or interpretations of what happened in the course of 1895. If Cecil Rhodes and the colonists were annoyed by what they dubbed the " pin prick " policy of Kruger, the Transvaal Boers in their turn were irritated by the high-handed action of H. M. Government in the Spring of 1895 when Pondoland and Amatongaland were annexed to Natal, thus cutting the Transvaal off from access to the sea.[5] H. M. Government was watching the Boers with considerable mistrust. If Rhodes had only exercised greater patience and if he had been willing to let events take their course, he might have had the full cooperation and sympathy of the Home Government in a defensive campaign against Kruger's pin pricks. Trouble was evidently brewing in 1895. Sir H. Loch, British High Commissioner, wrote to Kruger " that unless the grievances of the Uitlanders were redressed in good time a revolution was inevitable ".[6]

The British Government believed that the Boer Uitlander controversy was something more than a purely local affair. They noted anxiously that Kruger was increasing his military budget and they feared that he was seeking outside alliances. In particular, the British accused Oom Paul of flirting with the Germans. Various moves on the part of the Boer President and on the part of the German Government lent color to this accusation. In 1894, Kruger sent his State Secretary, Dr. Leyds, to Germany. The doctor was well received by the Kaiser and his ministers.[7] As already noted, in the summer of 1895, a deputation of German naval officers were present at the opening of the Delagoa Bay to Pretoria railway[8] and the Emperor sent President Kruger a telegram alluding to the railway as " a means of drawing closer the bonds which connect the two countries ".[9] It has been already pointed out that the Germans were supporting the efforts of the Transvaal to purchase the Delagoa Bay line.[10] Furthermore, on January 27, 1895, the Kaiser's birthday, Kruger drank a toast to the Emperor in which he remarked confidently: " I know I may count on the Germans in the future, and I hope Transvaalers will do their best to strengthen and foster the friendship that exists between them." [11]

Lord Kimberley, thereupon, informed Kruger that in many respects the attitude of the German Government towards the South African Republic was not in harmony with its international status. He warned him that under the London Convention of 1884, the Republic could not enter into an alliance with any other state without the previous consent of H. M. Government. He was afraid that there was a growing feeling in the Transvaal that they could count on Germany's support. In short, he feared that the Transvaal was coquetting with Germany.[12]

On November 23, 1895, Sir J. De Wet reported to Sir Hercules Robinson that he thought the Germans were " aiding and abetting the Transvaal in an endeavor to get possession of the Delagoa Bay Railway " and that Germans were buying up all the land they could at Delagoa Bay.[13]

Sir Edward Malet, British Ambassador at Berlin told von Marschall, the German Foreign Secretary, that the Transvaal was for England the " black spot " in Anglo-German relations and fully as important as the Egyptian question.[14] In fact, according to the Kaiser's account, Malet on the eve of his departure in the fall, hinted that England might go to war over the question.[15]

To be sure, Salisbury tried to soften the indiscreet utterances of the Ambassador. He insisted that Malet had no authority to call the Transvaal " the black spot " in Anglo-German relations. He reproved Sir Edward for his tactless words and for his threats and, further, expressed his regret to Count Hatzfeldt.[16]

The Germans, for their part, denied that they had any poltical interests in the Transvaal save in the maintenance of the *status quo*. Their interests there were chiefly commercial and they were particularly concerned with the fate of the Delagoa Bay railway in which, as noted before, German capital was heavily invested.[17] For the sake of their commercial interests, however, it was important that the Transvaal be maintained as an economically independent state. This was compatible with its status as defined by the London Convention of 1884. The Germans were ready to support that convention. The chief difficulty lay, they maintained, in the policy advocated by Cecil Rhodes and in the apparent willingness of H. M. Government to allow the Cape Premier to pursue his objective unchecked. Cecil Rhodes, they claimed, was talking about " a commercial union " and " amalgamation or federation of all the South African States." Such a union would run contrary to German commercial interests in the Transvaal and Delagoa Bay because it would mean a Cape monopoly of Transvaal trade and the exclusion of that of Germany. The Germans, thus, could not allow the absorption of the Transvaal by Cape Colony. Above all, the Pretoria to Lourenço Marques railway must not fall into Cecil Rhodes' hands.

There was, therefore, considerable resentment and suspicion on both sides. The clouds were piling up over the Transvaal. The storm broke, finally, when Dr. Jameson, Rhodes' right-hand man, led a band of Mashonaland and Bechuanaland police into the Transvaal on the night of December 29. In starting the Raid at that particular time, Jameson overstepped himself and very nearly wrecked all Rhodes' future plans. Rhodes, at the last minute tried to stop the raiders. Although he cannot, therefore, be implicated in the final steps leading up to the advance, he had been, as seen, largely instrumental in securing the jumping-off ground for the raiders and in organizing a prospective uprising at Johannesburg.[18] In fact, he and his colleague Alfred Beit supplied the funds for the uprising.[19]

The story of what happened is well known and has been discussed in detail before Parliament, in committees and in the press. It is not necessary here to rake over the ashes of that controversy. H. M. Government immediately repudiated this violation of the territory of a still friendly state and took steps to bring the ringleaders in the raid to justice. Rhodes resigned his position as Prime Minister of the Cape and also his place as director on the board of the British South Africa Company. Both in England and South Africa, he was obliged to submit to a thoroughgoing inquiry into his complicity in the plot. The evidence indicated that, although Rhodes could not be implicated in the final steps, his hands were not clean. As Prime Minister of the Cape, he was guilty of allowing a conspiracy against a neighboring state to be formed and, as previously noted, had even encouraged, aided and abetted the conspirators.[20]

In the fiasco of the Jameson Raid, Rhodes saw all his cherished plans and projects almost ruined. No longer could he realize his dream of cooperation between the Boers and the British in his work of expansion in the North.[21] No longer could he expect the backing of H. M. Government in his schemes. A British resident was appointed for Rhodesia and the High Commissioner was given direct control over the police force of the Chartered Company.[22] Cool cautiousness towards Rhodes' plans was now the mood in London.

Nevertheless, it is remarkable that Rhodes did not suffer more from his complicity in the conspiracy. To be sure, he was severely censured. Still he retained an immense popularity both in England and among the British at the Cape.[23] The shareholders of the British South Africa Company stood loyally behind their fallen leader. He was their mentor even when he was not on the board of the Company and he was unanimously and enthusiastically reinstated as a director on the board just two years after the raid. In fact, it was on the strength of his connection with the board that the company was able to finance its work in South Africa. In Cape Colony, in spite of the opposition of the Bond, he was elected again to his seat in the Cape House.[24] On his return from the investigation in England, his journey through South Africa " was more like a triumphal progress than the penitential pilgrimage of a culprit going to meet his judges." [25] In fact, he was able to go ahead with his plans for developing Rhodesia. In 1899, he addressed the British South Africa Company at the Cannon Street Hotel which was the largest hall available in the city. The place was crowded and Rhodes had to address an overflow meeting afterwards on the stairs and in the corridor.[26]

Rhodes, the great imperialist, was a national hero. In short, the people were willing to forgive his faults " for the greater purpose " which inspired his actions.[27]

The British people felt less inclined to condemn Rhodes for his participation in the Jameson Raid because of the irritating action of Germany at the time of its fiasco.[28] Count Hatzfeldt, German Ambassador at the Court of St. James, was ordered to demand his passports if the British Government did not immediately repudiate the violation of Transvaal territory.[29] Plans were made to send German troops to the Transvaal.[30] The German Government dispatched a note, later withdrawn, to London declaring that it would recognize no change in the international status of the South African Republics.[31]   To cap the climax, the Kaiser sent a telegram congratulating President Kruger upon the fact

that without appealing to the help of friendly Powers, you and your people have succeeded in repelling with your own forces the armed band which broke into your land as destroyers of the peace and you have defended the independence of your country against foreign aggression.[32]

There is some question about the actual authorship of this famous telegram.[33]   It was issued as a result of a conference held on January 3.   The Kaiser, however, had been working for some time to bring England into the Triple Alliance.   Indeed, according to Count Hatzfeldt, he had " been trying during the last six months to frighten England into joining the Triple Alliance." [34]   In fact, on October 25, 1895, he warned Colonel Swaine, the British Military Attaché, that England must abandon her selfish policy of isolation and decide either for or against entering it.[35]   So far, his efforts had been of no avail because, as Lord Salisbury told Queen Victoria, " the English people would never consent to go to war for a cause in which England was not manifestly interested; and Lord Salisbury during the present ministry and during his previous ministry, has always declined on this ground." [36]   The Kaiser, evidently, had the policy of forcing the British from their aloofness into the arms of Germany very much at heart.   It is, therefore, a plausible explanation of his actions in regard to the Jameson Raid to allege that he used the Raid as an excuse to frighten the British and to show them the dangers of their isolated position.[37]

At the conference on January 3, the Emperor talked about a German protectorate over the Transvaal, mobilization of marines and the transport of troops to South Africa.   The

Chancellor warned him that this would mean war with England. His Majesty agreed but said that it would only mean war on land. Then the suggestion was made that a German agent be sent to reconnoiter the Transvaal. Finally, the Kaiser was persuaded by von Marschall to retreat somewhat from his bellicose position and to expend his energies in sending a telegram of congratulations to Kruger. The telegram, according to von Marschall, was originally drafted by the Colonial Director, Dr. Kayser, and the wording stiffened by von Marschall.[38]

Kruger received the telegram with gratitude.[39]   In Germany, also there was wide-spread rejoicing over its dispatch. The Press stood stanchly behind the Kaiser's impetuous gesture. Von Marschall notes that all parties were united and that even the respectable Liberal paper, " die Tante Voss . . . will fight ".[40]

There is some evidence to show that the German Government was cautiously sounding the ground for concerted European action against England. On January 3, von Marschall wrote confidentially to President Kruger that if the Republic turned to the Powers and called a conference to decide upon the status of the Transvaal and perhaps to recognize its neutrality, Germany would support such a motion. The German Government, however, was unwilling to take any initiative in the matter because it feared that it might be suspected of pursuing its own self-interest.[41] Again after the dispatch of the telegram, on January 5, von Marschall advised Kruger to avoid a war with England but suggested, at the same time, that deliberation among the Powers would be advantageous for the Transvaal and would assure its position in the future. He insisted once more that Germany would stand behind such a move but could not take the initiative alone because of the suspicion, which such action would call forth, that Germany desired a protectorate over the Transvaal.[42]

On January first, von Marschall approached the French ambassador, M. Herbette, with the proposal that France act in concert with Germany to curb the insatiable appetite of England[43] but he excluded such questions as those of the Orient, Egypt and the Mediterranean from this concerted action. There were other issues, however, he hinted, in which the two governments could bridle England without running the risk of a European conflict. M. Herbette, for his part, received von Marschall's overtures with coolness and reserve. In excluding the Egyptian question, he insisted, von Marschall left out the principal reason for cooperation.[44]

This coolness of the French towards the Germans showed itself likewise in their reaction towards the Kruger telegram. When the news of its dispatch first arrived, the Press was kindled with enthusiasm for the cause of the South African Republic and with admiration for the Kaiser's telegram but twenty-four hours later the enthusiasm died down. The French newspapers began to talk once more of Alsace-Lorraine and of waiting until they could draw some advantage from the relations between England and Germany.[45] To be sure, the French blew now hot now cold. They were watching with considerable interest, De Courcel told von Hatzfeldt, what their ally Russia's reaction would be to the Transvaal situation. De Courcel warned Lord Salisbury, in fact, that he must not count too much on French moderation in regard to the Transvaal crisis.[46] On January 9, De Courcel negotiated an understanding with Germany over the Togoland hinterland. He went further and indicated that in the future, France and Germany might cooperate in many matters.[47] The French position was certainly influenced by the sympathy which the Russian Government was showing towards the Kaiser.

On January 4, the German Emperor wrote to the Tsar giving him his motives for sending the Kruger telegram and asking him to join with Germany in upholding treaties once concluded. " I hope," he said, " that all will come right but come what may, I shall never allow the British to stamp out the Transvaal." He informed Nicholas II that he had taken similar steps in France.[48]   The Russian Emperor, for his part, heartily expressed his friendship for the Kaiser and mentioned their community of interests. He, also, spoke with approval of the stand taken by the German Government in regard to the Transvaal. It is curious, however, that the Tsar linked the Transvaal question with the idea that the English were aiming at uniting South Africa with Egypt. It was this Cape-to-Cairo policy which the Tsar feared and could not countenance. He telegraphed the Kaiser, however, January 6, " quite agree with all you say." [49]

The Russian Government viewed the Transvaal crisis and the Kruger telegram as a matter of European concern. The Russian Ambassador told von Holstein that the Kaiser by his telegram represented not German but European interests and deserved, therefore, the greatest thanks.[50]   Von Marschall felt that if war developed out of the Transvaal question, Russia would fight on Germany's side.[51]   Nevertheless, in spite of this apparent approval of the Kaiser's action, there was some sympathy likewise for the British position in regard to the crisis. Prince Lobanow assured the German Ambassador, Prince Radolin, that Russia would never tolerate an extension of the British sphere of influence to Egypt such as Cecil Rhodes dreamed of but, on the other hand, he felt that the British stand in regard to the South African Republic was excusable. After all, the convention of 1884, prohibited the Transvaal from concluding any agreement with a foreign state without the previous sanction of Great Britain. It looked, in fact, as though the Russians were only lukewarm in their sympathy for the German position in regard to the Transvaal.[52]

The Italian Government was in a difficult situation. The Italians were torn between their allegiance to the Triple Alliance and their need of British support in Ethiopia and in the Mediterranean region.[53] To be sure, Crispi telegraphed to offer the Kaiser his good services in case of an Anglo-German conflict. Baron Blanc assured von Bülow that Germany would always remain the pivot of his policy. Nevertheless, the Italians did not follow Germany's lead with enthusiasm. Von Bülow was skeptical about their future support.[54]

In high quarters in Vienna, however, "the recent utterances from Berlin were considered reckless and unjustifiable."[55] Count Goluchowski assumed a reserved and temporizing attitude. The Austrian Foreign Minister asserted that he would in no case take the initiative in mediating between Germany and England.[56]

The European situation, therefore, in January 1896 was uncertain. Russia was sympathetic but wavering. France was cold. The Germans could not fully trust Italy's allegiance to the Triple Alliance. Hohenlohe felt that by pressing the French too hard they might be driven towards England. Russia, too, as France's ally might be alienated.[57] Italy had leanings towards a French-Russian combination.[58] Germany feared isolation.[59] The destruction of England's power, was, after all, of doubtful advantage to Germany. All things considered, the time was not ripe yet to form a continental coalition against England. It was wiser, Holstein concluded, for the Germans to be satisfied with a small diplomatic success for Germany and a little political lesson for England.[60]

The German ministers, in spite of the truculent tone of the Kruger telegram and in spite of the evident popular enthusiasm for the Kaiser's action, were inclined to a policy of moderation. They were willing to give England a scare and a lesson but they did not wish to press matters to the point of a conflict. To be sure, the German Government on December 31, asked Wissmann, the Governor at Dar-es-Salaam to send 400 to 600 men to Delagoa Bay. President Kruger, however, discouraged the sending of troops to the Transvaal. He feared that it would only complicate the situation. The troops were never sent but the German Government obtained permission from Portugal to land a detachment of 50 men to protect German lives and property.[61] The Portuguese granted this permission on January 8, with the stipulation that only fifty men should land and that the troops should be brought in only if further developments in the Transvaal threatened German lives and property.[62] According to the Marquis of Salisbury, the Portuguese " behaved very well " in regard to the Transvaal crisis.[63]

The Germans did not go any further than these preparations which the Kaiser later insisted were defensive measures.[64] Actually, no German troops were landed at Delagoa Bay. Furthermore, as noted before, the German ministers persuaded the Kaiser to send the telegram in lieu of taking more aggressive measures.[65] Von Marschall on January 5 urged Kruger to avoid war.[66] He also, in a letter to Hatzfeldt, January 6, tried to minimize the harshness of the Kruger telegram. It was, he insisted, not an unfriendly act towards England. How could it be called an unfriendly act if the Kaiser congratulated Kruger on repelling an armed band whom the British Government itself had declared to be " outlaws "? Also, Germany had a right to talk about the independence of the South African Republic when Great Britain had recognized that independence in the London

Convention of 1884.[67] Von Marschall contended that maintenance of the *status quo* was all that Germany desired from the beginning to the end of the controversy.[68]

The British people, however, were incensed by the Kruger telegram. It was in their estimation a recognition of the Boer claims of independence. Furthermore, who were " the friendly Powers " whose help Kruger did not need? Was there proof in this allusion that Germany was ready actively to take the part of the Transvaal? Was Germany intriguing with other Powers to come to the assistance of the South African Republic? The telegram, indeed, " was regarded by the British people, if not as a menace of war, as at least a provocative attempt on the part of a foreign Power to interfere in a matter of purely British concern." [69] The German specter hovered over Parliamentary debates. The Government must take care that " the Transvaal was not made a nursery that could be used by continental Powers to destroy our interests in Africa." The Transvaal, in fact, might become a danger " to the peace of the whole of South Africa. Here it was thrust like a wedge into the very heart of our own territory. . . ." [70]

Feeling ran high. In the city, wrote Hatzfelt, where the excitement was greatest, there was scarcely any business dealings with Germans.[71] A press campaign began against Germany which, Dr. Lovell maintains, affected Anglo-German relations right down to 1914.[72] In fact, Hatzfeldt noted with anxiety the general feeling was so bitterly anti-German that if the Government had lost its head and had wished to declare war for any reason, the entire public opinion would have supported its decision. This was a serious situation because, as he was careful to point out, British administrations were dependent upon the support of the people for their existence. The British ministers, therefore, must be guided in some measure by the voice of the people.[73] In

short, "English public opinion was in such a dangerous state
of exasperation," as St. John, the British Minister at Berne
told the French Minister, "that if Lord Salisbury had declared war, his administration would have been the most
popular we had had in half a century." [74]

Rhodes profited personally by this excitement. Popular
resentment was directed towards the Kaiser rather than
against his own guilty part in the Raid. In fact, as already
noted, he was regarded by the populace rather as a national
hero. They remembered that Rhodes had once before exor-
cised the German bogey when Bechuanaland was at stake.
He had then fought the Germans away from the route north
and had done all in his power to prevent a Boer-German
coalition.[75] Now he was posing once more as the defender
of British interests against another Anglo-Boer coalition.

> . . . I must admit [he told the select committee in England],
> that in all my actions I was greatly influenced by my belief that
> the policy of the present government of the South African Re-
> public was to introduce the influence of another foreign power
> into the already complicated system of South Africa, and there-
> by render more difficult in the future the closer union of the
> different states.[76]

Fortunately, for the peace of the country, H. M. Government did keep its head. Queen Victoria called the Kruger
telegram "outrageous and very unfriendly towards us.
. . ." [77] She went further and reprimanded her grandson.
The telegram, she told him, made "a very painful impression" in England.[78] On the other hand, she asked Lord
Salisbury to do all he could to allay the public excitement
towards Germany; to urge the police to prevent ill-usage of
innocent German residents and to "hint to our respectable
papers not to write violent articles to excite the people" for,
she deplored, "these newspaper wars often tend to provoke
war, which would be too awful." [79]

Lord Salisbury scarcely needed this admonition from his Sovereign. He took from the start a conciliatory attitude. He realized, he told Hatzfeldt, that the Germans had large commercial interests in the Transvaal.[80] He expressed little sympathy for Rhodes.[81] He hastened to repudiate the action of the raiders.[82] On January 7, he assured Hatzfeldt that no further action against the Transvaal need be feared.[83] He wished to leave the question of the suzerainty of the Transvaal out of the discussion and to emphasize the maintenance of the *status quo*. On this basis, he was sure both Germany and Great Britain could agree.[84] Furthermore, Salisbury did what he could to make amends for the raid. He promised to compensate the Transvaal and to limit the powers of the Chartered Company so that there would be no danger of another invasion of the South African Republic.[85] To be sure, the British Government organized a Flying Squadron but it was prepared more for the Venezuela crisis than for that in South Africa.[86] " This measure," Goschen wrote Queen Victoria, " has not been intended to be of the nature of ' mobilisation ', though it has been so regarded. The press fasten at the present moment on every step taken, with a tendency to exaggerate and sensationalize it." [87]

President Kruger, for his part, was anxious to avoid a conflict. He was grateful for the sympathetic support of Germany but he did not care for the establishment of a German protectorate over his country any more than he did that of an English. In fact, he and his State Secretary, Dr. Leyds, seemed anxious to avoid too much interference from outside.[88] Kruger acted with commendable restraint and moderation. He avoided raising political issues.[89] He merely required compensation for the Transvaal and punishment of the offenders. He even released Dr. Jameson and his officers for trial in England. To be sure, he sentenced the four leaders of the Reform Movement, (Col. Frank Rhodes, Mr. Hays Hammond, Mr. Lionel Phillips and Mr. Farrar) to death but later allowed them to escape with the payment of £25,000 each.[90]

Moderate counsels then prevailed in Germany, Great Britain and South Africa. Germany's blustering policy subsided with the collapse of the Raid. The Kaiser wrote a letter to his grandmother apologetically from Neues Palais, July 1, 1898. The telegram, he insisted, was never " intended as a step against England or your Government ". It was sent in the interests of peace and to protect Germans in the Transvaal and German bondholders at home. It was, moreover, directed against rebels.

Now to me [he wheedled], rebels against the will of the most gracious Majesty the Queen, are to me the most execrable beings in the world, and I was so incensed at the idea of your orders having been disobeyed, and thereby Peace and the security also of my Fellow Countrymen endangered, that I thought it necessary to show that publicly. . . . I was standing up for law, order, and obedience to a Sovereign whom I revere and adore, and whom to obey I thought paramount for her subjects.[91]

Thus the crisis aroused by the Jameson Raid and the Kruger telegram blew over but it left behind suspicion and distrust, the seeds of future trouble.

Rhodes, after the Raid, threw himself, with fresh intensity and a new absorption, into the development of Rhodesia and into his plans for a Transcontinental telegraph and a Cape-to-Cairo railway. He was at first busy with plans for financing the railway section from Buluwayo to Tanganyika.[92] No section of the line, however, was constructed for purely sentimental reasons. Each extension of the railway northward had " some immediate and material objects in view." The railway to the North was ultimately, according to the Rhodes prospectus, to reach Cairo; but Rhodes was in no hurry to push his project until it was financially feasible. The whole line from Vryburg to Buluwayo, however, " was financially a success, and from this date ", 1897, Metcalfe continues, " until his death Rhodes was enthusiastic for railway extension." [93] As Sir Robert Williams demonstrated in his address entitled " The Milestones of African Civilization," the railway followed mineral discoveries northward.[94] Rhodes was an idealist but he was at the same time a level-headed business man. If his head was in the clouds, his feet were on the ground as far as finances were concerned. He wanted his Cape-to-Cairo railway to pay its way through Africa. It was only thus, he realized, that the project could be brought to a successful completion.

In connection, therefore, with the prospective Tanganyika line, Rhodes made strenuous efforts to find new mineral " milestones." In 1891, he turned to Robert Williams, who was later on to become an enthusiastic collaborator in his railway schemes, and to carry on the construction of the Cape-to-Cairo line after Rhodes' death in 1902. Rhodes sent Williams on a prospecting expedition first in the region north of Vryburg and south of the Zambezi River. Williams reported that there was mineral wealth in the country but that it would be better to construct a line in from Beira to tap the resources than bring a line north from Cape Town.[95] Rhodes proceeded on Williams' suggestion and, as already noted, started the Beira-Salisbury line in 1892 before he engaged in the more extensive program of the Buluwayo-Tanganyika line.[96]

By 1898, however, Rhodes was ready to proceed with the Tanganyika line. Williams was then in the employ of the Zambezi Exploring Company. Rhodes decided to enlist the company in his campaign. He, therefore, granted to them

a 2,000 square mile mineral concession, together with the right
to locate a township and a pier at the southern end of Lake
Tanganyika, which was intended to be the Rhodesian terminus
of the Cape-to-Cairo Railway. In return for this grant, Rhodes
stipulated that £20,000 must be spent in prospecting the mineral
areas, and that a steamer should also be put on Lake Tanganyika
for carrying material to build the telegraph line for the construction of which along the German shore of the lake he had
already obtained the Imperial sanction.[97]

To take over the rights granted by Rhodes the Tanganyika Concessions Company was formed. This new company sent out expeditions in 1899 and 1904 under the leadership of the late George Grey to explore for minerals on the
Rhodesian side of the Congo-Zambezi divide. It was these
expeditions which revealed the Kansanshi Copper mine in
Rhodesia and the famous Katanga copper belt, besides important gold, tin and diamond deposits. During the siege
of Kimberley in the Boer War, when Rhodes was shut up
in the beleaguered city, Williams cheered him with search-
light messages about the mineral discoveries.[98]

While Rhodes was hunting for mineral wealth to draw the
railway northward, he was also approaching H. M. Government for a collateral guarantee for the railway to Tanganyika. Chamberlain in the Colonial Office at first considered the scheme " commendable." [99] It also found warm
advocates in Parliament. The plateau through which the
railway would run, said the member from Dover, " is, in
fact, the backbone of South and Central Africa, and if you
construct this railway you will give that backbone a spinal
cord, and then this Dark Continent, which has lain so long
inert, will at last begin to live and move and have its
being." [100] " I for one," said another member, " hope that
it may not be long before there is a railway to connect Cairo
and the Cape. I can conceive of no more civilizing influ-

ence that could be brought to bear than the laying down of a railway throughout that great continent." [101]

Rhodes voiced his own hopes when he appealed to the shareholders of the British South Africa Company, on April 21, 1898, for £2,000,000 for his railway to Tanganyika:

> Look at the matter. You get the railway to Lake Tanganyika, you have Her Majesty's sanction for the railway to Uganda (it joins on at Tanganyika), and then you have Kitchener coming down from Khartoum . . . it is not imaginative; it is practical. That gives you Africa—the whole of it . . . the conquest of Africa by the English nation is a practical question now.[102]

He spoke again to the shareholders of the Bechuanaland Railway Company May 6, 1898. This speech, Michell thinks, had "a great effect in convincing the public that the Cape-to-Cairo Railway was not only a national obligation, but would materially benefit British trade." [103]   Rhodes obtained £450,000 to £500,000 for his railway from companies holding claims in the neighborhood of Gwelo, through which the line was to run. This was enough to start the line and lay it for 150 miles; but Rhodes asked for £3,000,000 more for the remaining distance to Lake Tankanyika. Alfred Beit offered to take up £500,000 of the new debentures. Rhodes himself took £200,000. Friends in the city subscribed £500,000. In all Rhodes received enough to build 500 miles of railway. Although the total fell short of the £2,000,000 first asked for, the public had shown a genuine readiness to cooperate in the undertaking.

There was, of course, some opposition to the project, especially among the die-hard Little Englanders of the Liberal Party. Sir William Harcourt, Leader of the Opposition,[104] ridiculed the scheme with biting sarcasm:

> It is only £2,000,000 for the railway [he scoffed] but the con-

sequence is that we are to take over Africa, " the whole of it ",
and so the conquest of Africa by the English nation is a practical
question now. . . . Will you not endorse our promissory note
to go to Tanganyika? That means giving you without expense
" the whole of Africa." What a noble and generous offer!
Only it is not the Chartered Company who is to pay for this—
it is the British taxpayer. You must remember that this prospectus is not only for English publication and English con-
sumption, but it is a notice to other countries who most wickedly
imagine that they have some claim to some share in portions of
Africa, even though it be in what Lord Salisbury calls " light
soil "; and when they are informed that the British Government
has embarked in an undertaking without expense, and only guar-
anteeing two millions of money, to take the whole of Africa,
they may be rather disturbed in their mind. . . . [105]

It is to be noted that H. M. ministers were undoubtedly
interested in Rhodes' project but they objected to Rhodes'
terms. They were indeed, fully appreciative of the value of
the railway in administering and developing the territories
through which the line would run. The Government even
offered to make a loan on the basis that the railway from
Vryburg to Buluwayo would, at the expiry of the period of
repayment, become the joint property of H. M. Government
and the Cape Government on payment to the shareholders of
£10,000 by the respective Governments. Rhodes, in turn,
rejected the Government's offer. He was not disposed to
accept the substituting of Cape Colony for Rhodesia as the
ultimate part owner of the line. The financial arrangements
of the Government's counterproposal he also found unsatisfactory.[106] Since neither side could agree, Rhodes was compelled to push ahead with his plans without a government
guarantee.

The Government's refusal to guarantee the Tanganyika
line was not the only obstacle thwarting the construction of

the " all red " line of communications as conceived by Rhodes. Years earlier, Germany had pushed a solid wedge of territory between the British sphere of influence in South and Central Africa and the British sphere in the North. The story will be told in later chapters.[107] It is sufficient here to remember that by 1898, when Rhodes was about to launch his Tanganyika railway project, he could no longer contemplate running the line entirely through British territory. The railway must run north either through German or Congolese land and concessions were, therefore, necessary from either King Leopold or the German Emperor.

In spite of setbacks and disappointments, Rhodes persisted in his railway plans. There is no doubt that Rhodes, at heart, ardently wished for an " all red " railway line.[108] As will be seen in a later chapter, he fought hard to keep Uganda, the corridor to the North through which his railway and telegraph would run in British hands.[109] He was probably behind the agitation against the Anglo-German Treaty of 1890 which placed the German bar across the Cape-to-Cairo route,[110] and he may have influenced Rosebery in negotiating the Anglo-Congolese Agreement of 1894 by which England tried to secure a railway strip from Lake Tanganyika to Lake Albert Edward.[111] Rhodes was forced, however, to bow before accomplished facts.[112] He could not have an all-red line after 1890 but he could have an international railway opening up Africa to European commerce and civilization and incidentally to British trade and commerce. He was a practical man; if he could not have all his dream, he would realize as much of it as he could. He threw himself, therefore, heartily into plans for an international line from the Cape to Cairo.

He had already secured funds for constructing 500 miles of the Tanganyika railway. The route from Gwelo to the Kariba Gorge on the Zambezi River, however, was surveyed and condemned by Metcalfe. The country was mountainous and difficult after crossing the Kariba Gorge. There was coal in the district of the Gorge but it was of inferior quality. On the other hand, an important colliery was opened up at Wankie far to the west.[113] If the railway line was diverted to tap this new source of potential wealth, it would run farther west than the line originally proposed by Cecil Rhodes. In 1901, as already noticed, Grey made important mineral discoveries in the Katanga District.[114] Copper was discovered at Broken Hill in Northern Rhodesia, considerably to the west of the Tankanyika line first proposed. Furthermore, Williams secured prospecting rights over 60,000 square miles of the Katanga district on the northern side of the Congo-Zambezi divide for the Tanganyika Concessions Ltd. Rhodes was himself very much interested in the Katanga district.[115] Economic opportunities, therefore, favored a railway to the Katanga district through Wankie rather than a line to Tanganyika. Rhodes, however, was seriously considering both routes for the extension of the railway to the North. The Wankie-Katanga line would naturally run through the Congo; the Tanganyika line, on the other hand, would run north through German East Africa to Uganda.

On his own initiative, Rhodes began negotiations with both Leopold and the Kaiser. The story of those negotiations will be taken up later.[116] He secured a highly unsatisfactory railway agreement from the Kaiser. " All ifs and ands," he said.[117] On the other hand, Williams was able to negotiate a satisfactory agreement with King Leopold for a concession for a railway to connect up the navigable Congo with the whole mining area of Katanga as far South as the Rhodesian frontier and west to the Ruwe gold mine.[118] Rhodes was satisfied. He abandoned his plans for a Tanganyika line and lent his support to a Cape-to-

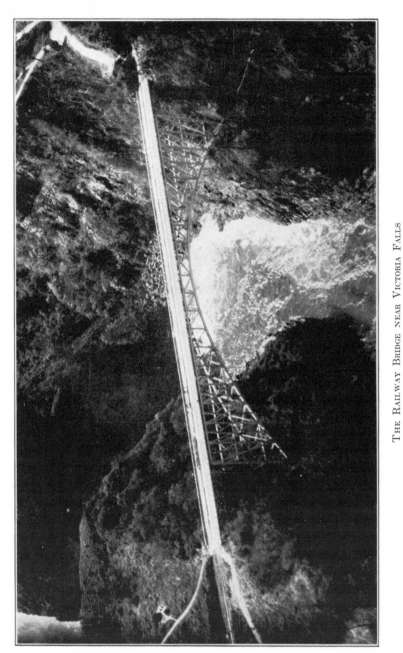

THE RAILWAY BRIDGE NEAR VICTORIA FALLS

Reproduced with the permission of the South African Railways and Harbours Administration

Cairo railway internationally owned and operated through the Congo.[119]   The last letter he wrote to Williams was an offer to build the Cape to Cairo Railway through the Congo State.[120]   The railway was thus brought north by the new route.   It reached Victoria Falls in 1904, two years after Rhodes' death, too late for the imperial dreamer to feel, as he had wished, the spray of the Falls on his face when the first train pulled across the bridge.[121]

The attitude of the Imperial Government, during these years, was one of embarrassed sympathy towards Rhodes' projects.   Although H. M. officials were inclined after the Raid to regard him as an overrash and dangerous imperialist and although they pigeon-holed the railway proposal,[122] they still showed considerable appreciation of his plans and purposes.   They might reject concrete proposals; they were not willing to become implicated in any new madness; but they were at heart still in accord with Rhodes' determination to colonize and occupy the country from Bechuanaland to the Lake District.   H. M. Government continued to support the work of the Chartered Company in Rhodesia.   There was some agitation in Parliament to withdraw the company's charter,[123] but this was not done.   When Rhodes was, finally, restored to the board of the British South Africa Company, there were some murmurs in Parliament against his reinstatement.[124]   The British Government disclaimed all responsibility for the action of the board but at the same time indicated its approval.[125]   As Harcourt put it: " We are willing to express not our condemnation, but really what amounts to our approval of these transactions in the past by entrusting the same responsibility to the same individual in the future." [126]

When a Matabele war broke out again in Rhodesia in 1896, H. M. Government stood stanchly behind Rhodes.   The Government maintained that it was ready to dispatch any military force required by the situation and that it was prepared to fill up the Cape garrison with reinforcements whenever it was depleted because of sending troops to Rhodesia.[127] "The policy of Her Majesty's Government," said Chamberlain, "was to supply at once whatever forces the authorities on the spot might ask for."[128]

The chief result of the Jameson fiasco as far as Rhodes' career was concerned was to direct his attention from Cape politics to his imperial schemes in the north. He was, for a time, under a political cloud in South Africa. Hofmeyr drew away in disgust from his friend and colleague. When he heard of Jameson's advance, he said, "If Rhodes is behind this, he is no more a friend of mine."[129] With Hofmeyr went the members of the Bond. For awhile, Rhodes was politically inactive. In 1898, however, he entered the field again as a member for Namaqualand and Barkly West. He regained his old seat for Barkly West but his party lost throughout the country. He never regained the full confidence of the Boers although many of his former friends among them remained faithful to him personally.[130]

His future work lay in the north in the settlement and development of Rhodesia and in the promotion of his railway and telegraph projects. He pushed forward with his Cape-to-Cairo schemes with a new vigor and earnestness. In fact, he told his friends: "I am just beginning my career."[131]

CHAPTER X

The Final Struggle for South Africa

WHILE Rhodes was thus proceeding with his program in the north, troubled conditions continued at the base of his contemplated empire, i. e., in Southeast Africa, particularly in the region of the Transvaal and the Portuguese colony of Mozambique. The British Government still suspected the Germans of carrying on intrigues in the Delagoa Bay region; of doing all that they could to sow distrust between Great Britain and Portugal, and of trying to gain a footing in Delagoa Bay territory.[1] The French, too, had commercial interests in the Transvaal and in the Portuguese Railways.[2] There was grave danger that Delagoa Bay and the railway might come under international control. The Transvaal might, then, with the encouragement of outside Powers shake off the last vestige of dependence upon Great Britain. Thrust like a wedge in between British South African territory, it might become a hot-bed of international intrigues and the storm center of South Africa.

Outwardly, however, there was a decided improvement in the relations between England and Germany during the years 1896 to 1899. As will be noted in a later chapter, the German Government lent diplomatic support and encouragement to the British campaigns in the Sudan which commenced in the Spring of 1896.[3] In the trouble between England and France, at the time of the Fashoda crisis in 1898, the Germans maintained a position of neutrality which was in reality advantageous to Great Britain.[4] In the summer of that year, the two countries had drawn so close that Sir

Frederick Lascelles, British Ambassador at Berlin, hinted to the Kaiser that " in some influential quarters," there was a wish for an alliance which should be strictly defensive and should only take effect if either power were attacked by two Powers at the same time.[5] To be sure, this conversation never led to a definite agreement. In fact, the following December Lascelles told the Emperor that he had spoken without authority and " that no formal alliance was necessary between England and Germany, as, if it became advisable for them to take common action, the arrangements could be made in twenty-four hours." [6]

Behind this show of friendship, however, there were danger spots. The Kaiser, for instance, was still playing with the idea of a continental coalition against England. In June 1898, in fact, Bernhard von Bülow, German Minister for Foreign Affairs, instructed the Ambassador at Paris, Count Munster, to sound out the French Government in regard to the Portuguese possessions in South Africa. He was to point out that the two countries possessed an identical interest there " whether in preventing or having a say in such an alteration of the Portuguese *status quo* both in politics and business." He was, also, to suggest diplomatic cooperation between Germany and France, not against England directly but against Portugal, possibly leading to an international control of Portuguese finances. The main object of the conversation, however, was " to ascertain clearly whether all practical cooperation between Germany and France in all individual questions, whatever they may be, is out of the question as a principle, as it was at the time of the Jameson Raid." He was reminded that " the clearing up of this point will be of wide importance in the future shaping of our foreign policy." [7]

On June 22, von Bülow told Count Hatzfeldt to warn the British that they must be careful in regard to their actions in

Portuguese Africa. Germany had supported Great Britain's policy in Egypt up to that time but if Great Britain acted too independently that support might be withdrawn. Germany could, probably, win over both France and Russia by suggesting a general settlement of all African questions. De Courcel was anxious for such a settlement because of France's interest in Egypt. Russia, in turn, wanted to drive England away from the Suez Canal. " Germany ", Count Hatzfeldt was to intimate, " is not in a position to render political services gratis, we expect a corresponding return." Germany would be forced to react energetically against an English attempt to seize silently a considerable portion of Africa.[8]   On January 19, 1898, the Kaiser warned Lt. Col. Grierson, British Military Attaché, that a European combination against England was not an impossibility.[9]   On August 19, when Count Hatzfeldt and Mr. Bertie, British Assistant Under Secretary of State for Foreign Affairs, reached an impasse over the Portuguese loan, Hatzfeldt threatened that the German Government " would give a greater extension to the matters at issue " and would " be obliged to seek other means " to settle the question. " Other means " he hinted " naturally meant other Powers." [10]

In short, the Portuguese Colonies presented a decided danger spot in Anglo-German relations during the years 1896-1898 because the Portuguese Government was once more in desperate straits for money. There was, in fact, some danger that Portugal might eventually have to part with its African possessions in order to extricate itself from its financial distress. In May 1897, M. de Soveral began conversations with Chamberlain over a scheme to assist Portugal financially and at the same time to guard against the alienation of the Portuguese colonies on the southeast coast to the Transvaal or any other foreign Power. The negotiations were unsuccessful but Germany's suspicions were aroused and in November 1897, the Kaiser recalled his Minister at Lisbon because he was not sufficiently firm in upholding German against British influence in Portugal.[11]

In 1898, Portugal again appealed for help. M. de Soveral was dispatched to London and Major Mousinho da Albuquerque to Paris and Berlin to negotiate for a loan.[12]

The British were suspicious not only of German but also of French interference in South Africa. Furthermore, they feared that Russia might join with France with the result that they would be " squeezed—Portugal willingly assenting—into a financial arrangement which would constitute Delagoa Bay and the railway an international concern under Portuguese sovereignty. This might soon be followed by the assertion by the Transvaal of entire independence of England." [13]

Moreover, if the Portuguese negotiations succeeded at Berlin, Germany would as a result secure a right of pre-emption over the Portuguese territories in Southeast Africa southwards from the German frontier down to the Zambezi. German territory would then encircle a large part of the British Central Africa Protectorate. The Germans might also, thereafter, encourage bad administration and sedition in the Portuguese possessions. The British were bound by the ancient treaty of 1661 to protect the Portuguese possessions. They also had, as already noted, under the treaty of 1891, a pre-emptive right on the east coast up to the Zambezi.[14] If, however, the Portuguese territory disintegrated by internal dissension, the British might lose their rights. It was to their advantage, therefore, to see order maintained and to eliminate as far as possible international interference.[15]

With these danger spots in mind, Chamberlain and De Soveral carried on negotiations in May and June for a loan to the Portuguese Government. The loan Chamberlain suggested should be secured on the mortgage of all their African possessions, including the railways as well as the general revenues. He suggested, also, an arrangement between the two countries by which Great Britain would guarantee to Portugal her African possessions. Portugal, in return, would promise that there should be no access to the Transvaal from the sea, without British concurrence, except by the port and railway of Lourenço Marques both of which were to be worked by an Anglo-Portuguese Company. The company would, however, provide money for the Berne Award. The Portuguese Government was, furthermore, to undertake not to confirm or grant concessions within a certain radius of Lourenço Marques without the concurrence of H. M. Government.

The Portuguese Government, at first, rejected these expansive terms. It insisted that public opinion " would be opposed to any alteration in the *status quo,* and would be strongly supported by the moral influence of Germany and France." Nevertheless, wherever the Portuguese turned, they were invited to throw in Lourenço Marquez and its port and railway for security. They finally turned back to Great Britain as the Power perhaps least interested in the disruption of their empire.[16] The chances of the two countries coming to an agreement looked more hopeful in the summer of 1898 than it had in May.

In the meantime, Hatzfeldt warned Lord Salisbury, June 14, that any one-sided action involving actual or contemplated passing of Portugal's sovereign rights in the African colonies into British hands would " make a very bad impression " on the Germans and would not tend to produce the improvement in relations which both countries desired.[17] In fact, the Germans were beginning to contemplate some cooperative action with Great Britain.

On June 14th, the Méline Ministry in which Hanotaux held the portfolio of foreign affairs, resigned and with it fell any hopes of cooperation between Germany and France. Hanotaux believed that France and Germany had interests in common in the maintenance of the *status quo* in Africa.[18] The Méline Ministry, however, was succeeded by that of Brisson in which Delcassé was Foreign Minister. Delcassé distrusted the Germans and was inclined to lean upon the Russian Alliance. Thenceforth, von Bülow decided that Germany would " attain more by negotiation with England than by combining our South African interests with those of France." [19]   The Germans, in fact, swung to the other extreme and determined to keep France from any participation in the Portuguese loan and from any benefits if Portugal had to renounce its territory.[20]   To be sure, as noted before, the Germans continued to use the idea of a European coalition to frighten England but in the summer of 1898, this threat appears to be more bluster than anything else.

On June 21, Count Hatzfeldt asked Lord Salisbury if Great Britain would join with Germany in a common action in regard to financial operations desired by the Portuguese Government.   At first Lord Salisbury was inclined to reject the proposal and declared that the question of financial assistance was a matter which exclusively concerned Portugal and Great Britain.   If there was any question of Portuguese territory passing to new owners, however, it would be most desirable for the governments of Great Britain and Germany to communicate with each other.[21]

On June 23, however, Lord Salisbury appeared inclined to consider Hatzfelt's proposals for parallel loans to be made by Great Britain and Germany to Portugal.   These loans were to be secured upon the customs revenues of the Portuguese possessions.   It being understood on both sides that in selecting places where these revenues were collected, the two countries would in reality be establishing a footing in case of a future partition of the territories in question. Germany chose for its share in the future spoils of a dismembered Portuguese southeast Africa the territory beyond the Zambezi up to the Rovuma including the Shire. The Germans were willing, however, to abandon Delagoa Bay and the rest of the Mozambique Province to the British.[22]

On this basis a series of discussions began which ended in the Anglo-German Convention of August 30. There is no need here to go into the details of those discussions. There was much dickering and bargaining on both sides. The field was widened to include Angola on the West Coast, Zanzibar and Pemba, Portuguese Timor, the Sulu Archipelago, and the Caroline and Samoan Islands. The British were insistent upon maintaining their rights on the Shire, particularly upon retaining Blantyre. They also insisted upon a fair division of the spoils in regard to Angola.[23] The Germans felt that they were making considerable sacrifice in surrendering all their claims to interfere directly or indirectly in affairs of the Transvaal and at Delagoa Bay.[24] They were, therefore, entitled to large compensations.

In the Convention signed August 30, 1898, the two countries agreed upon joint action in regard to a Portuguese loan on the security of the customs revenues of Mozambique, Angola and the Portuguese Island of Timor. The British were to receive the revenues of Mozambique south of the Zambezi and also the part of the province lying on the left bank of that river above its confluence with the Shire. Thus Blantyre was secured from German interference. They were also to receive the revenues from part of Angola. In case of default of payment, the custom houses were to be turned over to the two countries; those assigned to the German loan to Germany and those to the British to Great Britain.[25]

At the same time, the two Powers signed a secret convention by which they proceeded to partition the Portuguese provinces between them in case it was found impossible to maintain the integrity of the African possessions of Portugal south of the Equator. The division was to be made along the same lines as those laid down in that of the customs receipts. Further, both parties pledged themselves "to oppose the intervention of any third Power in the Provinces of Mozambique, Angola and in Portuguese Timor, either by way of loan . . . on the security of the revenues of those provinces, or by way of acquisition of territory. . . ." [26]

There was danger for a time that the Portuguese, who knew that some agreement had been reached between England and Germany and who suspected the character of the secret arrangement, might turn once more to France for financial assistance. In fact, there was evidence that Portugal had been sounding out that country in regard to a loan.[27] The Portuguese, however, failed in this attempt.

Portuguese finances were improving gradually. On June 7, 1899, M. de Soveral informed Lord Salisbury that there now appeared to be no necessity for an external loan.[28] In July, Count Tattenbach admitted "that a marked improvement had lately taken place" and "that a loan under the Anglo-German agreement was now out of the question." [29] In fact, the two governments were never called upon to use either of the conventions of August 30, 1898.

Thus in the fall of 1898, African interests seemed to be drawing the two nations together. The Kaiser went so far as to call the Anglo-German agreement a "new base . . . for mutual understanding and goodwill in colonial questions." [30] Nevertheless, even before the negotiations leading to this agreement over South Africa were concluded, trouble arose in another quarter which seriously threatened to destroy rapprochement and to embitter relations between the two governments.[31]

The roots of the new disturbance lay in the rivalry between Germany, England and the United States over the Samoan Islands. In 1889, as a result of a civil war in Samoa, a joint control by the nations of the three countries was established over the islands. Fresh trouble, however, broke out in the summer of 1898 with the death of King Malietoa and with the preparations of the United States Government to erect a coaling station at Pago Pago.[32] The succession to the throne was disputed by Mataafa, a former pretender and Malietoa Tanu, young son of the late ruler. Civil war broke out in which the German officials supported Mataafa while the British and American officials took the other side. There is no need here to go into the details of the controversy save to note that the Germans and the British were bitterly opposed to each other and could come to no agreement until the fall of 1899.[33]

On first consideration, these islands in the mid-Pacific seem too small and too far away from Africa to have any bearing whatsoever on African affairs. As a matter of fact, however, the British opposition to German ambitions in Samoa was likely to have repercussions elsewhere. Feeling ran high in both Great Britain and Germany over the Samoan controversy. British colonists in Australia and New Zealand were protesting loudly against allowing the control of Samoa to pass into the hands of a foreign Power. Samoa, they insisted, lay directly in the track of steamers plying between Australia and New Zealand and America.[34]

Although the islands were of no great commercial value, the German people considered them of great importance in building up their overseas empire. The loss of Samoa would be a blow to German prestige.[35] Von Tirpitz, Secretary of the Navy, was particularly vehement in his opposition to giving up the islands and insisted that whatever else Samoa was, " it was German and must forever remain

German." [36]   Furthermore, and perhaps this was the fundamental reason for the firm stand assumed by both sides, both
governments saw in the Samoan difficulties opportunities for
driving a bargain and for asking for compensations elsewhere. [37]

The German Government threatened and stormed.   Hatzfeldt talked of a realignment of the Powers and possibly of
a rapprochement between Germany and France and an understanding with Russia if the British remained recalcitrant. [38]
The German Foreign Office even hinted darkly that the
Kaiser " would break off diplomatic relations if a satisfactory agreement were not reached forthwith." [39]   Salisbury,
however, remained impervious to threats and warnings.
Relations became so strained during the summer of 1899
that Salisbury refused to see Hatzfeldt, the German Ambassador, for " whole weeks." [40]

The German Government, however, worked through unofficial as well as the regular diplomatic channels to break
down the British resistance.   Lord Salisbury, according to
Hatzfeldt, might be less moved by his colleagues than by
public opinion. [41]   Lord Rothschild's assistance was sought. [42]
Cecil Rhodes, the German Foreign Office decided, might also
prove a useful intermediary.   Rhodes was at the head of the
powerful British South Africa Company.   He was known
to be an influential " wire puller of British South African
policy." [43]   Furthermore, a bargain might be driven with
this South African.   As noted, after the Raid, Rhodes threw
all his energies into promoting his Cape-to-Cairo railway and
telegraph schemes and in developing Rhodesia.   He was
already contemplating taking his railway and telegraph north
either through the Congo State or through German East
Africa. [44]   He might be induced through concessions to his
cherished Cape-to-Cairo schemes to throw his influence on
the side of German interests in the Samoa controversy and

in regard to other contentious questions. He was more-over, a friend of Chamberlain, the influential colonial secretary.[45]

According to the account in *Die Grosse Politik,* General von Liebert, Governor of German East Africa, took a keen interest in Rhodes' Cape-to-Cairo railway schemes and was anxious to have part of the line run through the German territory. He, therefore, willingly lent his support to ar-ranging for an interview between Cecil Rhodes and the Kaiser. As early as February 5, the German Emperor was contemplating the possibility of such a visit from the South African politician.[46] On February 24, Holstein wrote to Hatzfeldt that it was known that Cecil Rhodes wished to come to Berlin. Holstein was sounding out Hatzfeldt about the man. He wanted to know whether Rhodes' influence was strong enough to overcome Lord Salisbury's inertia. Would Rhodes take an interest in the Moroccan question and in the Zanzibar controversy? Would he be prepared, in return for railway concessions, to take a part in the Samoa controversy? [47]

On the same day, Hatzfeldt wrote a letter to Holstein. Apparently arrangements had already been made for Rhodes' visit to Berlin because Hatzfeldt expressed delight that Rhodes was coming. He felt that it would be useful to establish good relations with the railway promoter. Rhodes would undoubtedly be interested in a bargain regarding his railway plans. He would hardly be interested, however, in questions which did not directly concern Cape Colony or the union between Cape Colony and North Africa. Further-more, Hatzfeldt shrewdly cautioned Holstein not to over-estimate Rhodes' influence. After the fiasco of the Jameson Raid, Rhodes' influence was on the wane. Chamberlain might listen to the would-be African Caesar but Salisbury certainly would not.[48]

Cecil Rhodes had just returned from a visit to Belgium where he had had an unsuccessful interview with King Leopold.[49]

> I found the King of the Belgians [he wrote to the Prince of Wales] was not in want of money . . . there is quite a Congo Stock Exchange at Brussels.
> The more serious matter was that under the Anglo-Belgian Treaty of '94 made by Lord Rosebery, we had given the King, (1) a strip of country along the Nile for his life; (2) the Bahr-el-Ghazal for so long as the Congo remained a Belgian colony. The King told me practically that he would not let my telegraph come through until we had given him the Bahr-el-Ghazal . . . now that we have settled with the French we must hand it over to him . . . I felt that there is likely to be a pretty squabble over the matter, and that between the two my telegraph would go to the wall.[50]

Cecil Rhodes was much incensed by Leopold's refusal to cooperate in his Cape-to-Cairo scheme. The story goes that, as he came out of the King's room, he caught hold of the British Military Attaché " and hissed in his ear: ' Satan, I tell you that man is Satan '." [51]   He later on confided to Sir Robert Williams, " I thought I was clever, . . . but I was no match for King Leopold." [52]   Rhodes was, thus, in a receptive mood to listen to German proposals. Furthermore, he realized that the only chance of getting his telegraph on at once was to get permission from the Emperor of Germany. He was delighted, therefore, to hear unofficially that the Kaiser would like to see him.[53]

Rhodes, finally, came to Berlin on March 10 and on the eleventh he was interviewed by the Kaiser.[54]   Rhodes came as an unofficial guest. H. M. Government was careful to say that he " acted entirely on his own initiative." [55]

Of the interview on March 11 and of a subsequent conversation between Rhodes and the Kaiser at an Embassy dinner, there are only fragmentary accounts. Apparently, Rhodes " found himself at once on the best of footing " with the German Emperor.[56] Their conversation ranged over a wide field. According to the Kaiser's own story, the two men discussed the Jameson Raid and the Kruger telegram. Rhodes claimed that Kruger's refusal to let his Cape-to-Cairo line come through the Boer country was the basis of " the stupid Jameson Raid." If Kruger had allowed him " such stretches of land as were needed for his rail lines . . . a demand which was not unjust and would certainly have met with German support," there would have been no Raid and no unfortunate telegram.[57] As far as the telegram was concerned, Rhodes told the Kaiser that the excitement raised in England diverted attention from his own misdemeanors. " I was a naughty boy," Rhodes explained archly, " and I never got whipped at all." [58]

The Kaiser expressed great interest in Rhodes' railway and telegraph schemes. In fact he claimed:

When Cecil Rhodes came to me, in order to bring about the construction of the Cape-to-Cairo Railway and Telegraph line through the interior regions of German East Africa, his wishes were approved by me, in agreement with the Foreign Office and the Imperial Chancellor; with the proviso that a branch railway should be built via Tabora, and that German material should be used in the construction work on German territory. Both conditions were acquiesced in by Rhodes most willingly. He was grateful at the fulfillment of his pet ambition by Germany, only a short time after King Leopold of Belgium had refused his request.[59]

Furthermore, the building of the Cape-to-Cairo line through German territory was also made dependent upon the cession to Germany of Samoa.[60] Rhodes' help was thus enlisted on Germany's side in this controversy.

The conversation then drifted further. Rhodes took the whole world into his purview and suggested Mesopotamia as a sphere of German activity. He spoke of a Bagdad railway. He advised the Kaiser to build the railway and to open up Mesopotamia. " This was Germany's task, just as his was the Cape-to-Cairo line." [61]

On March 16, von Bülow also had a confidential conversation with Rhodes. The latter promised the Secretary of State to exert all his influence in London, especially on Salisbury and Chamberlain, to bring the British Government to agree to a partition of the Samoan Islands in which America would receive Tutuila. The much coveted Upolu would go to Germany and England would have to be satisfied with the less desirable Savaii.[62]

Rhodes returned to England well pleased with his interviews with the Kaiser and with his cordial reception at Berlin.[63] He was, according to the Kaiser's account, " full of admiration for Berlin and the tremendous German industrial plants." [64] " I can tell you," Rhodes afterwards said to a Cape Town audience, July 18, 1899, " that in my humble opinion, he [the Kaiser] is a big man . . . he met me in the fairest way, and gave me, through his ministers, every assistance." [65]

Rhodes' conversion was complete. Up to the present time he has appeared as an outspoken opponent of German colonial ambitions. How he conjured up the German bogey to stimulate the colonial activity of his fellow countrymen and to promote his own plans of northward expansion has already been noted.[66] After his visit to Berlin, however, he became an ardent champion of German interests. He was willing to do all he could to support German colonial efforts (not in Africa to be sure—that was his special preserve), but in other parts of the world.[67] He worked strenuously to promote a feeling of goodwill toward the Kaiser and the Germans in England. Finally, in his will in 1902, Rhodes included German students under the provisions for Oxford scholarships.[68] Baron von Eckardstein, considers this conversion as a master stroke in German policy. "Cecil Rhodes," he writes, "became one of Germany's surest friends; and he used his very great influence and his still greater energy for the bringing together of Great Britain and Germany in their political and economic relationships."[69]

Rhodes left no stone unturned on his arrival in England to fulfill his part of the bargain with the Kaiser and to bring the British Government to consent to Germany's demands in Samoa. "Rhodes did not stop," writes Krause in the *Deutsche Revue,* "with expressing his discontent with the foreign office and the Yankees but he energetically recommended that the preponderant German claims to Samoa should receive justice. In this direction, he influenced the press organs which were favorable to him and made his influence felt in administrative circles."[70] He wrote to the Prince of Wales, pleading with him to forget past grievances and to receive the Kaiser cordially at Cowes that summer.[71] He talked with Balfour, with Chamberlain and with Salisbury.[72] There is some question, nevertheless, just how far Rhodes' strenuous efforts actually affected the Samoan situation. To be sure, the controversy was, finally, adjusted to Germany's satisfaction, by a treaty signed at London, November 14, 1899.[73] It must be remembered, however, that in October the Boer War broke out in South Africa. The German threats that the situation in Samoa might aggravate conditions and seriously damage a cordial understanding between the two countries probably did far more than Rhodes' ardent campaign to break down Salisbury's resistance. Rhodes, himself, admitted that he could make no headway with the British Prime Minister.[74]

The reward which Rhodes received for his efforts in the German cause was an agreement which allowed him to bring his Cape-to-Cairo telegraph line through German East Africa. Rhodes was delighted with his success. He called the arrangement " a most just bargain ".[75] The German Emperor made feasible a project which a few years before was only " a wild-cat scheme ". There were at least three conditions attached to the agreement. (1) After forty years the line was to pass into German hands [76] and (2) Rhodes promised that if the telegraph wire were carried through German East Africa, the Chartered Company would, not make a railway line to connect with the West coast except through German S. W. Africa.[77] (3) The Telegraph agreement was made dependent upon a favorable settlement of the Samoan controversy.[78] Under these conditions, the German Government was willing to grant Rhodes every facility to bring the line through German territory and promised to maintain the through line at actual cost.[79] After a little further dickering the final arrangements were completed and within less than a year the telegraph was laid for over fifty miles through German territory.[80]

Rhodes also secured a railway agreement but apparently it was of a very unsatisfactory character. He told Sir Robert Williams that it was " all ifs and ands ". It seems to have been principally useful as a bargaining lever with King Leopold.[81] The Kaiser in his memoirs indicates that Rhodes was given permission to extend the Cape-to-Cairo railway through German East Africa " on the proviso that a branch railway should be built *via* Tabora." [82] Another condition was that the materials for making that part of the line should be purchased in Germany.[83] It is safe to surmise also that the railway, like the telegraph agreement, was dependent upon a solution of the Samoan controversy which was favorable to Germany. Rhodes, however, seems to have made little use of the railway agreement.

Back of the unsatisfactory character of the railway understanding probably lay a determined opposition of an influential group in Germany. The Germans seem to have been more suspicious of Rhodes' railway plans than they were of his telegraph project.[84] There were, however, two camps. One group was in favor of taking the Cape-to-Cairo line through German East Africa because of the traffic advantages which would result.[85] The idea was that the German line from east to west and the British line from south to north would cross at Tabora.[86] Then, once the line from the east coast to the lakes was finished, German East Africa would possess a complete system of railways toward the east, west, north and south. The opinions of this section were so decidedly in favor of the railway that it almost seemed as though Rhodes' project would be wholly successful. A Berlin bank had already shown a disposition to make certain guarantees.[87]

There was, however, a strong group opposed to Rhodes' railway scheme. The opinion of this group was expressed in an article in the *Täglische Rundschau*. The railway, the author of this article claimed, was of no economic use to German East Africa and was very dangerous as a wedge of British influence. It would end in anglicizing the country. Two leaders in the Reichstag were absolutely opposed to the scheme and the negotiations fell through.[88] Sir Charles Metcalfe attributes the failure to the effort to bring a considerable section of the Cape-to-Cairo route under German official control.[89] Although Rhodes succeeded rather well with the Kaiser, he could not under the circumstances obtain a guarantee for the railway from the Reichstag representatives if the opinion of the voters was against the measure.[90] The maintenance of friendly relations between the English and the German people was, therefore, essential to the future success of Rhodes' schemes.

The growing friendship between Germany and England was outwardly manifested by the Kaiser's visit at Windsor from November twenty-second to the twenty-fifth, 1899.[91] Nevertheless, behind this seemingly cordial gesture there were some discordant notes. One minor source of irritation was the inclusion of Admiral von Senden in the Emperor's suite. The admiral was a *persona non grata* to the Prince of Wales.[92] Furthermore, just at this time, there were some " sour leading articles in the *Times* concerning Anglo-German relations ". Mr. Balfour, however, " complained of the German Press as being much more anti-British than the British Press was anti-German." [93]

On November 24, moreover, Chamberlain had a long and not altogether satisfactory conversation with the Emperor. The British Colonial Secretary suggested a general understanding between Germany, England and America. His Majesty rejected the proposition and maintained that it was better for Germany and England to agree together on individual points as they came up. He took this occasion to point out " that it was to England's interest to handle carefully the sensitive, obdurate and rather sentimental German and not to make him impatient, but to show him good-will in small matters. The German was ' touchy '; the more this was borne in mind by the British the better for the relations between the two countries." [94]   In short, the Germans evidently did not want their hands tied at this time. Chamberlain, however, persisted in the idea of building up an alliance between the two countries. On November 30, at a meeting at Leicester, he advocated such an agreement as the " most natural alliance " for England. His speech, however, met with a storm of Anglo-phobe fury in Germany.[95]

The real strength of the Anglo-German rapprochement received its acid test in the Boer War which broke out in October 1899. It is necessary, however, to return to 1896 to pick up the threads of that story. The Transvaal was from 1896 to 1899 the storm center of South Africa. Because of its strategic position sandwiched in between the British Possessions and the Portuguese, its fate was a determining factor in the question of whether Great Britain would be able to maintain its position as the predominent colonial Power in the South.

After the Raid, the relationship between the Boers and the British went from bad to worse. The failure of the Raid greatly strengthened Kruger's position in South Africa.[96] Rhodes' blunder, in fact, threw the Cape Dutch on the side of their Transvaal brothers. Kruger, therefore, could proceed towards his ultimate goal of "Africa for the Afrikanders" with more confidence and a firmer step. In Cape Colony, he could now count with assurance upon the support of Hofmeyr and the Bond.[97]

The grievances of the Uitlanders multiplied. There is no need here to give a detailed account of their alleged wrongs. Chief among them was Kruger's reluctance to give them the vote. By a system of franchise laws, the Uitlander could have no voice in determining the affairs of the Republic for fourteen years. There is, of course, much to be said on the side of the Boer president. The Uitlanders formed a considerable element in the population. There was danger that an English or foreign majority might elect an English president of the Transvaal and might some day bring about annexation of the country to the Cape.[98]

The British Government, for its part, however, after it had taken formal steps to make amends for the Raid, was insistent upon reforms in the Transvaal and that the grievances of the Uitlanders be redressed. British Colonial affairs were in the hands of the masterful Joseph Chamberlain. Under his leadership the British Government continued to press for reform.

The fundamental issue, however, between the Boers and the English, went far deeper than the franchise question. It was the claim of the Boers to complete independence.[99]

It would be beyond the scope of this study to probe into the arguments on either side or to go too deeply into the history of that conflict. It is sufficient for our purposes to note that the misunderstanding between the two parties was so deep and so provocative that it led to war and that the chief issues at stake were, for the Boer Republics, their complete independence and for the British their position of dominance in South Africa.[100]

The Boer War was a bitter one. The sturdy Dutch farmers put up a remarkably strong resistance. Much depended upon whether they would receive substantial support from outside. Indeed, the courageous struggle of the Boers awakened a lively sympathy among people all over Europe and a general popular condemnation of the English.[101] " Popular opinion," however, " was nowhere more universally and aggressively hostile to Great Britain than in Germany and nowhere was such hostility more frequently reflected than there in the public utterances of responsible statesmen. . . ."[102] Furthermore, the German press raged against the British, and as Sir Valentine Chirol points out, the German press was under the supervision and control of the government.[103] Might not the Germans forget their recent rapprochement with the English and in view of their past friendly relations between the Boers and the Germans, in view of the Kaiser's behaviour at the time of the Jameson Raid, come to the aid of their supposed kinsmen in South Africa?

As a matter of fact today, it looks suspiciously as though the Kaiser was playing a double game during the war. Technically his conduct towards England was correct and in line with the recent advances made between the two countries. Actually, he was trying to bring about a diplomatic intervention to stop the war. He was still dallying with his persistent idea of a continental coalition against England.

While the storm was brewing, von Bülow invited the Dutch Government " when it was in the act of offering conciliatory advice in its own name to President Kruger at Pretoria, to add that Germany also advised all conciliation." Von Bülow hinted that it might be well to apprise Chamberlain or Lord Salisbury of this move.[104] On June 8, Baron von Holstein refused to mediate between England and the Transvaal but suggested America as a possible intermediary.[105] There was some talk about American arbitration but the project fell through, probably because President Kruger objected to calling in American mediation at that time.[106] On August 10, Biermann, German Consul at Pretoria was told to maintain the " *strictest reserve* " about the Anglo-Transvaal difficulties.[107] " On the grounds of general policy and in consideration of the Anglo-German Agreement," Count von Bülow wrote to the German Foreign Office, August 12, " we must naturally avoid being forced into a false position, both in England and the Transvaal, in connection with the present troubles in South Africa. . . . Germany will not let herself be dragged into the Transvaal dispute in any form whatever." [108] The other continental Powers seemed at the time rather indifferent to the approaching crisis in South Africa. Von Bülow felt, therefore, that " it must be explained throughout the country that since France, Russia, Italy and Austria are not thinking of becoming enemies with England on account of South African questions, Germany cannot step forward and commit herself there all alone." [109]

The conduct thus far of the German Government seems unimpeachable although it was known that Chamberlain and Lord Salisbury suspected the Germans of disloyal conduct in the Transvaal. Possibly, they had heard that certain German business men in Southwest Africa had been trying to obtain a concession to build a railway through the Transvaal to connect with a line through Bechuanaland and the mining district of German Southwest Africa to go from there to the Atlantic Coast. In fact, such a proposal was actually made to the Transvaal Government but said von Bülow, it was after all a purely private enterprise.[110]

After the outbreak of hostilities, the conduct of the German Government continued to be ostensibly correct. Dr. Leyds, the Transvaal's chief European agent was sent on a tour to the European capitals to solicit aid. Count von Bülow instructed the German Chargé d'Affaires in Brussels, October 16, to do his best "quietly to prevent Dr. Leyds from travelling to Berlin, as I could not receive him." [111] Nevertheless, although they would not receive him at Berlin the Kaiser's Ministers kept in touch with Dr. Leyds through other channels.[112] The Kaiser's visit, as will be recalled, to Windsor took place in November after the war had commenced.[113] The Kaiser, moreover, gave strict orders to all army corps that none of their members, including even troops that have been disbanded, are permitted to go to Africa. Nevertheless, there were rumors that there were German officers and German soldiers enlisting in the Boer Army.[114] The Emperor carried on a lively correspondence with the Prince of Wales during the war even giving him military advice as to the campaign in South Africa.[115] The Kaiser even went so far as to assert that he had prevented a collective intervention with Russia and France, to bring England to make peace. The Emperor gave the impression that the invitation had first come to him from the Imperial

Russian Government.[116] Finally, in November 1900, the Kaiser refused to receive President Kruger.[117]

In fact, some years later, the Kaiser tried to coin an advantage from his apparent friendship with the English during this troubled period. On October 28, 1908, *The Daily Telegraph* published an anonymous article purporting to be an interview with the Kaiser. Although the authorship of the article was not disclosed, it had the approval of the Kaiser and the German Foreign Office.[118] The dominant theme of the reported interview was the Kaiser's friendship for Great Britain during the Boer War both openly and secretly maintained by the German Emperor though not shared by his people nor recognized by the British. The British people read the article with some skepticism. "When the Kaiser confessed that his subjects as a whole were unfriendly to England," Gooch remarks dryly, " he was generally believed; but when he affirmed his own undeviating good-will, he failed to carry conviction." [119]

Mr. Bertie, British Ambassador at Rome, gave a somewhat different version of the Kaiser's friendship to Great Britain during the Boer War. Mr. Bertie's account is embodied in a minute submitted to Sir Edward Grey in September 1907. According to him, " the extraordinary campaign of calumny " directed against Great Britain during the war " was undoubtedly fostered and encouraged in every way by the German Government and directly by Prince Bülow himself in the Reichstag." Also there was good evidence to show that the attempt to bring about a collective intervention was not made on the initiative of Russia, as the Kaiser claimed, but on that of Germany. In fact, " the Emperor made several attempts during the war to form a coalition to force Great Britain to bring the hostilities to an end." The Kaiser's refusal to receive Kruger, furthermore, meant very little because " by that time the ex-President was a discredited fugitive, and . . . to have received him in Berlin would have been a tactical blunder of the first order." Moreover, Mr. Bertie points out that a navy bill was passed in 1900 which aimed " at placing Germany in a position to challenge British maritime supremacy." In short, Anglo-German relations were in reality " correct rather than cordial." [120]

According to the French and Russian versions of the attempt to bring about an intervention, the German Government suggested to the Russian Government that there should be an intervention by Russia, Germany and France to put a stop to the War and to secure the independence of the South African Republics. The Tsar was unwilling to take any steps which would be regarded as hostile to England but decided that the Russian Government might join with the other two Powers to put a stop to the bloodshed on condition that there was reason to suppose that the step would be acceptable. It was from a humanitarian feeling and not with a political object hostile to England that the Emperor of Russia consented to enter into discussions on the subject with Germany and France. The Russian Government then, at the instance of the Germans, sounded out the French. Monsieur Declassé asserted " that France had no particular interests to protect in South Africa " but that he would, nevertheless, like to know the attitude of the other Powers if the mediation failed. Thereupon, the German Government replied that " in order to render the mediation or intervention effective it would be necessary that the three Powers should first enter into a guarantee for the maintenance of the *status quo* in Europe." France drew back from the far-reaching political implications of such a proposal and the discussion was dropped.[121]

There were no doubt pourparlers between the three governments from October 1899 to March 1900.[122] Whether

Germany acted in a Machievellian manner or not at the time is perhaps not so important as the fact of the failure of these negotiations.

Indeed, although the Boers elicited general sympathy, they received very little substantial support. France had no particular interest in South Africa. To be sure, when Kruger came to Europe, he was enthusiastically received by the French populace and even was granted an audience with the President.[123] The British, also, watched with some alarm Dr. Leyd's negotiations at Paris.[124] The French Government, however, was not sufficiently interested to champion Kruger's cause. In fact, Declassé was intent upon bringing France and Great Britain together by a comprehensive settlement of all principal questions that divided them.[125]

The Tsar as noted, was anxious to stop bloodshed but not anxious to enter into hostilities with England.[126] He had, in fact, just been instrumental in summoning the Hague Peace Conference.

Kruger sent emissaries to the United States but with no better success than in Europe. The Boer delegates received an enthusiastic popular welcome but this popular reception did not influence the Government. The Government refused all support, probably according to von Bülow, because the United States wished to emphasize " their solidarity of interests with England," [127] or because it was following its traditional policy of non-intervention in European affairs.

On October 14, 1899, the British Government concluded a convention with the Portuguese confirming the ancient treaties of alliance, amity and guarantee of 1642 and 1661. The Portuguese likewise, undertook " not to permit, after the declaration of war between Great Britain and the South African Republic, or during the continuance of the war, the importation and passage of arms, and of munitions of war destined for the latter." [128]

Early in 1900, the Emperor Francis Joseph, Germany's most intimate ally, declared himself " entirely on the side of England." [129]

England, therefore, was left free to deal with the South African situation. After an arduous, bloody and costly war, the Boer Republics were finally forced to come to terms.[180]

With the end of the Boer War an important chapter in the history of British expansion in Africa came to a close. The British were now undisputed masters of South Africa. They held the road to the North and they also held the position of dominance at the base of their ever growing empire in Africa. A vast stretch of territory was painted red from Cape Town to the great lake region. Cecil Rhodes' hand can be seen in much of this work of expansion and consolidation. H. M. Government had been led half unconsciously, half willingly into helping him realize the first part of his great dream of a British Africa from the Cape to Cairo. In the ensuing chapters, the story will be taken up of the spread of British influence from Egypt to the great lakes and the attempts to link the two spheres in the south and in the north. Cecil Rhodes will again be found working behind the scenes but his influence upon this phase of the expansion will be less direct.

CHAPTER XI

INTO THE HEART OF THE DARK CONTINENT

LONG before Cecil Rhodes began to color Africa red, other British empire-builders had done their bit to open up the Cape-to-Cairo route.[1] Their objective, to be sure, was not necessarily Cape Town. They had much more immediate goals in view, i. e., to reach the sources of the Nile, to open a new path to the Upper Sudan through East Africa and Uganda, to develop the fertile land in the lake region, or to forestall the operations of rival Powers in the Sudan, Uganda and East Africa. Nevertheless, the explorers and travellers who penetrated into Equatorial Africa, between 1857 and 1884, and by their accounts of its riches awakened a new interest in the Dark Continent, were veritable Cape-to-Cairo pioneers, because they were continually breaking paths along that great route. Moreover, mingled with their interest in science, and in the development of trade and commerce one may detect prophetic visions out of which more expansive dreams and projects would grow.

The search for the sources of the Nile was one of the first objectives which let British explorers into Equatorial Africa. As early as 1856, Burton and Speke travelled into the lake region from Zanzibar on the East Coast. In 1857, they discovered Lake Tanganyika and explored its northern half.[2] In 1858, Speke, on a branch trip of his own, sighted a great inland sea and named it Victoria Nyanza. In October 1860, Speke started out again for Africa. He was accompanied this time by Colonel J. A. Grant previously mentioned as a sponsor of the Overland Telegraph scheme.[3] They proceeded from the East Coast to the southwestern corner of

Lake Victoria. Finally, Speke alone entered Uganda in 1862 where he was later rejoined by Grant. While there, he made friends with Mtesa, the ruling monarch. In July 1862, Speke discovered the Ripon Falls and " saw the Nile pouring out of Lake Victoria." He realized that he had reached the great head reservoir of the White Nile.[4]

Meanwhile in 1861, Sir Samuel Baker and his wife began an expedition up the White Nile. At Gondokoro, February 1863, they met Speke and Grant who urged them to continue their journey. The Bakers agreed and proceeded on their way. Eventually, after many vicissitudes, they reached Kamrasi's capital in Unyoro, just north of Uganda. On March 14, 1864, they discovered and named Lake Albert. From the lake they travelled in canoes up the Victoria Nile and discovered the Murchison Falls. Finally, they returned to Khartoum, May 1865.[5]

The upper reaches of the Nile were further explored by Colonel Gordon and his collaborators. Gordon, himself, traced the course of the river between the Murchison Falls and the Karuma rapids. An American, Colonel C. Chaillé-Long, followed the Nile from the Ripon Falls to the Karuma rapids and discovered Lake Kioga. In 1874, Stanley circumnavigated Lake Victoria and demonstrated that it had only one outlet. He also partly explored the Kagera River, which he called the Alexandra Nile. By 1874, therefore, it was well known that the White Nile issued from a great lake reservoir, the Victoria Nyanza, which in turn was fed by streams coming from regions where the rainfall was particularly heavy.[6]

Baker again set out for Africa in 1869. This time, he was sent by the Khedive, Ismail Pasha, to establish a chain of military stations and commercial depots through Central Africa with Gondokoro as the base of operation and to suppress the slave trade.[7]

He reached Unyoro, just north of Uganda, and established two or three posts, but was unable to make much headway against the slave traders. He returned, however, in 1873 enthusiastic about the possibilities of the Sudan.[8] " In the magnificent equatorial portions of Africa," he wrote, " there is a great field for British enterprise." [9] He spoke, too, of the Khedive's project to improve communications in the Sudan and of the completion of a railway from Cairo to Khartoum. There would be, he was confident, direct communication by rail and river with countries that were eminently adapted for the cultivation of cotton, coffee, sugar, and other tropical products.[10]

These discoveries of Baker, Speke and Grant opened the heart of Africa and aroused British interest in the latent possibilities of the continent. It has already been seen how these discoveries awakened interest in the first Cape-to-Cairo project, the Overland Telegraph.[11]

Colonel Charles Gordon took up the work where Baker had left it. In 1874, the Khedive appointed him to succeed Baker as governor of the tribes of the Nile basin.[12] When Gordon arrived in the Equatorial Sudan, he found only three miserable posts still occupied by the Egyptians: Gondokoro, Fatiko and Toweira. In 1877, Gordon was raised to the rank of Governor-General of the whole Sudan, including Darfur, the provinces of the Equator and the Eastern Sudan. While Governor-General, he did much to spread Egyptian influence. He sent a mission to Mtesa in Uganda and he extended the rule of the Khedive almost to the Nile-Congo divide.[13]

Unlike Baker, he was not optimistic about the country. " People," he wrote, " says in the papers that the Soudan and most of the good places in Egypt are in the hands of the English. I declare I do not think you would get a man to take the Soudan. You might get him to come up but he would soon go down again and require compensation for having come." [14] In another place, he writes: "all the northern part of my province is marsh and desert ", [15] and again he complains that all the Sudan, south of Khartoum was a "wretched marsh." [16] When asked for his opinion concerning the prospects of an overland telegraph through the Sudan, he commented sourly, "If they made the telegraph through Africa, each station would be a nest of robbers in the shape of slave dealers." [17]

Nevertheless, Gordon looked beyond the marshes of the Equatorial Provinces and saw promising land to the South. He found a fertile territory near the great lakes, capable of maintaining a large and prosperous population. The center of Africa, the highlands near Mtsa's Kingdom, became his goal. He wanted "to push on to the lake [Victoria] to hoist the flag and to enable the Khedive to claim its waters." He dreamed of placing the Nile in free communication with the great lakes, of putting boats on Victoria Nyanza, of bringing Kabba Rega, the warlike slave-trading chief north of Uganda, into submission. The only way to open up Africa, he claimed, was to come in from the east at Mombasa and develop the lake district. He even urged the Khedive to send an expedition by steamer to Mombasa, to establish a station there and then to push on to Mtesa's capital in Uganda. Gordon made friendly contact with Mtesa and was successful in persuading the Khedive to send a small force to Juba [18] but he never lived to see his dream fulfilled. In 1882, the Mahdist revolt broke out in the Sudan. Gordon, as is well known, was killed by the Madhists at Khartoum in 1884. His work in the Sudan was destroyed but his dreams survived.

Gordon, Baker, Speke and Grant, although they did not talk about a Cape-to-Cairo empire, all pointed the way to opening up the heart of Africa through the lake district and to the building up of a long chain of British commerce and influence from Mombasa to the confines of Egypt. They were pioneers, breaking the way for British influence from East Africa to Uganda and from Egypt to the Equator.

It was left to Henry Morton Stanley to awaken a sustained popular interest in Uganda. His remarkable journeys (1874-1877) have already been mentioned.[19] His purpose was to open the center of Africa to European commerce and civilization. He turned first to England. " Before he touched English soil," his wife writes, " on his return at the end of 1877, his letters in the ' Telegraph ' had hinted at the vast and inviting political possibilities which the new country offered to England." When he reached home, he threw himself " into the work of persuading, preaching, imploring, the ruling powers in English commerce and in public affairs to seize this grand opportunity." [20] His interest was spread over all the central African strip from the mouth of the Congo to East Africa; but Uganda, he declared, was the " Pearl of Africa." [21] Uganda was important to Great Britain, he insisted, and Great Britain had a right to include this territory within its sphere of interest.[22] Stanley's appeal was premature as far as H. M. Government was concerned. " Little Englanders " were still in the saddle at home and the Government was apparently blind to his enticing dreams of empire. Stanley, thereupon, sought the more attentive ears of the Belgian King Leopold.

Some of Stanley's ideas, however, fell on fruitful ground in England. As a result of his campaign, a fund was started and missionaries dispatched to Mtesa's country. Her Majesty's Government, moreover, distinctly favored the sending out of the English missionaries and a letter to Mtesa from the Secretary of State for Foreign Affairs was given to the party. The letter stated that the missionaries were not agents of the Government but had its friendly support. A second lot of missionaries was next sent into the country by way of the Nile. This group also carried with them an official letter from the British Foreign Office. Later, the British consul at Zanzibar wrote to Mtesa, November 1879, confirming the fact that the letters, especially Lord Salisbury's of May 1878, came from the Government. Mtesa thereupon sent envoys to the Queen and the envoys returned home with presents from England.[23]

About the same time, 1879, the French people also became interested in the souls of the natives of Uganda and the White Fathers arrived from a French mission in Algeria.[24]

Other countries were awakening to a new interest in the great Equatorial belt. Leopold of Belgium, in particular, was already growing restless within the bounds of his tiny kingdom and was looking overseas for an outlet for his imperial ambitions. His attention, finally, fastened upon Africa. He felt his way carefully. To his palace at Brussels he summoned an international conference of explorers and scientists on September 12, 1876. From Great Britain came such well-known African specialists as Sir Bartle Frere, ex-governor of Cape Colony and William Mackinnon who was soon to become the " leading spirit " behind the Imperial British East Africa Company. The representatives had no official mandates. They were merely representatives of geographical societies, or prominent men in fields of exploration, or philanthropy. The chief result of the conference was the creation of the African International Association with its seat at Brussels and the establishment of branch national committees in various countries. The primary objective was the encouragement of the exploration of the civilization of Central Africa.[25]

The British Royal Geographical Society refused to form an English National Committee. National committees, however, were formed in other countries but the leadership fell to King Leopold and centered at Brussels. The African International Association held its first and only plenary session at Brussels in June, 1877. At this meeting a special flag was adopted for the association, a golden star on a blue background and definite principles were laid down for establishing a chain of posts from Zanzibar to the great lakes. The association was completely dominated by King Leopold and most of the funds provided came from Belgian sources; probably a large portion was supplied by the King himself. As a result of the activities of the Association, some highly unsuccessful expeditions were sent out between 1877 to 1885.[26]

Meanwhile, King Leopold was following with keen interest Stanley's expedition of 1874-1877 which revealed to the world the possibilities of development in the Congo region. "The power," Stanley declared, "possessing the Congo, despite the cataracts, would absorb to itself the trade of the whole of the enormous basin behind. This river is and will be the grand highway of commerce to West Central Africa."[27] Although Great Britain was not prepared to snatch at this golden opportunity, Leopold was. He dispatched commissioners to Marseilles to welcome Stanley upon his return and tried to enlist his services. As already seen, Stanley wanted to make his appeal first to the British; he, therefore, did not accept Leopold's offer immediately. His cold reception by the home authorities, however, drove him back to Leopold, and, finally, led him to cooperate in that ambitious monarch's schemes for developing the Congo region.[28]

Leopold's attention was fastened more and more intently on the Congo basin. On November 25, 1878, he summoned another international gathering at his palace at Brussels. This time, the conference was composed of representatives of the financial world of England, France, Germany, Belgium and Holland rather than of geographers and scientists and the interest centered specifically on the Congo. The result was the formation of a Comité d'Études de Haut Congo to investigate the commercial possibilities of the Congo basin. A fund of £20,000 was raised and a scheme drawn up for establishing a chain of posts along the Congo River and for acquiring areas suitable to cultivation in their vicinity. There were further meetings, December 9, 1878 and January 2, 1879. Stanley's services were enlisted and on January 23 he left England for Zanzibar. He was sent ostensibly to aid a Belgian expedition to open up the country but actually he was laying the foundations of what was soon to become the Independent State of the Congo. He carried with him the flag of the old International Association which the Comité d'Études was permitted to use.

He seems to have been following to some extent Colonel Strauch's plans of forming a negro confederation under a European president appointed by King Leopold. The confederation thus formed might in turn grant concessions to societies for the construction of public works.[29]

On this mission, Stanley arrived at the mouth of the Congo, August 14, 1879. On November 7, 1880, he met, near Ndambi Mbongo, a French naval officer, le Comte Savorgnan de Brazza.[30] De Brazza, too, was staking out claims. On July 27, 1881, Stanley met an agent of De Brazza at Bwala Njali who produced a treaty purporting to grant to De Brazza, as the representative of France, the territory from the Gordon Bennett river and Impila on the north bank of Stanley Pool. In short, the Frenchman had stolen a march on Stanley.

In spite of this check, Stanley did all he could to secure control over the district south of the French field, to found a series of stations and to conclude treaties. On April 23, 1884, he was able to report to the International Association of the Congo, which had replaced the Comité d'Études, that he had secured the country from Boma to the Niari-Kwilu.[31] The association, itself, however, was in an anomalous position. It had not yet been recognized as a body with power to accept cessions of territory and found sovereign states. Unless the Great Powers granted these rights, Stanley's work was in vain.

France was already claiming extensive territory both north and south of the Congo River, on the basis of De Brazza's exploration. The Congo Association, while willing to concede that France had rights over country north of the river, insisted that the land to the south belonged to the Association on the basis of treaties which Stanley had concluded before the arrival of De Brazza.[32] The fundamental question still remained, however, what was the status of the Congo Association in the eyes of the other European powers? Did it have the right to create a new state?

The question was urgent. France was not the only other rival Power. Portugal was reviving ancient claims to the mouth of the Congo River and England agreed to support the Portuguese contention, February 1884. King Leopold was annoyed at this " corking of the Congo bottle." [33] Stanley, on the other hand, seems to have favored the arrangement, probably in the belief that, on completing the organization of an administration on the Congo, the King of the Belgians would hand over the territory to Britain. The British would then have no reason to regret that the mouth of the river was in Portuguese hands.[34] The French, however, strenuously objected to the Anglo-Portuguese agreement as a distinct menace to their own operations in the Congo basin. The German Government also wanted to be heard. Bismarck announced that Germany could not recognize so farreaching an agreement in which she had not been consulted.

Fortunately for Leopold's interests, the United States formally recognized the flag of the Congo Association as that of a friendly government, on April 22, 1884.[35] Leopold also persuaded France to give up its claims on the south bank of the river in return for a right of preemption over the Congo Association's territory. On April 23, 1884, the International Association of the Congo formally declared that it would not cede its stations to any Powers.[36]

In the meantime, the difficulties arising out of the Anglo-Portuguese agreement just mentioned were growing acute. On April 17, Bismarck sounded France as to the desirability of an international conference. On October 8, Germany together with France summoned the leading Powers to a conference on " (1) freedom of commerce in the basin and mouths of the Congo; (2) the application to the Congo and the Niger of the principles adopted by the Congress of Vienna with a view to preserving freedom of navigation on certain international rivers . . . (3) a definition of the formalities necessary to be observed so that new occupations on the African Coast should be deemed effective." [37] The European Powers and the United States accepted and their representatives met at Berlin, November 15, 1884, for a discussion which lasted until February 26, 1885.

The Conference concluded its labors with a General Act.[39] The Berlin Act, as it was called, was most significant in the future partition of Africa because it laid down certain rules which were more or less accepted by the Powers as governing principles. The Act declared freedom of trade in the basin of the Congo. It defined the limits of this free trade belt and declared the territories within it to be neutral. France, later on, tried to claim that the Act recognized an independent Congo State within fixed limits. There is, however, very little if anything at all in the Act to justify this contention. Article I merely defines the limits of a free trade zone and does not in any sense create or recognize a new sovereign state within that zone.[39] Article X declares the zone to be neutral but also speaks of countries and territories of other Powers comprised within that neutral zone.[40] Article VIII places the supervision over the application of the General Act " in all parts of the territory . . . where no Power shall exercise rights of sovereignty or Protectorate " in the hands of an International Navigation Commission.[41]

The assembled representatives were not particularly interested in Leopold's newly created state. They were primarily engrossed in safeguarding their own commercial interests in the Congo basin. In short, they were concerned with the regulation of conditions most favorable to the development of trade and civilization, free navigation on the two chief rivers flowing into the Atlantic Ocean, the avoidance of " misunderstanding and disputes which might in future arise from new acts of occupation [*prises de possession*] on the coast of Africa." [42] To effect the last objective, the conference evolved two important rules which henceforth continually disturbed the peace of mind of the Great Powers who were busy " pegging out " claims in Africa. Article XXXIV of the General Act reads:

Any Power which . . . takes possession of a tract of land on the coasts of the African Continent outside of its present possessions, or which, being hitherto without any such possessions, shall acquire them . . . shall accompany the respective act with a notification thereof, addressed to the other Signatory Powers of the present Act, in order to enable them, if need be, to make good any claims of their own.[43]

Article XXXV pledges the Signatory Powers:

to insure the establishment of authority in regions occupied by them on the coasts of the African Continent sufficient to protect existing rights, and as the case may be, freedom of trade and of transit under the conditions agreed upon.[44]

The last mentioned Article lays down the rule of effective occupation. The principle was enunciated more than once in the scramble for East Africa and the lake region.[45]

CHAPTER XII

The German Barrier Across the Cape-to-Cairo Route

While Stanley was breaking a path into Central Africa from the west coast, other adventurers were pushing their way through East Africa towards the lakes. In fact, a race had already begun for East Africa, Uganda and the surrounding regions.

During the years 1882-1883, Mandara, an ambitious slave-raiding chief who was trying to subdue the other chiefs of the Kilimanjaro region, opened up relations with the Sultan of Zanzibar. Sir John Kirk saw an opportunity of turning these advances to good account and to send a British expedition into the friendly chief's territory. He prompted the British Association and the British Royal Society to finance a scientific mission to Mt. Kilimanjaro to investigate its fauna and flora. At the same time, he communicated his purpose to the Foreign Office. Sir Harry Johnston was chosen to head the expedition. The ostensible purpose of the mission was purely scientific but when Johnston arrived at Zanzibar, Kirk supplied him with treaty formulae and talked about the possibilities of negotiating tentative treaties with " Mandara or other potentates of the mountain." Johnston was, however, not to press negotiations on the chieftains and " only to deal with such a matter if a French traveller seemed to be coming to the neighborhood." [1] Evidently, Kirk was afraid of French colonial ambition and had his eye upon the movements of a certain French explorer, Révoil, who appeared at Zanzibar in April 1884. Révoil purported to be particularly interested in the remains of

244

helot-negro, Gala-speaking tribes in the coast region north of Malindi. Sir John Kirk, however, knew that he had been treaty-making in Somaliland and he was afraid that the French had designs of alienating from the over-rule of Zanzibar the tribes between the Juba River and Kilimanjaro.[2]

Johnston arrived at Zanzibar in 1884. He was, himself, as noted, turning over ambitious Cape-to-Cairo schemes in his mind.[3] He was especially anxious to forestall the work of any agents of other European powers in the Kilimanjaro region. In this connection, he seemed more disturbed by the operations of the Germans, who were becoming quite active in East Africa, than by the designs of the French. On his so-called scientific expedition, therefore he concluded several treaties and hoisted the British flag on Kilimanjaro and at Taveita. Sir Harry Johnston then considered his work done and returned to England. On his return, however, he made over his Taveita concession to the nascent committee of a great imperial trading company, the Imperial British East Africa Company.[4]

The Foreign Office for its part was surprised and disappointed to see him back so soon.

We thought [they told him] you were remaining — on that mountain, you know, where you made the treaties? After we heard what the Germans were doing we got the Government to agree to ratify your treaties for Kilimanjaro—and now here you are back, and goodness knows what is going on in East Africa! . . .[5]

Johnston was followed in 1885 by General Mathews, a British officer sent out by the Sultan of Zanzibar. Mathews, also, concluded treaties, in the name of the Sultan, with the native chiefs in the Kilimanjaro district.[6]

The race, however, was close. In 1884, Dr. Karl Peters led the first German expedition from Bagamoyo into the interior. Peters, like Johnston, made treaties with the chiefs. The German flag was raised at Usagara, Ukama, Nguru and Useguha. In May and June, 1885, another German, Dr. Karl Jühlke appeared in the Kilimanjaro region and concluded treaties with the natives. The Germans followed up Jühlke's treaty by making definite settlements. The British, on the other hand, made no settlement in the Kilimanjaro area. On February 17, 1885, a charter of protection was granted by the German Government to the Society for German Colonization founded by Karl Peters for the acquisition of territory in this region.[7]

Meanwhile as noted, Johnston had made his treaties over to the nascent committee of the British East Africa Company. In fact, Salisbury in a dispatch to Germany, May 25, 1886, mentioned a scheme of " some prominent British capitalists . . . for a British settlement in the country between the coast and the lakes, which are the sources of the White Nile, and for its connection with the coast by a railway." [8]   He then suggested a delimitation of the Sultan's territory.

Germany received the suggestion favorably and accordingly an agreement was signed in the fall of 1886, between the British and German governments, delimiting the Sultan's dominions and marking off spheres of influence for the British and German activities in East Africa. By this agreement, the Sultan's shadowy claims to a vast dominion on the mainland were disregarded and his kingdom was reduced to the Island of Zanzibar, certain other islands, and a strip ten miles wide on the mainland from Minegani River at the head of Tunghi Bay to Kipini. North of Kipini certain stations were also allotted to the monarch.

The two European Powers then proceeded to divide up East Africa between the Rovuma River on the south and the Tana River on the north. The dividing line ran from the mouth of the Wanga or Umbe River between Taveita and the Kilimanjaro range to the point on the eastern shore of Victoria Nyanza which is intersected by the first degree of south latitude. The German sphere of influence lay below this line and the British above. The two countries, however, failed to set any western limits to the territory under discussion, or to say anything about their operations north of the Rovuma River save that the stations of Kismayu, Brawa, Meurka and Magadisho with a radius landwards of ten sea miles and Warsheik with a radius of five miles, belonged to the Sultan of Zanzibar. These important omissions were bound shortly to give trouble.[9]

In fact in the following year, the question arose as to the respective rights of the two powers concerned to expand westward. The issue grew out of the attempt of a British expedition to rescue Emin Pasha. Emin Pasha, whose real name was Edouard Schnitzer, was a doctor, born and educated in Germany. He spent, however, some years in Turkey and became so enamoured with his foster country that he adopted a Turkish name and became a Turkish citizen. His wanderings, finally, brought him in the capacity of a physician to Gordon at Lado. Thereafter, Gordon sent him on important contact missions to Uganda and Unyoro. In fact, Emin Pasha seems to have been fully in sympathy with the Governor General's plan to open communications to the Equatorial Provinces from the East Coast and to make the Upper Sudan independent of the Nile. He went so far as to establish stations towards the southeast.[10]

When the Madhi, in 1882, overran the Sudan, the Doctor held his own at Wadelai in the Equatorial Province. He managed to keep the loyalty of his Egyptian and Sudanese troops. In fact, as late as 1886, when all the rest of the Sudan was ravished by the Mahdists, Emin Pasha could boast: " What I have striven for and longed for—the holding of this province intact for Egypt . . . I have done." [11] In spite of this brave boast, however, the Pasha was faced with difficulties. He was very much cut off from the outside world. It was not, indeed, until the Spring of 1886 that he received authentic news of the murder of his chief, General Gordon, which had taken place in 1884. Furthermore, he needed reinforcements and help and was beginning to grow anxious about the fate of his Equatorial Province. He realized by this time, that there was a strong probability that Egypt intended to evacuate the province.[12]

He was in a quandary as to the best course to pursue. He debated the question of whether he should leave the employ of the Khedive to set up an independent kingdom of his own in the Sudan, or appeal to some European Power for aid. If he did turn to outside aid, there was some question as to whether he would ask for help from Great Britain, or from Germany, his mother country. At heart, it seems that Emin Pasha was eager to maintain his Equatorial kingdom as an independent state " like the Rajah of Sarawak." [13] He was worried, however, about the practicality of such an undertaking and, finally, decided to seek help from some European Power.

Germany, however, was at first slow in making up to the importance of the Equatorial Province and to Emin Pasha's plight. England was the first country to show any interest in the stranded doctor.[14] He was, therefore, in the years 1885 to 1887 inclined to turn to that country for help. He couched an appeal to his Scotch friend, Felkin, in glowing imperialistic terms:

The time is now come [he wrote], for England to secure her part in North East Africa before it is too late . . . I believe that a state (this province) which should I think, include Uganda and Unyoro, if under British control, would be indeed a great blessing to Central Africa, and it would form a central point

from which the annexation and exploitation of a healthy fruitful and compact district could be easily carried out . . . if
England forsakes us, I must seek in some other direction for
support . . . [15]

There is some reason, to be sure, to doubt Emin Pasha's
sincerity because he told his German friend, Junker, " I have
written to England asking for support in my work. Rather
cool for one who is not an Englishman. A truce now to
this mendacity; I am beginning to fear that on the whole it
is not a very difficult profession." [16]

What Emin Pasha wanted fundamentally was some outside support in the form of diplomatic protection and the
tangible assets of guns and ammunition. As far as his own
work was concerned, he wanted as little interference as possible. He liked the Sudan. Irrespective of which country
came to his assistance, he wanted to be left in a position of
authority in his own Equatorial Province. " I shall on no
account desert my people," he told Felkin, " . . . There is
no question about it; I shall remain here." [17]

A group of Britishers did answer Emin Pasha's appeal
but in a manner which was much more thorough-going than
the doctor expected or wanted. In fact, " English people
were full of the idea that Emin had necessarily to be
rescued " rather than just relieved.[18] There was undoubtedly a genuine humanitarian desire to help the forsaken and
destitute Pasha. The motives, however, leading to the
rescue were mixed. The British people, possibly, were not
deaf to Emin Pasha's imperialistic pleadings. At any rate,
they heeded his warning that he might turn to other Powers
if the British did not help him. They were inclined to mistrust the rugged individualism of the good doctor. They
did not believe that he would be able to maintain an independent State. Furthermore, they remembered his accounts
of the fertility and commercial potentialities of the Equa-

torial Province and Uganda. There were rumors, indeed as early as 1884, that there were a number of British mercantile capitalists who were interested in the Sudan and that these gentlemen had even tried to " form a ' Royal Soudan Company' on the lines of the Old East India Company," i. e., another great imperialistic trading concern was contemplated.

The famous explorer, H. M. Stanley, for one, was keenly interested in a scheme for developing the Equatorial Provinces and the lake district.[19] He was anxious to utilize the commercial and political possibilities of this region either for the British Empire or for his friend, King Leopold. He also mistrusted the doctor and believed that with foreign and especially German competition so strong in the scramble for Africa that it was not safe to allow the Pasha to set up an independent state which he probably could not permanently maintain. Stanley contemplated three alternative solutions of the problem. (1) Emin Pasha should be removed altogether from his Equatorial Kingdom and taken back to Europe, or, if that course were impossible, (2) his services should be enlisted by the then nascent British East Africa Association for work in their employ in the country northeast of Lake Victoria. (3) Another alternative was to engage Emin Pasha's services as Governor-General of the Equatorial Province but under the King of the Belgians.[20] Emin Pasha, at all events, must not be left alone to prejudice British or Congolese interests in the Upper Sudan.

With these proposals in mind, but with the Belgian proposition still a secret, Stanley headed in 1886 an expedition to rescue Emin Pasha.[21] It is significant that a large part of the funds for the expedition were furnished by Sir William Mackinnon, the founder and leading spirit behind the abovementioned British East Africa Association. The expedition started on its way in the early part of 1887.[22]

Germany now sensed the dangers lurking in a British expedition into the fertile country back of the lake district. Stanley travelled into the Equatorial Province through the Congo State and his route lay through the country back of Victoria Nyanza. The directors of the German East African Company were disturbed by the news that a British expedition was headed towards this region because they feared that Stanley's mission, although ostensibly simply to rescue Emin Pasha, would pave the way for the establishment of a British Protectorate back of the German sphere of influence as laid down in the previously mentioned agreement of 1886.

The German Government shared the company's alarm. Baron von Plessen wrote to Lord Salisbury that such a turn of events would be contrary to the understanding upon which the treaty of 1886 was based. The letter is significant because in it von Plessen first set forth the main argument upon which the Germans later based their contention to the region between the Congo and their sphere of influence in East Africa. The primary object behind the agreement of 1886, Baron von Plessen maintained was " the arrangement of a line of demarcation on the north of which the English were free to operate, while the Germans were to operate south of it." He admitted that it was true that no special line had been expressly fixed by that agreement for the delimitation on the west but he contended that

the Imperial Government had started from the idea that England would leave Germany a free hand for the future in the territories south of the Victoria-Nyanza Lake, and, without interfering with the territories lying to the east of Lakes Tanganyika and Nyasa at the back of the German Protectorate, would confine herself to opening up territories lying to the north of the agreed line.[23]

Baron von Plessen further stated that he felt it expedient to lay an early explanation of his Government's views on this question before H. M. Government because of the suspicious character of Stanley's expedition. The money for that mission, he pointed out, was largely contributed by a certain Mr. Mackinnon whom he was sure was actuated by views of a commercial and political as well as a philanthropic character. Mackinnon, he further stated, was indeed at that moment treating with the Sultan for the collection of customs at Mombasa.[24]

Her Majesty's Government replied soothingly that Stanley's expedition would not interfere with the territory "under German influence or in the rear of it." Furthermore, H. M. Government took

the same view of the question as is entertained at Berlin, and are prepared to discourage British annexations in the rear of the German sphere of influence, on the understanding that the German Government will equally discourage German annexations in the rear of the British sphere.[25]

This is a significant statement of the views of H. M. Government. It meant that as early as 1887, Lord Salisbury was willing to acknowledge that the strip between Germany's sphere in East Africa and the Belgian Congo belonged to Germany's sphere of activity. In other words, the German sphere was made conterminous with the Belgian Congo. Lord Salisbury, thereby, precluded the realization of the dream of an all-British line of communication running through all-British territory from the Cape to Cairo.

To be sure, in 1887, " from the Cape-to-Cairo " had not yet become a popular slogan. The popular interest in a transcontinental railway, for instance, was manifested for the first time in the agitation over granting a charter to the British South Africa Company in 1886.[26] Possibly, Salisbury had never heard of a Cape-to-Cairo scheme. He, therefore, cannot be accused in 1887, of betraying any great imperial project. However, even if he knew about embryonic Cape-to-Cairo plans at this time, he, probably, would have disregarded them. In fact, a few years later in 1890, he was inclined to consider a thorough-going Cape-to-Cairo project as impracticable.[27] He was essentially a realist but nevertheless a stanch imperialist at heart. He was in no position in 1887 to fight for a still abstract Cape-to-Cairo ideal but, as later events proved, he was prepared to defend and promote British imperial interests in Africa and to encourage the extension of British influence throughout the heart of the Dark Continent wherever he could.[28]

The agreement of July 2, 1887, embodied, as will be noted later on, the fundamental principle behind the better known Anglo-German treaty of 1890 as far as German East Africa and the British sphere of influence to the north were concerned. It embodied the idea that " where one Power occupies the coast, another Power may not, without consent, occupy unclaimed regions in its rear," [29] i. e., the German " Hinterland Doctrine." The treaty of 1890 and a discussion of the further development of this doctrine will be taken up later on but, before this point is reached, it is necessary to revert once more to the scramble which was going on in East Africa, Uganda and the Upper Sudan.

In spite of the British government's denial of imperialistic designs, the Germans were justified in fearing the activities of Stanley in the region back of Lake Victoria. As later events proved, he was busy not only in the rescue of Emin Pasha but also in concluding numerous treaties with the native chiefs upon which later British claims were based.[30]

A new interest in Emin Pasha was springing up in Germany in 1886 and 1887. This interest was, as in England, inspired by mixed motives. The Germans as well as the

English had political and commercial ambitions. Dr. Junker, a friend of Emin Pasha and a famous African explorer, wrote an article in the *Kölnische Zeitung,* November 17, 1886, calling for an armed expedition to Uganda, to depose the monarch there, substitute " a chief friendly to Europeans " and then to rush to the relief of Emin Bey with the aid of the Uganda people themselves. The prestige of Europe was almost lost in those regions. He demanded " The deliverance of Uganda! The support of Emin Bey and reoccupation of those provinces! " Germany was at last, after a period of complete neglect, ready to claim the doctor as " her distinguished son." [31]

In the Spring of 1888, a committee of the German East Africa Company started agitating for an Emin Pasha relief expedition. The proposals of the committee were welcomed by the German Emperor and Prince Bismarck. Funds were subscribed and plans laid for an expedition to be jointly headed by Dr. Karl Peters and Lieutenant Wissman. [32]

While Germany was thus preparing to send relief, Stanley reached Emin Pasha in the Equatorial Province, April 29, 1888. He, then, presented his three proposals to the Pasha. The doctor sturdily refused to leave the Equatorial Province unless his men consented to go with him. He was, however, inclined to accept the proposal to establish himself and his followers along the northeast corner of Lake Victoria, in the employ of the British East African Association. Stanley then left the doctor, for the time being, to collect some of his force whom he had left behind. [33] When he returned, he had evidently changed his mind about Emin Pasha's joining the East African Association. The Pasha's Sudanese soldiers had, at last, revolted against their leader. Stanley became convinced that it was not safe to leave the doctor and his unreliable followers behind. In other words, he was determined to carry Emin Pasha back with him *to*

Europe. The doctor, however, was reluctant to leave his beloved Province. Stanley, thereupon, forcibly compelled the Pasha to accompany him to the coast.[34]

On his way to the coast, Emin Pasha officially received word that the Germans, who had once neglected him, were now making great efforts to send him aid. He also received a hint that Germany was planning to make use of him in East Africa. Furthermore, when he arrived at Bagamoyo on the East Coast, he was delighted to receive a telegram of welcome from the German Emperor. Shortly, thereafter, he received from him the Second Order of the Crown, with a Star. The days of indecision were over. " After this," he declared, " one might willingly lay down his life for the Emperor." Successfully resisting all of Stanley's attempts to carry him off to Europe, the Pasha enlisted his services for a German expedition into the interior, this time with the avowed determination to forestall British activity in the lake district.[35] There are of course two versions to the story but apparently, Stanley by his masterful conduct had turned a potential friend into a dangerous enemy to British imperialism in East Central Africa. Emin Pasha's instructions from Wissman, Imperial Commissioner of East Africa were:

(1) . . . to secure on behalf of Germany the territories situated south of and along the Victoria Nyanza Lake, from Kairrondo Bay and the countries between Victoria Nyanza and Tanganyika up to the Muta Nzige and Albert Nyanza, so as to frustrate England's attempt at gaining an influence in those territories. I consider that the extension of the line from Kilmanjaro and the Kairrondo Bay to the north-west, up to the frontier of the Congo State, constitutes the Anglo-German frontier [he remarked]. Any extension warranted by circumstances, of the sphere of influences just described, would be regarded by me as redounding to your Excellency's special merit.

(2) When marching towards the Victoria Lake, your Excellency will everywhere make known to the population that they are placed under German supremacy and protection . . . [36]

Germany openly was in the race. There was no longer talk of humanitarian and scientific expeditions. Emin Pasha proceeded, April 26, 1890, towards the lake region on a frankly imperialistic mission.

Meanwhile, a German Relief Expedition led by Karl Peters, had been sent to aid Emin Pasha, and had made its way into Uganda by February 1890.[37] At the request of Mwanga, the much harassed native chief, and Père Lourdel of the French White Fathers, Peters made a loose treaty with the chief " agreeing that Uganda was to be free to the commerce of all nations and to accept the decrees of the Berlin Treaty." Peters, thereupon, hoisted the German flag in Uganda. He then departed for the coast just before Jackson, an agent from the British East Africa Company, arrived in the same country. Jackson, in turn, tried but unsuccessfully to secure a treaty from Mwanga.[38] The race for the lake district was on in dead earnest and feeling ran uncomfortably high in both Germany and Great Britain.

Trouble was also brewing in other directions. In May 1887, the Sultan of Zanzibar granted a fifty-year concession of his powers on the mainland and within the British sphere of influence to Mackinnon's company then called the British East African Association.[39] In 1888, the founders of the company applied for a charter which H. M. Government granted September 3, 1888. The group, then, took the name of the Imperial British East Africa Company or the Ibea Company as it was commonly called.

Like the British South Africa Company, the Ibea was frankly and openly imperialistic in character. It was, for instance, formed to:

(1) to take over the concession of the Sultan of Zanzibar of May 24, 1887, . . . (4) to acquire territory from native chiefs in the British sphere of influence by treaty, purchase or otherwise . . . (5) . . . generally to exercise all the rights pertaining to sovereignty over acquired districts . . . [40]

Furthermore, its imperialistic nature was definitely recognized by outsiders. " The company," said an article in the *Times,* " as the nation's agent was bound to secure the lake regions of Central Africa for British dominion and commerce." In return for this service, " if the company can put Englishmen and English money into its territory upon any considerable scale, it need not doubt that due protection will be forthcoming." [41]

The new organization took its imperial responsibilities seriously. It did not limit its activities to the mainland strip granted it by the Sultan of Zanzibar. The directors were looking far into the interior to the fertile country of Uganda where English mission stations were already forming nuclei for the spread of British influence.[42] They were, moreover, determined to forestall the operations of foreign powers in this attractive interior. In fact, even before the grant of the charter, the company's agents had pushed inland from the sultan's concession and concluded 21 treaties with the chiefs in the interior of East Africa.

Rival German companies, however, were equally active both in the interior of East Africa and on the coast. Their activities on the coast were not only in the region definitely assigned as a German sphere of influence by the agreement of 1886 but centered also around Witu north of the demarcated spheres near the Tana River in territory actually allotted to the Sultan of Zanzibar. At first glance, German activities in this region on the East Coast seem far removed from any question of British expansion along the Cape-to-Cairo route.

It must be remembered, however, that Baron von Plessen stated the famous "hinterland doctrine" in 1887. If this doctrine were accepted whole-heartedly, the growing German sphere of influence around Witu might be extended far back into the interior until it actually shut out the Upper Sudan to British activity.[43]   The question of whether the German or the British Company, therefore, could establish control over the Coast north of the Tana River was of far-reaching significance.

Lord Salisbury, indeed, was awake to the importance of the German and British rivalry on the east coast.   He later told Parliament:

As long as the sultanate of Witu was in the hands of another Power, there was a possibility of annexations and expeditions to the north of us, which would have cut off British influence and British dominion from the sources of the Nile, from Lake Albert Nyanza and the valley which lies at the base of the mountains of Abyssinia.[44]

There is no need to go into the complicated story of the clashes between German and British companies on the east coast, north of the Tana River save to note that both countries were anxious to secure paramount control along the coast.   That rivalry was a serious point of friction between the two countries and pointed to the urgent need for a new delimitation of the German and British spheres of influence.[45]

Further south, the Nyasaland district was another point of dispute between the Germans and the British.   A strict application of the "hinterland doctrine" would cut through the Nyasaland district where, as already noted, there were a number of English mission stations and coffee plantations and where the African Lakes Company was in full operation.[46]   Such a southern boundary would also enclose the

Stevenson Road from Lake Nyasa to Lake Tanganyika.[47] Salisbury, however, insisted on the basis of " effective occupation " and in disregard of the " hinterland principle " which he had apparently accepted in 1887 that Germany must not interfere with British operations in Nyasaland. He rested his case solidly on the explorations of Livingston, the work of the missionaries and the activities of commercial companies in developing trade and keeping the slave trade at bay in those regions.[48]

The storm clouds, therefore, were piling up in various quarters. Germans and Britons were at loggerheads on the east coast, in the region back of Lake Victoria and in the Nyasaland district. Both countries were too deeply involved in the operations of imperialistic trading companies to back out of these regions without loss of prestige. Nevertheless, both countries needed each other's help. England needed Germany's diplomatic support in Egypt.[49] Germany wanted Great Britain to cede the island of Heligoland, which might one day serve as a strategic naval base protecting the Kiel Canal which was then under construction.[50] As early as 1884, Bismarck had sounded the British out as to the cession of this island. " The acquisition of Heligoland," the German Ambassador in London insisted, " would be extraordinarily popular in all of Germany." Germany felt that, above everything else, it was necessary to be master at her own gate.[51] H. M. Government, however, did not immediately warm up to the German suggestion. The island was not of any great value to England but Granville felt that its cession would be unpopular.[52] Possibly, too, the British Government was looking for more substantial compensation for the island than Germany was willing to offer in 1884.

In December 1889, both countries, at last, seemed disposed to discuss the points at issue in their colonial contacts.[53] The following May, Sir Percy Anderson was dispatched to carry on negotiations at Berlin with Dr. Krauel over African questions. At the same time, discussions were proceeding in London between Lord Salisbury and Count Hatzfeldt.[54]

The negotiators were chiefly concerned with the definition of the spheres of influence of their respective countries in such a way as " to avert the danger of the revival of ' hinterland ' disputes." [55]   The discussions ranged over a wide field from the question of the recognition of a British protectorate over Zanzibar, and that of British claims to Witu and the islands of Manda and Patta to a definition of spheres of influence in the heart of Africa from the Upper Nile Valley down to the Zambezi River.   This book, however, is mainly concerned with the delimitation of spheres of influence in the center of the continent along the south to north route.

The heart of the controversy centered around two disputed areas one in the north behind Lake Victoria and one in the south between Lake Tanganyika and Lake Nyasa.   The extremists on the British side laid claim to all the territory covered by Stanley's treaties,[56] i. e., roughly " the ground between Uganda and the northern end of Lake Tanganyika." [57]   In the south, they wanted a stretch of territory which would include the famous Stevenson Road and would be shoved like a wedge between Lake Nyasa and Lake Tanganyika with the point touching the north end of Lake Tanganyika.[58]   If the British obtained the limit of these demands, they would have an unbroken line of territory running from their sphere of influence in the south to that in the north.

The Germans on their part, wished the boundary lines of the agreement of 1886 extended westward.   This would make them conterminus with the Congo State along their western border and give them also part of Uganda.[59]

These were, of course, the extreme demands.   Between them lay plenty of ground for compromise.   Lord Salisbury, himself, preferred to take the middle road.   He criticized both extremes.

The claims of the Germans [he said], rest simply upon the doctrine of " Hinterland ", which they have to a great extent invented, and which in their arguments appears to mean that, if you have possessions in an uncivilised country, you have a right to extend those possessions to an unlimited distance inland from the sea, until you strike the frontier of another civilised country. On this ground they claim to extend their territory westward, both to the south and the north of Lake Tanganyika, till it abuts on the frontier of the Congo State.

He was, however, equally critical of some of the demands of his own countrymen:

. . . The English, on the contrary, rest their claims upon two grounds. In the first place they have a claim, for which it is not very easy to discover any international foundation, that they shall have an unbroken stretch of territory from Cape Town on the south to Lado, the point at which the Nile becomes navigable, on the north, and that this stretch of territory shall only be broken by the waterway of Lake Tanganyika. Secondly, a far more tenable ground of claim consists in the fact that, on the south of Lake Tanganyika the English originally discovered, and have now for many years, through the African Lakes Company, through Mr. Stevenson and through the Scottish Missions, occupied the territory which the Germans claim. . . . To the north of Lake Tanganyika the English claim rests wholly upon the treaties which Mr. Stanley, and possibly Mr. Jackson, have made with the King of Uganda and other natives. The weak point of such treaties, as a ground of title, is that generally they are confronted by a parallel set of treaties made with another European Power by the same native Potentates or by native Potentates claiming the same country; and Mr. Stanley's and Mr. Jackson's treaties do not seem to be exempt from this inconvenient flaw.[60]

Lord Salisbury wanted two main objectives; " the rounding off of a large and fruitful opportunity for the development of England's enterprise in what is now Northern Rhodesia " and " the safeguarding for all time of her southern approach to the Nile Valley. . . ." [61]

He was, however, hard pressed by the extreme demands of two great imperial trading organizations. The British South Africa Company was agitating particularly for the territory in the south between Lake Tanganyika and Lake Nyasa.[62]   The Imperial British East Africa Company were interested in the country behind Lake Victoria and between lakes Edward and Tanganyika.[63]   Stanley, at the time, was touring the country arousing popular enthusiasm for the lake region and for the demands of the Ibea Company. The Ibea Company were unwilling to surrender any of Stanley's treaty-bought provinces and their importunate demands made it difficult for Lord Salisbury to arrive at a satisfactory solution of the East African question.[64]   In fact, he complained that the requests of the Ibea were more unreasonable and that the company was harder to deal with than the British South Africa Company.[65]   Hatzfeldt reported that the greatest difficulty of the negotiations lay in satisfying the demands of these two companies.[66]

There was also, according to Sir Edward Malet, a considerable group, possibly belonging to both companies, which was demanding a passage through from the Cape to Cairo.[67] This group was insistent upon a corridor between Lakes Albert and Edward and the northern end of Lake Tanganyika,[68] and free transit across Lake Tanganyika.

But [said this group], Germany must not be tempted to aspire to block the free movement of British commerce and civilization north and south. Lake Tanganyika, though Germany possess the one shore and the Congo State the other, must remain an open highway, and British enterprise must have undisputed access to it at its northern point. This is the subject of Mr. Stanley's warnings and objurgations . . . Germany must not be allowed to sever the line of actual or possible connexion between British influence in South Africa and British influence in the Lacustrine region.[69]

The strip from Tanganyika to lakes Albert and Edward, however, said Salisbury, could not have been obtained without breaking off the agreement altogether.[70] Great Britain, after all, could not produce effective claims to the corridor. There were no British settlements between 1° south latitude and Lake Tanganyika. Stanley's treaties only extend to the latitude 1° S, or some 20 or 30 miles beyond it.[71] Salisbury, therefore, yielded to Germany in this case and gave up the " wasp waist " between the British empire in the South and the embryonic empire in the north. In the agreement of July 2, 1887, however, Salisbury had already made the major decision to acquiesce in the German " hinterland principle " wherever Great Britain could not produce evidence of effective occupation.[72]

Lord Salisbury has been severely criticized by Cape-to-Cairo enthusiasts for this surrender of " the wasp waist " to Germany. " A wedge of German territory," writes Sir Lewis Mitchell, " was allowed to be driven between the Nyanza lakes and Tanganyika . . . a Cape-to-Cairo line all British was thus rendered impossible by the shortsightedness of ministers on this side." [73] This criticism seems unfair. Salisbury believed he could not have insisted upon this strip without repudiating the agreement of 1887 and ruining the chance of coming to any accord at all in 1890.

There were other issues which entered into the negotiations. The British wanted to establish a protectorate over the Island of Zanzibar. They were also anxious to have a British protectorate over Witu and the islands of Manda and Patta recognized. The Germans for their part wished access to the Zambezi River from their colony in Southwest Africa.

There was some discussion and dispute but the offer of Heligoland made to the Germans on May 14, was tempting and in the end proved decisive. Von Marschall telegraphed Hatzfeldt May 25: "From a military point of view the possession of Heligoland because of the North Sea Canal is of the greatest importance." [74] On May 29, he telegraphed again " the possession of Heligoland . . . is for us of the greatest importance and is by far the most important subject of the now pending negotiation . . . without Heligoland, the North Sea Canal has no significance for our fleet." [75] There was further bargaining but the Germans appeared willing to go almost to the limit of concessions in Africa to obtain the coveted Heligoland. There is some reason to believe that Lord Salisbury might have pushed the Germans even further than he did, and insisted upon the cession of territory above Lake Tanganyika which would have given the British the corridor to the north. In fact, Count Hatzfeldt was instructed that if the negotiations came to an impasse over the British East African Company's demands north of Tanganyika, " he was to ask for further instructions." [76] Lord Salisbury, however, did not press the point. Possibly he was not aware of the final note of hesitation. Perhaps he considered hard bargains bad bargains.[77] He had been willing to yield on this point anyway in 1887.[78] Finally, the two countries came to an agreement in the early summer.

By the Anglo-German treaty of July 1, 1890, Lord Salisbury exchanged Heligoland for Germany's acquiescence in British spheres of influence in (1) Nyasaland and the northeastern corner of Rhodesia including the Stevenson Road, (2) Uganda, (3) territory to the north extending from the Juba River to the confines of Egypt, east of the western watershed of the basin of the Upper Nile. The Germans

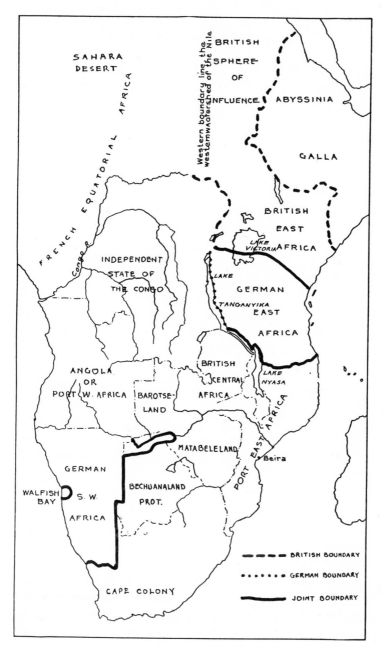

ANGLO–GERMAN TREATY, 1890

also withdrew their claims to a protectorate over Witu and the adjoining eastern coast up to Kismayu.[79]

In Southwest Africa, Great Britain, in turn, conceded to Germany a strip of territory no less than 20 English miles in width from German Southwest Africa to the Zambezi, i. e., the so-called " Caprivi's finger." [80]

Furthermore, while confirming freedom of trade and navigation in the free trade zone defined by the Berlin Act of 1865, the Anglo-German agreement also especially stipulated that there be freedom of commerce between lakes Nyasa and Tanganyika and also on the latter lake.[81]

Both countries were well satisfied with the bargain although, of course, there was some grumbling.[82] There was, in England, a loud protest over the cession of Heligoland without the full consent of the inhabitants,[83] and severe criticism in that country came from the Cape-to-Cairo enthusiasts.

. . . I think [said Lord Salisbury], there has been only one strong criticism adverse to that agreement. It has arisen from a very curious idea which has become prevalent in this country, that there is some special advantage in handing a stretch of territory extending all the way from Cape Town to the sources of the Nile.[84]

And again in a dispatch from Sir P. Anderson to Sir E. Malet, Berlin, June 28, 1890:

The delimitation of the spheres may not correspond with the desire which has been expressed in some quarters that an uninterrupted British sphere should extend through Central Africa, but it must be remembered that the realization of this idea was already impracticable when the negotiations commenced; Germany and the Congo State being riverains throughout the large territory comprised in the eastern and western shores of Lake Tanganyika.[85]

Protests of the Cape-to-Cairo group demonstrate clearly how quickly and deeply the idea had taken root in the minds of Englishmen.   The treaty, lamented one M. P.

will be the perpetuation in Africa of the separation between the British sphere of influence in the North and the British sphere of influence in the South.   It will be impossible to get from Lake Tanganyika to the Victoria Nyanza without passing through German territory.[86]

Conybeare believed that

We ought to have insisted at all hazards on the retention of the right of way—not an imaginary easement between Lake Tanganyika and the Victoria Nyanza. . . . Those who look beyond the immediate present, and take a fair view of the future, know that one of these days a trunk line of railway must be constructed north and south, and by the limitations involved in the acceptance of the Hinterland Doctrine laid down by the German Government, and allowing them to push their territory from the coast to the boundary of the Congo territory, our Government have cut off this country from all right to lay down such a means of communication to connect our territory on the Zambesi with that north of the German sphere of influence.   This is a fatal blot in the agreement, however beneficial it might be in other respects.[87]

This criticism, although strong, was not, however, the predominant note in Parliament.   That is perhaps voiced better by the optimism of another M. P. who summarized the general satisfaction with the treaty:

From the coast we have a stretch of country extending 500 miles inland to the lake region at the head of the waters of the Nile; and geographically this is one of the most important positions in all Africa.   In that region we have got a range of snow-clad mountains and a country fit for habitations by Europeans . . . Besides all this, we have kept Germany out of two places within that region, where German influence would have been very inconvenient to us—namely Uganda and Witu. This alone is worth the cession of many islands like Heligoland.

The Anglo-German agreement, he estimated, added 1,000,-000 square miles to the British Empire.[88]

Lord Salisbury seems to have been well pleased with the bargain. He told the Queen:

Under this arrangement the whole of the country outside the confines of Abyssinia and Gallaland will be under British influence up to Khan, so far as any European competition is concerned. On the other hand, we could not without this arrangement come to a favourable agreement as to the Stevenson road, and any indefinite postponement of a settlement in Africa would render it very difficult to maintain terms of amity with Germany, and would force us to change our system of alliance in Europe. The alliance of France instead of the alliance of Germany must necessarily involve the early evacuation of Egypt under very unfavourable conditions.[89]

The Anglo-German Treaty of July 1890 was, however, only a paper delimitation. It was, moreover, the recognition of a British sphere in Uganda and the Nile basin by only one of the Great European Powers. As Salisbury pointed out: " the whole doctrine of paper annexation," was " in a very fluid condition." [90] A paper annexation must be followed up by effective occupation and the recognition of its validity by more than one Great Power. To obtain a really secure foothold in Uganda and the Nile Valley was the program before the English people for the next nine years.

France, for example, never gave a formal adherence to the treaty. The French Government, in fact, at first, protested against the recognition of a British protectorate over the possessions of the Sultan of Zanzibar. This clause,

France declared, violated a declaration of 1862 by which France and Great Britain agreed to respect the independence of the sultans of Muscat and Zanzibar.[91] To be sure, France withdrew its protest after H. M. Government offered to recognize a French protectorate over Madagascar and further to compensate the French by concessions in West Africa.[92] Nevertheless, the French Government, afterwards claimed, that the withdrawal of its objection to the Zanzibar section did not signify approval of the rest of the treaty. In fact, the French, Hanotaux declared, in 1895, never acknowledged the delimitation of the spheres of influence as set forth in the treaty.[93] Under international law, a convention binds only its signatories and is not binding upon a third party. There was, therefore, no legal hindrance to a French advance into the territory recognized by Germany as a British sphere of influence.[94]

The British had the problem, therefore, of " implementing " the treaty of 1890. They tried to strengthen their claims both by obtaining the sanction of other European Powers to their operations in the new sphere and also by gradually occupying the country and establishing an effective control over the immense area from German East Africa to Egypt. This was not consciously a Cape-to-Cairo movement but the history of this spread of British influence falls properly into this book because out of it grew the establishment of British hegemony along the south to north route from Egypt to the lake district.

CHAPTER XIII

Uganda, the Key to Africa

THE British directed their efforts first to the occupation of British East Africa and to the development of Uganda. Liberal and Conservative administrations applied themselves with equal zeal to this task. The work was carried on largely, as it was in South Africa, by an imperial trading company, the Ibea. In the summer of 1891, the Salisbury Government negotiated with the Company for the construction of a railway from Mombasa to Lake Victoria. The railway, which the Government proposed to subsidize and guarantee, was planned with the purpose distinctly in mind of opening up the interior and of facilitating the work of the Company in Uganda.[1] It was, in fact, called the " Uganda Railway," although it was not to go any farther than the lake, i. e., from Mombasa to Lake Victoria.

Furthermore, H. M. Government in 1890 assumed special obligations to suppress the slave trade in the interior. Through Great Britain's own initiative coupled with that of Germany, another international conference met at Brussels in 1890 to consult upon the best methods of putting an end to the slave trade in Africa. The conference recommended:

(1) Progressive organization of the administrative, judicial, religious, and military services in the African territories placed under the sovereignty or protectorate of civilized nations.
(2) The gradual establishment in the interior, by the responsible Power in each territory, of strongly occupied stations.
(3) The construction of roads and particularly of railways connecting the advanced stations with the coast, . . . to substitute

economical and speedy means of transport for the present means of portage by men.

(4) The Powers exercising sovereignty or protectorate in Africa, in order to confirm and to give greater precision to their former declarations, undertake to proceed gradually, as circumstances permit, either by the means above indicated, or by any other means, which they may consider suitable, with the repression of the Slave Trade; each State in its respective Possessions and under its own direction . . .

To fulfill these objectives, the engagements of the Powers might be delegated to Chartered Companies but the Powers remained responsible.[2]

According to a broad interpretation of these principles, Great Britain was responsible for carrying out these measures in the new sphere of influence. To be sure, the words " sphere of influence " were not used but a loose interpretation of the expression " the African territories placed under the sovereignty or protectorate of civilized nations " [3] might be stretched to include spheres of influence.[4] Germany was certainly doing its part in East Africa to the south by commencing railways and developing the country under its responsibility. The British, who prided themselves on their traditional war against the slave trade, must not fall behind. The program suggested by the Brussels Conference furnished another incentive for the British effort to penetrate into the interior as far as the inner borders of Uganda. Uganda, indeed, might easily become a stronghold for the Arab slave dealers.[5]

Furthermore, the Ibea Company, said Joseph Chamberlain, was given certain powers by its charter. " Not only was the company entrusted with discretion, but distinct and definite pressure was put upon it to go forward and to prevent other countries from coming in and taking possession of territories which were within the sphere of British influence." [6]

In the meantime, the Company had been busy negotiating treaties with the natives in East Africa and bringing the whole country from the coast to Uganda under their control. In 1890, they stepped into Uganda itself. Uganda was at this time in a parlous state. It was torn by quarrels between various religious factions: the Mohammedans, the Roman Catholic and Protestant missionaries. Behind these factions, political parties were developing which seriously threatened the independence of the kingdom. The Christians united for a time to drive out the Mohammedans. Then, when the Mohammedan danger was seemingly past, in 1889, considerable friction grew up between the White Fathers and the Protestant missionaries. The Roman Catholic party or the " Wa-Franzas " looked first to their parent country, France, for aid. They, at one time, even persuaded the native king, Mwanga, to accept a French protectorate.[7] This was France's golden opportunity to step in and to secure a foothold in the country which commanded the source of the White Nile. Fortunately for British interests, the French, were, at this time, too preoccupied with internal politics to realize the importance of their interest in this remote territory in the heart of Africa. Although a few years later, they were awake and engaged in keen competition with the British for access to the Upper Nile, they now let the opportunity slip through their fingers and turned a deaf ear to the appeal of Cardinal Lavigerie.[8]

The policy next adopted by the White Fathers was to invite to Uganda " traders of all nationalities on the same terms and to cede political influence to no European nation." They wanted the neutralization of Uganda and Cardinal Lavigerie even tried to obtain from the international Brussels Conference a formal declaration placing Uganda as a neutral territory outside the spheres of the European Powers. Failing this, rumor had it that the White Fathers, some of whom were Germans, were inclined to favor German trade.[9]

The " Wa-Englesa " or Protestant party steadily favored English support. The missionaries, especially Mackay, considered themselves as representatives of British interests and spread propaganda for their country's supremacy.[10]

The native king, Mwanga, was swayed first one way and then the other by the various factions. On June 15, 1889, for example, he dispatched a messenger to Jackson, an agent of the Ibea Company, then exploring the interior in the direction of the lake region. Mwanga asked for Jackson's help against the Mohammedans. Jackson, at first declined to go, but upon a second letter from Mwanga, received December 7, he decided to accept Mwanga's invitation. Nevertheless, when he arrived, he found as noted before, that Karl Peters had forestalled him.[11] Mwanga, influenced now by Père Lourdel and the French party had been persuaded to sign a treaty with Peters. Mwanga, however, agreed to send envoys to the coast to inquire to which European Power Uganda was to be assigned.[12]

The Peters mission took place just at the time Emin Pasha was dispatched on his imperialistic mission into the interior.[13] It was high time that H. M. Government hastened to secure the British position in Uganda. Public opinion in Great Britain called for prompt and energetic action.[14] The Government turned to the Imperial British East Africa Company at this juncture. Her Majesty's Government very clearly intimated that they looked to the Company to assert and maintain British rights in Africa, which were represented to depend on effective occupation.[15] " Public feeling in this country," one M. P. testified, " almost denounced us for our inactivity. Was Uganda to be left to other nations or to perpetual slavery? Were the missionaries to be sacrificed? ' Certainly not,' we said, and we echoed the voice of Great Britain and we sent Captain Lugard." [16]

The Ibea Company, patriotically but not wholly unselfishly, responded by sending an expedition under Captain Lugard to make a treaty for the Company in pursuance of the Anglo-German agreement which had just been concluded, and to place Uganda under the Company's protection. Lugard was already dreaming "that British Central and British East Africa might be the embryo empires of an epoch already dawning—empires which in the zenith of their growth and development [might] rival those mighty dependencies which are now the pride of the Anglo-Saxon race." [17]

Fortunately for the British, the Anglo-German agreement had been concluded and Lugard carried a copy of it with him. Thanks to that agreement, his way was made easier. Emin Pasha, indeed, was at Bukoba, on the southern frontier of Uganda. It would have been easy, Lugard pointed out, for the Germans to have stepped in and gained a footing and a treaty, while prior British efforts would have been nullified, and resulted only in collapse and failure. No sooner, however, was the agreement received than Emin Pasha offered his assistance and cooperation to Lugard. [18]

Lugard fulfilled his mission with complete thoroughness. Before he left for home in June, 1892, he brought all Uganda, by actual conquest, under the authority of the Ibea Company. He came back with a treaty signed by Mwanga acknowledging the suzerainty of the Company and that Uganda was within the British sphere of influence. Mwanga promised "to fly the flag of the Company and no other " at his capitol and to grant no concession to or allow any Europeans to settle in his country without the consent of the Company's resident in Uganda. [19]

In sending the expedition to Uganda, however, the Ibea Company had exceeded its own financial capacity. As early as December 1891, Lugard received word that the Company would have to temporarily withdraw from the territory. H. M. Government came to the rescue, however, and offered a grant-in-aid for a survey of the railway between Mombasa and Lake Victoria.[20]   The construction of the railway would greatly promote the development of Uganda and enable the Company to carry on its work there.   In fact, a railway was essential to a permanent occupation, as Salisbury recognized.[21]

To be sure, the Ibea Company did not obtain all that they wished for from the Government.   They wanted a Government subsidy for the construction of the railway but the Treasury refused to allow anything more than a grant-in-aid for the survey.   Nevertheless, the Government signified thereby its willingness to cooperate to some practical extent.

Furthermore, friends of the Protestant missionaries, alarmed for the safety of the Uganda missions, offered to finance the Company's occupation for another year. The Ibea agreed to postpone withdrawal until December 31, 1892.[22] Lord Salisbury expressed satisfaction with the liberal contributions which had been made to the Company but expressed no opinion whatsoever as to its determination to retire at the end of the year.   Perhaps, this failure to outline a future policy, was due to the fact that the Salisbury administration was on the edge of withdrawing and did not wish to tie the hands of the incoming ministry.

When the new Liberal Cabinet with Gladstone at its head came into power, the question of what would happen to Uganda, when the company would retire, was in an acute stage.   The Liberal Party had traditional leanings towards the principles of " the Little Englanders."   Gladstone, himself, was opposed to adding to Great Britain's responsibilities. In his own words:

Those dreadful missionaries, Mr. Rhodes, [he said] are dragging us into all sorts of new complications I don't like. I don't find fault with *you*; you give us no trouble, but to this extension in Uganda I am opposed.[23]

The Liberal Party did not, however, have complete unanimity among its own members. In fact, a very large wing of the party were in favor of a British " forward policy " in Africa. There was only a small but vociferous group of radical die-hards who still loudly bewailed England's march through the Dark Continent, and who dubbed the new imperialists " Jingoes." [24] Furthermore, Gladstone had appointed Rosebery as Secretary of State for Foreign Affairs. Rosebery believed stoutly in " the continuity of British foreign policy." [25] He was also intensely interested in Uganda. He called it " the key to Central Africa." He maintained that it also commanded the Nile basin. It was, finally, a field lately of heroic enterprise and a land that had been watered by the blood of saints and martyrs. " I for one," he said, " as a Scotchman can never be indifferent to a land which witnessed the heroic exploits of Alexander Mackay, that Christian Bayard, whose reputation will always be dear, not only to his own immediate country, but throughout the Empire at large." [26]

Rosebery was also a great friend of Cecil Rhodes and Rhodes was girding himself for the battle for this second key position on his road north from Cape Town to Alexandria.

The web of British interests in Uganda was growing stronger. There were the missionaries who were asking for British protection. They claimed that there would be a general massacre if Uganda were evacuated.[27] Before the Ibea Company came, the missionaries had managed to survive without the protection of H. M. Government but after the Company came in, conditions changed. The Ibea had definitely taken the part of the " Wa-Englesa." After the commotion and bitter feelings aroused by Lugard's conquest of Uganda, the missionaries could never survive the savage civil war which would ensue if the Company retired and Great Britain refused her protection. Great Britain by enrouraging the Ibea to enter Uganda had incurred thereby greater responsibilities than heretofore for the lives of the missionaries.[28]

In the second place, Lugard had concluded fresh treaties on behalf of British interests and had proclaimed that the territory was under British protection. Great Britain could not, therefore, without loss of honor and prestige, repudiate these contracts.[29]

Moreover, if the British could not maintain peace and order in Uganda and effectively occupy the country, there were other nations ready to step in.[30] The Anglo-German agreement would furnish slender protection in such a case. " However, others may deceive themselves," the member from Cambridge University warned the House, " as to the intentions of Foreign Powers, those who know the situation practically cannot believe that if we quit Uganda—that is, if we give up command of the head waters of the Nile some foreign Power will fail to find some excuse for occupying them." [31]

Retention, indeed, was advocated by both the Conservative Lord Salisbury, and the Liberal Lord Rosebery. The argument for retention, furthermore, was supported by public organizations of various kinds all over England and especially in Scotland; chambers of commerce, dignitaries of the Church of England, moderates of all three churches in Scotland, missionary societies, anti-slavery societies.[32]

Lugard himself toured the country " beating the big drum " for the retention of Uganda.[33] Lord Rosebery

LORD ROSEBERY

Addressing the House of Lords

Reproduced from Coates, F. C., *Life of Lord Rosebery,*
with the permission of E. P. Dutton & Co., Inc.

spoke in and out of Parliament putting pressure on reluctant colleagues to fall in with his scheme, which meant a first step towards the permanent establishment of a great Empire in the Valley of the Nile and up towards Uganda and the Lake District.[34]

Cecil Rhodes did what he could to fasten his important link in the Cape-to-Cairo chain. His founding of the Transcontinental Telegraph Company, at this time, was, as noted before,[35] part of his scheme to save Uganda.[36] He sent a most confidential letter to the Secretary of State for Foreign Affairs.

Understanding [the letter read] that Her Majesty's Government is considering the question of the retention of Uganda under her protection, I think it well to state for their information that I am prepared to extend at once the line of Telegraph from Salisbury, the capital of Mashonaland to Uganda without asking Her Majesty's Government for any contribution.[37]

Rhodes, also, offered to take over Uganda from the financially embarrassed Ibea Company and to run it for £25,000 a year.[38] Both these offers, he presented to Harcourt in a conversation with that harassed Little Englander but Harcourt was horrified.

Rhodes appealed to Gladstone but at first the Prime Minister remained unmoved. There was, however, one person to whom Gladstone would listen and that was his Secretary for Foreign Affairs, Lord Rosebery. Rosebery threatened to resign if Gladstone remained obdurate. Gladstone yielded and consented to a compromise. H. M. Government agreed to prolong the Company's occupation for three months and to send an expedition under Sir Gerald Portal to investigate conditions in the country.[39]

This arrangement seems to have been only a cloak, however, to cover the real purpose of the Government to keep Uganda and to relieve Gladstone of embarrassment. The very character of the Portal mission portended that Great Britain would not abandon the country. Gladstone might argue, elaborately and somewhat pathetically, in the House that the expedition was merely one of inquiry and that the fate of Uganda was not a foregone conclusion. His words were received with laughter by the opposition.[40] Sir Gerald Portal was known to be an advocate of the British retention of Uganda. In a letter to the *Times,* Portal pointed out that " Lugard, Martin, missionaries, natives and everyone who has come from there are unanimous in saying that the withdrawal of the English officers will be the certain signal for a general war and the inevitable massacre of Christians— a massacre such as the world has not seen for centuries." [41] Cecil Rhodes' brother Frank was also sent with Portal.[42] Furthermore, Portal was instructed to investigate the best means of dealing with the country, whether through Zanzibar or otherwise.[43] Moreover, Lugard claimed that complete withdrawal would not make the territory in any sense less a sphere of British influence. On the contrary, the government would them become directly responsible for the sphere.[44]

It was not a question of giving up the sphere of influence that sent Portal out to Africa but just the question of what next was to be done there. Portal was to establish friendly relations with King Mwanga and even if necessary to subsidize him. He was also to acknowledge a letter of June 17 to the Queen from Mwanga pleading for the retention of the Ibea, and to assure him of the interest taken by the British Government in the country.[45]

Portal reported in favor of a British Protectorate. H. M. Government after due consideration of the report determined to accept this recommendation.[46] " That announcement . . . met throughout the country an approval so general that, in spite of some dissentient voices it might fairly be said to have obtained a national ratification." [47] A Liberal Government, thus, with the approval of the country forged one more link in the Cape-to-Cairo chain.

CHAPTER XIV

THE SOUTHWARD MARCH FROM EGYPT

WHILE Cecil Rhodes and fellow empire-builders were painting the map red from Cape Town to the lake region, British influence was also spreading from Egypt into the Sudan.

In 1876, Lord Goschen, special commissioner to investigate financial conditions in Egypt, appointed Sir Evelyn Baring, as British Commissioner of the Public Debt. This appointment was an important step in a series of events leading to the occupation of the country. To be sure, Sir Evelyn received his commission, not from H. M. Government, but from Lord Goschen. In fact, H. M. Government was careful not to assume any responsibility in the matter. The officials were anxious not to interfere in the internal affairs of Egypt. They refused even to make a nomination.[1] Nevertheless, the presence of a British Commissioner of the Public Debt in Egypt was indicative of how deeply rooted British commercial interests were in the country. British bondholders held about £30,000,000 of Egyptian debts. All the Khedive's shares in the Suez Canal were in British hands and English capital was invested heavily in Egyptian Railways. Furthermore, H. M. Government had growing imperial interests in the country. The Suez Canal was a short-cut to India. In time of war or in case of trouble in the Far East, the Suez route might be of vital importance for Great Britain's hold on India. In short, the best security for the right of way to India was occupation of Lower Egypt. While the bondholders, therefore, were clamoring for more effective control over Egyptian finances, the statesmen were demanding greater control over the Suez Canal. Imperial and commercial interests were soon to drag a reluctant government into active interference in Egyptian affairs.[2] In fact, British interests in 1877 were so strong in the Nile country that there was a feeling prevalent both at home and abroad that the occupation of Egypt by England was only a matter of time.[3]

In 1882, the Government finally yielded to the pressure of events. British battleships bombarded Alexandria; British troops landed on Egyptian soil and definitely occupied the country. There is no need here to unravel the tangled story which led up to this occupation but it is well to remember that in the summer of 1882, Egypt was in a chaotic condition which threatened European interests. The reins of government were in the hands of a mutinous Egyptian army whose leaders were hostile to foreigners. There was rioting in Alexandria; some fifty Europeans were killed and among them the British consul. An exodus of Christians had begun and Arabi, the leader of the mutinous army, proposed that the property of all Egyptians leaving the country be confiscated.[4]

H. M. Government felt that conditions were alarming enough to warrant intervention. Before embarking on such a policy, however, the British made serious efforts to enlist the cooperation of other European powers, particularly that of France.

We feel [Gladstone told the House on July 22] that we should not fully discharge our duty if we did not endeavor to convert the present interior state of Egypt from anarchy and conflict to peace and order. We shall look during the time that remains to us to the co-operation of the Powers of civilised Europe, if it be in any case open to us. [But, Mr. Gladstone continued while the Commons cheered], if every chance of obtaining cooperation is exhausted, the work will be undertaken by the single power of England.[5]

The other European powers refused to join with Great Britain. The British, therefore, entered the country alone and commenced the task of reorganization.

The British occupation of Egypt was undoubtedly a popular measure. Parliament voted the money for the venture by a majority of 275 to 19. The English people, however, probably had no conception of the full significance of the step which they had taken. They were in Egypt to restore order. " This was," says Viscount Milner, " not merely our professed but our true and only object." [6] Milner's words ring true. The evidence leads to the conclusion that H. M. Government entered Egypt with reluctance for this definite purpose and that it was anxious to limit rather than extend its responsibilities. It was, however, vital for British interests to establish a stable administration under which the rights of foreigners would be protected, European property and persons would be safe, debts could be collected and the Suez Canal would be brought more closely under British guardianship. The intervention was, in large measure, simply the answer to the insistent demands of the bondholders and the Englishmen interested in the Suez Canal. In general, the practical English people were not pursuing, at this time, a policy so visionary as the establishment of British hegemony from Alexandria to Cape Town.

Nevertheless, the occupation of Egypt was only the first link in a long chain of events which finally ended in the development of a British sphere of influence from Egypt to the Equator almost touching the British sphere in the south. To be sure, one statesman at least, glimpsed this wide portent of the occupation of Egypt but he of all Englishmen was the one least likely to sponsor a Cape-to-Cairo movement. In 1877, Gladstone, the stanch " little Englander," prophesized gloomily:

Our first site in Egypt . . . will be the almost certain egg of a North African Empire, that will grow and grow until another Victoria and another Albert, titles of the Lake-sources of the White Nile, come within our borders; and till we finally join hands across the Equator with Natal and Cape Town, to say nothing of the Transvaal and the Orange River on the South, or of Abyssinia and Zanzibar to be swallowed by way of *viaticum* on our journey.[7]

Not only was Gladstone's prophecy nearly fulfilled during the years 1877 to 1902, but his words, also, aptly describe the character of British expansion from Egypt to the Equator. Like the development of an egg, the movement was, in the main, almost organic in its nature. Each stage seemed to be the logical outgrowth of the previous advance. The British people were apparently led from one objective to the next.

After the entrance of English troops on Egyptian soil, it became more and more difficult to withdraw. In order to bring stability to Egypt, the British reformed the administration root and branch. Legislative, judicial and financial reforms were instituted, new administrative machinery set up, British influence spread throughout the country and the control of Egypt rested actually in British hands.[8]

Behind the Khedive stood the British Agent and Consul General. The function of the Consul General was chiefly to tender advice. Advice, however, was often tantamount to a command. The Consul General in turn was supported by a large group of British officials who, although nominally servants of the Khedive, were actually powerful instruments of British authority throughout the country. The commander-in-chief of the Egyptian army, the Sirdar, was British, as were the Financial Adviser and Financial Secretary. Furthermore, back of the British officials stood the army of occupation, "the outward and visible sign of the predominance of British influence."[9]

In short, Great Britain had established a veiled protectorate over Egypt. H. M. Government, to be sure, refused to acknowledge a protectorate over the country. Nevertheless, in 1895, Sir Edward Grey maintained, " Towards Egypt this country stands in a special position of trust, as regards the maintenance of the interests of Egypt; " [10] and a year later, the Prime Minister, the Marquis of Salisbury, called his countrymen, the " trustees of Egypt." [11]

So firm was the British control over the affairs of Egypt that the Khedive became a mere puppet in British hands. For example, when on March 3, 1896, Kitchener, British Sirdar, received an official telegram announcing the decision of H. M. Government to send a force into the Sudan, he proceeded to consult Lord Cromer, British Consul General, on the necessary measures to be taken. Together they worked at high pressure for several hours mobilizing the Egyptian army before they remembered that they had not yet observed the formality of informing the Khedive. " Surely," writes Arthur in his *Life of Lord Kitchener* " in no land but the land of Paradox could British Officials have calmly disposed of the resources of the army without the sanction or even cognizance of the ruler." [12]

Whether as " trustees " or " protectors," the British assumed a certain guardianship over Egyptian affairs and interests when they entered the country in 1882. At first, the Government desired to limit its responsibilities. It was too much occupied with building up the internal administration of the country to care to look beyond the confines of Egypt proper. Nevertheless, as masters of Egypt, the English people could not entirely shake off responsibility for the Egyptian hinterland to the south. Almost, in spite of themselves, they were brought face to face with serious conditions in the Sudan.[13]

Egypt possessed a loose but extensive empire in the Sudan, from Wadi Halfa on the north to the frontier of Unyoro on the south and from the western boundary of Kordofan to Ethiopia on the east. The existence of this empire, in 1883, was seriously threatened by hordes of fanatical Dervishes under a religious leader, Mohammed Ahmed, the supposed Mahdi or Saviour of the Sudan.

Far from indulging in any chimerical dreams of extending British influence from Cairo to the Cape, H. M. Government was inclined to disclaim all responsibility for this region infested by Mahdi hordes. In fact, Lord Granville refused to have anything to say in regard to Sudanese affairs. When General Hicks, at the head of an ill-fated Egyptian force, was commissioned by the Egyptian Government to march into Kordofan, he telegraphed: " Her Majesty's Government are in no way responsible for the operations in the Soudan, which have been undertaken under the authority of the Egyptian Government, or for the appointment or actions of General Hicks." [14] Again, Granville informed General Hicks that it was " the policy of Her Majesty's Government . . . to abstain as much as possible from interference with the action of the Egyptian Government in the Soudan." [15] Nevertheless, the British Government did not absolutely forbid the Hicks expedition. It could not divest itself, therefore, of all responsibility for the complete disaster which followed. As Cromer points out, the British were in military occupation of Egypt. They were the temporary masters of the country and the civilized world fixed on England a certain responsibility for the actions of the Egyptian government. Mere disclaimers could not relieve the Home Government of this responsibility. [16]

The Egyptian treasury was exhausted. The Egyptian army was unpaid and undisciplined, " worthless as a fighting machine ". It was madness to attempt an aggressive campaign against the Mahdi at this time. Even under more auspicious circumstances, however, the anti-imperialistic administration of Gladstone, then in power, would probably have been reluctant to intervene in the Sudan.[17]

After the Hicks disaster, the British embarked on a definite policy of withdrawal from the Sudan. In December of 1883, H. M. Government recommended the ministers of the Khedive to abandon " all territory south of Assouan, or, at least, of Wadi Halfa." [18] At the same time, the British asserted that they were prepared to maintain order in Egypt proper and to defend the Red Sea ports. The real purposes of the British Government are clearly revealed in the adoption of this line of action. The policy was the same as that which first brought British troops into Egypt, i. e., the maintenance of security and order in Egypt and the defense of Britain's short route to India. The people were not interested as yet in Egypt's hinterland and the great transcontinental route to the south.

The British Government, in fact, insisted on the adoption of the policy of withdrawal from the Sudan in spite of considerable opposition from the Egyptian ministers. The Khedive, however, was forced to yield, the Chéref Pasha ministry resigned and the Khedive " accepted cordially the policy of abandoning the whole of the Soudan." [19]

The next step which H. M. Government took in carrying out its policy of withdrawal was to dispatch Colonel Charles Gordon, Ex-Governor General of the Sudan, whose work has already been mentioned in a previous chapter,[20]

to report . . . on the military situation in the Soudan, and on the measures which it may be advisable to take for the security of the Egyptian garrisons still holding positions in that country, and for the safety of the European population in Khartoum. [He was also instructed] to consider and report upon the best mode of effecting the evacuation of the interior of the Soudan,

and upon the manner in which the safety and the good administration by the Egyptian Government of the ports on the seacoast can best be secured . . . [and] to perform, such other
duties as the Egyptian Government [might desire to intrust
to him].[21]

The choice of General Gordon for this delicate mission
had a significant bearing on the course of future events.
By his previous experience as Governor-General of the
Sudan, he was supposedly well qualified to shoulder his new
responsibilities. Furthermore, the selection was immensely
popular. The tales of his past exploits, his heroism and
unimpeachable integrity of character caught the imagination
of his fellow countrymen. In short, Gordon's great popularity played a decided part in the subsequent development
of events in the Sudan.[22]

There is no need here to go into the controversy as to
how Gordon carried out his mission. He was apparently
more interested in establishing some form of government
and in " smashing the Mahdi " than in evacuating the country. Furthermore, evacuation, he believed, should not mean
abandonment. " Any solution was better than allowing the
country to fall into the hands of the Mahdi." In any event,
the Sudan must not be left to anarchy and chaos. The
British Government must not scuttle out of the country
without some provision for the future.[23]

H. M. Government, however, was intent on complete
evacuation within as short a time as possible. It was, furthermore, exceedingly reluctant to send troops into the
country.[24] The rest of the story is well-known. Conditions went from bad to worse as far as the Gordon expedition was concerned. The Mahdi surrounded the ill-fated
General at Khartoum. There was no longer a question of
establishing a stable government in the Sudan : the vital
question was how best to relieve the beleagured commander.

H. M. Government, finally, consented to the dispatch of an expedition. The expedition was for the relief of the general and H. M. Government was careful to limit its sphere of military operations as much as possible. In fact, Lord Wolseley was instructed " not to advance any farther southwards than is absolutely necessary to attain the primary object of the expedition." [25]

The relief expedition was, as everyone knows, sent too late. Gordon was killed before the troops reached Khartoum. The death of Gordon aroused great indignation at home. " A wave of Gordon *cultus* passed over England in 1884." [26]   At the end of 1884 the nation was intent on one subject, and on one subject only, the position of Gordon at Khartoum. " His imprisonment in Khartoum was the anxiety of a nation." His death raised him to the rank of a national martyr.[27]   Khartoum rankled in the hearts of the English people. Both the nation and the army were smarting under a sense of failure.[28]

The first reaction to the news of Gordon's death was a determination to carry on his work, to " smash the Mahdi " and to avenge his death. H. M. Government ordered Wolseley to overthrow the power of the Mahdi at Khartoum. An immediate advance on the city, however, was impractical at the time and Lord Wolseley determined to capture Berber and Abu Hamed. The campaign had already begun when the policy of the British Government veered completely in the opposite direction, back to the former determination to abandon the Sudan. The Russians were advancing towards the Indian frontier and the services of the army were required on this front. Great Britain ordered a retreat to Wadi Halfa.[29]

The desire to wipe out the disgrace of the Gordon fiasco, however, continued to smoulder in the hearts of the English people. In fact, this blow to British pride and prestige contributed to the development of a new and more aggressive spirit. Great Britain did not remain long behind the Wadi Halfa frontier to which the Egyptian troops were withdrawn in 1885. As early as 1891, there were unmistakable signs of an awaking interest in the Sudan; an interest which was eventually to lead to the reconquest of the country, 1896-1898.

The memory of Gordon, although an important factor in this change of mood, was only one of various influences. In the first place, England was in a far better position in 1896 to contemplate aggressive action in the Sudan than in 1885. Two conditions, Cromer points out, were essential before Egypt could undertake a reconquest. One was an efficient army and the other sound finances. The British Sirdars were rapidly transforming the disorganized Egyptian army of 1884 into a well ordered fighting machine. In 1884, General Baker's Egyptian troops threw down their arms and fled before a small force at Suakin. In 1887, however, the tide began to turn. Egyptian troops defeated the Dervish forces at Ginness near Suakin in a " brilliant skirmish." In December 1888, the Egyptian soldiers inflicted a far more serious defeat upon the enemy in the neighborhood of Suakin. In 1889, Egyptian troops under Colonel Wodehouse prevented a formidable invasion at Toski near Wadi Halfa. The Dervish forces must henceforth respect the fighting ability of the Egyptian Fellah. The Egyptian soldiers no longer fled in panic before the enemy. " The engagements which took place in 1888-89," writes Cromer, " in the neighbourhood of Suakin and in the Nile Valley, showed that some confidence could be placed in the Egyptian army." [30]

The financial condition of the country was also improving. In 1883, the Treasury was exhausted. The British administrators were engaged in a long, hard struggle against bankruptcy. Egyptian resources were wholly inadequate to meet the needs of aggressive action in the Sudan. By 1888, however, the battle was almost over. Financial equilibrium was assured and the Egyptian treasury was even in possession of a surplus. For the first time in years, Egypt had sufficient resources to embark on new ventures.[31]

There were, furthermore, powerful motives for Egyptian reconquest of the Sudan. The defeats suffered by Egyptian troops in past years called for revenge. Then there was the argument that Egypt was never secure from invasion unless the hinterland to the south was at peace.[32] Already, the Dervishes had attempted one invasion of Egypt proper. In 1896 there were rumors of " a contemplated advance by the Dervish troops in large numbers into Upper Egypt." [33] As early as 1891 there was a military party at Cairo which clamored that it was " indispensable for the safety of Egypt that the frontier of Egypt should not be, as Her Majesty's Government promised in 1888 it should be, namely at Wady Halfa, but at Khartoum." [34]

Moreover, the Nile Valley and the Eastern Sudan were fertile and attractive regions for the development of trade. The district around Tokar (near the Red Sea) was a rich granary. It also was a cotton-producing area and before 1883, it furnished about 175,000 cwt. annually of cotton of the finest staple, superior to that of Egypt proper.[35] Furthermore, it was the key to trade with the Sudan. The ambitious English businessman felt that it was a burning shame to let this promising district be exposed to the ravages of the Dervishes.[36] The raids of Osman Digna and the stoppage of trade were doing great damage to Lancashire and Manchester trade.[37]

South of Egypt, in 1887, General Grenfell and Sir Hollis Smith advanced to a station in the Sudan called Boshee, for purposes of trade, but later the trade was closed and the

British force withdrawn.[38]   In Dongola, lay another great granary and through Dongola, passed another important trade route.[39]   It has already been noted how British commercial men were becoming interested in the Upper-Sudan, still farther south in connection with the Emin Pasha rescue.[40]

Another reason for British interest particularly in the Eastern Sudan was that the rule of the Dervishes in this region gave a stimulus to the slave trade.   The British cruisers on the Red Sea could not stop the traffic.   The best remedy for this evil appeared to be the occupation of Tokar. If Tokar were occupied, Osman Digna, leader of the Dervishes, could no longer obtain supplies and would be forced to leave the Eastern Sudan.[41]

Accordingly, the Egyptian troops occupied Tokar in 1891 and thereby cleared the Eastern Sudan of the Dervish hordes.   The British argued, at first, that the occupation of Tokar and the region near Suakin was not a departure from their former policy.   H. M. Government were careful to state that no advance would be made from this position into the interior.[42]   To be sure, as stated before, the British, when in 1883 and 1884 they decided to evacuate the Sudan, " bound themselves to protect the Egyptian Government in Egypt and also in the ports of the Red Sea." [43]   The British claimed that they were occupying Tokar to strengthen Suakin, a Red Sea port and to check the slave trade.   There was " no newly annexed territory to be defined on a map." Incidentally, however, Tokar was a district which is peculiarly calculated to revive trade and industry in the Eastern Sudan.   In fact, it was considered " the open door of the Soudan " to British trade.[44]

While Egyptian troops under British leadership were occupying Tokar and establishing an Egyptian civil and military government there, British officials at home were refurbishing old claims to the Sudan. "In the opinion of Her Majesty's Government," Sir John Ferguson, Secretary of State for Foreign Affairs, told the House, March 2, 1891, "the withdrawal of the Egyptian troops from the Soudan did not constitute an abandonment of the sovereignty of that region."[45] It was a little difficult, to be sure, to reconcile this point of view with the Khedive's statement in 1884 that he "accepted cordially the policy of *abandoning the whole of the Sudan*."[46] Also the theory that Egypt still maintained sovereign rights in the Sudan was hardly consistent with Granville's reply to Gordon's proposal in April, 1884 that Turkish troops be sent into the region. In that reply, Granville insisted that "such a course would involve a reversal of the original policy of Her Majesty's Government, which *was to detach the Soudan from Egypt, and restore to its inhabitants their former independence*."[47]

Sir John Ferguson evidently sensed the inconsistency of his theory. A few days later, March 5, he presented a new argument. The rights of sovereignty, he insisted, belonged to the Sultan, not the Khedive. The Sultan of Turkey had never abandoned his rights over the Sudan. Indeed, in 1885, the Turkish ambassador made a formal statement to that effect to the British Foreign Secretary. The Turkish ambassador, furthermore "pointed out to Her Majesty's Government that . . . neither the Sultan nor the Khedive, his great feudatory, had ever abandoned his right to the Soudan. Consequently he [the Khedive] is entirely within his rights in re-occupying that portion of the Sudan, [i. e. Tokar]".[48]

These labored arguments about the Khedive's and Sultan's rights and the establishment of an Egyptian civil and military government at Tokar all lent color to the current belief that Great Britain was taking the first step towards a reconquest of the Sudan. The Secretary of State for Foreign

Affairs protested that the troops proceeded to Tokar on the " distinct assurance that there was no intention to proceed further." Nevertheless, the *Times* published a telegram from Cairo which regarded the capture of Tokar " as a first step towards the occupation of the Soudan." [49]

The Egyptian Government [said Labouchere, an anti-imperialist leader in the House], are rejoicing because they see the possibility of going to Berber and laying hold of the Soudan again . . . financiers and pashas interested. . . . They think that if they can induce us to assent to the Egyptians laying hold of the Soudan, they can inaugurate a frontier war, that they can push on to Berber and Khartoum, . . . [50]

Another Little Englander warned the House gloomily:

You will have to go on, step by step, into the interior of the country, ever advancing to put down the resisting Dervishes until, in the end, you will be again obliged to occupy equatorial Africa. This is what those in Cairo want.[51]

In the occupation of the district around Suakin, in the reviving interest in the Sudan, can be traced the beginning of a new period of expansion. The movement southwards was destined " to grow and grow," as Gladstone had prophesied until Britishers not only pushed on to Berber and Khartoum but up the Nile, through Central Africa until they almost touched the British sphere in the South.

CHAPTER XV

Guarding the Nile Valley

THE close connection between Egypt and its hinterland to the south has already been noted in the previous chapter. As members of Parliament were fond of repeating, " the Nile was Egypt and Egypt was the Nile." It is true that the fertile country below Wadi Halfa was dependent upon the Nile River not only for its prosperity but for its very existence. Any tampering with the sources of that great life-giving river, therefore, was a matter of grave concern to the guardians of Egypt. Furthermore, the Nile Valley offered the main avenue of approach to invaders from the south. The Masters of the Upper Sudan, therefore, held a strategic position from which they could threaten all Egypt.[1]

The chief danger to Anglo-Egyptian interests before 1890 was, as already noted, an invasion of Mahdist forces from the south. The Mahdists, however, held a strategic position the advantages of which they were too ignorant to utilize. The situation would be more alarming with a European Power ensconced in the Sudan.

A civilised nation [Sir Colin Scott Moncrieff [2] pointed out], would surely build regulating sluices across the outlet of the Victoria Nyanza and control that great sea as Manchester controls Thirlmere. This would be an easy operation. Once done, the Nile supply would be in their hands, and if poor little Egypt had the bad luck to be at war with this people in the upper waters, they might flood Egypt or cut off the water supply at their pleasure.[3]

294

It was undoubtedly better, British imperialists argued in the era of the scramble for Africa, for the safety and prosperity of Egypt to have the administration of that country and the whole length of the Nile waterway under one-unified control.[4]

Furthermore, if it was of vital importance to Egypt to hold the Nile along its entire length, it was of some significance also to hold the approaches to that river. As early as the seventies, it will be recalled, Gordon pointed out that Mombasa on the east coast of Africa was the best entrance of approach to the Upper Nile Valley.[5] In the Anglo-German controversy over Witu, as already seen, the German claims to the east coast near Witu actually threatened Anglo-Egyptian interests in the Sudan because of the " hinterland doctrine." Germany, by a firm insistence upon this doctrine, might gain exclusive control of the Nile valley and the line of access to it from the east coast.[6] Thus, the destinies of East and Central Africa were tangled also in the web of Anglo-Egyptian interests.

The story of British expansion from Egypt to the great lakes is, in some measure, therefore, simply a logical outgrowth of the occupation of Egypt. The defense of this country led to the adoption of an aggressive policy in the Sudan: the protection of the Nile, Egypt's source of life. This policy, in turn, developed into that of protecting the approaches to the Nile Valley. Thus, Great Britain was brought step by step from Egypt into the Sudan and from there into East and Central Africa. It might almost be said that, when they once determined to hold the country of the Lower Nile, the very nature of the land drew Britishers irresistibly southwards from one advance to the next.

There was, however, as mentioned in the previous chapter, a marked difference in the character of the British advance into Equatorial Africa after 1890.[7] Previous to this date, the Government was impelled, almost against its will, to interfere in the Sudan. It was dragged reluctantly down below the frontier of Egypt proper. After 1890, a new and more adventurous spirit was prevalent among politicians and statesmen. A wave of imperialism swept over the country. This spirit has been met in the foregoing pages in the story of the occupation of Rhodesia and in the efforts of the Imperial British East Africa Company to push into the central lake region. There were already huge spheres of British influence developing in the south and east. It was, perhaps, only natural that a few aggressive leaders of this time should think of bridging the gaps and of building a continuous empire from " the Cape to Cairo." The imperialistic dreams, for example, of Sir Harry Johnston, of Rhodes and of Lugard will be recalled.[8]

In Parliament, Labouchere, ardent anti-imperialist, was fighting, as early as 1890, " the Jingo dream " of a great empire stretching from Alexandria in the north down to Simons Bay in the south.[9] In 1894, Sir E. Ashmead-Bartlett, a stanch imperialist, pointed out that:

At this moment in the North of Africa British influence, British administration, and British civilisation were predominant in Egypt. In the South likewise the influence of the British power was extending rapidly northwards. Already it reached from Cape Town to the Zambesi. Comparatively small districts intervened between the regions in the north and in the south which already were under British power and civilisation. . . . We might very soon learn with pride that the whole vast region from Alexandria to Cape Town was under British hegemony.[10]

The foregoing chapters have shown how the Conservative and Liberal leaders of this period were distinctly influenced by this spirit of imperialism. In particular, Lord Rosebery was an exponent of the Cape-to-Cairo idea. He was, it will be recalled, Foreign Secretary under Gladstone from August 1892 to February 1894 and Prime Minister, from February 1894 to June 1895. He was a friend of Cecil Rhodes and was regarded by Rhodes " as the English statesman most in harmony with his general outlook." [11] It may be well to remember, also, that Lord Rosebery was Baron de Rothschild's son-in-law and that the house of Rothschild was substantially interested in the country both in the north and south along the Cape to Cairo route.[12]

On the other hand, Lord Salisbury, Prime Minister from August 1886 to August 1892 and again from June 1895 to July 1902, was, as noticed, not in sympathy with the South African Empire builder. In fact, it was during his second administration in the period from 1887 to 1890 that Germany successfully asserted claims to territory which stretched from the Indian Ocean to the Congo State and thus blocked the British road to the North. Indeed, he spoke with scorn of Cape-to-Cairo dreams. Nevertheless, even if he was not an ardent supporter of Rhodes' schemes, he worked steadily and effectively in a practical way to establish British control over vast stretches of Africa.[13] Furthermore, the British nation stood behind a vigorous " forward policy " in the north as well as in the south. Each advance of H. M. Government into the heart of Africa met with ready support in the House.[14]

The chief stimulus which roused popular enthusiasm for British expansion in Africa was the sharp competition between England and European neighbors for a controlling influence in the continent, especially in the Sudan. By the late eighties, a race had set in for the Upper Sudan. In a previous chapter, German colonial aspirations in Uganda and the Equatorial Provinces have been discussed in some detail. German rivalry with the British in this region, however, ceased with the Anglo-German treaty of 1890. Germany by this treaty, it will be recalled, recognized the Nile Valley as a British sphere of influence.[15] There were other dangers, however, looming upon the horizon in the south.

King Leopold, for example, had long cherished dreams of obtaining control of the headwaters of the Nile. As the Southern provinces fell from Egypt's grasp because of the Mahdist ravages, he hoped that they would drop into his hands.[16] He discussed the idea with Gordon at Brussels, in January 1884, when Gordon was just setting out on his ill-fated journey to evacuate the Egyptian garrisons. In fact, he almost succeeded in enlisting Gordon's services. The General contemplated at one time retiring to the South and placing the Bahr-el-Ghazal and Equatoria under the protection of the Congo Association but was discouraged by the British Government.[17] Again in 1887, when Stanley set out to rescue Emin Pasha, King Leopold offered him assistance if he went through the Congo State.[18] As already noted, Stanley carried with him a secret offer from the King to make Emin Pasha " administrator of the country for him " with the rank of General, an offer which the independent Pasha refused.[19]

Leopold was not discouraged by the failure of these two attempts. He determined to realize his ambition through the efforts of his own people. Belgian explorers pushed beyond the fourth parallel of north latitude from the Congo into the Upper Sudan and planted a series of stations in the valley of the M'Bomo and in 1893, they reached Liffi, not far from Demi-Zibur in the province of Bahr-el-Ghazal. Thence they penetrated as far north as the frontier of Darfur. They directed their efforts also towards the Upper Nile. In 1891, an expedition led by Van Kerchoven, left Stanley Pool and travelling by way of the Welle arrived in Equatoria, then pushed north establishing stations at Dufile and Lado on the Nile.[20]

Leopold, however, foresaw trouble with England if he advanced into the western watershed of the Nile. In fact, the strip between the eastern boundary of the Congo State, (i. e. East longitude 30° and Lake Victoria), was claimed by the Imperial British East Africa Company. Stanley, as already noted, on his expedition to rescue Emin Pasha, made treaties with the natives in this region and then on his return, handed the country over to the East Africa Company which had largely supported the relief expedition.[21]

Early in 1890, Stanley presented a solution to King Leopold. He suggested that the eastern limit of the Congo State should " be the centre of the Albert Edward Nyanza and the course of the Semliki River "[22] instead of 30° E. longitude as previously recognized. He believed that an exchange of territories could be effected in this section which would be advantageous to both the company and the Congo. His Majesty was pleased with the idea. In the spring of 1894, Leopold came over to London where he talked with Lord Salisbury and the principal directors of the British East African Company. On May 24, 1890, Leopold entered into an agreement with the company which followed Stanley's ideas.[23]

The agreement of 1890 is of peculiar significance because it foreshadowed to some extent, the Anglo-Congolese Convention of 1894, and because it embodied the Cape-to-Cairo idea of a route under British control from one end of the continent to the other. The boundaries between the Congo State and the sphere of operations of the British East Africa Company were agreed to be the Albert, and (Albert) Edward lakes and the course of the river Semliki from the center of the southern shore of the (Albert) Edward to the northern head of Lake Tanganyika. The words of the agreement, as given by Stanley in his *Autobiography* are not precise but apparently, the agreement provided for the reser-

vation of a strip of ten miles in width to Great Britain for
free transit, through the lake region in territory formerly
part of the Belgian Congo. In short, it circumvented the
provisions of the Anglo-German agreement of 1890 and
allowed the British a Cape-to-Cairo corridor from Lake
Tanganyika to Lake Albert. At any rate, this is the construction given by Stanley, for he wrote triumphantly:
" There was now, a free broad line of communications between Cape Town and British Equatoria." [24]

Stanley was too exuberant. Although the treaty was
honored by King Leopold and the Company, it never received
the official sanction of H. M. Government.[25] On the contrary, part of the territory under discussion was recognized
by Great Britain as belonging to Germany by the Anglo-
German Treaty of July 1, 1890.[26] By this treaty the
northern boundary of German East Africa was drawn
from the western point of Lake Victoria intersected by the
first parallel of south latitude along that parallel to the frontier of the Congo State.[27] A glance at the map will show
that this made German East Africa and the Congo State
contiguous from above Lake Kivu to Lake Tanganyika and,
therefore, precluded the Ibea Company from any activities
below the first parallel of south latitude. Furthermore, as
mentioned already, Lord Salisbury by the treaty of 1890
definitely blocked the British road to the north by recognizing that German East Africa bordered on the Congo State
from the Nyasa-Tanganyika Plateau to the first parallel of
south latitude.

Nevertheless, the abortive agreement of May 24, 1890,
between King Leopold and the Imperial British East Africa
Company is important. In the first place, King Leopold,
evidently considered that an agreement signed by the responsible director of a royal chartered company was an authoritative instrument and that by virtue of these arrangements he

was justified in sending exploring parties into the territory affected by them. Indeed, expeditions sent out by the Belgian King travelled over a considerable portion of the territory, and their leaders made treaties and established posts. To be sure, H. M. Government protested from time to time that the "territory thus explored was well known to be included in the British sphere of influence." [28] Nevertheless, expeditions did take place apparently on the faith placed by Leopold in the agreement.

Furthermore, although it did not seem feasible at this time to secure the strip, the Cape-to-Cairo corridor, between Lake Edward and Lake Tanganyika, the idea was tempting. The subject was not definitely dropped, but the scheme continued to ripen and, finally, bore fruit in the Anglo-Congolese agreement of 1894. This agreement will be discussed later on. [29] It is well here to note, however, that H. M. Government was, evidently, more fascinated by Leopold's proposal in regard to "the corridor" than Salisbury cared to admit. In fact, the Earl of Kimberley, Foreign Secretary in 1894, asserted that the later Anglo-Congolese agreement was no new idea but "the result of communications which have been going on for some time." [30] Salisbury, himself, pointed out: "I do not think it," [i. e., the Anglo-Congolese treaty of 1894], "differs very largely from one which was under discussion at the time I left office." [31] There seems, therefore, to be some continuity between the abortive agreement of 1890 and the later one of 1894.

Before the agreement of 1894 is taken up, however, it is necessary to examine further the growing competition between Europeans in the Sudan. The Congolese were not the only rivals of the British in the Upper Sudan. H. M. Government was watching with even greater anxiety the operations of another Power. The French, also, had designs upon the upper reaches of the Nile. They were indeed building a magnificent African empire. From colonies along the Atlantic coast, from Algiers and Tunis in the north and in from Obok on the east coast the French were pressing into the interior. As explorers worked their way in towards Timbuctoo and Lake Chad, the idea grew of uniting French Equatorial Africa with the west coast colonies on one hand and with the expanding colonies in the north on the other. In 1889, France possessed an energetic Colonial Minister, M. Étienne, who set to work to effect the union of the various French colonies by systematic exploration and conquests.[32]

Furthermore, ever since France refused to cooperate with England in the occupation of Egypt in 1882, the imperialists rued their decision. They recalled England's promise to withdraw from Egypt as soon as the state of the country and the organization of proper means from the maintenance of the Khedive's authority will admit of it.[33] As their influence spread through Equatorial Africa towards the Nile Valley, they conceived a new plan for forcing H. M. Government to come to terms. They were well aware of the strategic advantages of an occupation of the Upper Nile Valley. They knew that the masters of the Upper Nile would be masters also of Egypt.[34] Access to the valley of the Nile from the south, said de Brazza, " is the only way in which we might be enabled one day to settle the Egyptian question in a way consistent with our interests. It is easy to join the Congo territory to the Soudan by way of Darfur." [35] On May 5, 1893, President Carnot told Monteil that he was planning to reopen the Egyptian question by arriving on the Nile from the south. Monteil pointed out that Fashoda would be a strategic post which could be reached by way of the Ubangi River. Carnot's schemes, moreover, contemplated the construction of barricades on the Nile. He went so far as to discuss the question with an engineer. The most important barricade was to be constructed in the province of Fashoda. As early as 1893, therefore, the idea of grasping the Sudan and fastening a strangle-hold on Egypt was sufficiently familiar in France to interest the President of the Republic.[36]

French colonial enthusiasts, likewise, were anxious not only to reopen the Egyptian question but also to resist the British advance across the continent. They were determined not to let Britain " dominate exclusively from the Mediterranean to the Lakes and from the Lakes to the southern seas." [37] Finally, what the French wanted, primarily was a strategic position which would give them a deciding voice in the ultimate partition of North Africa. They wanted a good bargaining stand in future diplomatic arrangements.[38] They desired, in short, to bring England to terms.

Frenchmen were advancing slowly towards the Western Nile Basin and were laying plans for future development of the district. In 1891, a post was established at the confluence of the Ubanga and Kamo rivers at 5° north latitude. In the same year, M. Liotard was commissioned to occupy the territories which the French claimed to be under their influence and to open a door towards the Nile. Frenchmen arrived at Abiras in that year and came face to face with the Belgians.[39] In 1892, on the initiative of the energetic M. Étienne, a credit was granted of 300,000 francs to send a mission into these regions to investigate the country and to make settlements. To be sure, nothing came of the movement. The Under-Secretary refused to sign the necessary measures and the credits set aside for the expedition were unused.[40] In 1893, as pointed out above, plans were discussed for erecting a barricade on the Nile at Fashoda.[41] The year 1894 was one of renewed activity on the Ubangi river. The French had at last succeeded in establishing a civil administration in the region of the Upper Ubangi near Wadi and the Egyptian Sudan.[42]

French activity in the Upper Sudan was regarded by the British as a serious menace to their interests in Egypt and to British expansion southward. If their rivals succeeded in establishing themselves in the Nile Valley, they could block Great Britain's road south, they could wrest Egypt from England's grasp and they could build up a powerful empire controlling all North Africa. H. M. Government decided, therefore, to concentrate its forces against the French and to use the Congolese as pawns in the game.

They found an opportunity to woo the friendship of King Leopold in the growing rivalry between the French and the Congolese in the Ubangi and Bahr-el-Ghazal regions in the Upper Sudan. As noted before, the Belgians were pushing up through the Bahr-el-Ghazal in one direction and along the Nile Valley as far as Lado in another. The British, although, as previously seen, they had opposed this north-ward advance,[43] now began to look upon it with more favor. They commenced to think that it would be preferable to have the Belgians rather than the Congolese as neighbors in the Upper Sudan.

The French and the Congolese came to a clash in the Ubangi region. Both rivals put forth claims to the country. The French maintained that the Belgians could not go be-yond the 4° parallel of north latitude. In the first place, the fourth parallel was the northern frontier assigned to the Independent Congo State by a series of conventions (1884-1885) between the International Association of the Congo and four European powers: Germany November 8, 1884;[44] France February 5, 1885;[45] Portugal February 14, 1886;[46] and Belgium February 23, 1885.[47] The frontier which resulted from these agreements was depicted on an official map drawn up by M. Friedericksen and annexed to the protocols and documents of the Berlin Conference.[48] The northern line was similarly defined in a circular issued by the Administrator General of the department of Foreign Affairs of the Independent State of the Congo, August 1, 1885. The same circular declared the neutrality of the new state.[49] France claimed that these agreements definitely fixed the frontier of the Congo State at the fourth parallel of north latitude and that the Congo, as a neutral state, had no right to extend its activities beyond this limit.[50]

The Belgians protested, however, that they were the first in the field and that Belgian explorers were the first occupants of the region north of the Ubangi River. As to the neutrality of the Congo State, that had been proclaimed by the independent State itself by virtue of the right conferred on it by the Berlin Act. The proclamation of neutrality, was, therefore, a unilateral act which the independent state could break at will. It could not prevent the sovereign Independent State of the Congo from extending beyond its original boundaries. In fact, in 1887, the Franco-Congolese frontier had already been modified by a protocol without a protest from any European power. Similarly, in 1889, no power had protested against the partition of Muata-Yamvo with Portugal.[51]

The French, further, insisted that the Congo State in advancing into the region above the fourth parallel, was violating its treaties of 1885 and 1887 with France.[52] The issue centered around the exact boundary line between the French sphere of influence in Equatorial Africa and the frontier of the Congo State.

The controversy was highly technical.[53] It is not necessary here to pass upon its merits. It is enough to keep in mind the position of both parties and to note that the Congo State refused energetically to withdraw from the disputed region. Some useless negotiations took place in 1892. In 1893, the French government tried to reopen negotiations but Leopold refused. The discussion was renewed on April 16, 1894 but the plenipotentiaries separated April 25 without agreement except an admission in principle that a recourse to arbitration was necessary.

Leopold next turned to H. M. Government. The British decided that the best policy was to pit one power against the other and that, while safeguarding their claim to a sphere of influence in the Nile Valley, it was safest to espouse the cause of the weaker of the two powers, Belgium.[54] The idea grew up of creating " a buffer state between the Nile waterway and the French forces." The King of the Belgians, the British began to think, was a neighbor they " might be very glad to have " and one whom they could " perfectly trust " to undertake for them what they had most at heart, the care of territories which for a time he could reach more easily than they.[55] The important point was that there should be no French occupation of the western basin of the Nile.[56]

CHAPTER XVI

The Surrender of the Cape-to-Cairo Corridor

The British Government was faced in 1894 with a grave situation in the Upper Nile Valley. The French were about to push forward, establish themselves at some strategic location on the upper reaches of the Nile and to challenge the British position in Egypt. As noted in the last chapter, H. M. Government decided to support the Congolese as a counter force to the French and to set up a buffer state.

The British, however, had insisted ever since the Anglo-German treaty of 1890 that the Nile Valley was their sphere of influence. They had, in fact, protested against Belgian as well as French encroachment into this region. The problem before them was how to maintain their claims to this vital strip and at the same time to use Congolese colonial ambitions to oppose the French advance.

The British found, however, a clever and novel solution of this knotty question by borrowing a rule of private law for the situation. They decided to lease to King Leopold the territory which he coveted. Great Britain could thus keep the ultimate title to the Nile Valley in its hands and could likewise obtain Leopold's recognition of a British sphere of influence in the Nile Valley. H. M. Government could at the same time shift to the shoulders of the Belgian king the burden of developing the country and warding off French encroachments.

Leopold as pointed out in the previous chapter, appealed to Great Britain for support in his controversy with the French over the Bahr-el-Ghazal.[1] London listened sym-

307

pathetically to his advances and on May 12, 1894, Great Britain and His Majesty King Leopold II, Sovereign of the Independent State of the Congo, signed an agreement relating to their spheres of influence in East and Central Africa.[2] In the first place, Leopold recognized the British sphere of influence, as laid down in the Anglo-German agreement of July, 1890.[3] Great Britain in turn, by Article II, agreed to lease to Leopold certain territories in the western basin of the Nile. The territories leased comprised, roughly, the block now called the Lado Enclave, along the Upper Nile, and the Bahr-el-Ghazal region. The lease of all this territory was to " remain in force during the reign of His Majesty Leopold II, Sovereign of the Independent Congo State." At the expiration of his reign, the lease was still to remain in force as far as the territories situated to the west of the 30th meridian were concerned, i. e., the Bahr-el-Ghazal. The lease was to continue here as long as " the Congo Territories as an Independent State or as a Belgian Colony remain under the sovereignty of His Majesty and His Majesty's successors." [4] Furthermore, a strip 25 kilometers in breadth stretching from the watershed between the Nile and the Congo up to the western shore of Lake Albert and including the port of Mahagi, i. e., the Lado Enclave, was, also, to be leased to the Belgian King with the same tenure as that of the territory west of the 30th meridian. The rest of the territory was leased only during the reign of Leopold.[5]

In short, Article II allowed Leopold, as Great Britain's tenant, to set up a buffer State in the Sudan and thus secured a friendly ally to guard the route north through the Upper Nile Valley. This defense of the Nile Valley from French encroachment was probably the primary consideration leading to the signing of the agreement.

H. M. Government, however, had another important objective in view. In the previous chapter, the abortive agreement of 1890 between Leopold and the Ibea Company was discussed. It was, also, noted that H. M. Government never officially recognized the agreement but that H. M. officials were attracted by the idea of a Cape-to-Cairo corridor suggested by the arrangement of 1890. In fact, conversations on this subject continued.[6] In 1894, the British Government, with Rosebery at the helm, was still very much interested in Leopold's tempting offer of a railway strip from Lake Tanganyika to Lakes Albert and Edward embodied in the abortive agreement between Leopold and the Ibea Company in 1890. The Congolese, however, had entered into treaty arrangements with various European countries involving economic and political considerations. The Congo State, furthermore, had declared itself a neutral state.[7] It would hardly be consistent with these treaty engagements or with the neutrality of the State if the Congolese granted the British an outright cession of territory for the Cape-to-Cairo railway and telegraph line. Here again, the device of a lease offered a useful solution of the difficulty and resulted in the provisions of Article III of the Anglo-Congolese agreement. Article III is a genuine Cape-to-Cairo measure and shows how far Cecil Rhodes' influence had spread. Because it embodied a Cape-to-Cairo policy, it will be well to give the exact words of the article here:

The independent Congo State grants under lease to Great Britain, to be administered when occupied, under the conditions and for a period hereafter determined, a strip of territory 25 kilometers in breadth, extending from the most northerly port on Lake Tanganyika, which is included in it, to the most southerly point of Lake Albert Edward.

This lease will have similar duration to that which applied to the territories west of the 30° meridian east of Greenwich.[8]

Furthermore, the Anglo-Congolese agreement not only secured a lease of the Cape-to-Cairo corridor for a railway but it also made possible the fulfillment of another one of Cecil Rhodes' projects, the Cape-to-Cairo telegraph. By Article V, the Congo State authorized the construction of a telegraph through its territories by Great Britain or by any company duly authorized by the British Government. The telegraph, the article specifically stated was to connect " the British territories in South Africa with the British sphere of influence on the Nile." [9]

The Anglo-Congolese Agreement of May 12, 1894, then, accomplished four major purposes. It secured the definite acknowledgment by the Belgian King of a British sphere of influence in the Nile Valley as defined by the Anglo-German agreement of 1890. It delimited the boundary between the Congo State and the British sphere of influence to the southwest. It set up a buffer state against French incursions into the Nile Valley, a state which British and Congolese troops would be prepared to defend at need. Lastly, it secured under lease to Great Britain an important strip of land running between Lake Tanganyika and Lakes Albert and Edward, the connecting link between the British sphere of influence in the South and in the North.

The agreement was signed during Rosebery's administration. It was the work of a stanch friend and ally of Cecil Rhodes. The convention was Rosebery's second great contribution towards the realization of the cherished dreams and plans of Rhodes because he, as will be remembered, was chiefly instrumental in keeping Uganda, the key to the Cape-to-Cairo route in the Lake district, in British hands.[10] Now, in this new agreement, he strengthened British claims to a vast sphere of influence along the Cape-to-Cairo route. Furthermore, Rosebery secured permission to carry a transcontinental telegraph through the Congo State. Finally, he

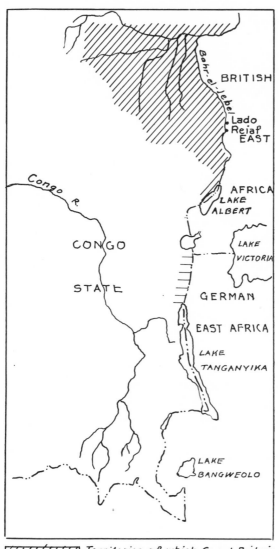

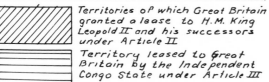

Territories of which Great Britain granted a lease to H.M. King Leopold II and his successors under Article II

Territory leased to Great Britain by the Independent Congo State under Article III

ANGLO–CONGOLESE TREATY, 1894

made progress toward securing an easement over an unbroken strip of territory between Lake Tanganyika and Lakes Albert and Edward.

To be sure, the corridor was only held under lease and was regarded by H. M. Government simply as a right of way. " In obtaining a lease of that strip of territory the object of the Government was not to acquire a right of occupation or administration in that territory, but simply to acquire a right of way." [11] A right of way, nevertheless, was an opening wedge. It was the first step in securing an unbroken stretch of territory from Cape Town to Cairo. It was largely, therefore, under the Rosebery administration that H. M. Government definitely shaped and sponsored a genuine Cape-to-Cairo measure. In fact, in this instance, the British Government was pursuing a clear-cut Cape-to-Cairo policy. Whether it would develop and follow that policy consistently, whether it was really heartily interested in securing a line of communication from Egypt to South Africa, remains to be seen.

The agreement of 1894 was apparently well received in Parliament. The Earl of Kimberley, Secretary of State for Foreign Affairs, emphasized the fact that it was urgently necessary for Great Britain to come to some distinct arrangement with Leopold and to put upon a regular footing the Belgian occupation of the Upper Nile Valley. He believed that the rights of no other Powers were violated. A friendly neighbor had been secured and at the same time British responsibilities were diminished rather than increased. With the Nile Valley in friendly Belgian hands, the British could devote themselves to the immediate duty before them, namely, the consolidation of the Protectorate of Uganda and the administration of the vast region which is implied in that term.[12] It is significant also that the Marquis of Salisbury, on the other side of the House, gave the agreement his blessing and condescended to call it "a sensible arrangement." He thought the King of the Belgians would prove a useful and trustworthy neighbor.[13] The satisfaction of H. M. Government over the Anglo-Congolese agreement was, however, not shared by outside Powers. In fact, the agreement encountered the determined opposition of France and Germany.

France felt deeply injured by the convention.

. . . the question of Egypt and one can even add of Africa [Hanotaux explains], was regulated by a single stroke. The policy followed by France, for fifteen years, was only a vain parade. No means of reprisal, no element of exchange or of compensation remained for her, at the time when the great African negotiation would take place.[14]

France at first limited its action to an official protest against the Anglo-Congolese agreement and provisions of which appeared to be incompatible with arrangements made between France and the independent State of the Congo, and with the international position of certain countries in the basin of the Upper Nile. H. M. Government in turn took notice of this communication without discussing or admitting the grounds on which the reservation was based.[15] A new ministry was about to be formed and Casimir-Périer, the outgoing premier, did not wish to involve his successor in a definite line of action.

The Casimir-Périer ministry was succeeded by that of Charles Depuy. Eight days after the constitution of the new ministry, June 7, 1894, Hanotaux, the Minister of Foreign Affairs, gave in the Chamber of Deputies, the fundamental objections of the French Government to the Anglo-Congolese agreement. He attacked primarily article II which concerned the lease of Bahr-el-Ghazal and Lado Enclave to Leopold. He established, in the first place, that the stipulations in Article II of this agreement infringed the rights of the Sultan and of the Khedive in the provinces of the Basin of the Upper Nile, and were incompatible alike with the firmans relating to Egypt and with the international acts by which the integrity of the Ottoman Empire was secured.[16] The provinces in the Upper Nile Basin, Hanotaux pointed out, had for many years been occupied and administered by Egypt and although, within recent years, the agents of the Khedive in consequence of events beyond their control had been obliged to abandon them, nevertheless, the Egyptian Government had never ceased declaring its wish to reestablish its authority there. The provinces were still claimed by Turkey.[17]

In the second place, Hanotaux maintained that the Congo State, as a neutral state, constituted by a conventual act, could not extend beyond the limits fixed by conventions with the bordering Powers. In other words, he was reiterating the arguments which the French Government had used repeatedly against the encroachment of the Congolese in the Bahr-el-Ghazal.[18]

He next attacked the competence of Great Britain to grant a lease over territory which it did not own and had never effectively occupied. " Real occupation," Hanotaux argued according to the newly developing African international law, appeared to be " the only practical means of preventing difficulties and conflicts." There was, however, no doubt that Great Britain had never " effectively occupied " the territories in question.[19] The whole conception of such a lease was, after all, a singular one.[20]

Lastly, he attacked Article III of the Anglo-Congolese Agreement. The lease of a strip of territory between Lake Tanganyika and Lake Albert Edward appeared to the French to be contrary to the principle of equal treatment set forth in Article V of the General Act of Berlin and incompatible with the preferential right of France recognized in the Agreements of 1884 and 1887 with the Congo State.[21] France had interests and rights to protect which could not be annulled by an agreement to which she was not a party.[22]

The Earl of Kimberley replied point by point to the memorandum of Hanotaux' speech in the Chamber of Deputies.[23] As to the rights of Turkey and Egypt, the two contracting parties did not ignore the claims of Turkey and Egypt in the basin of the Upper Nile. They specifically declared this in the official dispatches attached to the agreement.[24] H. M. Government, however, was perfectly willing to enter into a discussion with the French government as to how those claims could be better protected or to give their careful consideration to any well-substantiated claims of the Porte.[25]

Concerning the status of the Congo State, H. M. Government flatly denied that the Congo State was " constituted by a conventional Act, or restricted within certain defined frontiers." The Berlin Act in Article I only laid down the limits of the Conventual Basin of the Congo, *not* the limits of the Congo State. There was nothing in these stipulations to prevent a Power which had proclaimed itself neutral from extending its territories either within or beyond the limits assigned to the Conventual Basin of the Congo.[26]

Furthermore, the limits of the Congo State had not been laid down in any general international convention. The Congo State had *itself* issued a circular to the various Powers in August 1885, in which it proclaimed its neutrality, and stated its limits as they then existed. But it neither entered into any undertaking not to extend or modify its frontiers, nor was any such obligation imposed on it by the other Powers Signatories of the General Act of Berlin. H. M. Government, here, was publicly espousing the side of King Leopold in the occupation of the Bahr-el-Ghazal and pouring a shattering broadside into the French position in this controversy.[27]

Concerning the peculiar character of the lease, Lord Kimberley admitted that it was a novel measure. He suggested, however, that " occupation by mutual agreement for a fixed or uncertain period " was " by no means unknown to European international law." [28]

In regard to effective occupation, H. M. Government concluded that it would not " be convenient to push too far the obligation of effective occupation of all territory within the spheres of influence of the several European Powers." [29]

At any rate, if H. M. Government could not lay claim to effective occupation of the Nile Valley, it, at least, held in its possession two conventual agreements. One was with Germany, the treaty of 1890 [30] and the other with Italy. The latter agreement made in 1891 will be discussed later on. [31] Both arrangements recognized a British sphere of influence in the Nile Valley. These conventions had been, furthermore, publicly announced and hitherto uncontested. [32] In addition, H. M. Government pointed out to Hanotaux that the British lessee had already occupied a portion of the territory while French occupation had not approached to that point. [33]

In regard to the contention that Article III of the Anglo-Congolese agreement infringed France's special rights and privileges in the Congo State, H. M. Government pointed out that the conditions of the lease, as well as the period assigned to the lease precluded any contravention of rights which France might claim under her agreement of 1884 with the International Association of the Congo. At the same time, H. M. Government took the opportunity of remarking to the French government that " the claims of priority and preference " of the French Government might be regarded as incompatible with the neutrality of the Congo State. [34]

In short, both France and Great Britain were preparing for a struggle to contest their rights in the Upper Sudan.

The argument was not to end here. Hanotaux was not content with mere verbal protest. As will be seen in a later chapter, he set out to definitely occupy the regions in question and to oppose British paper claims with actual French occupation.

The French received, for a while, Germany's support against the Anglo-Congolese agreement. The Germans were annoyed, in the first place that England had concluded such an agreement without their consent.[35] Furthermore, they objected specifically to Article III granting the lease to Great Britain of a strip of territory between Lake Tanganyika and Lake Albert Edward. This clause, the Germans claimed, was injurious to their rights under the convention of November 8, 1884 between the German Empire and the International Association of the Congo. It must be admitted, however, in justification of the British position, that although the Agreement of 1894 granted certain rights and privileges, there was no clause in the treaty which directly stated that Germany must be consulted if the Association ceded or leased any of its territory.[36] Baron von Marschall, German Secretary of State for Foreign Affairs, claimed, however, that " from a legal point of view," the borderline between Germany and the Congo could not be altered without the consent of Germany. The Anglo-Congolese agreement did, nevertheless, change this borderline by leasing the strip between Lake Tanganyika and Lake (Albert) Edward to Great Britain. By the operation of this lease Germany and the Congo State ceased to be neighbors. The form of lease was of no consequence because it was in reality a grant of land for an indeterminate period of time which was a cession.[37]

From a practical angle, von Marschall insisted, the British Government had not acted in a friendly spirit in concluding the Anglo-Congolese agreement. In 1890, he reminded

Lord Kimberley, that in the negotiations of the Anglo-German treaty of that year, Sir Percy Anderson had requested a strip of land connecting Lake Edward with Lake Tanganyika.[38] Von Marschall had then flatly refused the request and had declared that Germany "would have to consider such an 'English belt' around our East African possessions as a political and commercial danger. . . ."[39] The request was dropped and Germany believed the matter closed. The Germans did not expect that the British Government would attempt to secure the same advantage indirectly through the Congo State. Finally, Great Britain's action, von Marschall warned Kimberley, would be considered as "a measure of its desire to maintain friendly relations" with Germany. In other words, Germany's consent was essential to Article III of the Anglo-Congolese agreement. This consent would be given only when the Germans were certain that their rights and interests were fully recognized. They considered that bilateral contractual as well as political rights were in question. They could not allow an encirclement of their territories in East Africa by England without previous agreements and guarantees.[40]

As early as May 26, the Chief of the Colonial department at the German Foreign Office told one of the secretaries of the French embassy that the government would not consent to the substitution of an English for a Belgian neighbor to her possessions in that region in Africa. June 13, von Marschall proposed common action with France in safeguarding the legal *status quo* in Africa. The German Chancellor, said von Marschall, was not decided about how this common action should be carried out, whether by a simultaneous proposal for summoning a conference or by some other procedure. "If the idea of a conference prevailed . . . it would not be necessary for the French and German representatives to speak in unison nor for them to support each other publicly under all circumstances. But loyalty constrained them not to desert the ground of their preconcerted resolutions." [41]

Hanotaux agreed that France and Germany should be ready to affirm the common point of view of the two governments in regard to the necessity of safeguarding the *status quo* in Africa. He suggested that the best course of procedure was for both to continue their negotiations at London and at Brussels. They should in these negotiations defend each other's position. They should not come to a definitive arrangement until they had each one obtained, respectively, complete satisfaction. Only if negotiations pursued thus at London and at Brussels did not succeed, could they consider the eventuality of a conference with the the other interested Powers. The French wished to safeguard their rights but at the same time to conciliate the interests of England and the Congo State and to save their *amour-propre*.[42]

The Germans were evidently prepared to do everything in their power to break up the agreement between the Congo State and England.[43] In fact, besides joining hands with France, they continually held the threat over England's head of a conference of the Powers.[44] At such a conference, von Marschall hinted, not only the Anglo-Congolese agreement would be discussed but other African and colonial questions would be scrutinized. For example, France would on such an occasion undoubtedly seize the opportunity of submitting the Egyptian question in its entirety to the Powers.[45] The Emperor, in corroboration of von Marschall's threat, refused diplomatic support for England's interests in Morocco, as long as the Congo question was not satisfactorily settled.[46] In short, he bluntly warned the British Ambassador that he would be very sorry if England's disloyalty to Germany in regard to the Anglo-Congolese agreement should make it impossible for Germany to support England's wishes towards other states in the same friendly manner as in the past.[47] Finally, the Germans made it plain that they meant business and that they could make the international situation very uncomfortable for the British.

In the meantime, von Marschall warned the Belgian King that the Anglo-Congolese agreement was " incompatible with the neutrality of the Congo State. The government of this state should not force Germany to go to extremes." [48] Apparently, von Marschall had in mind a suggestion of Hatzfeldt that Leopold could be coerced by the threat of a complete alteration of the relations, even treaty relations between the Congo State and the Triple Alliance.[49]

At first, Great Britain attempted to take a firm stand in regard to the Anglo-Congolese agreement. In France, Lord Dufferin, British Ambassador, spoke of an ultimatum which he held in his pocket.[50] Then, H. M. Government became more conciliatory. Lord Kimberley's reply to Hanotaux, discussed in detail above, although it firmly set forth the position of H. M. Government, at the same time indicated that Great Britain was willing to enter into negotiations over the question of safeguarding the rights of the Khedive and the Sultan.[51]

Towards Germany, the British protested stoutly that the offensive Article III did not " threaten either the progress or security of the German colonial possessions." [52] In the negotiations which preceded the signing of the agreement, the position of the Congo State in its relationship to Germany received the attention of the High Contracting parties. They were careful not to interfere in any way with the rights of Germany, with whom they had so long had cordial relations in East Africa. All the stipulations of the convention between Germany and the International Association of the Congo in February 1885 would remain in force. In accepting the lease of territory between the lakes, Great Britain fully recognized this fact.[53]   The projected lease was sedulously divested of all political significance by Article IV of the Anglo-Congolese Agreement.[54]   Furthermore, agreeing with Germany that the boundary line between the German and the Congo territories could not be altered without Germany's assent, H. M. Government denied that Article III altered that boundary.[55]

In spite of the fact, however, that the British professed a firm belief in the justice of their case, the diplomatic situation in Europe was so threatening that they decided to yield.   The Congo State was, on its side, anxious to crawl out of the embarrassments in which it was placed by the Anglo-Congolese Agreement.   As early as May 29, the government of the Independent Congo State admitted that the boundaries between German and Congolese territory could not be altered without the assent of the Imperial Government.[56]   To Germany's request that the band of leased territory be placed 20 kilometers from the German frontier, Leopold agreed readily.[57]   When Germany was not satisfied with this concession and demanded that Leopold actually cancel Article III, the Belgian King answered that he could not do so without England's approval but that he was willing to ask Great Britain to consent to the cancellation of the offending article.[58]

In this state of affairs, the British manoeuvred.   By sacrificing Article III, England might be able to save the rest of the agreement and secure German diplomatic support against France, especially on the Egyptian question.[59]

Article III was the only part of the agreement to which Germany objected.   This Article, therefore, was formally withdrawn on June 22, 1894.[60]   Once this article was withdrawn, Germany left France to fight its own battle alone for the revision of Article II.[61]   The French government, however, found Leopold ready to come to terms and on August 14, 1894, France and the Congo State signed a new boundary agreement which considerably modified the effects of Article II of the Anglo-Congolese as far as the two countries were concerned.

It is well to remember, however, that Article II was never really withdrawn. The new arrangement between France and the Congo State, although it changed the boundary lines between the French and Congolese spheres of influence, did not abrogate in any respect the principles of Article II of the Anglo-Congolese agreement of the previous May. If Germany had continued to give France support, perhaps, France could have gone farther in a conference of the other European Powers. As it was, although H. M. Government allowed the negotiations between France and the Congo State to take place, it was not a party to the new treaty.[62] In reality, Great Britain never retreated from the position which it had taken. Great Britain still claimed the Upper Nile Valley as a British sphere of influence.

In the new Franco-Congolese arrangement, France was permitted, as far as Leopold was concerned, a free hand in the Ubangi-Shari and Bahr-el-Ghazal provinces, i. e., in part of the territory previously leased to Leopold under Article II of the Anglo-Congolese agreement.[63] France thereby abandoned its previous contention that the Congo State was permanently fixed within the limits which had been assigned to it at its birth because France, itself, very illogically, allowed the Congo to push beyond the much-disputed fourth parallel as far as the fifth parallel of north latitude. France was, apparently, not fighting for abstract principles but for a foothold in the Upper Nile Valley.

Although Leopold thus included part of the leased territory in the French sphere of influence, there was nothing in the new treaty to abrogate the lease which Great

Britain had granted to the Congo State. As picturesquely stated by one M. P.,

France said, as it were, to the King of the Belgians: " You must only occupy the ground floor of that house " . . . The king agreed with somebody else to enter only into partial occupation of the territories leased to him [by Great Britain]. That was his affair [not England's]. The lease remained.[64]

The King of the Belgians, also, was still in full occupation of the Lado Enclave. The lease was only terminated in 1906 by a new agreement with Great Britain.[65]

The Anglo-Congolese Agreement of 1894 may be classed as a diplomatic blunder but not as a complete failure. Great Britain, it is true, suffered a humiliating rebuff from Germany.[66] The British consent to the withdrawal of Article III indicated decidedly how far the British position in Egypt and the Sudan depended upon Germany's diplomatic support. As Sir Edward Grey admitted, if the British

had been at all aware of the importance which the German Government attached to that particular part of the Treaty, it would not have been inserted. The moment it was found the German Government attached importance to it Her majesty's Government felt it would be only in accordance with a proper sense of what was due to the different Powers concerned that part of the Treaty of no great importance to us, but considered to be of great importance to the German Government— should be withdrawn.[67]

Furthermore, Great Britain did not succeed in creating " a buffer state between the Nile waterway and the French forces that were advancing from Central Africa toward the Nile." [68]

Germany and France had, at least, shown Great Britain that the British people could not spread, unchallenged, all the way across Africa from the Cape to Cairo. Germany would not allow the British the little narrow strip between the Southern and Northern spheres of British influence, "the wasp waist" which advocates of a Cape to Cairo policy coveted so much.[69]

To be sure, H. M. Government openly disavowed that it had any intention of pursuing a Cape to Cairo policy. Lord Kimberley declared to the French Ambassador at London and also to the British Parliament that "the royal government did not propose at all to establish English dominion from the Cape to Alexandria. 'That is a policy', he said, 'which must be relegated among absurd chimeras.'"[70] H. M. Government, likewise, insisted that in accepting the lease of the strip between Lake Tanganyika and Lake Albert Edward, Great Britain did not seek to acquire any political rights and that the rights of administration, therefore, conceded to her during the period of the lease, could only be used for purposes of commerce or communication.[71] In other words, H. M. Government avowed no intention of trying to obtain an "all-red" strip of territory throughout Africa. Nevertheless, article III of the Anglo-Congolese Agreement, obviously, and specifically, was designed to establish a line of communication between the British spheres of influence in the south and in the north.

Although Great Britain was obliged to give way before the pressure of the combined opposition of France and Germany, the Anglo-Congolese Agreement of 1894 was not a complete failure. Even after the withdrawal of Article III, Great Britain still retained substantial and permanent advantages in the remaining clauses. The King of the Belgians, for instance, still acknowledged a British sphere of influence in the Nile Valley.[72]

Furthermore, although Article III was gone, Great Britain still kept Article V which authorized the construction of a line of telegraph through the Congo State. Article III, in the first place, Lord Kimberley argued, gave Great Britain only a strip of land for the construction of a line of telegraph and eventually a road. The time for the construction of such a road had not come yet and as regards the more immediate object, the construction of a telegraph line, Article V provided well enough for that.[73]

The British were put on their guard by the determined opposition of France and Germany to the Anglo-Congolese Agreement; but the British advance continued. Politicians and business men still talked about a line of communication from the south to the north of Africa.[74] They were obliged to surrender the Cape-to-Cairo corridor; but the Cape-to-Cairo dream still persisted.

CHAPTER XVII

PLOTS LAID IN ETHIOPIA

As guardians of Egyptian interests, the British must keep watch along all the avenue of approach to the Nile Valley. One of these lay through Ethiopia. Indeed, this country, like the lake region and the Upper Sudan, furnished strategic ground which could be used by rival powers to weaken British control in Egypt. In the first place, three important tributaries to the Nile rose in the Ethiopian mountains: the Sobat, the Blue Nile, and the Atbara. These Ethiopian affluents were the principal sources of the annual flood so essential to the life and prosperity of Egypt.[1] It is to be expected, therefore, that the destinies of Egypt and Ethiopia would, in some measure, be linked together.

Furthermore, Ethiopia offered a tempting base for expeditions from the east coast into the Nile Valley. It was this danger which caused British statesmen and politicians much anxiety in the period of 1890 to 1902. They were afraid that the country might become a hotbed of intrigue hostile to their Egyptian interests and a starting ground for expeditions into the Upper Nile region.

They were watching with particular vigilance the operations of the French. French interests were, indeed strongly rooted in the country and in Somaliland. The French first gained a foothold on the Somali coast in 1856 at Ambabo and Obok. Their primary objective was to establish a naval base along the Red Sea. They, also, hoped that Obok would serve as a center of commerce for the interior, i. e., Harrar, Shoa, and southern Ethiopia. In a few years, they acquired possession over the coast from Das Dumeria on the Straits of Bab-el-Mandeb to Jibuti.[2] Between 1883 and 1887, a French protectorate was established in the region. French influence was also penetrating into the interior. In fact, the French held a treaty of friendship and commerce with the king of Shoa, as early as 1843. They were very much interested, likewise, in trade and commerce in the Harrar region. Harrar lay directly on the caravan route to Dongarita and constituted a natural hinterland for French exploitation. They were not the only competitors in this field, however, and they were suspicious that the British were helping the Italians to capture coveted trade there. They tried, at one time, to tie the hands of their rivals and to persuade the British to refrain from taking over Harrar and also to oppose the efforts of any other Power to annex it. The British needed Italian support against the Mahdists and were not willing to go as far as the French desired. On the other hand, they were unwilling to admit their cooperation with the Italians. They, finally, agreed in 1888 to a secret treaty with the French. The treaty was a masterpiece of ingenuity and vagueness. In it, the two governments agreed not " to endeavor to annex Harrar nor to place it under their Protectorate." They also agreed not to " renounce the right of opposing attempts on the part of any other Power to acquire or assert any rights over Harrar." [3]

In their Ethiopian adventures, the French worked hand in hand with the Russians. The Russians took an especial interest in the country because of the affinity between the Coptic Church of Ethiopia and the Greek Orthodox Church of Russia. At one time, Russia went so far as to propose that it be given a Protectorate over the country in order to properly represent Ethiopia in Jerusalem and the Red Sea area.[4] In 1888, a cossack, Atchinoff by name, visited Ethiopia. He was sent back a little while later by the Russian Government to Obok.[5]

In 1890, Menelik came to the Ethiopian throne. The new monarch was friendly to both France and Russia and prepared to cultivate relations with them. In fact, he made advances which were at first rejected. In 1894, however, a mission was dispatched by the Russian Geographical Society under the command of Captain Léontiff accompanied by the Monk Zaphraim. The mission was very influential for a time at the Ethiopian Court. Menelik even went so far as to assign to Léontiff the Government of his " Equatorial Provinces." As a result of the mission, Russia established diplomatic relations at Addis Ababa and placed several officers in Menelik's army. The object behind the Russian operations, Dr. Work believes, was to assist the French in breaking the British route to India.[6] Bourgeois speaks also of a Russo-French expedition to Ethiopia in 1895 which brought back the Ethiopian bishop of Harrar to Petrograd to establish closer relations between the Russian and Ethiopian clergy. Hanotaux, then French Minister of Foreign Affairs, was interested in a plan formulated by Léontiff to build a political entente with Menelik on the basis of a religious entente " in order to retard the already advanced progress of England on its way from the Cape to the Valley of the Nile." [7]

In 1894, the King of Kings of Ethiopia granted a concession to M. Ilg, a Swiss engineer with French sympathies, to construct a railway from Jibuti to the Nile. M. Ilg, in turn, became associated with M. Chefneux in founding a French company, *La Compagnie Impériale des Chemins de Fer Ethiopiens*. The railway grant, indeed, was regarded in France as a considerable success. It promised to make the town of Jibuti one of the principal ports on the Red Sea and the great entrepôt for Ethiopian commerce. It also signified that the French might exercise a preponderant political and economic influence in the country.[8]

With their influence so strongly entrenched in Ethiopia and with a king on the throne so friendly to French and Russian interests, the French might well speculate upon using Ethiopia as a base for further operations. The Nile Valley was their goal. They were now beginning to dream not only of uniting their possessions in North, West and Equatorial Africa but also of joining their growing empire in these regions with their sphere of influence in the East.[9] France would then become the paramount power in North Africa. They did not wish to establish a protectorate in Ethiopia, but they were desirous of maintaining a position of dominance there and to use the friendly monarch to promote their imperial schemes elsewhere. Finally, as mentioned in a preceding chapter, the French intended to drive the British out of Egypt by establishing themselves firmly along the upper reaches of the Nile River.[10] They planned to accomplish this by approaching some strategic position along the river from two directions. French penetration was to proceed towards the Nile Valley from both the west and the east coasts and French forts were to be placed on both the left and right banks of the Nile.[11]

In the previous chapter, their progress into the Ubangi and Bahr-el-Ghazal region from the west coast has already been noted. As early as 1894, plans were already forming for expeditions in from the east through Ethiopia. In that year, the French Government dispatched Lieutenant Mizon to Ethiopia " with instructions to make *un voyage de reconnaissance* to the Nile." The Government also ordered Captain Clochette to proceed with another group from Jibuti to the Nile.[12] To be sure, shortly after these expeditions were sent out, a period of inaction set in at home called in France " *cette néfaste période* ". They were not ready to proceed as fast as they had evidently expected. Lieutenant Mizon's expedition was recalled and Captain Clochette's expedition was allowed to remain at Addis Ababa for eighteen months without orders or resources.[13] Nevertheless, French agents were busy at the Ethiopian court and the ground was being prepared for a more active program in the future.

Although their influence was in the ascendant in Ethiopia, the French were not the only competitors in the field. Italian aspirations to control the Harrar trade have already been noted. They, as well as the French, had deep rooted interests in Somaliland and aspirations towards a sphere of influence not only over the coast but also over Ethiopia and regions in the Eastern Sudan.

Like the French, the Italians first planted a colony on the East Coast. In 1869, an Italian steamship company, the Rubattino, purchased Assab on the Red Sea Coast just north of the French seaport of Obok. The port of Assab was, at first, simply a coaling station to be used by the company. In 1882, however, after Italian aspirations in Tunis had been thwarted by France, Italy turned to the African Coast and took over Assab from the steamship company. In 1882, they acquired Massawa. Around Assab and Massawa, the Italian colony of Eritrea began to grow and expand.[14]

Just below the Italian and French colonies on the Somali Coast, a British sphere of influence was also growing. In fact, the British had had interests on the Somali coast for some time. The first connection with the region came from their trade with the Far East. The East India Company needed a harbor for their ships. Accordingly, as early as 1840, treaties were concluded with the Sultan of Tajura and the Governor of Zeila allowing the Indian Government to exercise considerable influence on the coast although British authority was not definitely established there. During the years 1872-1874, Ismail Pasha, Egyptian Khedive, occupied the ports of Tajura, Berbera and Bulhar; but during the revolt of the Mahdi in 1884, the Khedive garrisons were withdrawn.[15]   It will be remembered that in 1882, British troops occupied Egypt and the British became the guardians or trustees of the country.   It will, also, be recalled that when the British advised the Khedive to withdraw the Egyptian garrisons from the Sudan after the Mahdist onslaught, they promised to protect the Red Sea ports belonging to Egypt.[16]   As trustees and guardians of Egypt, therefore, to protect the Red Sea route to the east, the British occupied Zeila, Berbera and Bulhar.   Finally, during the years 1884 to 1887, they established the protectorate of British Somaliland from Loyi Ada to Bandar Ziada.[17]

Meanwhile, the Italian Colony of Eritrea was growing and the Italians were beginning to push back into the interior. As already noted, they coveted the trade around Harrar.[18] Their progress to the west was checked at first by a crushing defeat at Dogali.   In 1889, however, they partially retrieved their fallen fortune by espousing the cause of Menelik in a dispute over the succession to the Ethiopian throne.   Menelik, in return concluded a treaty with the Italians; the famous treaty of Uccialli of May 1889.[19]   By this instrument, the Italians obtained, they claimed a protectorate over Menelik's kingdom, because article XVII gave them control over Ethiopian foreign relations.   Indeed, the Italian version of this article read: " His Majesty the King of Kings of Ethiopia, consents to avail himself of the Italian Government for any negotiations which he may enter into with the other Powers or Governments." [20]   To be sure, Menelik refused to regard Italy as a protector.   He asserted that the treaty empowered him but did not compel him to use Italy as an intermediary. The Amharic text of the much disputed article XVII read differently from the Italian.   According to the Amharic version, " His Majesty the King of Kings of Ethiopia, *may if he desires to,* avail himself of the Italian Government for any negotiations he may enter into with the other Powers or Governments." [21]   Since both the Italian and the Amharic versions were agreed by the two contracting powers to be official,[22] the question at issue was a delicate one and boded trouble for the future amicable relations between the two countries. Italy, however, continued to regard the Ethiopian Kingdom as an Italian sphere of influence.

Two European Powers, therefore, were working for a position of dominance in Ethiopia; the Italians and the French.   As in the case of the rivalry between the French and the Congolese in the Bahr-el-Ghazal, the British decided to espouse the cause of the weaker and, therefore, less dangerous power.[23]   Although the Italians harbored expansive ambitions for a sphere of influence not only over Ethiopia but also in the Sudan and although the Italian aspirations were hardly compatible with Anglo-Egyptian interests in the Eastern Sudan, they were less formidable rivals than the French.   Italy, furthermore, as a member of the Triple Alliance was a desirable friend.[24]   Italians, likewise, might be useful as opponents of the Dervishes around Kassala in the Eastern Sudan.   Their influence, too, in Ethiopia would be beneficial to counteract the growing French ascendancy there.   Furthermore, according to Dr. Work, the British wished to secure high country at the back of Ethiopia upon which to construct the Cape-to-Cairo Railway and thus to avoid the swamps of the Nile Valley.[25]   The British thought that by recognizing an Italian sphere in the Ethiopian kingdom, they might be able to secure this highland strip.   In short, H. M. Government decided to use Italian colonial ambitions to safeguard British interests in the Nile Valley and the Eastern Sudan.

Great Britain decided, therefore, to recognize Ethiopia as an Italian sphere of influence.   In a series of protocols, the two Powers agreed to lines of demarcation between their respective spheres in East Africa, the Upper Sudan, the

Eastern Sudan and Somaliland. In two protocols, (one dated March 24, the other April 15, 1891), H. M. Government carefully guarded the Upper Nile Valley against Italian encroachment. The line of demarcation between the British and Italian spheres in these regions ran from the Indian Ocean along the mid-channel (thalweg) of the River Juba up to latitude 6° north. Kismayu with its territory on the right bank of the river remained to England. The line then followed the sixth parallel of north latitude up to the meridian 35° east of Greenwich which it followed up to the Blue Nile.[26] From the Blue Nile, the line continued after a dip around Kedaraf, in a northeasterly direction until it reached Ras Kasar on the Red Sea.[27] The boundary excluded Kassala, an important post in the Eastern Sudan, from the Italian sphere of influence but the Italians were permitted in case of military necessity to occupy Kassala and the adjoining country as far as the Atbara. Such an occupation, however, was in no case, to extend to the north or northeast of a certain line from Gos Rejeb on the Atbara to the Italian frontier. The two powers then agreed " that any temporary military occupation of the additional territory [i. e., that around Kassala], shall not abrogate the rights of the Egyptian Government over the said territory, but that these rights shall only remain in suspense until the Egyptian Government shall be in a position to reoccupy the district in question . . . and there to maintain order and tranquility." [28]   In other words, the Italians were to defend Egyptian interests against the dervishes in this important region in the Sudan but they were not allowed to establish themselves there. It looked very much as though they were being used as a " cat's paw " for the British in the Sudan.

On the whole, " It was a fortunate thing," Englishmen concluded; " . . . that the Italians were in the Eastern Soudan. It was clear that the future establishment of

British Dominion over the Nile waterway and the civilization of all those countries depended on a cordial co-operation between Italy and Great Britain in those regions." [29]

One other point about the protocols of 1891 is worth noting. The demarcation line, as Dr. Work points out, was drawn so as to reserve some high country for the British to the west of the Italian sphere. Over this route, they might someday build a south-to-north railway.[30]

The protocols of 1891 delimited the Italian sphere on the south and west. There was still, however, the question of the boundary in Somaliland. Accordingly, on May 5, 1894, Sir Francis Clare-Ford for the British and Francesco Crispi for the Italians signed a third agreement which concerned spheres of influence in Eastern Africa. Part of this agreement was published; part was supposed to be kept secret. There was nothing in the published portion to disturb European powers. As to Ethiopia, however, it finished the process of turning all that country into an Italian Protectorate as far as British recognition was concerned.[31]

The unpublished part, on the other hand, dealt with the region around Harrar and caused some anxiety in other quarters. According to Italian sources, this secret section stated clearly that England should have the right to take temporary control over Ethiopia including the Harrar region until Italy was in a position to assert its authority over the country. This temporary occupation, however, must not be considered as denying the position of Italy as the protector of Ethiopia and its dependencies.[32]

This portion of the protocol of May 5, 1894 was not a secret for long. As early as May 20, the Germans knew of its existence. Von Bülow, in a report to Caprivi, stated that in a secret arrangement with Italy, England was granted the right to control the Harrar Province and to consider it as within the British sphere until Italy was ready to extend its influence there. The French, likewise, soon heard about the agreement. In fact, they knew of it as early as June 18. Their version of the secret protocol was much the same as the German. According to M. Ernest Lavisse, " Italy would allow Great Britain to exercise a temporary intervention in the Harrar until she should be in a position herself effectively to establish her protectorate." [33]

On June 18, M. Hanotaux lodged a protest against the May Protocol with the British Foreign Office. It was, he declared, incompatible with the treaty of 1888 between France and England over the Harrar.[34] In that treaty, he reminded the British, the two countries had affirmed the independence of Abyssinia. Furthermore, he stated, there appeared to be a secret section which was repugnant to the Anglo-French agreement regarding the Harrar region. While the treaty of 1888, to be sure, did not bind the British to oppose a protectorate over the Harrar, it did bind them not to promote such a protectorate. This was the very thing, however, which the British had done in the secret Anglo-Italian agreement of May 1894.[35]

The British replied evasively to the French protest. There was some correspondence between the two governments. The treaty, however, was not withdrawn.[36] This protocol, therefore, taken together with the two concluded in 1891 gave Italy, as far as Great Britain was concerned, a free hand over all Ethiopia and in Somaliland from Eritrea to the Indian Ocean.[37]

With the British protocols and the treaty of Uccialli to support their claims, the Italians proceeded to pose as the protectors of Ethiopia. Trouble, however, was brewing between them and King Menelik. King Menelik was not behaving as though Ethiopia were a protectorate. Upon his ascension to the throne, he dispatched anouncements of his coronation directly to the different states of Europe instead of using the Italian Government as an intermediary. The thorny question arose of what was the true meaning of article XVII of the Treaty of Uccialli. Furthermore, the Italians were beginning to encroach upon territory claimed by Menelik as part of his kingdom. A boundary dispute ensued. There is no need to go any further into the quarrel over article XVII or the boundary disputes here but simply to note that there was growing irritation with the Italians between 1890 and 1893. There was also some grounds for suspicion that this ill-feeling was fostered by the French agents at the Ethiopian court.[38] Finally, February 12, 1893, Menelik denounced not only article XVII, but the whole treaty of Uccialli.[39] He not only informed King Umberto of Italy of his decision but proceeded to notify the European Powers of his action. " Ethiopia," he said, " has need of no one; she stretches out her hand unto God." [40] He also sent a deputation to Paris. It is significant that M. Chefneux of the French railway company headed the expedition and that M. Chefneux had been residing for sometime at the Ethiopian court. Some months later, he returned to Ethiopia with munitions of war among them ten rapid-fire cannon.[41]

War did not immediately follow the denunciation of the treaty of Uccialli. Apparently, the two sides were not ready. The Italians, spent a year trying to persuade Menelik to submit to a protectorate. In the meantime, they were intriguing with the native chiefs. Furthermore, they were having trouble with the Dervishes in the Sudan. The Italians, also, needed British support. It was in this period, as noted above, that they concluded the final protocol of May 1894 with the British.[42]

In 1895, the Italians began to move forward. They occupied Adowa " with great pomp and little resistance." [43] Finally, they clashed with Ras Mangasha's and Ras Makonnent's forces in the province of Tigré and were driven back to Macallé. War had then fairly commenced. The climax was reached in the overwhelming defeat of the Italians at Adowa, March 1, 1896.[44] It is significant that in this battle, the Ethiopians were reported to be armed with French rifles. Undoubtedly, the British Consul wrote, the French were supplying the Ethiopians through the port of Jibuti with quantities of arms and munitions. If it had not been for their help, Menelik would " never have been able to have gained (sic.) the crushing victory of Adowa." [45]

Whatever may have been the cause for this Ethiopian triumph, the fact remains that it was utterly disastrous to Italian prestige in Africa. It was, however, not the end of the conflict of Italians for supremacy in Ethiopia. It was merely the beginning of a struggle which has extended down to the present day. In its immediate consequences, the Battle of Adowa was bound to have repercussions in the Sudan. With Italian prestige lowered, the Dervishes would be encouraged. As will be remembered, the dervish forces of the Mahdi overran the Sudan in 1884. The Mahdi died but his followers under the Khalifa were still ravaging the country. In fact, the Italians were at grips with the Khalifa's sources in the Kassala region. There was danger, that after the Italian defeat under Menelik, the Khalifa's followers might become bold enough to invade the confines of Egypt. The British, as guardians of Egypt and as friends of the Italians felt that the time had come for action. The story of the British campaign falls properly in the next chapter. It is sufficient here to note that the defeat of the Italians at Adowa was the match which kindled a second conflagration in the Sudan.

CHAPTER XVIII

The Reconquest of the Sudan

By 1894, H. M. Government held four treaties recognizing a sphere of British influence in the Nile Valley: the Anglo-German Treaty of 1890, the Anglo-Italian protocol of March, 1891, the Anglo-German Agreement of November 15, 1893 and the Anglo-Congolese Agreement of 1894. These were Great Britain's paper titles to the region but Salisbury reminded the House:

It is not safe in these days to establish your title to large territory . . . and then to leave it there without any effort to assert your title in a more practical and more effective fashion. The whole doctrine of paper annexation is in a very fluid and uncertain condition . . . I believe that, in order to make your claim over these vast regions a genuine one, and one which the public opinion of Europe will respect, . . . you ought to show that you are gradually assimilating it, gradually making good your possession of it. . . . [1]

Her majesty's government was doing what it reasonably could, to make its control effective over the vast sphere of influence recognized in the Anglo-German treaty of 1890. In the few years elapsing between that date and the summer of 1894, Lord Rosebery, the prime minister, could point to the fact that " some 80 treaties of friendship and protection had been concluded with the neighboring tribes and nations that inhabit our sphere of influence." [2] In February, 1894, Major Owen reached Wadelai in the Equatorial Province and hoisted the British flag there. The British had also brought to a successful close a campaign in Unyoro, just north of Uganda. [3] Where the British could not go, they

337

had tried to find someone else to help them. They had, for example, in the Anglo-Congolese agreement of 1894, entrusted to the King of the Belgians the care of territories in the Upper Nile.[4]   Neither the Liberal Rosebery Government of 1894 nor the Conservative Salisbury Government which preceded it, could be accused of indifference to or negligence in regard to British interests in the newly acclaimed sphere of influence.

There was, however, need of haste.   The French government realized, too, that paper claims were weak arguments where the other side could produce positive proofs of effective occupation.   Furthermore, the Anglo-Congolese agreement of May 1894 created a bad impression in France. Following the Anglo-German Treaty of July 1890 and the Anglo-Portuguese treaty of 1891, it looked to the French as though the English having painted the map red in the south and in the north were now commencing work at the center.[5]   France refused to be ousted by a series of paper arrangements from the Upper Nile Valley.

To be sure, the French government did not begin immediately after the signing of the boundary agreement with the Congo State, August 1894, to make effective a French occupation of the Ubangi and Bahr-el-Ghazal.   Soothed by the apparently conciliatory attitude which Great Britain adopted towards the provisions of the Anglo-Congolese agreement in the summer of 1894, the French government stopped Colonel Monteil at Loango on his way to the Upper Ubangi and diverted his mission to the Ivory coast.   The 1,800,000 francs which were voted to improve communications between the coast and the Upper Ubangi were also employed elsewhere at Loango and on the Ivory coast.   Nevertheless, in the fall of 1894, as noted before, the French government decided to attack the problem of occupying the Upper Ubangi region with renewed energy.   In September, Liotard was named commissioner to the Upper Ubangi with the instruction to extend his work into the Bahr-el-Ghazal and as far as the Nile. The French were inaugurating a policy of peaceful penetration into the Nile country.[6] They were quietly preparing to oppose the English paper claims and blustering declarations with a *fait accompli*, an actual occupation of the Upper Nile Valley.

In 1894, however, the French still hoped to be able to settle their many African problems with England through diplomacy as well as through actual occupation. Their plan to occupy the Nile Valley by direct action was only one phase of the French program. While they were preparing for more decisive action in the Ubangi district, the government of the Republic was also consenting to a proposal by Lord Dufferin for negotiation on African affairs. A conciliatory spirit seemed predominant, at this time, in both countries. Numerous conferences were held during the autumn at the Quai d'Orsay. Towards the end of the year a general arrangement of African questions and especially that of the Nile Valley was agreed to by the plenipotentiaries.

France obtained thereby a definition and limitation of English claims in this region. The disputed territory was to be in some degree neutralized and placed under the surveillance of the two Powers. This agreement however, which might have prevented all future difficulties and changed the whole course of history in the Sudan, was rejected by both governments. Hanotaux, the French plenipotentiary, was reproached for having sacrificed too much and for an excessive desire to conciliate England. Similarly, in England, the imperialists assailed the Liberal Cabinet for going too far to conciliate France.[7] With the failure of this attempt at negotiation, both countries assumed a more aggressive attitude.

Englishmen watched with anxiety the growing colonial activity of the French in 1895. Never before had they seen France put forth such coordinated and effective efforts.[8] At home, the colonial group was bending every endeavor to arouse popular support for colonial ventures and to stimulate the government to greater activity. Abroad, French explorers penetrated in greater numbers and with new vigor into the heart of the Dark Continent. By 1895, Liotard had made considerable progress and had established French authority definitely over the sultanates of Zenio, Bamgasso, Rafai and Tambura.[9]

Towards the end of 1895, the French Government began preparations for sending an expedition under the command of Captain Marchand into the Bahr-el-Ghazal as far as the Nile. On February 24, 1896, Guieyesse, Colonial Minister, signed the first instructions given to Marchand. The object of the expedition, according to these instructions, was to extend French influence up to the Nile. Marchand was told to push ahead and to reach the Nile, before the English Colonel Colville arrived at the same place. In order to accomplish this, he was authorized to set up friendly relations with the Madhists.[10] In the meantime, the Méline ministry came into power in France and fresh instructions were issued to Marchand in June of a less imperialistic tone. The Méline ministry took great care to define the nature of the expedition. It was not a military enterprise for conquest. It was only an expedition to maintain the line of policy which France had already been pursuing for two years under Liotard in the Nile Valley. Its aim was the establishment of French influence in the Nile basin. Marchand was expressly subordinate to Liotard, who had just received the rank of Governor.[11]

The French Government, naturally, did not officially notify the British Foreign Office of its intentions in dispatching the Marchand expedition. Hanotaux, however, indignantly denies that the expedition was a surreptitious affair. It was not nearly so secretive an affair, he claims, as the English expedition which was then preparing to approach the Nile Valley from the South. All the acts concerning the Marchand Mission and the principal stages of its advance were published and a debate on the subject took place in the Chamber of Deputies, on February 7.[12] Furthermore, notice of the proposed Marchand Mission was sent to Constantinople, to Russia and to Menelik in Ethiopia.[13]

The British, indeed, were well aware that operations were going on in the Bahr-el-Ghazal and Ubangi region. As will be noted in the following pages, in the Spring of 1895, the disquieting rumors in regard to a supposed French expedition towards the Nile Valley led to the formulation of the famous Grey declaration. To be sure, Marchand had not started at this time, but vague suspicions and rumors were in the air. In the conversations between Kimberley and de Courcel, after the Grey declaration was made, Kimberley spoke directly about a French expedition which, it was rumored, had entered the territory under discussion. Lord Kimberley said that he hoped that the French Government would assure him that these rumors were unfounded. De Courcel in reply did not deny its existence. He merely answered evasively: " His Excellency said that no news had been received of the expedition in those parts, with which communication was extremely tardy and difficult and that he did not, therefore, see how it would be possible for the French Government to give assurances while they were in ignorance of the actual facts." [14] H. M. Government then was, at least vaguely, aware of the preparations of the French Government to dispute the British claims to a sphere of influence in the Nile Valley by actual occupation.

The occupation of the Nile Valley, however, was, as noted before, only part of a more comprehensive program.[15] The primary object of the French government was to secure an influential place in future negotiations over African questions. The French people wanted a point of vantage from which they could bargain and bring their arch-rival, England, to terms. The Nile Valley was not the only place where England and France were at loggerheads. On the West Coast of Africa, they had conflicting interests in Gambia, Sierra Leone, Liberia, the country of Kong and Nigeria. They were disputing the navigation of the Niger and the Benoue and the subject of a boundary line in the Lake Chad district. While off the south-west coast in the French protectorate of Madagascar, English missionaries and English adventurers were making trouble for the French among the native Hovas. The Egyptian question, however, dominated all the others. Once the English were ousted from Egypt, France would become the paramount power in North Africa. It has been noticed already, how closely bound up with the Egyptian question was that of the occupation of the Nile Valley. In fact this question, Hanotaux believed, was the knot holding all the others together. Once the question of the Nile Valley was settled, all the others could be solved.[16]

Vague rumors of French activities in the west and in the east reached England. The British were alarmed also by the fact that the Russians were taking at least a momentary interest in Ethiopia. In January 1895, the conclusion of a military alliance between France and Russia was officially revealed. For sometime, the British had known that there was close cooperation between France and Russia.[17] As pointed out in an earlier chapter, about this time there had been an attempt on the part of Ethiopians and Russians to bring about a religious entente between their respective churches and there was some danger of this religious rapprochement developing into a political accord. Léontiff was especially active in these transactions.[18] In reality, the Russians although they were involved in Franco-Russian intrigues in Ethiopia, were reluctant to have their ally France drag them into a war against England over an African question.[19] Nevertheless, English observers, who were not at all clear about Russian and French movements in North Africa at this time, suspected that the Russian expedition into the country foreboded trouble.

It was a significant fact [Sir E. Ashmead-Bartlett warned the House on March 28], that while the French were threatening the Nile waterway to the west, a very remarkable mission from another Great Power, also our rival, was working on the eastern side of the Upper Nile waters. There was a coincidence about this action which was not accidental. A large and influential and well equipped Russian mission went, about six weeks ago, into Abyssinia, bearing costly presents and large sums of money, for distribution among the chieftains and the people.[20]

There was a growing appreciation in England of the gravity of the question of the British sphere of influence in the Nile Valley and the danger of French encroachment.

. . . As to the question of the Nile waterway [Sir E. Ashmead-Bartlett told the House, March 28, 1895], of all the questions abroad of political rivalry and power which were likely to arise in the next few years, with the exception, perhaps, only of the future of Asia Minor and the passage of the Straits—the security of the Upper Nile waterway was undoubtedly the principal. There was a race at present proceeding for Transafrican Dominion between France and Great Britain. . . . If they [the French], once succeeded in establishing the position of Transafrican Dominion, the whole of North Africa was bound to become a French possession, Egypt included; and the Mediterranean was almost bound to become a French Lake. Then there was the British race from South Africa to the north, from Cape

Town to Alexandria—a great dominion which had been very nearly achieved, which only required the small completion of a chain already stretched the greater part of the way, to render it perfect and permanent, and to give this country such advantages of imperial influence and commerce in Africa as it was almost impossible to overrate.[21]

Disquieting rumors were rife of the French expeditions in Central Africa towards the Nile Valley. Some excited members of parliament even urged H. M. Government to take defensive measures against this ominous advance. " Our government ought to have gunboats on the upper waters of the Nile," Sir E. Ashmead-Bartlett, an ardent exponent of a Cape-to-Cairo policy, insisted. They ought to " patrol the river as far as Lado and even Fashoda and ought to take steps to find out where this French force really was at the present time." [22] " If the French were advancing," another pugilistic M. P. urged " the government to send a small force to place the British flag on the junction of Bahr-el-Ghazal and Bahr-el-Jebel." [23]

The Rosebery government was not willing to go this far but it was willing to take a firm and decided stand for British rights in the Nile Valley. On March 28, Sir Edward Grey, then Under Secretary of State, made a declaration in the House giving France " full warning " that Great Britain would not tolerate French encroachment in the Nile Valley. Concerning the British sphere of influence in this region, he insisted that

there was an agreement made in 1890 with Germany and another with Italy defining the British sphere of influence, and obtaining from those two great countries a recognition of the British sphere of influence. . . . Besides this, there is the question of the claims of Egypt. Towards Egypt this country stands in a special position of trust, as regards the maintenance of the interests of Egypt, and the claims of Egypt have not only been admitted by us, but they have been admitted and emphasized lately by the government of France. I stated the other day that in consequence of these claims of ours, and in consequence of the claims of Egypt in the Nile Valley, the British and Egyptian spheres of influence covered the whole of the Nile waterway. . . . I am asked whether or not it is the case that a French expedition is coming from the West of Africa with the intention of entering the Nile Valley and occupying up to the Nile. . . . I cannot think it is possible that those rumours deserve credence because the advance of a French expedition under secret instructions right from the other side of Africa, into a territory over which our claims have been known for so long, would be not merely an inconsistent and unexpected act, but it must be perfectly well known to the French government that it would be an unfriendly act, and would be so viewed by England.[24]

To be sure there was no special French expedition, other than that of the Liotard mission sent out the previous autumn, operating in Central Africa with the object of reaching the Nile Valley. Marchand had not started at this date. Nevertheless, London was nervous about the aggressive attitude which France was assuming towards colonial activities in Africa. H. M. Government considered that the time was ripe to give the French Republic a warning of the British point of view.[25] This statement of Sir Edward Grey, therefore, was an important step taken to clear the issues. It was distinctly an official communication and formed the basis of the subsequent policy of H. M. Government. Lord Rosebery, himself, accepted full responsibility for this policy. He said some years later at a speech at Epsom, October 12, 1898 that he was " personally and ministerially responsible for the declaration made on behalf of the government by Sir Edward Grey in March, 1895 " and that he had " no disposition to recede from a word or syllable of that declaration." [26] It was the foundation of the policy adopted by the

Conservative government which succeeded Rosebery's Liberal Cabinet. In 1897, Sir E. Monson informed Hanotaux regarding British claims to a sphere of influence in the Nile Valley in the following words:

The views of the British government upon this matter were plainly stated in Parliament by Sir Edward Grey some years ago during the administration of the Earl of Rosebery, and were formally communicated to the French government at the time. Her Majesty's present government entirely adhere to the language that was on this occasion employed by their predecessors.[27]

Before the advance on Khartoum, Lord Salisbury told Lord Cromer that the policy of Her Majesty's Government as regards the territories shortly to be conquered was exactly defined by the language used by Sir Edward Grey and subsequently by Sir Edward Monson.[28]

Six months before Grey warned France through an official declaration in the House to keep away from the Nile, Rosebery also let the French ambassador know through unofficial channels that British claims in the Nile Valley were to be respected. Cecil Rhodes was his spokesman. Rhodes recounted the story in a speech at Good Hope Hall, Cape Town, on October 25, 1898.

I was staying with Lord Rosebery and we were talking about many things. I said, I believed the chief risk to us in the world was through the delay of the people getting up from Uganda, if the French got across and cut in between Khartoun and Uganda; and he said, " all I can say is that if they do that, that is a question I would fight upon " . . . About a week or a fortnight afterwards, the French ambassador said he would like to see me, and I went and saw him . . . he saw, " now, what do you think is the risk of war in the world? " I said, " I think the risk in the world is your going on to the Nile either from the east or west." And he said, " What would England do? " and I said, " I am sure she would fight." He said, " Why

do you think that?" I said, "Because Lord Rosebery told me
so two days ago, and he represents the Liberals, and if the Conservatives were in, they would be worse."

Now, why do I tell you that story? I tell it to show that the
French are perfectly well aware that Marchand is not on the
Nile without plenty of warning to the French government. If
I, as an outsider, was privileged to know that, and told the
French ambassador, you may be sure they were told by the
English government four years ago. . . . I may finish my story
by saying that I told Lord Rosebery afterwards that I had told
the French ambassador this, and he said he was glad. He said,
" I am glad you let them know that, that was my feeling as the
Liberal Prime Minister." [29]

France had certainly received sufficient and clear warning
that H. M. Government considered the Nile Valley as a
British sphere of influence. Sir Edward Grey's speech was
ominous. As Rosebery pointed out later the use of the word
" unfriendly " was especially serious. " The word ' unfriendly ' ", said Rosebery, " which socially among us has,
perhaps, no particular meaning, or perhaps, too common a
meaning, is among diplomatists a word of exceptional weight
and gravity; and when that word is used to denote an act
committed by one government against another the situation
is grave." [30]

Hanotaux replied immediately to the English threat, by a
speech before the French Senate, on April 5, 1895. His
speech reflected the indignation of the French people over
the Grey declaration. According to the French point of
view, the vast stretch of country between the Lake district
and Wadi Halfa was under the high sovereignty of the Sultan with the Khedive as lawful master. The Anglo-German
treaty of 1890 which set up a British sphere in this region
was merely

one of those annexations on paper which an enterprising diplomacy afterwards cultivates as germs of a future claim and title.

. . . Germany, not having any right or claim to put forward in those regions, gave her assent to a claim which did not cause her any inconvenience.[31]

Furthermore, France never consented to the parts of the Anglo-German convention which related to a British sphere of influence in the Nile Valley. To be sure, an agreement had been reached between Great Britain and France over another part of the Anglo-German treaty, i. e., that relating to Zanzibar.[32] " But," Hanotaux insisted, " France was not called upon to discuss the articles of the convention which related to other parts of Africa. By the fact of signifying her assent to certain articles only, she reserved her assent as regards the others." Indeed, France had shown her open disapproval of a British sphere of influence in the Nile Valley by protesting against clause II of the Anglo-Congolese Agreement of 1894.

Furthermore, Hanotaux asked the English just what was the sphere of British influence as defined by the Anglo-German convention. The terms of that convention were exceedingly vague as far as the sphere on the left bank of the Nile was concerned.[33]

Not only were the French people indignant over the Grey declaration but they felt that it had come at an inopportune moment. Negotiations were still in process for settling disputed points between the two countries. The relations between France and England had always been friendly and courteous. It was, therefore, undiplomatic to interject a declaration so uncompromising in tone into the situation just at a time when France was trying peacefully to settle its difficulties with England by diplomacy. Although the negotiation over the general situation in Africa had failed,[34] France and England had not yet given up hope of settling their differences, section by section. Already negotiations on this new basis had begun and as early as January, the two Powers had come to an agreement over one vexatious question, i. e., the boundaries of Sierra Leone.[35] Conversations were still going on. The Grey declaration was calculated to prejudge the question and to obtain from France an adhesion to this vague sphere of influence. The British wished the French to settle the future of these regions prematurely. Hanotaux begged for at least a discussion. It was a wiser plan, he thought, to leave the whole knotty question of the Nile Valley to the patient work of the diplomatists.[36] In short, although Hanotaux' speech was strong, it also left the door open for further discussion.

At first, H. M. Government seemed somewhat disturbed by the excitement in Paris over the Grey declaration and was disposed to soften the harshness of the under secretary's speech. There was not complete unanimity in the cabinet. There were still some of its members who adhered to the old Liberal school of " Little Englanders " and who disapproved of the declaration. On the other hand, Lord Rosebery, the Prime Minister, and Lord Kimberley, the Secretary for Foreign Affairs, considered Grey's speech " sensible and salutary ".[37] In general, the opinion of Rosebery and Kimberley prevailed but Grey was persuaded to make a significant correction of his speech in the *Times* for April first. He changed the words the " British sphere of influence covered the whole of the Nile waterway " to " the British and Egyptian spheres of influence together cover the whole of the Nile waterway." [38]

This correction, according to the French point of view, made an important difference. They claimed from the beginning that the Nile waterway belonged to the Khedive. If Great Britain was willing to admit that there was an Egyptian as well as a British sphere of influence there, this left the door open for further discussion as to where and what was the Egyptian sphere. As Hanotaux pointed out in his speech above, France was anxious for further discussion and negotiation. The French objected primarily to the dictatorial manner of the original Grey declaration which seemed to debar all discussion. In fact, they regarded that declaration as a virtual " *prise en possession* " on the part of Great Britain of the whole basin of the Upper Nile.[39]

H. M. Government was disposed to accept the olive branch which Hanotaux proffered. Conversations were immediately begun in London between de Courcel, the French Ambassador, and Lord Kimberley. Lord Kimberley, while not retracting at all the claims of Great Britain to a sphere of influence in the Nile Valley, contrived to leave de Courcel with the impression that the question was still open to debate.[40] The declaration was, after all, only a statement by an Under Secretary and had less solemnity and gravity, therefore, than a pronouncement by the Foreign Minister or the Prime Minister. The declaration, furthermore, was not a " *prise en possession* " but simply a statement of the British side of the case, an affirmation of British claims in this region. France had her point of view and was at liberty to accept or reject the British thesis. At bottom, said Lord Kimberley, the real point of irritation between the two countries was the British occupation of Egypt. When H. M. Government, however, said that the provinces in the Sudan should follow the destinies of Egypt, H. M. Government was contemplating that it would not always be responsible for Egyptian frontiers. In fact, it sincerely looked forward to the end of the occupation.[41]

The situation was grave in the spring of 1895, but neither country wished as yet to go to extremes. The issue was not yet ripe. H. M. Government merely indicated that it did not wish to quarrel with France, at this juncture. As a matter of fact, the claims of both countries were none too secure; both governments needed time to substantiate their pretensions, "to implement the rights they claimed in that district." [42] Both sides realized how faulty their legal arguments were. Neither side possessed an authoritative mandate for their actions in the Nile Valley.[43] To strengthen their respective positions, both sides must leave the realm of legal sophistries and oppose facts with facts. Effective occupation was the only solution of the problem and effective occupation would take time.

The storm clouds blew over for the moment but the issues were left still unsettled. Great Britain had not retracted her claim to a sphere of influence in the Nile Valley. Great Britain, as well as France, was planning to secure its claims by actual occupation. In August 1895, the Salisbury administration came into power. The new conservative cabinet was not likely to yield in the least to French claims in the Sudan. Furthermore, Salisbury appointed Joseph Chamberlain as Colonial Minister. Chamberlain was an outstanding imperialist and a fiery opponent of French encroachments in Africa.[44] He was, also, to a large extent, in sympathy with Cecil Rhodes' policy of colonial administration at the Cape. He was particularly interested in the extension of the railway to the north.[45] As far as rival colonial interests, especially those of the French, were concerned, Chamberlain was a dangerous man to place at the head of the British Colonial Office.[46] His appointment boded ill for the patient and peaceful adjustment of controversies in Africa. Moreover, in 1895, as noted before, "there was a tidal wave of Jingoism rising throughout the country."[47] The nation was ready to stand behind a forward policy in Africa.

From the very outset, the new administration contemplated the reconquest of the Sudan.[48] In fact, in the early part of 1895 Salisbury confidentially told the French ambassador that England was preparing for an expedition to Dongola.[49]

He proposed an understanding with France on the basis that " the expedition undertaken on Egyptian territory with the collaboration of the arms and financial help of the Khedive would not go beyond Dongola." If in consequence of this operation, the English felt it was necessary to go beyond this point, they would not take this advance step without a previous understanding with France.[50] The French ambassador wanted to continue the negotiations but his Government absolutely opposed recognizing in any way the British right to enter the Sudan in concert with the Egyptians. The Quai d'Orsay firmly insisted on maintaining the integrity of the Ottoman Empire and considered acceptance of such an arrangement as Salisbury proposed as a diplomatic heresy. The British were warned further, through the French newspapers, as early as March 17, 1896, of the gravity of the consequences of a campaign in the Sudan.[51]

Just at this juncture, Leopold made another proposal. The King of the Belgians, still, had his eye on the Upper Sudan. In spite of his previous failures to enlist the help of either Colonel Gordon or Emin Pasha, in spite of the fact that he had recognized a French sphere of influence in the Bahr-el-Ghazal by the treaty of 1894,[52] he was yet on the lookout for an opportunity to secure a foothold in the Sudan. The idea of a lease continued to be tempting. Furthermore, he clung to the idea that if the British were seriously contemplating " smashing the Mahdists," perhaps, it would be convenient to have him as a tenant in the Mahdist country. On January 17, therefore, he approached Lord Salisbury for a lease from the Khedive to himself of that part of the Nile which is now in the hands of the Mahdists. He dwelt with fervour on their excellent military qualities and on the profit which the English could draw from them when the country was under his control as lessee.

Salisbury, probably with the ill-success of the Anglo-Congolese treaty in mind, was inclined to ridicule the idea. " It really seems," he later told Queen Victoria, " as if he King Leopold had taken leave of his senses." The ambitious Leopold was obliged to retire from his interview with a shower of compliments but in despair.[53]

Although Salisbury laughed at Leopold's schemes, the British Government, itself, continued to contemplate aggressive action against the Mahdi. Speaking of Egypt, Lord Salisbury said that the ultimate object and intention was to go to Khartoum and restore it to Egypt, but time was needed for that.[54]

We have been for a long time of opinion [Salisbury maintained on June 12, 1896], that sooner or later it would be necessary to take a step in the direction of reclaiming for Egypt the territory that was lost to her in the years 1882 and 1884. . . . In 1884 the trust of which we had become the trustees was diminished by something like one-half. It was not a satisfactory state of things, and I freely admit that I did not consider that Egypt would be safe, under whatever guidance, if Khartoum was left permanently in the hands of a hostile Power. That is the general policy which impressed itself upon my mind. . . . For myself, I repeat the opinion that we shall not have restored Egypt in that position of safety in which she deserves to stand, until the Egyptian flag floats over Khartoum.[55]

The decision of H. M. Government was received with enthusiasm. " I have never remembered," said Broderick, Under Secretary for War, " a step taken by any ministry and carried to its conclusion which secured so universal a commendation as this advance into the Soudan." [56] Indeed, among the populace, the desire for the reconquest of the Sudan had been smouldering ever since the murder of Gordon at Khartoum. This desire for revenge added fuel to the already mounting spirit of imperialism which swept over the country. British enthusiasts, in fact, were not willing to stop at Khartoum. " On to Cape Town " was the cry.[57] The man in the street was ready to stand behind Salisbury, when finally in March 1896, H. M. Government decided on an advance in force to Dongola.[58]

The immediate excuse for this decision was the defeat of the Italians at Adowa.[59] Previous to this disaster, however, in January, 1896, the defeat of Italian troops at Amba Allagi rendered probable a Dervish attack on Kassala. Kassala was a strategic post in the Eastern Sudan and its fall would mean a serious loss of prestige for the European forces. A catastrophe to the Italians at Kassala would probably throw on the Khalifa's side many of the Arab tribes which were at that time either neutral or wavering. A reenforced Dervish army would constitute a serious menace to Egypt itself.[60] As early as January, the British were discussing plans for a demonstration towards Dongola to divert the Dervish forces and relieve the Italians.[61] Then, March 1, came the crushing defeat of the Italian forces at Adowa. Rumors were also abroad, of a contemplated advance by the Dervish troops in large numbers into Upper Egypt.[62] H. M. Government decided to act immediately and to prepare not only a demonstration at Dongola but to send troops there in force for a real military expedition.[63] With the expedition to Dongola, the reconquest of the Sudan began and it did not end until the Egyptian army had gone far beyond this point to Khartoum, and even beyond Khartoum. In fact, the campaign which started with the Dongola expedition ended only in an effective British and Egyptian occupation of the whole of the Nile Valley.

H. M. Government, however, made no serious attempt to conceal the fact that the Italian disasters merely furnished a convenient occasion for inaugurating a larger program. In fact, the First Lord of the Treasury told the House:

We have been quite clear in our statements that, although the particular moment for the advance was one on which Italian interests had important bearings, the advance towards Dongola itself is, in our opinion, necessitated by Egyptian interests, and by Egyptian interests alone—[cheers]—and that, even if the Italians had never been heard of in that part of Africa, that advance would sooner or later have had to be undertaken.[64]

The more impelling reason perhaps for the advance was the French activity in the Bahr-el-Ghazal. The decision, thinks Giffen, sprang from a wish to anticipate the ambitions of French annexationists.[65] It was an answer to Marchand's expedition, which, H. M. Government was well aware, was advancing towards the Nile Valley.

There were, of course, behind these immediate causes many underlying motives leading to the reconquest of the country. Undoubtedly, the tales of the ravages of the Dervishes shocked Englishmen. Undoubtedly, too, the national chagrin over the death of Gordon and the desire for revenge played its part in rousing popular sympathy for the Sudanese War.[66] Furthermore, the movement was popular with British commercial leaders. As Salisbury pointed out, the country around Dongola was very fertile and of great value to Egypt. " We believe," he said, " the reconquest of it and the opening up of the Nile so far will draw great, rich and vivifying streams of commerce into Egypt." [67]

The Egyptian authorities, likewise, were interested in the reconquest of their lost provinces. They had never ceased to look forward to the day when Egyptian power would be restored over the former empire.[68] It was only just, the British argued, that as trustees of Egypt, they should make a serious effort to restore to the country what Egypt had relinquished to England's bidding in 1884.[69] The reconquest of the Sudan, also, meant greater protection for the Egyptian frontiers from the inroads of barbarians and it was assuredly of vital importance to keep the control of the waters of the Nile in friendly hands.[70]

Not only the interests of Egypt required the reconquest of the Sudan but also the British occupation of Uganda pointed to British control over the Equatorial Provinces on its border. The reconquest of the Sudan, Grey claimed, was simply the logical outcome of the British occupation of the countries north and south of that area.[71]   The Sudanese campaign, according to this argument, had its roots in the British entrance into Egypt in 1882. It, also, had its roots in the Uganda controversy of 1893. It would even be possible to go behind this controversy and say that the reconquest was an outgrowth of the policy of 1890 and the Anglo-German treaty of that year. The occupation of the country between Egypt and Uganda was, then, the last triumphant step forward to the effective occupation of the vast sphere of influence assigned to Great Britain under that treaty. In a larger sense, the reconquest of the Sudan was the culmination of a long series of events which led to the establishment of British hegemony from the Cape to Cairo.

The leader of the Egyptian army during the successful campaigns of 1896-1898 was Sir Herbert Kitchener. Kitchener was, in a sense, the Cecil Rhodes of the North. He did more, in his direct practical way, than any man except Rhodes to make the Cape-to-Cairo dream a reality. In the first place, he completed a long and important stretch of the railway which was Cecil Rhodes' cherished project. In the second place, he made British control secure at last from the Great Lakes to the Mediterranean. Kitchener was heartily in sympathy with Cecil Rhodes. He had the greatest admiration for the empire builder in South Africa. He was a personal friend of Rhodes and the two men discussed their plans together.[72]

As early as 1893, Rhodes talked over with the British Sirdar his scheme for connecting North and South Africa

LORD KITCHENER

Reproduced from Weinthal, Leo, *The Story of the Cape to Cairo Railway and River Route,* with the permission of the Pioneer Publishing Co., Ltd.

by telegraph and railway. The two men went into the details of route and gauge. They began a friendly rivalry as to who would be the first to carry the railway and telegraph to the center of the Dark Continent. In the early part of 1896, Rhodes visited Kitchener again in Egypt and obtained from the Sirdar a cargo of Sudanese donkeys for use in Rhodesia. Long before the campaign in the Sudan, they had come to an understanding about the junction of their respective spheres of work on the railway and had even made arrangements for securing identical gauges on both the Egyptian and South Africa systems. Later on, in 1899, Kitchener and Rhodes met frequently in London. They discussed their plans and projects together as they rode on horseback in the park. During this critical year, when Rhodes was trying vainly to obtain a government guarantee for the first section of the Tanganyika railway, he had at least one comforting satisfaction; his friend, Kitchener, stood behind his Cape-to-Cairo railway project.[73] In fact, during 1899, the two men reached another distinct understanding about their plans. " I think," Rhodes hinted in this connection, " you will hear before long that funds have been provided for Lord Kitchener to proceed from Khartoum to Uganda." [74]

In short, there is good evidence that Rhodes and Kitchener were working together under a concerted arrangement. There is no doubt that Kitchener was thoroughly embued with Cecil Rhodes' ideas of a Cape-to-Cairo railway when, as Sirdar, he led the Egyptian forces in the victorious Sudanese campaigns of 1896 to 1898.

An integral part of the story of those campaigns is the history of the building of the " Desert Railway," the Sudanese section of the famous Cape-to-Cairo line. The worst obstacle which Kitchener had to overcome in the River War was not the already waning power of the Khalifa nor yet the feeble but valiant show of resistance from Marchand and his handful of French soldiers at Khartoum but the impediments which nature itself placed in the way of the advancing soldiers. One of his major problems was the actual transport of food and stores for the army through a barren and desolate country. Without a railway "every pound of biscuit and every extra round of ammunition" had to be carried over a large portion of the way on the backs of camels because the Nile could only be used where it was not obstructed by rapids.[75] Progress of an army under such conditions was hazardous and, at best, aggravatingly slow. With disturbing rumors abroad of French activities in Ethiopia and in the Bahr-el-Ghazal, it was important to proceed as expeditiously as possible to forestall a French occupation of the Upper Nile Valley.[76]

For a long time Kitchener had been contemplating the problem of reconquering the Sudan. He had decided that the best method of conducting the campaign was by a gradual advance along the Nile, immediately followed by the construction of railways.[77] Kitchener turned to the railway which had been built south of Cairo under the auspices of Ismail Pasha. It will be recalled in 1885 the railhead of this line was at Sarras.[78] During the progress of the Gordon Relief expedition, fifty more miles had been constructed to Akasheh, but upon the British retirement from Khartoum the rails were pulled up on the Akasheh extension and the railhead once more was at Sarras.[79] The rails, however, still lay along the abandoned line. On the outbreak of hostilities in March, 1896, Kitchener arranged for the reconstruction of the Akasheh line and its extension to Kerma, 203 miles south of Wadi Halfa in the Dongola province. This extension was at last completed under extreme difficulties, both from climate, pestilence, and floods in 1897.[80] Meanwhile Dongola was reoccupied by Kitchener's troops in 1896.

During the campaign, negotiations over African affairs still continued between England and France on the basis of dealing with each particular difficulty at a time.[81] In 1897, the question under consideration was the boundaries in the Lake Chad country. Great Britain took this occasion once more to assert its claims to the Nile Valley. Sir E. Monson wrote to Hanotaux concerning the French claim to the northern and eastern shores of Lake Chad:

> . . . If other questions are adjusted, Her Majesty's Government will make no difficulty about this condition, i. e., French claims in the Lake Chad region. But in doing so they cannot forget that the possession of this territory may in the future open up a road to the Nile; and they must not be understood to admit that any other European Power than Great Britain has any claim to occupy any part of the Valley of the Nile. . . . [82]

Sir E. Monson, thereupon, proceeded to reaffirm Sir Edward Grey's words as correctly stating the position of H. M. Government in regard to the Nile. Evidently, the Salisbury administration was willing to give to the language of the former Under Secretary the weight and solemnity of a definite statement of policy on the part of H. M. Government.[83]

Hanotaux replied with equal firmness that the French Government must again repeat the reservations " which it had never failed to express every time questions referring to the Valley of the Nile were under discussion." [84] He reminded Monson, as a case in point, that the Grey declaration called forth an immediate protest from the French representative in London. This protest the French ambassador had developed at greater length in subsequent conversations with the Foreign Office. Hanotaux, himself, had objected to the declaration in his speech of April 5, 1895, and the British Government had never replied to that speech.[85] In short, in 1897, neither side was willing to yield and the negotiations over the Lake Chad region were carried over into the next year.

Meanwhile the campaign in the Sudan continued. Kitchener had next to make plans for the reconquest of the whole Sudan. The railway was, again a major feature in his program. The course of the Nile below Wadi Halfa presented a serious problem. Below this frontier post, the river makes a great dip before it returns to its former southerly course below Abu Hamed. To follow the great bend of the river with the railway was too long a procedure. Kitchener conceived the bold idea of throwing the railway line straight across the desert from Wadi Halfa to Abu Hamed. It was a daring project because, at that time, the intervening country was totally unknown. The estimated distance for the line was 250 miles. There was a possibility that no water would be found over all this distance. Fortunately, however, water was found at mile 77 and three wells sunk. Wells were also sunk at mile 126 but no water was found after that between this point and Abu Hamed.[86]

There was some discussion about the gauge to be used on the Desert Railway. Lord Cromer favored a 3 ft. 3 in. gauge. Kitchener wanted the 3 ft. 6 in. gauge which was used on the South African and Rhodesian systems.[87] " . . . the Sirdar was obdurate," writes Grew, " just because he was looking ahead " to a Cape-to-Cairo line. " He was determined to do his share from the northern end . . . he foresaw the eventual junction of the future Cape—Abu Hamed—Halfa line with the Luxor Assuan line " and the final adoption of the regular South African standard throughout the transcontinental system.[88]

Kitchener realized the need for haste and he built the Desert line as expeditiously as possible. He was constantly overseeing the work on the railways. He was aware of the fact that a French expedition was moving in from the Congo and that he must proceed quickly to forestall an occupation of the country by the French. Railway construction was pushed ahead at a record pace. On October 31, 1897, the rails reached Abu Hamed at Mile 232.[89] " A record in manual tracklaying and earth work had been established, namely 5,030 yards in one day; and 220 miles of complete railway had been constructed between May 15 and the end of October (169 days)." [90] Locomotives for the new railway were collected from various places. Cecil Rhodes showed his interest in the Sudan section of the Cape-to-Cairo line and his willingness to cooperate with Kitchener by letting the Sirdar have some locomotives originally intended for use in Rhodesia.[91]

In the meantime, Egyptian troops occupied Abu Hamed. The railway was pushed ahead as far as Genenetteh and helped to transport the British brigade for the important battle on the Atbara. On April 8, 1898, the British inflicted a crushing defeat there on the Dervish forces. By July 3, the railway was extended to the Atbara River.[92] " The question of supply was then settled, and with it," says Grew, " the fate of Dervish rule was sealed." [93] The British met their foes victoriously again at Omdurman, September 2. Finally, on September 4, the British and Egyptian flags were hoisted over the Mahdist stronghold at Khartoum.[94] Railway construction continued and the line reached the bank of the Blue Nile opposite Khartoum on the last day of 1899 bringing Khartoum within four days' journey of Cairo, 1,360 miles distant.[95]

Kitchener's successful conquest of the desert hordes was largely due to his railway. " The bayonet action waited always till the railway action had piled the camp with supplies and munitions of war. Patient and swift, certain and relentless, the Soudan machine rolled southward." In short, the Sirdar overwhelmed the Khalifa by means of superior supplies and communications.[96]

Cecil Rhodes was eagerly watching from South Africa the triumphant progress of the Sirdar's army and the Sirdar's railway. After the British victory at Omdurman, Rhodes telegraphed from Kimberley to Kitchener, " Glad you beat the Khalifa. . . . My telegraph will shortly be at south end of Tanganyika. If you don't look sharp, in spite of your victory, I shall reach Uganda before you." Kitchener replied, " Thanks . . . My southern station Sobat. Hurry up." [97]

Rhodes' speeches at this time were full of anticipation and show plainly how important he considered the Sirdar's work. In September, 1898, Rhodes told a Port Elizabeth audience: " As you know, Sir Herbert Kitchener only started the other day, and we can fancy we see them marching to-night towards Khartoum. We are coming up from the South, and we are going to join him as sure as I am standing here. . . . What was attempted by Alexander, Cambyses, and Napoleon we practical people are going to finish." [98]

It was fitting that the two Cape-to-Cairo empire builders, Kitchener and Rhodes, should receive the degree of D.C.L., *honoris causa,* at Oxford at the same time. It is, likewise, significant that Rhodes, the principal exponent of the Cape-to-Cairo idea, experienced the warmer reception. [99]

Kitchener's victory at Omdurman was the decisive battle of the Sudanese campaign. After that all the territories which were subject to the Khalifa passed by right of conquest to the British and Egyptian Governments. [100] With the establishment of an Anglo-Egyptian condominium throughout the Sudan, Rhodes' Cape-to-Cairo dreams seemed less imaginative. Furthermore, says Decle: " Englishmen realised that it was no longer the possibility of laying a wire across Africa which had to be considered, but the foundation of an Empire extending from the Mediterranean to the Cape of Good Hope." [101]

CHAPTER XIX

THE FASHODA CRISIS

THE victorious march to Khartoum, the capital of the Khalifa's kingdom, placed his dominions in the hands of the Anglo-Egyptian forces by right of conquest. The British and the Egyptians held the country, Lord Salisbury was careful to state, by conquering the central Power as William the Conqueror held England with his invading army. All past claims and titles were swept away by the triumphant march of the army through the Sudan.[1]

While the Anglo-Egyptian army had routed the Khalifa's forces and were masters in his territory, they were still faced by serious problems. Order must be restored and their power firmly established throughout the country. Kitchener's march to Khartoum was only a part, a major part to be sure of a larger plan. Furthermore, the British had one more potential enemy to encounter. The French, as already noted had penetrated far into the Upper Sudan. In fact, two months before Kitchener's army reached Khartoum, Marchand with a handful of followers raised the French flag over Fashoda.[2]

As already noted, Marchand's expedition was only part of a much larger program. The intrepid commander expected to meet a Franco-Ethiopian force from the East when he arrived at his destination on the Nile River.[3]

Indeed, the French had for some time been contemplating a march in through Ethiopia and had laid elaborate plans for approaching the Nile Valley from the east. It will be recalled that in 1896, Captain Clochette was at Addis Ababa

363

waiting for instructions and provisions to proceed on an exploring expedition to the Nile.[4]

In 1896, also, instructions were sent from Paris to Lagarde, the French Governor at Jibuti " to press for permission to explore the Sobat through Abyssinia and westward."[5] He was, furthermore, to encourage Menelik in an effort to establish control over his dominions which he claimed stretched as far west as the Nile and as far south as the 5th parallel of north latitude. Finally, Lagarde was to pave the way for an alliance with Menelik[6] and in general " to spread a pacific influence in Abyssinia."[7]

It will be remembered, likewise, that from 1894 to 1896, a period of comparative inaction set in as far as French colonial operations were concerned. By 1897, however, this *néfaste période* was ended which had kept Clochette waiting at the Ethiopian Capital. Lagarde chose him to head an expedition to connect with Marchand on the Nile. The expedition had instructions to establish a French fort on the left bank of the Nile and an Ethiopian fort on the right bank of the river. The expedition was to consist not only of French officers among whom were Bonvalot, Bonchamps, Faivre and Potter, but also of some two hundred Ethiopians.

In order to enlist Ethiopian cooperation, the French were careful to persuade Menelik that they were aiding him to establish his ancient claims to territory east of the Nile. Indeed, Lagarde in his negotiations with Menelik found that monarch was anxious to claim the whole course of the Nile between the fifth and the fourteenth degrees north latitude as the western boundary of Ethiopia. He was, however, afraid of England and glad to accept the cooperation of France. He entered sympathetically, therefore, into the French schemes for sending the expedition into the west and even tried to win the Mahdists over to a friendly reception of the explorers.[8]

Captain Clochette set out with his force but in spite of an auspicious beginning the expedition failed utterly. Captain Clochette died. Bonchamps then took his place. Bonchamps led the force as far as Nasir on the Sobat river but he never reached the Nile. He was forced to return to Addis Ababa before Marchand reached Fashoda because of sickness and lack of boats.[9]

M. Lagarde next tried to induce Menelik, himself, to occupy all the territory which he claimed east of the Nile. His efforts were so far successful that at the close of 1897 there were four Ethiopian columns moving towards the Nile but little was accomplished. The expeditions were poorly equipped for work in lowland countries. They were defeated largely by disease and physical obstacles. Furthermore, a revolt in Tigré diverted Menelik's attention from the Nile.[10]

Lagarde did, however, succeed in concluding an alliance with the Ethiopian King. On March 20, 1897, Menelik signed a Franco-Ethiopian agreement providing that Ethiopia should extend to the Nile between the 5th and 14th parallels of north latitude. The treaty was never published but it undoubtedly anticipated common action between the countries and offered France decided advantages.[11]

In addition to the expeditions led largely by Frenchmen, there were rumors of others with which certain Russians were associated. Count Léontiff, especially, was in Menelik's good graces. As seen in a previous chapter, Menelik granted him the governorship over his " Equatorial Provinces." There was some vagueness about where these provinces were located for a while. At this juncture, however, it appeared that they constituted the territory southwest of Ethiopia extending to the south beyond any claim Menelik had previously made, probably the 2nd parallel of north latitude. On the west, they touched the Nile. Léontiff collected a formidable expedition to proceed to these provinces. Associated with him was the Frenchman, Prince Henry of Orleans. Léontiff, however, was accidentally shot through the legs and as a result the expedition came to nothing.[12]

In spite of these failures, one expedition did almost reach its goal in 1898. A large Ethiopian mission travelled down the Sobat to the White Nile. It was the main Ethiopian division led by Dedjazmach Tessama. It was sent to follow up Bonchamps, to occupy for Menelik the territory from the White Nile to the Ethiopian plateau and to give aid to Marchand at Foshoda. Tessama arrived at the mouth of the Sobat, June 20, 1898. Here, however, sickness again forced him to return just ten days before Marchand's boats passed the mouth of that river.[13]

Although the British possibly had very little definite information about the French operations in Ethiopia, disturbing rumors reached them from time to time, as already noted.[14] They were determined to forestall French activity wherever they could and to prevent their rivals from establishing themselves in the Upper Nile. In 1897, Sir James Rennell Rodd was dispatched by the British Government on a good-will mission to King Menelik. He was, at the same time, to watch the movements of the French and Russians in that country and to counteract any influence which was likely to harm British interests. He was, also, to make sure that there would be no co-operation between Menelik and the Khalifa during the Sudanese campaign.[15]

While at Menelik's court at Addis Ababa, Rodd learned that Ethiopians were on the Sobat River, south of Fashoda. He learned also that Clochette had left Addis Ababa on a relief expedition to the Nile to join hands with Captain Marchand. He discovered, likewise, that Menelik was anxious to restore the ancient limits of Ethiopia and was putting forward " the most extensive claims to a dominion " covering half the British Somali Protectorate and extending westward to the Nile. The various Ethiopian border governors were even then engaged in extending Ethiopian control in many directions. Sir Rennell's work was on the whole successful. He and his followers were well received and sent away, he wrote, with a pomp and ceremony never accorded before to any other mission.[16]

He returned with a treaty which delimited the eastern boundary between Ethiopia and the British protectorate on the Somali coast but wisely did not mention the question of the Nile Frontier. Such a question could be better decided after British troops reoccupied Khartoum. The chief merit of the treaty, however, seems to have been that it established a good understanding between the King of Kings and H. M. Government and disposed of a possibility of an alliance between Menelik and the Khalifa. Rodd succeeded, therefore, in conciliating Ethiopia during the last phase of the Khartoum campaign and secured the friendly neutrality of the Ethiopians. Salisbury, indeed was more anxious about the French advance towards the Nile and the news which Rodd had in this respect than about the boundary arrangements on the Somali coast. Sir Rennell Rodd urged speed in the British advance on Khartoum and felt that the situation was becoming critical in the Upper Nile region.[17]

Sir Edward Grey saw in the Ethiopian treaty more than just a readjustment of a boundary line. He appreciated that its chief merit was the establishment of good relations with the Ethiopian Monarch. Furthermore, he saw wide possibility for the future in this evidence of good will.

. . . the question of this part of Africa [he pointed out], is an important question and it may be a very critical question in the future. Abyssinia is undoubtedly a great factor in that part of Africa, and must be a great factor in any future settlement; and I think the real justification of this Treaty is to be found in the fact that as other nations have entered into relations with Menelik and have had an understanding with him, it became vital that we should also have an understanding to recognize him . . . [18]

In short, the Rodd mission to Ethiopia was a supplementary part of the British program of reconquering the Sudan. Had Ethiopia joined the Khalifa under French influence, a knot would have been tied across Africa which it would have been difficult for the British to cut.[19]   The Lion of Judah, however, by the skillful and timely diplomacy of the Rodd mission, was converted from a potential enemy into a real friend to British interests.

Furthermore, the British were speculating upon the probable behaviour of the Congolese.   It has been seen how Salisbury rejected Leopold's offer to take the Mahdist country under a lease.   Now, the British felt that the ambitious Monarch rebuffed by them, might have turned to the French. As early as September, 1896, Lord Salisbury confided to Sir Arthur Bigge that " we have shrewd suspicions that the King of the Belgians will give them the French, a helping hand." [20]   There seems to have been some grounds for this suspicion for in September, 1898, Delcassé admitted to Sir E. Monson that Marchand's expedition was " undertaken in virtue of an understanding with the Congolese Government." [21]

H. M. Government was also preparing the ground in the South for the reconquest of the Sudan.   The object of the British Government was to make good its claim to the entire upper valley by effective occupation.[22]   As early as 1897, the Government was planning for expeditions northwards from Uganda to join hands with Kitchener's forces coming down from the North.   The advance from Uganda was to be carried out in two directions.   One expedition under Colonel Macdonald was to proceed across country ostensibly to explore the districts adjacent to the Italian sphere along the course of the river Juba and make treaties with the chiefs in that portion of the British region; but really to join forces with the Anglo-Egyptian army coming down from Khartoum. The other expedition, under Major Martyr, was to work its way down the Nile from the Lake in order to establish a chain of posts along the White Nile.[23]

The British Government was more secretive than the French about their expeditions.[24] For a time, H. M. Government tried to keep even the British Parliament in ignorance of the true objective of the Macdonald mission. The mission, Balfour, first Lord of the Treasury, insisted, " was to explore and delimit the boundary between the Italian and British spheres of influence, fixed by the Treaty of 1891." [25] Sir Charles Dilke, however, pointed out incriminatingly the rather unusual choice of men from the Dinka and Shilluk tribes to accompany the so-called Juba expedition. The territory of the Dinkas and the Shilluks did not lie at all near the sources of the Juba River, towards which the expedition was ostensibly directed. These tribes had their home on the western side of the Nile in the Bahr-el-Ghazal region. The Juba rose on the eastern side of the Nile. The Dinkas and Shilluks, Dilke surmised, were to be taken along as interpreters and guides. It certainly was curious that an expedition to explore the source of the Juba River should take with it, as assistants, men from two tribes in the Bahr-el-Ghazal.[26] The implication was that the expedition was directed, in reality, towards the province claimed by the French as their sphere of influence.

The Macdonald expedition should have started in 1897, but was delayed by troubles in Uganda and particularly by the revolt of the Sudanese troops whom Macdonald was employing for his missions.[27] When he finally was ready to start, Macdonald divided his force, leaving one part at the base, sending a second under Captain Austin to the north of

Lake Rudolph and leading the third northwards himself toward the Latuka Sultanate.   Here he was forced to turn back because he mistrusted the loyalty of his troops.   The column was already exhausted, the transport of food and provisions was exceptionally difficult and the force was in no condition to meet a probable attack of the Dervishes. He returned to his base at Save intending to make a second attempt after reprovisioning his troops.   He failed, however, to find the needed supplies at Save and decided to break up the expedition.

Major Martyr, on his part, pushed north as far as Rejaf on the Nile.   There his way was blocked by the sudd and he likewise was obliged to return.[28]

When Marchand, therefore, after a long and hazardous march, arrived at Fashoda in July, 1898, he was opposed by no British columns coming down stream from Uganda. He also reached his chosen destination more than two months before Kitchener and his victorious troops pushed their way down from Khartoum.   Marchand could thereby claim prior occupancy.[29]   He wrote as early as March to his friend Paul Boudarie: " . . . to-day, the entire Bahr-el-Ghazal can no more belong to England except with the wish of France or by an international conference: it is no longer to be taken." [30]   Marchand did what he could to secure his position and to make the French occupation effective.   He set up eleven French fortified posts in the Bahr-el-Ghazal and established a rudimentary form of administration there.   He built a road ninety miles long from Kojali to the upper M'Boku.[31]   He repulsed, on August 25, a Dervish attack.   He next concluded, on September 2, a treaty with the Shilluks placing their country under French protection.   Marchand sent the treaty to France by way of the Sobat and Ethiopia, and a second copy by way of the Bahr-el-Ghazal with a request for reinforcements.[32]   The

French claimed that they had established themselves with heavy sacrifices in the Bahr-el-Ghazal, that they were maintaining several posts there at great expense, that they were assuring the country of security and protecting commerce, in a word, that they were fulfilling all the requirements of the Berlin Act for effective occupation.[33]

Marchand, however, was in a weak position. The Ethiopian expeditions, as above, failed to reach Fashoda. He had only one hundred and fifty men with him.[34] His supplies were inadequate. The French, however, stressed the point that, even with his small force, he had successfully repulsed an attack by the Dervishes. As a matter of fact, there was good reason to believe that the Dervish flotilla which he drove back had merely retired for reinforcements.[35] The Shilluks were doubtful friends. As soon as Kitchener arrived with his superior forces, the cunning Shilluk Mek denied ever having concluded a treaty with the French and expressed great delight at returning to Egyptian allegiance.[36] Nothing could have saved the Marchand expedition, Kitchener claimed, from annihilation by the Dervishes if the English had been a fortnight later in arriving.[37] In other words, it was decidedly questionable whether the French occupation was really effective.[38]

The French, themselves, in spite of their insistence that Marchand had effectively occupied the Bahr-el-Ghazal were anxious about the safety of the Captain at Kitchener's army proceeded up the Nile. Delcassé informed Sir E. Monson, that Marchand was only an " emissary of civilization " and had " no authority to assume the decision of questions of right." Such authority belonged " exclusively to the competence of the British and French Governments." He hoped that H. M. Govrnment would, therefore, prevent a collision " by reserving all questions of principle for direct discussion at home." [39]

Against the insecure French occupation of the Bahr-el-Ghazal, the British advanced the positive and ancient rights of the conqueror. As early as September 9, after the battles of the Atbara and at Omdurman, the Marquis of Salisbury wrote to Sir E. Monson about the possibility of a meeting between Kitchener and Marchand. Sir E. Monson was instructed to tell Delcassé " that, by the military events of last week, all the territories which were subject to the Khalifa passed by right of conquest to the British and Egyptian Governments. Her Majesty's Government do not consider that this right is open to discussion. . . ." [40]

With the victorious Anglo-Egyptian army approaching Fashoda, the French were in a difficult position. They were unwilling to recognize a British sphere of influence in the Upper Nile Valley yet they realized the weakness of Marchand's position. Once more on the eve of the meeting between Kitchener and Marchand, Delcassé told Monson, British Ambassador, that there was no Marchand Mission in the political sense of the word. Marchand was a subordinate officer and received all his orders from M. Liotard. M. Liotard had been sent out in 1893 as commissioner to Ubanga to secure French interests in the North-East. The British had not protested then and, therefore, why should they protect against France's sending out Marchand to aid Liotard? " If Her Majesty's Government would meet that of France in a friendly spirit, there could be no reason why a satisfactory arrangement should not be quickly arrived at."

Monson replied firmly " that the situation on the Upper Nile is a dangerous one ", that Fashoda distinctly fell within the territory of the conquered Khalifate and, therefore, belonged to the conquerors. On that point there was no hope for a compromise. [41]

Kitchener met Marchand at Fashoda on September 19. The incident was a tense one; " the high point," says Giffen, " in thirty years of Anglo-French rivalry in Africa." [42] The Sirdar informed the French commander, courteously but firmly, that " the presence of the French at Fashoda and in the Valley of the Nile was regarded as a direct violation of the rights of Egypt and Great Britain," that he was instructed to " protest in the strongest terms against their occupation of Fashoda, and their hoisting of the French flag in the dominions of His Highness the Khedive."

Marchand replied with equal firmness

that as a soldier he had to obey orders; the instructions of his Government to occupy the Bahr-el-Ghazal and the Mudirieh of Fashoda were precise, and, having carried them out, he must await the orders of his Government as to his subsequent action and movements.[43]

The Sirdar, thereupon, warned Marchand that although he wished to avoid hostilities, he must carry out his instructions to re-establish Egyptian authority in the Fashoda Mudirieh. If Marchand wished to retire, he would supply him with gunboats.

The French commander gallantly answered, that if Kitchener felt obliged to take action, " he could only submit to the inevitable, which would mean that he and his companions would die at their posts." He begged, however, that the question of his remaining at Fashoda be referred to his Government.

The Sirdar then diplomatically offered a way out of the difficulty. He suggested that Marchand allow the Egyptian flag to be hoisted over the fortress. The Frenchman hesitated and then admitted that he could not resist the hoisting of the Egyptian flag.

The flag of Egypt was accordingly raised with due pomp and ceremony on a ruined bastion on the south portion of the old Fashoda fortifications about 500 yards from the French fort, and on the only road leading from Fashoda to the interior.[44]

Kitchener left a written protest with Marchand on behalf of the Egyptian and British Governments, against any occupation by France of the countries in the Valley of the Nile.[45] He then proceeded on his way south to Sobat on the White Nile.[46]

There was some hesitation on the part of the authorities at home about publishing the news of this fateful meeting. The subject was, too, dangerous. Indeed, the first news reached the public on the 26th, seven days after the actual encounter.[47] Feeling ran high in both France and England. The reconquest of the Sudan had been an exceedingly popular measure among the British. Each advance had been greeted with cheers in the House.[48] The general feeling had been right along that France had no business to interfere in the Nile Valley. It has already been noted how intense the feeling was at the time of the Grey declaration.[49] After the Fashoda incident, the British nation as a whole was ready to stand behind Lord Salisbury's firm policy in regard to France.

There was perhaps, a feeling, too, of resentment that France was trying to block British expansion from the Cape-to-Cairo. It is significant that Sir E. Monson, British Ambassador to France, should voice this resentment. On October 21, he wrote to Salisbury:

. . . It seemed, however, impossible for any one to deny that that expedition, i. e., the Marchand . . . had been a deliberate attempt to obstruct our advance up the Nile Valley, and to intercept our line of communication between north and south Africa, the establishment of which, as all Europe knows, is the object of our policy.[50]

Was Great Britain then following a definite Cape-to-Cairo policy in the reconquest of the Sudan? These words of the British Ambassador certainly lend color to this theory.

Lord Rosebery boasted that his administration was largely responsible for the Government on which the policy in connection with Fashoda was founded. The Marchand and Kitchener encounter was one " of extreme—of supreme gravity " in view of the fact that France had been duly warned that an encroachment into the Nile Valley would be an "unfriendly act." The "untiring and united strength of the nation itself" stood behind the policy of the British Government in this matter. He warned outsiders:

. . . If the nations of the world are under the impression that the ancient spirit of Great Britain is dead or her resources are weakened, or that her population is less determined than ever it was to maintain the rights and honour of its flag, they make a mistake which can only end in a disastrous conflagration.[51]

Sir Michael Hicks Beach, vigilant guardian of the national exchequer, told France that Great Britain had put its foot down. He said truculently:

If, unhappily, another view should be taken elsewhere, we, the Ministers of the Queen, know what our duty demands. It would be a great calamity—I do not underrate it—that, after a peace of more than eighty years . . . those friendly relations should be disturbed and we should be launched into a great war. But there are greater evils than war. We believe that we have in this matter the country at our back; and we shall not shrink from anything that may come.[52]

The Government did not restrict itself to uncompromising language. Preparations portending a complete rupture were under way. A reserve squadron was placed in the Channel. Work was said to be going on day and night in Plymouth and Portsmouth. The fleet was sent to Alexandria to protect the Suez Canal.[53]

When Delcassé inquired of Monson: " You surely would not break with us over Fashoda? " Monson replied that that was exactly what he feared.[54] Furthermore, H. M. Government was doing as little as possible to help Marchand at Fashoda. Lord Salisbury telegraphed to Rodd, the British agent at Cairo:

M. Marchand's position should be made as untenable as possible. If he is in want of food supplies, it will be very necessary to use circumspection in helping him to obtain them. Until he expresses his intention of going down the river, no such supplies should be furnished to him except in the case of extreme necessity.[55]

Unless Marchand retired from Fashoda, H. M. Government refused to negotiate with the French.[56]

The French people were also excited. The Paris press was particularly hostile to England. *Le Matin,* the mouthpiece of the French Government, sturdily maintained that the Government " will not retreat before menaces from the press or any other menaces." Monson wrote to Lord Salisbury " it needs but the whisper of a possible insult to the French flag to arouse a tempest of excitement throughout the country." In view of the fact that the Chamber was about to meet, France was " within measurable distance of very dangerous excitement." [57]

Delcassé stated that any formal demand that France give up Fashoda

would be considered as an ultimatum and rejected. Already by the occupation of Sobat, and Sirdar has committed what is practically an act of war or at any rate a more than unfriendly act, of which, however, his Excellency does not yet wish to make a complaint. . . . He could not think that it is wished in England to go to war over such a question, but France would, however unwilling, accept war rather than submit.[58]

The French fleet was ordered to Cherbourg. Stores and ammunitions were collected at Cherbourg and orders to march were in the hands of commanding officers.[59] War was imminent.[60]

At this crucial juncture, however, the French were in a weakened condition at home and in a doubtful position abroad. Internally, the country was disturbed by dissensions. The Brisson cabinet fell on October 26. The notorious Dreyfus case had been reopened. The country was torn almost as if by Civil War.[61]

One way out of the French difficulties might be to call a conference of European Powers. There was some question whether one of the great Powers to whom peace was of importance might not submit the question to the deliberation of the other Powers. In fact, Delcassé hinted to Monson " that this contingency " had " suggested itself to his mind ". In such a case, the Fashoda dispute would probably be coupled with Near Eastern questions.[62]

Russia, however, was indifferent to the African situation in spite of its interest already noted in Ethiopian intrigues [63] and seemed reluctant to be dragged into a war against England over a " miserable swamp " in the heart of the Dark Continent. Fashoda was after all a purely African question, and one which did not in any way affect Russia, who had no interest in Africa.[64] Nevertheless, as Sir Edmund Monson pointed out to the Marquis of Salisbury, October 21, " any tendency towards the disturbance of international peace must be eminently distasteful to Russia." Furthermore, Russia, as France's ally was under certain obligations to it. Sir Edmund noted with uneasiness that Count Mouravieff's visit to Paris and then to Vienna gave encouragement to the French Government. It would, in fact he thought, be difficult for Count Mouravieff to decline to show some intention of giving his best support to France in the existing emergency.[65]   It later turned out that Count Mouravieff had advised Delcassé not to give England any pretext for attacking at present.   At a later date, Russia would find an opportunity for opening up the whole Egyptian question.[66]   Salisbury did not believe that " Russia's support was either contingently promised or categorically refused in the present emergency."   War at that time would be inconvenient for Russia and she would like to stop it but she was indifferent as to whether it was stopped by France yielding or England yielding.[67]   On the whole, the Emperor of Russia seemed unwilling to raise difficulties for England.[68]

Italy, Sir P. Currie informed Salisbury, in an event of war between France and England, " could only remain neutral or side with England." [69]

France at this juncture, could not count on any support from Germany.   The Anglo-German rapprochement of 1898 and 1899 has been discussed at some length in a previous chapter.[70]   There were, to be sure, pitfalls behind that rapprochement and it had its weaknesses.   Nevertheless, it was important that just at this time Germany was turning towards England rather than France.   In fact, all during the Sudanese campaign, Germany supported England.   The Germans favored the British campaign in the Sudan by voting for a grant from the Egyptian General Reserve Fund for the campaign.[71]   After the British victory at Atbara, the Kaiser wrote to the Queen, " most glad at good news. I beg to express my sincerest congratulations at the brilliant victory in the Soudan.   The Sirdar has done his work ably and well."   After the battle of Omdurman, the German Emperor, moreover, took occasion to show his good-will towards the English by congratulating the British ambassador on Kitchener's victory.[72]   Furthermore, at Hanover, where he was reviewing the German troops, he called for three cheers for the Queen.[73]   Just after Kitchener and

Marchand met at Fashoda, it will be recalled, Great Britain and Germany came to an agreement over a loan to Portugal which Germany regarded as the inauguration of a common colonial policy.[74]

Unstable as Germany's friendship might be, Great Britain and Germany were in accord over their African ambitions at a time when Great Britain needed Germany's support. Any evidence that Germany stood by England even on a single question could not but be favorable to England's general position. It was not so much on legal and fine-spun arguments that the Fashoda issue was decided but on the relative strength of France and England both at home and in Europe.[75] The balance of strength was on the side of England.

To be sure, as far as the Fashoda incident itself was concerned, the German Government maintained a formal neutrality but it was a neutrality which clearly worked to the advantage of Great Britain. " The truth was," Giffen maintains, " that German neutrality did not weigh equally on each side; by a sort of paradox German neutrality was not neutral." " Germany's neutrality alone," said von Bülow, " would probably suffice to secure England against a conflict with France and Russia together. . . . It would not be necessary for England to make any sacrifice whatever in order to purchase French complaisance, since that was immediately conditional upon German neutrality." [76]

Whatever may have been the argumentative merits of Delcassé's case, France was actually in a difficult position. With Marchand at the mercy of Kitchener's army in Africa, with a united England behind the uncompromising British stand, with no help from Germany or Russia, France, torn by dissension at home, could do little to defend itself. From the first Delcassé appeared willing to enter into negotiations with England. He maintained, it will be remembered, that it was not for either Kitchener or Marchand to decide upon the political consequences of their expeditions. That was a question to be regulated by the two governments.[77] The French Ambassador at London believed that they would find a basis for an understanding.[78] The French objected, however, to the peremptory demand of Great Britain that Marchand evacuate Fashoda before discussions began. To demand evacuation before discussion, Declassé declared, was fundamentally tantamount to an ultimatum.[79]

In spite of Delcassé's " brave words ", however, France could not risk a war with England at this time. At first, the French tried to gain time. They asked H. M. Government to wait until they received an official report from Marchand himself regarding the Fashoda incident before they recalled the intrepid commander.[80] Lord Salisbury, while refusing to accept any responsibility for the health or safety of Marchand during the interval yielded so far as to allow the French government to convey a message asking for a report, through Cairo, to Marchand.[81]

On October 4, Delcassé hinted that there was a way out of the impasse. The Fashoda issue, he suggested, might be linked with the question of delimiting the spheres of influence of the French colonies in the Congo and Upper Ubangi regions. The French, he admitted, would not contest their rights as first occupants of Fashoda under all conditions but they could not abandon their position at Fashoda without some discussion, without some friendly understanding in regard to other matters. They wanted, especially, some amicable arrangement completing the agreements already arrived at in the Lake Chad region.[82] Baron de Courcel made a similar proposition, the following day, to Lord Salisbury. The French, he added, were particularly anxious for an opening on the Nile.[83] Lord Salisbury, while not accepting immediately Delcassé's proposal, was willing to discuss it with his colleagues and seemed to be in a conciliatory and friendly mood.[84]   As far as British and French statesmen, therefore, were concerned, the door appeared to be gradually opening for an accord between the two countries.[85]

Popular feeling, however, especially in England, was growing more and more tense.[86]   There was still talk of war.[87]   Furthermore, H. M. Government continued, in spite of Salisbury's more friendly mood of October five, to take a firm stand.   On October 12, Lord Salisbury demanded that the French retire to the watershed.[88]   The French Government decided to yield and to order the evacuation of Fashoda.   On November 4, Lord Salisbury received the official announcement of this decision.[89]

Even after the evacuation of Fashoda, however, feeling was still tense in England.   Naval preparations were continued.   There were many vexatious questions which were as yet unsettled.   The French had withdrawn from Fashoda but they continued to occupy other posts in the Bahr-el-Ghazal; at Mesha-er-Rek, Wau and Tembura.[90]   The question of where the French sphere ended and the Anglo-Egyptian began was a debatable matter.   Even as late as December, the Kaiser told Sir F. Lascelles that the danger of trouble between France and England was by no means past. " . . . it was probable war would break out in the spring." The Emperor seemed to delight in the idea and to egg the British on to further trouble.

From a military point of view [he said], the moment was well chosen.   France was by no means the equal of England at sea, and she would receive no assistance from any other Power. . . . England would, therefore, have an excellent opportunity of settling accounts with France.

Germany, for its part, would maintain a strict neutrality so long as the struggle was confined to England and France.

If any other Power stepped in, the Kaiser hinted at putting into operation a previously discussed defensive alliance between England and Germany.[91]

Nevertheless, in spite of the threatening atmosphere, new negotiations over questions yet pending began finally on January 12. The French were willing to give up their original plan of a political establishment in the Upper Nile region and to confine themselves simply to the request for a trade route on the Upper Nile and a favorable delimitation of their sphere of influence east of Lake Chad. Finally, they asked only for freedom of trade along certain avenues and a favorable delimitation of spheres of influence.[92] On this basis, negotiations proceeded and ended in the Anglo-French agreement of March 21, 1899, completing the convention between Great Britain and France of June 14, 1898.

The agreement was, in reality, a supplement to Article IV of the Convention of the previous June, defining British and French spheres of influence in Central Africa and the Sudan. It was, therefore, the final act in the series of negotiations, which have already been noted, respecting these regions.[93] By the new agreement, the French Republic gave up all political claims in the Bahr-el-Ghazal. The treaty, however, implied that France, in return for the Bahr-el-Ghazal, might have a free hand in the southern hinterland of Tripoli.[94] Furthermore, although France gave up all political rights in the Bahr-el-Ghazal, she was allowed certain commercial privileges there.[95]

The arrangement of March 21, 1899, was undoubtedly a hard blow for the French and the press was bitter against the English. It meant a distinct renunciation by them of their hotly contested rights in the Bahr-el-Ghazal. The French statesmen also were forced to relinquish their plan, cherished since 1893, of reopening the Egyptian question by securing a strong position on the Upper Nile. Their whole scheme of extending French influence into the Nile Valley and perhaps farther to Obok on the Red Sea was a failure.[96] They were also singularly unsuccessful in blocking the seemingly steady advance of the British across the continent from Cairo to the Cape. To be sure, as far as this latter point was concerned, Hanotaux denies that it was ever an objective of the French to cut the Cape-to-Cairo line.[97] Nevertheless, other writers give evidence that the French people were watching the progress of the British from south-to-north with a great deal of alarm and jealousy.[98] Darcy maintains that the French policy was distinctly " to dispute with England the sovereignty of all one half of Africa." [99] Opposition to the supposed British Cape-to-Cairo movement was probably at least one stimulating element in the extension of French influence into the Upper Nile Valley. At any rate with the withdrawal of the French from Fashoda and the signing of the Declaration of March 21, Anglo-French rivalry ceased in the Sudan. Henceforth the section of the Cape-to-Cairo route which lay in this region was left free for the British advance.

The agreement of March 21, 1899 was the reluctant recognition by one more great European power of a British sphere of influence in the Nile Valley.[100] In short, the Anglo-French declaration of March 21, 1899 was the culmination of the African policy which commenced with the Anglo-German agreement of July, 1890. By the reconquest of the Sudan and by a series of treaties concluded with three European Powers, Great Britain had, at last, made secure her prescriptive rights from the Great Lakes to the Egyptian frontier. This advance was enthusiastically supported by the British nation. It voiced a popular desire for a forward movement in Africa.

CHAPTER XX

Epilogue

THE INFLUENCE OF THE IDEA

In the preceding chapters, the development of specific Cape-to-Cairo projects has been discussed such as the Overland Telegraph of Arnold, Nicholls and Grant and the transcontinental railway and telegraph schemes of Cecil Rhodes.

The primary interest, however, has centered not so much on the development of these projects as on the influence of the idea behind them; i. e., the opening up of the Dark Continent from the south to the north to British commerce and civilization. This has led the reader deeply into the tangled story of British expansion and international rivalry along the south to north route.

In this expansion, the British Government did not follow a Cape-to-Cairo policy. In fact, Lord Salisbury in 1887 [1] and 1890 [2] definitely sanctioned the interposition of a German barrier across the road to the north. Furthermore, although Lord Rosebery sponsored a Cape-to-Cairo measure in Article III of the Anglo-Congolese Agreement of 1894, the Government yielded to the insistence of France and Germany that this article be withdrawn. [3]

Nevertheless, the Cape-to-Cairo dreams exercised a real influence over the activities of certain individuals who played important rôles in opening up the heart of the continent to British commerce and civilization. Sir John Kirk, Sir Harry Johnston, Captain Lugard, and Kitchener as well as Cecil Rhodes, were Cape-to-Cairo imperialists. The idea also was sponsored by influential business groups in England. It found supporters in the British Parliament,[4] and it found ministerial favor in the Rosebery Cabinet in 1894.

Although the British did not pursue a definite Cape-to-Cairo policy, outsiders often accused them of doing so and the belief that Great Britain was contemplating an empire from the Cape to Alexandria influenced to some extent the operations of other Powers. As early as 1795, it will be recalled, Lacerda warned the Portuguese that the recent conquerors of Table Bay would in time spread north across the continent.[5]

The fear that English hotspurs longed to see the British flag floating over Africa from Table Mountain to Egypt disturbed the minds of German colonial promoters in the early eighties and was a factor in leading them to talk about planting a transcontinental empire from east to west across the northward path of the British.[6] The suspicion that the English wished to join their spheres of influence in the south and in the north and thus to shove a strip of British territory between the Congo State and German East Africa aroused the Germans to protest against Article III of the Anglo-Congolese agreement of 1894.[7] They were also afraid in 1898 to allow Cecil Rhodes' railway to run from the south to the north of German East Africa lest it be the entering wedge for British influence along that route although at the same time, they were willing to cooperate in plans for building an east to west railway.[8] They were afraid of the iron rails with which Cecil Rhodes threatened to span the continent. " The placing British South Africa in communication with the Sudan by a railway," said an article in the *Täglische Rundschau,* " would be equivalent to the premeditated ruin of our colonial empire in Africa. This railway would be of no economic use for our colony and would result in anglicizing our protectorate and, if this project could be realized, it would give such an extraordinary impetus to English influence that we would soon be forced to decamp from Africa." [9]

The fear of a British advance from the Cape-to-Cairo, also, haunted the French people. Although Hanotaux denies that this was a determining factor in the attempt of the French to secure a footing in the Upper Nile Valley,[10] he talks with some uneasiness about the Anglo-Congolese agreement of 1894 being a British attempt to seize the center of the continent as they had already done in the south and in the north.[11] Darcy in his *Cent Années de Rivalité Coloniale* attributes a definite Cape-to-Cairo policy to the British,[12] and maintains that French activities in Ethiopia aimed at retarding the already advanced progress of England in her route from the Cape to the Valley of the Nile.[13] These may have been phantom fears which the English could declare were without foundation but they played, nevertheless, some part in shaping the policies of other nations.

Even as late as 1910, E. de Renty felt that British negotiations in Ethiopia in 1902 and discussions with Belgium over the Lado Enclave pointed to the conclusion that they were still pursuing the Cape-to-Cairo idea and that at some opportune moment the transafrican question might once more come up resolved in favor of the English.[14] In 1912, M. E. Cammaert tried to conjure up the Cape-to-Cairo bogey. He wrote an article on the present state of the Cape-to-Cairo railway in *le Bulletin de Colonisation comparée* in which he stressed the fact that the economic purpose of building such a line was only secondary and that at that moment there was behind the railway scheme an imperialistic movement to join the British possessions in the south and north and to isolate the possessions of the other countries on the east and west; forever forbidding any other power to pursue a panafrican or transafrican policy.[15]

This point of view seems exaggerated when it is noted that in 1911, Sir Edward Grey assured the German Ambassador Count Metternich that " if the Congo should be for sale it would be no object of ours, as some people supposed, to prevent German territory from extending across Africa from East to West." [16] Nevertheless, during the same conversation, Sir Edward Grey showed that the British were still interested in a Cape-to-Cairo line of communication as an economic project. " No doubt," he added, " we would ask for wayleave for a railway from North to South." [17]

In fact, the Cape-to-Cairo idea is alive today but rather as an economic than a political concept. In this book, on the other hand, the interest has chiefly been in the Cape-to-Cairo dream as a force in the scramble for Africa. The great diplomatic struggles over which it had some influence occured before 1900. Attention, therefore, has centered on the period between 1875 and 1900.

There has, however, been considerable progress made since 1900 in opening up the Cape-to-Cairo route for communication. In this last chapter, therefore, without pursuing the subject deeply, the high spots of that development down to 1936 will be lightly sketched. No attempt, however, will be made to give a complete account of this period. Such an account would, indeed, fill another volume and lies outside the scope of this book.

OBSTACLES SURMOUNTED

As the nineteenth century drew toward its close, the partition of eastern Africa between Cairo and the Cape was virtually completed. Great Britain had succeeded in reserving all but a small portion of the territory required for the great transcontinental railway of which Rhodes had dreamed. There remained three considerable obstacles to building an unbroken line of communications from Cape

Town to Alexandria: first, the sudd in the upper Nile; second, the Lado Enclave, held by Leopold; third, the lake region still in Germany's grasp. The influence of the Cape-to-Cairo idea on British policy may be gauged by the official interest shown in surmounting these barriers.

The first of these difficulties was an impediment not so much to an all-rail route as to the combined rail-and-water system which 19th-century pioneers envisaged. Had the upper Nile been navigable throughout its course, it would have supplied water transportation for a considerable section of the proposed route. But the Nile was not navigable. As Sir Harry Johnston reported in 1900:

> The River Nile, from the place where it issues from the Victoria Nyanza is interrupted by constant series of rapids and falls until it reaches Kakoge. From this point it is navigable . . . as far north as Foweira. After Foweira the Victoria Nile ceases to be navigable until Fajao is reached. From this point it can be navigated by small steamers as far north as Dufile. Then begins a stretch of about 70 miles of rapids, and the Nile is scarcely navigable again until it reaches Beden or Fort Berkeley. From this point, but for the occasional obstruction of the sudd, the Nile is navigable to Khartoum.[18]

Johnston speaks lightly of the sudd but in reality it was a very serious obstacle in the way of any practical progress. Sudd is an Arabic word meaning "barrier" and is generally used to signify the great masses of papyrus and other floating vegetation which clog the Nile between Beden and Khartoum.[19] As noted before, the Martyr expedition was forced to return because the river was blocked with sudd below Rejaf.[20] Still earlier, Gordon planned to open up a road from the east coast to the Equatorial Province in order to become independent of the Nile River because of the difficulty of navigation through the sudd region.[21]

Various attempts have been made to open a clear-water passage. In 1899, for example, the British succeeded in cutting their way through the floating barrier. The islands of sudd, however, closed in again and blocked the way. In 1900, another channel was cut through the northern and heaviest portion and in 1901 the remaining blocks were removed by a British expedition. By 1904, freedom of communication was permanently secured between Khartoum and Gondokoro, and after that transport and communication were regularly maintained up to Rejaf. The sudd is a formidable but not an impassable barrier. A way can be kept clear by a patrol of two gunboats [22] and with the further development of irrigation works in the region of the Nyanza Lakes much of the difficulty may be overcome.[23] Better roads are being built around the portions of the river which are obstructed by rapids in Uganda. There is now actually a through route from the south to the north of Africa, part rail, part motor road, and part waterway but the section through the upper reaches of the Nile is not of much commercial use or importance yet.

There is, however, a possible alternative route which if utilized in the future would avoid the marshes of the Upper Nile Valley and the difficulties of navigation in this section. From Uganda, a railway might be pushed north through Ethiopia. The firm highlands of this country offer distinct possibilities for the construction of a railway between Uganda and the Lower Sudan.[24] Darcy in his book, *Cent Années de Rivalité* hints that the British were fully aware of the possibilities of such a line and that they coveted Ethiopia not only as the guardian of the Nile tributaries but also as ground for this railway connection between the Nile and Uganda.[25]

Certainly the treaty of 1902 between England and Ethiopia lends color to this theory. On October 28, 1902,

Menelik II, King of Kings of Ethiopia, signed a treaty of friendship delimiting the frontier between the Sudan and his dominions. By article V he specifically granted to " His Britannic Majesty's Government and the Government of the Soudan the right to construct a railway through Abyssinian territory to connect the Soudan with Uganda." [26] " Thus," says Darcy, " England obtained at one stroke the exclusive control and the guardianship of all the rivers running from the Ethiopian mountains. She obtained free passage for her Cape-to-Cairo railway as far as the heart of the Ethiopian plateau through the vast and fertile valleys of the Blue Nile and Didessa." [27]

The railway through Ethiopia was never constructed. Nevertheless, the railway clause in the treaty of 1902 is significant and raises some important questions. Did H. M. Government consider this prospective Ethiopian line as a link in the great Cape-to-Cairo chain? Or was the line regarded merely as an aid in administering the Sudan and Uganda or as a commercial railway to open up the fertile valley of the Blue Nile? Was H. M. Government contemplating the construction of this railway when, as will be noted later, Cromer refused to grant Leopold a pier on the Nile for a Congo railway and told Williams: " The Nile is Egypt's . . . we will build the connecting link ourselves."? [28]   If the first question can be answered in the affirmative, it shows that H. M. Government took a much greater interest in a Cape-to-Cairo railway at this time than its refusal to sponsor a trans-Congo line would indicate.[29] It is perhaps unwise, however, to press Darcy's theory too far.

Dr. Work, however, in his recent book on Ethiopia lends some support to this theory. As noted before, he points out that the British safeguarded a highland route west of Ethiopia in the protocols of March and April 1891 between

England and Italy.[30] Although a Cape-to-Cairo route is not mentioned in these agreements, nevertheless, they did allot territory to the British sphere of influence which might in the future be used for railway construction.[31] Furthermore, Dr. Work definitely attributes a Cape-to-Cairo motive to the negotiations between Colonel John Lane-Harrington and Menelik in 1898 which led up to the conclusion of the 1902 treaty between Ethiopia and England. In short, he maintains:

Enough highland territory east of the Nile for the construction of her long desired Cape-to-Cairo railway was essential to England. That she might have this and the control of the waters of the Blue Nile and the Atbara had been England's main purpose all along.[32]

By the treaty of 1902, England did secure plenty of upland territory upon which to build her railway.[33]

The second obstacle was the Lado Enclave, leased to Leopold II in 1894.[34] To secure ultimate ownership of the Lado Enclave, Great Britain made an agreement on May 9, 1906, with Leopold II annulling clause II of the Anglo-Congolese Agreement of 1894. The Belgian King renounced his lease to all the territory between the twenty-fifth meridian East of Greenwich and the Nile, but was permitted to continue during his reign to occupy the territory now held by him and known as the Lado Enclave. Within six months, however, of the termination of His Majesty's occupation, the Enclave was to be handed over to the Sudanese Government. A strip of territory 25 kilometres in breadth stretching from the watershed between the Nile and the Congo up to the western shore of Lake Albert and including the port of Mahagi was to continue in the possession of the Congo State on the conditions laid down in Article II of the Anglo-Congolese agreement of 1894.[35]

In the agreement of 1906, the British negotiators evinced a keen interest in railway development. Article IV arranged for

a concession . . . to be given, in terms to be agreed upon between the Soudanese and Congo State Governments, to an Anglo-Belgian Company for the construction and working of a railway from the frontier of the Independent State of the Congo to the navigable channel of the Nile, near Lado, it being understood that, when His Majesty's occupation of the Enclave terminates, this railway shall be wholly subject to the jurisdiction of the Soudanese Government.

The Egyptian Government, moreover, undertook, to guarantee at a rate of interest of 3 per cent, on a sum not to exceed £800,000 the capital expenditure required for the construction of this line. Finally, a port open to general commerce, with suitable provision for the storing and transhipment of merchandise was to be established at the terminus of the railway.[36]

As far as the German barricade across the Cape-to-Cairo line was concerned, the diplomatic defeat of 1894 seemed to have been definitive until 1914. The most that the British could hope for was permission to run the transcontinental telegraph through German East Africa. When, however, Great Britain entered the World War in 1914, " almost the first dispatch from South Africa spoke of the hope that the end may see an ' All Red ' Cape-to-Cairo Railway in a way with every turn and angle planned for a quick defense. . . ."[37] The end of the War, although it did not hasten the construction of the railway, did destroy completely the German barrier across the Cape-to-Cairo route. Most of German East Africa was placed under British mandate. Along the whole route from Cape Town to Alexandria, Great Britain had no European rival.

The map of Africa is now red from Cape Town to Alexandria. To be sure the color is deeper in the section from the Cape to the Lake region but there is a distinctly reddish tint throughout. How long this red tint will remain, is, of course, a matter for future speculation and depends much upon what happens in Egypt, in Ethiopia and in the Mandated territories. Already Egypt has won nominal independence and there are hints of future trouble in the growing nationalism of the Egyptians.[38] The Germans, too, may cause trouble in the future. They have not forgotten their lost overseas empire nor their dreams of a " Mittel Afrika " from the east to the west coast.

RAILWAY PLANS AFTER 1898

The railway, after 1898, even in Cecil Rhodes's estimation, became purely an economic proposition. It was still important to extend British commercial interests and to open new avenues for British commerce and enterprise, but this could be done, he believed, by an internationally owned and operated line through the Congo. Thwarted by Germany in his plans for a British-owned railway up to Tanganyika, through East Africa into Uganda, he devoted, as already noted, all his remaining energies to the international Katanga line.[39] His able lieutenant, Robert Williams, carried on the work in this spirit both before and after the death of the great empire-builder.[40]

Before turning to Sir Robert Williams' work as continued after Rhodes' death, it is necessary to turn back and to pick up some of the threads of the story already related in previous chapters. It will be recalled that after Cecil Rhodes abandoned his original plan of bringing the railway north to Lake Tanganyika, he decided to take the line through the Congo State.[41] He was, however, unsuccessful in his personal negotiations in 1899 with King Leopold for such a line.[42]

Robert Williams, on the other hand, had been successful about this time in securing from the Belgian King a grant of the sole prospecting rights for minerals over 60,000 square miles of the Katanga district of the Congo State adjoining Northern Rhodesia.[43] As a result of these transactions, Rhodes turned to Williams, the successful negotiator, with his railway problem. The two men studied the map of Africa.

That is the way we will go [Rhodes said, pointing through the Congo State], but your mineral concession is only for thirty years: it is too short. Get King Leopold to extend it to ninety-nine years—the British public love a ninety-nine years' lease. The King will agree to this, he will ask for something, a sort of fine. Give him what he wants, and when you have done all this you can afford to give me a share of your minerals to assist me with my railway.[44]

Williams went to King Leopold and did obtain an extension of the mineral concession together with a railway agreement. In fact, he secured a concession from the King for the construction of a line from the Rhodesian frontier through the Congo State to the Nile. He offered this to Rhodes together with a half-share in the mineral rights which he had also obtained from Leopold. Rhodes' financial supporters, however, would not agree to the terms. Sir Robert Williams attributes the failure of the scheme to Beit who was behind Rhodes. Beit, he said, " demanded such an extravagant share of the mineral rights of Katanga (not only of mine, but also of King Leopold's) as the price of bringing the railway forward to the Congo frontier, that the scheme fell through." [45] Behind Beit, he saw German machinations. " The Germans," he claimed, " were particularly anxious to quash this Cape-to-Cairo scheme, and one of their agents went to Brussels ' to put a spoke in Williams' wheel.' " [46] Germany, he thought, was even then scheming to secure the Congo State and " the British Government was too blind to see it, and too supine to realise the vital importance to the British Empire of Rhodes' great scheme."

Rhodes died shortly after the failure of the above transaction, but not before Williams, his faithful collaborator, had promised to do his best to see his line north.[47]

Before the Congo was reached, there was still a little stretch through Rhodesia from Broken Hill to the border to be completed. The construction of this line to the Congo border was a private undertaking financed largely through the efforts of Williams himself, George Pauling and the Erlanger brothers, London bankers.[48] H. M. Government felt that it could not afford to back the undertaking and even the British South Africa Company was unable to find the money. The Beit trustees of Rhodes' will were, likewise, unwilling to finance the little link between Broken Hill and the Katanga border.[49]

Williams was still turning over plans for carrying the railway through the Congo. Undaunted, by the failure of his first attempt to bring the line through the Congo, he proceeded to come to a fresh agreement with Leopold. This time, he reduced the request for the railway concession to a line connecting the navigable Congo with the mining area of Katanga as far south as the Rhodesian frontier and west to the Ruwe gold mines. Sixty per cent of the railway was to be owned by the Belgians and forty per cent by Williams' Company, the Tanganyika Concessions Ltd. This was, said he, the inception of the *Chemin de Fer du Katanga*, or Katanga Railway Company, which now connects the Rhodesian Railway with the navigable Congo.[50] In fact, it connects the Benguella Railway with the Cape-to-Cairo line.[51] The railway was brought to Victoria Falls in 1904 and to Broken Hill in 1907. After strenuous efforts by Robert Williams, the Katanga Copper Mines were reached in 1909.[52]

Williams had, furthermore, begun to lay plans for linking the line with the Egyptian railway system. He talked his schemes over first with King Leopold.[53] He hoped, at the time, to interest his home Government in carrying the Cape-to-Cairo Railway through the Congo State. Leopold suggested that he see Lord Cromer and ask him to settle the Lado Enclave difficulty and to give the Belgians a pier on the Nile for the Belgian end of the railway. He likewise suggested that Williams try to secure Chamberlain's support for his scheme.[54] Thereupon, the railway promoter solicited the help of both Chamberlain and Cromer.

He went first to Egypt. Cromer " quite agreed that the best and only practical route for the Cape to Cairo Railway was through the Congo State, utilising the great navigable Congo River." [55] " But why call yours the Cape to Cairo Railway, Mr. Williams? " Cromer said, " . . . call it the ' Cape to the Nile ' for *there* it will meet the Egyptian system of railways." He refused to give Leopold a pier on the Nile because, he maintained: " The Nile is Egypt's . . . we will build the connecting link ourselves." [56]

Williams then proceeded to London where he interviewed Joseph Chamberlain. He asked the British Government for a guarantee of interest on £10,000,000. If this guarantee were granted, he undertook to bring the Cape-to-Cairo railway through the Congo State. Chamberlain appeared interested and said he believed it would all be carried out in time but that then it would be impossible to get the Chancellor of the Exchequer to agree to the amount on the grounds that the expense of the Boer War was too great to permit consideration of a new enterprise.[57] Also, Chamberlain appeared to be influenced by the fact that Lord Cromer had refused assistance.[58] " Had the guarantee been granted," said Williams in 1917, " the railway would now have been built." [59] As it is, the railway is still pushing slowly north through the Congo.

The scheme for constructing the railway north through the Congo, the Katanga railway, was undertaken as a co-operative enterprise. It was linked with two other schemes: one the Benguella railway from Lobito Bay on the west coast to the Katanga railway; and the other, a line to connect up the Lower Congo railway and Leopoldville with the Katanga Railway at Bukama. The earnings of these railways were to be pooled. The Cape-to-Cairo railway, therefore, as it started north through the Congo was part of an international railway plan carried on by British, Belgian and Portuguese companies. Monsieur Jean Jadot, the great Belgian banker, helped largely in financing the work in the Congo. The plan was ably seconded by King Albert and his Colonial Minister, Monsieur Rankin. The Portuguese Government was also most co-operative.[60] Under this arrangement, the railway reached Bukama in 1916.[61]

Williams next planned for the systematic exploration of the Sudanese side of the Nile-Congo Divide. Close to the Divide on the Congo side, the Kilo and Moto Gold Mines were already being exploited by the Belgians.[62] He hoped to find more mineral wealth on the Sudanese side. He had formerly demonstrated that mineral discoveries of South Africa had generally been found on the watersheds dividing the great river systems, and how these discoveries had led the Cape to Cairo Railway step by step into the interior of the continent.[63] Now he hoped to find this northern divide equally rich in minerals. His paper entitled " Milestones of African Civilization " read before the Royal Colonial Institute in May 1917, embodied this theory.

As a result of the paper, Williams received a call from Major C. Christy. Christy believed that the Nile-Congo divide must be the future route for the extension of the Cape to Cairo line from Khartoum southward. He also believed in the great mineral wealth of the Divide. He was anxious to undertake an exploration of the region. The investigation was, finally, carried out at the instance of Williams' Company, The Tanganyika Concessions, Ltd., and by the Nile-Congo Divide Syndicate. A concession was first obtained by Major Christy from the Sudanese Government of some 60,000 square miles along the Sudanese side of the Divide, and then in 1923 Christy led the expedition to explore the area.[64]

The following year, Christy presented a paper at the Toronto meeting of the British Association of the Royal Scottish Geographical Society. Without prophesying an immediate extension of the railway in the region of the Nile-Congo Divide, he maintained that " in the Bahr-el-Ghazal portion of this great watershed discoveries have recently been made which will, it is believed, act as the last great mineral milestone needed to lead the Sudan Railway southward and ultimately to link up with the Congo system." [65]

The scheme of Williams and Major Christy contemplated that the Cape-to-Cairo route would run north through the Congo, up over the Nile-Congo divide and join with the Sudanese railway. This plan would make possible a railway from one end of the continent to the other end and would obviate the difficulties and inconveniences of transhipment over a rail-and-water line.

In brief, there are now, at least, three possible routes for a Cape-to-Cairo line of communications to follow. One is an all-rail route through the Belgian Congo over the Nile-Congolese Divide. The next is a rail-water-motor-route through Uganda and the Upper Sudan. The third is, again, an all-rail route through East Africa, along the Ethiopian Highlands into the Lower Sudan.

PRESENT AND FUTURE

Notwithstanding the efforts of Rhodes and Williams and despite the successes won by British diplomacy and British arms in the early twentieth century, the Cape-to-Cairo railway was not completed. Neither through the Belgian Congo, nor through East Africa, nor through Ethiopia were rails laid to connect the lines that had been extended down from the north and up from the south. From the North, the Egyptian trunk line reached to Aswan, and a little beyond, but not to the frontier of the Sudan. In the Sudan, there were rails from Wadi Halfa, on the northern border, to Sennar and El Obeid, south of Khartoum, but the southern Sudan was not yet spanned. Nor was the Belgian Congo. From South Africa, northward through Rhodesia, a trunk line bravely entered the Congo, only to veer westward toward an Atlantic outlet.

The fact that the railway has not been completed, can no longer be explained by reasons of international politics. The international barriers have long since been razed. Nor is the neglect of the project now any proof that it was not once vital. Circumstances have changed. Above all, two changes should be noted. First, as already observed, the railway is no longer necessary as an entering wedge for British imperialism in unclaimed hinterlands. The hinterlands have been appropriated, and Great Britain has a considerable share. Second, the locomotive now has to compete with airplane and automobile. A bi-weekly air mail service has been established by the Imperial Airways from the Cape to Alexandria, via Uganda and East Africa. The trip is made regularly in seven days.[66] There have been, however, much faster trips made by individual private flyers.[67]

Furthermore, people have from time to time made the trip using motor and water transportation. Major and Mrs. Court Treatt travelled from the Cape to Cairo principally by motor starting August 24, 1924 and arriving at Cairo,

January 23, 1926.[68]   In 1924 to 1925, two Americans, Mr. and Mrs. Felix Shay, using motor and water transportation to fill in the gaps in the railway, made the Cape to Cairo trip in 135 days.[69] According to *The South and East African Year Book for 1935*, at the close of 1928, it became possible to pass from Cape Town to the Egyptian border by public mechanical conveyance and at fixed fares, without quitting territory either belonging to or administered by Great Britain.[70]

Allowing for delays, about 40 days were necessary to make this journey.   There is further an all-British motor route from Cape Town to Juba in the Sudan.   Cars have gone also from Khartoum to Luxor but for 1,000 miles north of Mongalla, there is a swamp which will probably defy road construction for many years.[71]   With the extension of motor highways to link the existing railways, the Cape-to-Cairo route may quite possibly become important long before the Cape-to-Cairo railway is a reality.

It may even be questioned whether the railway will ever be completed.   At any rate, the view has often been expressed that the rail project is economically unsound.   The critics concede that the Cape-to-Cairo idea has had a great influence upon the development of Africa.   They are willing to concede that the idea will remain as a stimulus to further development of railways in Central Africa.[72]   They think, however, that the project will never be completely realized.   This group believes that the construction of lateral lines from the coast into the interior is the practical and feasible method of tapping the rich sources of the continent and developing the country.   To them the development of a mammoth line from the south to the north, is only a sentimental idea.   Such a great transcontinental railway would parallel two ocean lanes: the Atlantic and the Indian Ocean

—Red Sea route. Ocean transport is much cheaper than the carriage of goods by rail. The south-to-north railway could never compete with the sea lines.

As early as 1899, in the April number of *Munsey's,* the late Colonel Prout disparaged the idea of a Cape-to-Cairo railway. Colonel Prout was editor of the *Railroad Gazette,* 1887-1903, and an engineer of experience in the Sudan. The construction of the railway was, he considered, in the first place, too gigantic an undertaking. He gave a discouraging estimate of the probable cost of construction. Furthermore, it was an uneconomic proposition. It was a railroad which would run for at least a quarter of its distance alongside navigable waters. Furthermore, it would go for half its length through uncivilized country and for three fifths of its length through land unsuitable for white men.[73] He was astonished that such an experienced and intelligent business man as Cecil Rhodes could ever have seriously promoted the project and that " other men of brains and experience should receive it kindly."

He was willing to admit, however, that the idea was enticing:

The scheme [he wrote], is so grand and brilliant that it captures the swift imagination, and the laggard judgment cannot catch up . . . suddenly a whole vast continent, one of the great divisions of the earth, is captured by a *coup de main,* or perhaps by a *coup de théatre.* Nothing quite so spectacular has been done in history since the time of Alexander the Great.[74]

Prout was enthralled by the dream of conquering and holding Africa but he believed that this could be done more easily by building short lateral railways in from the east and west rather than by long inland lines.[75]

Other writers and scientists agree with Colonel Prout's

pessimistic opinion of the economic value of the line. T. L. Gilmour thought the idea unsound from its inception because such a railway would parallel the two great existing ocean routes. The lateral lines should come first.[76] Again, Professor A. Demangeon, thought that a south-to-north railway, was a mere dream because there was no real flow of traffic in this direction. If a transcontinental line were constructed, it would be a transverse one.[77]

On the other hand, another group see not only economic but also strategic and administrative advantages in the Cape-to-Cairo railway. They believe that the line should be finished. They are willing to grant the paramount commercial importance of lateral lines to tap the economic resources of Africa. They believe, however, that the great south-to-north line has some importance in linking together the lateral systems. In their estimation, the south-to-north railway then " would be the backbone and spinal cord to direct, consolidate and give life to the numerous systems of side railroads which will connect the vast central road with the seas on either hand." [78] " The chief object " of the Rhodes' line, said Viscount Milner, " was not so much to connect its one extreme end with the other, as to connect those otherwise isolated points along the great backbone of the continent, from which lateral lines ran to the coast." He admitted that it " was undoubtedly, in the first instance, the lateral lines which were of importance for trade." The points, on the other hand, of greatest importance were isolated points on the central high plateau. " They might each have their separate communication with the sea, but the trunk line linked them together, and in that way alone could the scattered centers of civilization in the heart of Africa be united into one country, and effectively brought within the influence of the British Empire." [79]

Sir Robert Williams feels that this great south-to-north backbone linked to the now recently opened Benguella line may be of great strategic importance if the Suez Canal is closed for any reason. It might form a back-door entrance to the Sudan and Egypt which would be extremely useful in the event of a blockade of the Mediterranean Sea. Furthermore, the Benguella Railway with the Cape-to-Cairo connections to the Sudan would belong in their entirety to Britain or to friendly countries. Portugal was Britain's ancient ally and Belgium " a recent and gallant ally " during the Great War.[80]

One other writer saw the Cape-to-Cairo railway as the ridgepole holding up the Anglo-Saxon empire in Africa. " Politically," he claimed, " the railway is intended to make Africa finally and predominantly British." He, too, saw the strategic advantages of the south-to-north line and pointed out that if the Strait of Gibraltar were ever closed an enormous British colonial army could be thrown in seven days into Egypt from the south. If the railway were completed, England would then have in its grasp the three corner points of the African triangle: the Niger, the Zambezi, and the Nile. The predominant English influence would then gradually pervade the whole, and practically the continent would be more Anglo-Saxon than America.[81]

If the Cape-to-Cairo railway is ever brought to completion, it will probably run, thought Sir Lewis Michell, along the " Great African watershed," especially along the Nile-Congo Divide. Michell was confident at the time that although there might be delay, there would be no permanent abandonment of the project.[82]

In 1924, as noted, Dr. Christy declared that the Bahr-el-Ghazal portion of the Nile-Congo watershed offered mineral resources enough to draw the railway south from El

Obeid.[83] On the southern side of the divide are the Kilo and Moto gold fields. If these fields become profitable enough, the Katanga railway will be brought north to tap them. That would enhance the probability that a junction will be made between the El Obeid and the Katanga line. Already, short stretches of line have been built from Kongolo to Kindu and from Ponthierville to Stanleyville, along the Congo River north of Bukama.[84] Dr. Christy felt that " There is little doubt that in the not-very-distant future the Cape-to-Cairo Railway, or one of its alternative routes, will traverse the great western volcanic or Lakes Rift, passing along the shores of Lakes Kivu, Edward and Albert, and the Semliki Valley " skirting " the base of the great Ruwenzori range—the Mountains of the Moon—between Lakes Albert and Edward." [85] It is true that the Cape-to-Cairo railway probably will not be finished in this direction, unless there are substantial reasons for extending it, section by section, north through the Congo and South from El Obeid. The process, however, has already begun and the day may not be far distant before the various links which are already forged will be joined. Then, there will be an unbroken line of rails running from one end of the continent to the other.

In reality it will be a series of railways rather than one great line. It will be more accurate to call it the Cape-to-Cairo system rather than the Cape-to-Cairo railway. It will, morever, be an international system, not a British line running through all-British territory, as Cecil Rhodes at one time dreamed. It will, however, be a line in friendly hands throughout. At present part of the system is under the management directly of Cape Colony and part under the Rhodesian Railways, closely related to the British South Africa Company. The section starting north through the Congo is already under the international direction of British, Belgian and Portuguese companies. Belgium and Portugal are traditional friends of England. The Sudanese section is under government control again and so is the Egyptian.

Finally, in the words of the president of the Royal Geographical Society, Sir Thomas Holdich: " Even if the idea of the railway from the Cape to Cairo remains an idea, it is . . . a very inspiring idea. It may not eventuate in a concrete form, but at all events it will always remain as a spur to further development of railways in Central Africa." [86]

NOTES

CHAPTER I

Paths into Africa

[1] According to the late Sir Harry Johnston, well-known writer on African subjects, the phrase "Cape to Cairo" was coined by Sir Edwin Arnold and used by Arnold in a pamphlet published in 1876. Weinthal, Leo, *The Story of the Cape to Cairo Railway and River Route, 1887-1922* (Pioneer Publishing Co., London, 1923), vol. i, chapter entitled "My Story of the Cape to Cairo Scheme" by Sir Harry Johnson, pp. 77 and 81-83.

I have found, however, a similar expression, to wit: "Cairo to Cape Town" used as early as 1875 by H. B. T. Strangway in connection with the proposal for a transcontinental telegraph. *The English Mechanic and World of Science*, November 26, 1875, vol. xxii, p. 278.

The phrase from "the Cape to Cairo", whatever its origin, was adopted and popularized by Sir Harry Johnston. He used it in various press articles and in conversations with Rhodes and Salisbury in 1889. Weinthal, *op. cit.*, vol. i, pp. 77 and 81-83.

[2] "... dans cette région des grands lacs qui donnant à la fois naissance au Nil, au Congo, et au Chiré, est la clef de voûte de toute l'Afrique." Darcy, Jean, *France et Angleterre, Cent Années de Rivalité* (Paris, 1904), pp. 354-355.

[3] "Great Britain's Policy in Africa" by an African Explorer, *The Times*, August 22, 1888, p. 8, cc. a, b, c.

[4] Vernon, S. P., "The Cape to Cairo Railway," *Liberia Bulletin*, no. 15, November, 1899, pp. 30-40.

[5] Speech by the Marquis of Salisbury, Hansard, series 3, vol. 346, cc. 1267-1268.

[6] *Infra*, pp. 309-311.

[7] Speech of Burdett-Coutts, Hansard, series 4, vol. 43, cc. 722-723.

[8] Hobson, C. K., *Export of Capital* (London, 1914), p. 95.

[9] See *Commerce and Industry, a historical Review of Economic Conditions*, edited by Wm. Page (London, 1919), pp. 282 and 284. Schuyler, R. L., "The Climax of Anti-Imperialism in England," *Political Science Quarterly*, vol. xxvi, December, 1921, pp. 543-560. Egerton, H. E., *A Short History of British Colonial Policy* (London, 1897), p. 368.

[10] *Cf.* Williams, Judith B., "British Trade with West Africa, 1750 to 1850," *Political Science Quarterly*, vol. l, June, 1935, pp. 194-213.

[11] For an outstanding illustration of the British desire to curtail responsibilities in South Africa, read De Kiewiet's discussion of the subject

in *British Colonial Policy and the South African Republics, 1842-1872* (London, 1929), *passim.*

[12] Lacerda, *The Lands of Cazembe, Lacerda's Journey to Cazembe in 1798* (London, 1873).

[13] The Prince of Orange was a refugee in England in 1795. Holland was at that time an ally of France and under the domination of Napoleon. The British, as opponents of Napoleon, offered aid and protection to the refugee Prince and took up the cudgels on his behalf. Hazen, C. D., *The French Revolution and Napoleon* (New York, 1917), pp. 187 and 225.

[14] For a graphic picture of conditions in Cape Colony before 1855 read Newman, W. A. (Dean of Cape Town), *Biographical Memoir of John Montague* during his administration as Colonial Secretary, 1843-1853 (Cape Town, 1855).

[15] Walker, Eric A., *A History of South Africa* (London, 1928), chapter viii, " The Great Trek," pp. 202-241.

[16] C. O. 51, nos. 131-159, *passim.*

[17] See Weinthal, *op. cit.*, vol. i, pp. 71-73. Hertslet, *The Map of Africa by Treaty* (London, 1909), vol. i, no. 39, p. 300. Johnston, Sir Harry, *History of the Colonization of Africa by Alien Races* (Cambridge, 1913), p. 71.

[18] Johnston, "My Story of the Cape to Cairo Scheme," Weinthal, *op. cit.*, pp. 71-72.

[19] Hansard, series 4, vol. 42, c. 811.

[20] Hallberg, C. W., *The Suez Canal* (New York, 1931), *passim.*

[21] *Ibid.*, pp. 77 and 101-103 and also Weinthal, *op. cit.*, vol. ii, " The Railway System of the Sudan " by Lieut-Col. W. E. Longfield, R. E. (Deputy General Manager of the Sudan Government Railways and Steamers), pp. 309-325.

[22] " The Railway System of the Sudan," Weinthal, *op. cit.*, vol. ii, p. 309.

[23] Rose, J. Holland, *Development of the European Nations* (London, 1905), vol. ii, p. 147.

[24] Livingstone, David, *Missionary Travels and Researches* (London, 1899), *passim.* Cameron, V. Lovett, Letters appended to *The Report of the Royal Trade Commission on Depression, Accounts and Papers*, 1886, vol. 23 [c.—4893], Appendix E, pp. 71-74.

[25] Blaikie, William Garden, *The Personal Life of Livingstone* (New York, 1881), *passim.* See especially articles in *The Newcastle Journal*, October 17, 1889 and *The Scotsman*, June 8, 1889 on the operations of the I. B. E. A. and B. S. A. companies in relation to stopping the slave trade.

[26] General Act of Brussels Conference, Article i, *Accounts and Papers*, 1889-1890, vol. 50 [c.—6048].

[27] See Weinthal, *op. cit.*, vol. i, section entitled "Memoirs of the Pioneers of the Cape-to-Cairo Route," for brief but convenient sketches of the work of some of these travellers.

[28] Blaikie, *op. cit.*, pp. 213-214.
[29] Speech by the Earl of Harrowby, Hansard, series 3, vol. 328, c. 538.
[30] Blaikie, *op. cit.*, pp. 461-462.
[31] Stanley, Henry Morton, *How I Found Livingstone* (New York, 1872).
[32] Stanley, H. M., *The Autobiography of Sir Henry Morton Stanley* (New York, 1902), pp. 296-330.
[33] *Infra*, pp. 239-241.
[34] Weinthal, *op. cit.*, vol. i, "My Story of the Cape to Cairo Scheme" by Sir Harry Johnston, pp. 68-69.
[35] Weinthal, *op. cit.*, vol. i, "Kimberley and the Cape-to-Cairo Route" by George Beet (an esteemed journalist pioneer of Kimberley), p. 671.
[36] Walker, *History of South Africa, op. cit.*, p. 333.
[37] Williams, Basil, *Cecil Rhodes* (New York, 1921), p. 19.
[38] Walker, *History of South Africa, op. cit.*, pp. 333-350. Walker, *Lord De Villiers and His Times* (London, 1925), p. 186. Williams, *Cecil Rhodes, op. cit.*, pp. 19 and 107. Weinthal, *op. cit.*, vol. i, "The Discovery of the Rand," pp. 695-701.
[39] The Governor's speech at the opening of the Cape Parliament, C. O. 51/177, Minute No. ii, p. 4, *cf.* Dispatch from Governor Barkly to the Earl of Kimberley, July 2, 1874, C. O. 48/469, vol. ii, no. 83.
[40] For a further history of railways in South Africa, *infra*, pp. 110-119. The whole story can be traced in great detail in the Colonial Dispatches for the years 1853-1886, C. O. 48, series nos. 342 to 500 and in the Cape Parliamentary Papers, C. O. 51 series for the years 1855-1886, nos. 100-257.
[41] Williams, *Cecil Rhodes, op. cit.*, pp. 20-23. Hertslet, *op. cit.*, vol. i, p. 177.
[42] Williams, *op. cit.*, p. 22.
[43] *Report of the Colonial Survey Committee, Accounts and Papers,* 1906, vol. 73 [c.—2684-46].
[44] *Peace Handbook*, vol. 15, *The Partition of Africa* (London, 1920), pp. 13-14.
[45] See, for example, the 1853 treaties made by Pieter Johannes Potgieter and Jacobus Pretorius with Lobengula. These treaties were later on to cause the British difficulty. *Accounts and Papers*, 1890 vol. 51 [c.—5918], Enclosure in No. 4.
[46] *Report of the Royal Commission on Trade Depression, Accounts and Papers*, 1886, vol. 23 [c.—4893], pp. vii-xx.
[47] "American Competition in the Cotton Trade," *The Economist*, December 11, 1880. Earle, E. M., "Egyptian Cotton and the American Civil War," *Political Science Quarterly*, 1926, vol. xli, pp. 520-545.
[48] *Commerce and Industry, op. cit.*, pp. 305 and 261. *Report of the Royal Trade Commission on Depression, op. cit.*, pp. x-xv.

⁴⁹ Livingstone, himself, seems to have approved of giving firearms to the natives particularly as a protection against Boer raids. In fact, he remarks, in connection with a Boer attack on the natives of Kolobeng: "Had the people of Kolobeng been in the habit of raising the raw materials of English commerce, the outrage would have been felt in England; or, what is more likely . . . the people would have raised themselves in the scale by barter, and have become, . . . possessed of fire-arms, and the Boers would never have made the attack at all. We ought to encourage the Africans to cultivate for our markets, as the most effectual means, next to the Gospel, of their elevation." *Livingstone, Missionary Travels and Researches, o'p. cit.,* p. *720. Cf.* statements in the same book, pp. 719 and 723-725.

⁵⁰ Milner, Viscount, *England in Egypt* (London, 1904), p. 527. Earle, *op. cit.*

⁵¹ Letter from V. L. Cameron appended to the *Report of the Royal Commission on Trade Depression, op. cit.,* Appendix E, p. 72.

⁵² Address of Sir Rutherford Alcock to the Members of the Royal Geographical Society, November 12, 1877, *Proceedings of the Royal Geographical Society,* old series, vol. 22, pp. 25-28.

⁵³ Letter from V. L. Cameron appended to *Report of the Royal Commission on Trade Depression, op. cit.,* Appendix E, p. 72.

CHAPTER II

WIRES ACROSS AFRICA

¹ Sir Edwin Arnold stated that the South African Colonies were a month distant from home and Colonel Grant maintained: "at present we cannot communicate with the Cape within two months." Pamphlet listed under the name *Nicholls* (printed by Wm. Clowes & Sons, 1876 and kept in the library of the Royal Geographical Society), sections 2 and 3.

² *Nicholls Pamphlet, op. cit.,* section 3 by Colonel Grant.

³ *Ibid.,* section 1 by Nicholls.

⁴ *Ibid.,* section 3 by Grant.

⁵ *Ibid.,* section 1 by Nicholls.

⁶ *Ibid.,* section 1.

⁷ *Ibid.,* section 2 by Arnold.

⁸ Michell, *The Life of the Rt. Hon. Cecil John Rhodes* (London, 1910), vol. i, p. 286 and Weinthal, *op. cit.,* vol. i, "The Trans-African Telegraph Line," p. 212.

[9] Weinthal, *op. cit.*, vol. i, "My Story of the Cape to Cairo Scheme" by Sir Harry Johnston, p. 69.

[10] *Proceedings of the Royal Geographical Society*, 1879, n. s., vol. i, pp. 217-218.

[11] Pamphlet Z. 68, 13 (kept in the library of the Royal Geographical Society), Appendix O-O², Frere to Sir M. E. Hicks Beach, Government House, Cape Town, April 20, 1878.

[12] C. O. 48, nos. 356-359, *passim.*

[13] Pamphlet Z. 68, 13, *op. cit.*, Appendix M, Thomas Watson to Grant, July 26, 1878.

[14] *Ibid.*, Appendix K, Dr. Atherstone to Grant, Grahamston, July 4, 1878.

[15] Sir Samuel Baker described Grant as "one of the most loyal charming characters in the world, perfectly unselfish." *Dictionary of National Biography*, supplement 2, vol. i.

[16] *Dictionary of National Biography*, supplement 2, vol. i.

[17] *Supra*, pp. ——.

[18] Weinthal, *op. cit.*, vol. i, "The Exploration of the Dark Continent" by Archibald Hurd, p. 481.

[19] Weinthal, *op. cit.*, vol. i, "My Story of the Cape to Cairo Scheme" by Sir Harry Johnston, pp. 483 and 485.

[20] *Ibid.*, p. 485. It might be of passing interest to note here the further activities of the enterprising staff of this newspaper after Arnold was no longer editor. In 1913, they commissioned Captain R. N. Kelsey to conduct a motor-car expedition from the Cape to Cairo. The party started July 19, 1913 but ended after Kelsey's death without completing the journey.

In 1920, *The Daily Telegraph* was associated with the project of an aeroplane flight from Cairo to the Cape. Unfortunately, this project was also unsuccessful. The plane crashed at Shereik about eight hundred miles from Cairo. Weinthal, *op. cit.*, vol. i, "The Exploration of the Dark Continent," pp. 487-489.

[21] Weinthal, *op. cit.*, vol. i, "My Story of the Cape to Cairo Scheme" by Sir Harry Johnston, p. 69.

[22] See Grant's own account in *A Walk Across Africa* published in 1864.

[23] *Dictionary of National Biography*, supplement, vol. ii.

[24] Kerry-Nicholls, James Henry, *The King Country, or Explorations in New Zealand* (London, 1884), pp. viii and 15-16.

[25] *Nichols Pamphlet, op. cit.*, section 1.

[26] *Ibid.*, section 1.

[27] *Ibid.*, section 2.

[28] *Proceedings of the Royal Geographical Society*, n. s., vol. i, p. 123.

[29] *Minutes* of the Geographical Conference at the Brussels Palace, Sept. 12-14, 1876 (lithographed copy kept in the library of the Royal Geographical Society).

[30] *Proceedings of the Royal Geographical Society*, o. s., vol. 21, p. 606.

[31] *Ibid.*, vol. 21, p. 17.

[32] *Ibid.*, n. s., vol. i, p. 63.

[33] *Ibid.*, o. s., vol. 21, p. 616.

[34] C. O. 48/492, Royal Geographical Society, Jan. 16, Notes on the report of the Committee.

[35] Pamphlet Z. 68, 13 in the Library of the Royal Geographical Society, Appendix D, C. Giegler to Grant, Khartoum, September 5, 1878. A perusal of extracts from Gordon's diary indicates that Gordon did not approve of an Overland Telegraph through the heart of the continent.

[36] Pamphlet Z, 68, 13, *op. cit.*, Appendix A, Cameron to Grant, the United States Club, Pall Mall, July 15, 1878.

[37] *Ibid.*, Appendix I, Kirk to Sivewright, Zanzibar, May 10, 1878.

[38] C. O. 48/492, vol. iv, 1879, Note on the back of the dispatch.

[39] Pamphlet Z, 68, 13, *op. cit.*, Stanley to Grant, Paris, August 11, 1878.

[40] C. O. 48/492, vol. iv, 1879, comment on the back of the dispatch.

[41] Pamphlet Z, 68, 13, *op. cit.*, Appendix C, Baker to Grant, July 16, 1878.

[42] *Proceedings of the Royal Geographical Society*, n. s., vol. i, p. 125.

[43] C. O. 48/488, F. O., April 18.

[44] C. O. 48/492, *Royal Geographical Society*, Jan. 16, comment on back of the dispatch.

[45] C. O. 48/485, No. 90, Comments on the dispatch.

[46] *Infra*, pp. 63-64.

[47] C. O. 48/485, No. 90, comments on the dispatch.

[48] C. O. 48/487, Agents April 11, comments on the dispatch.

[49] C. O. 48/492, *Royal Geographical Society*, Jan. 16, comments on the report.

[50] *Ibid.*

[51] Pamphlet Z, 68, 13, *op. cit.*, Appendix M, Sivewright to Sabine, Cape Town, July 21, 1878.

[52] Michell, Sir Lewis, *The Life of the Rt. Hon. Cecil J. Rhodes* (London, 1910), vol. i, pp. 284-286. Williams, *Cecil Rhodes, op. cit.*, pp. 187 and 196-198. *Who was Who.*

[53] Williams, *Cecil Rhodes, op. cit.*, p. 187.

[54] Weinthal, *op. cit.*, vol. i, "The Trans-African Telegraph Line," p. 217. *Cf.* Williams' statement that the African Transcontinental Telegraph Company was "almost entirely a creation of Rhodes' forethought and private capital." Williams, *Cecil Rhodes, op. cit.*, p. 181.

[55] Paper by J. Sivewright read at the meeting of the Institute of Electrical Engineers, March 26, 1879, *Journal of the Institute of Electrical Engineers*, 1879, vol. viii, pp. 201-204.

[56] *Ibid.*, pp. 203-204.

[57] Michell, *op. cit.*, vol. i, p. 285.

[58] Pamphlet Z, 68, 13, Appendix O-O², Frere to the Rt. Hon. Sir M. E. Hicks Beach, Government House, Cape Town, April, 1878. Appendix O³, Leading Article, *Cape Argus*, March 30, 1878. Appendix M. Sivewright to Sabine, Cape Town, July 21, 1878.

[59] C. O. 48/489, No. 23, The Governor and High Commissioner to the Rt. Hon. the Secretary of State, Pietermaritzburg, Natal, January 22, 1879.

[60] C. O. 48/492, F. O., Jan. 6, notes on the back of the dispatch.

[61] Pamphlet Z, 68, 13, Appendix H, Frere to Sir Henry Barkly, Cape Town, August 7, 1878.

[62] C. O. 48/488, John Pender to Sir M. E. Hicks Beach, November 14, 1878.

[63] Pamphlet Z, 68, 13, Appendix M.

[64] C. O. 48/492.

[65] *Journal of the Institute of Electrical Engineers, op. cit.*, vol. viii, p. 203.

CHAPTER III

THE RED PAINT BRUSH

[1] Williams, *Cecil Rhodes, op. cit.*, p. 51.

[2] *Ibid.*, p. 51. *Cf.* W. T. Stead, *The Last Will and Testament of Cecil John Rhodes* (London, 1902), p. 59.

[3] Macdonald, J. A., *Rhodes, A Life* (London, 1927), p. 8.

[4] Stead, W. T., "Character Sketch: Cecil Rhodes of Africa," *Review of Reviews*, 1899, vol. xx, p. 462 and also Garrett, F. Edmund, the editor of the *Cape Times*, "The Character of Cecil Rhodes," *Contemporary Review*, Jan.–June, 1902, vol. 81, p. 769.

[5] Low, Sidney, "Personal Recollections of Cecil Rhodes," *The Living Age*, 1902, vol. xv, p. 582.

[6] Lovell, R. I., *The Struggle for South Africa, 1875-1899* (New York, 1934), p. 119.

[7] Warren, Charles, "Cecil Rhodes' Early Days in South Africa," *Contemporary Review*, 1902, vol. 81, p. 645.

[8] Low, Sidney, "Personal Recollections of Cecil Rhodes," *op. cit.*, p. 587.

[9] Général Bourelly, "Cecil Rhodes," *Le Correspondant*, 1900 (n. s.), vol. 162, p. 572.

[10] Michell, *op. cit.*, vol. i, p. 90.

[11] Vindex, *Cecil Rhodes, His Political Life and Speeches, 1881-1900* (London, 1900), pp. 610, 647, 696 and 704. Fuller, Sir T. E., *The Right Honourable Cecil John Rhodes* (London, 1910), p. 29.

[12] Vindex, *op. cit.*, pp. 315, 625, 630, 644, 696, 703 and 704.

[13] Lockhart, J. G., *Cecil Rhodes* (London, 1933), p. 130.

[14] Alfred Beit, for example, left a trust fund expressly for the Cape-to-Cairo Railway. Fort, G. Seymour, *Alfred Beit* (London, 1932), pp. 32-42 and Weinthal, *op. cit.*, vol. i, "History and Finance of the Rhodesian Railway System" by Baron Émile Beaumont D'Erlanger, pp. 657-659.

[15] Rhodes was not quite 49 years old when he died.

[16] Williams, *Cecil Rhodes, op. cit.*, pp. 52 and 122.

[17] "Rhodes", Edmund Garrett maintains, "was not a rich man who took up the Empire as a hobby when he was tired of making money. He formed the ideal first, the fortune afterwards." Garrett, F. Edmund, "The Character of Cecil Rhodes," *op. cit.*, p. 769.

[18] Michell, *op. cit.*, vol. i, pp. 21 and 195. Fort, G. Seymour, *Alfred Beit, op. cit.*, pp. 72-73.

[19] See accounts of it in Williams, *Cecil Rhodes, op. cit.*, pp. 102-104 and Michell, *op. cit.*, vol. i, pp. 183-186.

[20] Michell, *op. cit.*, vol. i, pp. 184-185. Williams, *Cecil Rhodes, op. cit.*, p. 104.

[21] Plomer, William, *Cecil Rhodes* (New York, 1933), pp. 34-36 and Lovell, *The Struggle for South Africa, op. cit.*, p. 116.

[22] Garrett, F. E., "The Character of Cecil Rhodes," *op. cit.*, p. 771.

[23] Macdonald, *Rhodes, A Life, op. cit.*, p. 119.

[24] Fuller, Sir T. E., *op. cit.*, p. 58.

[25] Macdonald, *op. cit.*, p. 50.

[26] Michell, *op. cit.*, vol. i, p. 89. Walker, Eric A., *History of South Africa, op. cit.*, p. 390. Walker, Eric A., *Lord de Villiers and His Times* (London, 1925), p. 157. Williams, *Cecil Rhodes, op. cit.*, p. 57.

[27] Macdonald, *op. cit.*, p. 57.

[28] Rhodes evidently did not make as favorable an impression on the House at first as he did later. Sir Lewis Michell (one of his most flattering biographers), writes about his first speech: "A candid friend remarked afterwards that he would be a Parliamentary failure." Michell, *op. cit.*, vol. i, p. 91.

[29] Williams, *Cecil Rhodes, op. cit.*, pp. 190-191.

[30] *Ibid.*, pp. 191-192 and Michell, *op. cit.*, vol. i, p. 93.

[31] Lovell, *The Struggle for South Africa, op. cit.*, p. 118.

[32] See, for example, his offers of financial assistance made to Parnell, Sir Harry Johnston and W. T. Stead.

[33] See Garrett's eulogistic article "The Character of Cecil Rhodes," *op. cit.* and also Whyte, Frederic, *The Life of W. T. Stead* (London, 1925), vol. ii, pp. 94-98 and 203-205.

[34] Williams, *Cecil Rhodes, op. cit.*, p. 192.

[35] See for examples: The newspaper's championship of Rhodes' Kimberley Railway policy in 1882 and Rhodes' policies in regard to Bechuanaland and the Interior in 1884.

[36] Williams, *Cecil Rhodes, op. cit.*, p. 192.

[37] Whyte, *op. cit.*, vol. i, p. 311.

[38] *Ibid.*, vol. i, p. 270.

[39] *Ibid.*, vol. i, pp. 182-185 and 270-271.

[40] *Ibid.*, vol. ii, pp. 206-210. To be sure, in 1890, Rhodes had Stead's name expunged from the list of trustees in his last will. Rhodes claimed that he was afraid of Stead's "extraordinary eccentricity," i. e., probably his pro-Boer sympathies.

[41] Williams, *Cecil Rhodes, op. cit.*, pp. 234-235.

[42] Weinthal, *op. cit.*, vol. i, "My Story of the Cape to Cairo Scheme" by Sir Harry Johnston, p. 81.

[43] Williams, *Cecil Rhodes, op. cit.*, pp. 234-235. Vindex, *op. cit.*, p. 319.

[44] Weinthal, *op. cit.*, vol. i, "The House of Rothschild and the Cape to Cairo Route," pp. 633-635.

[45] *Ibid.*, vol. i, "The History and Finance of the Rhodesian Railway System" by Baron Émile Beaumont d'Erlanger, pp. 639-659.

[46] *Infra*, p. 145.

[47] Weinthal, *op. cit.*, "The History and Finance of the Rhodesian Railway System," p. 639.

[48] Williams, *Cecil Rhodes, op. cit.*, p. 238.

CHAPTER IV

Cape Colony as the Base of Operations

[1] Vindex, *op. cit.*, p. 225.

[2] Lovell, *The Struggle for South Africa, op. cit.*, p. 114.

[3] *Cf.* in this connection, Rhodes' statement in regard to a gift to the Irish party funds in order to promote the cause of Home Rule in Ireland: "I gave," said Rhodes, "Mr. Parnell's cause £10,000 because in it I believe lies the key of the Federal system, on the basis of perfect Home Rule in every part of the Empire, and in it also the Imperial tie begins." Vindex, *op. cit.*, p. 210. *Cf.* also his talks with Stead on the subject of imperial federations. Whyte, *op. cit.*, vol. i, p. 270 and also statements by Williams in his *Cecil Rhodes, op. cit.*, pp. 133-134.

[4] Williams, *Cecil Rhodes, op. cit.*, pp. 80-81 and Vindex, *op. cit.*, pp. xii-xxv.

[5] Time and again, Rhodes insisted upon loyalty to the British flag as a cardinal principle in his work in South Africa. See especially, his

speech July 18, 1886, Vindex, *op. cit.*, pp. 51-52 and Williams, *Cecil Rhodes, op. cit.*, pp. 66-67; his speech September 28, 1888, Vindex, *op. cit.*, p. 226 and his speech, September 6, 1890, Vindex, *op. cit.*, p. 243.

"To Rhodes' South African friends," writes Hans Sauer, a Cape politician, "it has always been a matter of surprise that he should have been so misunderstood by his own countrymen. To us, I speak as an Afrikander born, he was first an Englishman, a passionate lover of his country. Hence the greatest libel ever passed upon him was the accusation of ulterior motives in his policy of Imperial aggrandisement. . . . To all who knew him it was evident that patriotism was the mainspring of his life. . . . " Sauer, Hans, "Cecil Rhodes," *Empire Review*, 1902, vol. iii, p. 364.

[6] Vindex, *op. cit.*, pp. xxvii and 225-226.

[7] Lovell, *The Struggle for South Africa, op. cit.*, p. 120.

[8] Michell, *op. cit.*, vol. i, pp. 94 and 228 and Lovell, *The Struggle for South Africa, op. cit.*, pp. 123-124.

[9] Michell, *op. cit.*, vol. i, p. 94.

[10] *Ibid.*, p. 94.

[11] Lovell, *The Struggle for South Africa, op. cit.*, pp. 120-121; Michell, *op. cit.*, vol. i, pp. 93-95; Williams, *Cecil Rhodes, op. cit.*, pp. 193-195 and Plomer, *op. cit.*, pp. 68-69.

[12] Vindex, *op. cit.*, pp. 62, 63-64, 67-68, 224-225 and 286-287.

[13] *Accounts and Papers*, 1890, vol. 51 [c.—5918], No. 16.

[14] Michell, *op. cit.*, vol. i, pp. 89 and 94. Williams, *Cecil Rhodes, op. cit.*, pp. 185-186. Lovell, *The Struggle for South Africa, op. cit.*, p. 124.

[15] Michell, *op. cit.*, vol. i, p. 94.

[16] Walker, *History of South Africa, op. cit., passim* and Vindex, *op. cit.*, p. 61.

[17] " . . . the well-marked track by which explorers, hunters, missionaries and traders travelled into the interior, and which was the main approach to the Tati Gold Fields opened in 1869, Matabeleland and the hunting grounds of the Zambesi." Williams, *Cecil Rhodes, op. cit.*, p. 69.

[18] *Accounts and Papers*, 1884, vol. 57 [c.—3947], *passim*.

[19] Walker, *Lord de Villiers and His Times, op. cit.*, p. 47.

[20] *Ibid.*, p. 47.

[21] Lovell, *The Struggle for South Africa, op. cit.*, pp. 108-109 and 112-113.

[22] Walker, *History of South Africa, op. cit.*, pp. 408-409.

[23] *Ibid.*, pp. 409-410 and Walker, *Lord de Villiers and His Times, op. cit.*, p. 253.

[24] Walker, *History of South Africa, op. cit.*, p. 352.

[25] *Ibid., passim*.

[26] Lovell, *The Struggle for South·Africa, op. cit.*, p. 114. Williams, *Cecil Rhodes, op. cit.*, p. 85.

[27] *Accounts and Papers*, 1890, vol. 51 [c.—5903], enclosure no. 27, p. 26.

[28] Kruger, Paul, *The Memoirs of Paul Kruger* (New York, 1902), pp. 174 and 177.

[29] *Mémoire présenté par le Gouvernement du Portugal en réponse aux Mémoires . . . présentés par les Gouvernements des États-Unis de l'Amérique du Nord et de la Grande Bretagne. Tribunal Arbitral du Delagoa Bay* (Berne, 1892), p. 9.

[30] " . . . un tramway à vapeur, dit le mémoire Américain lui-même, *est connu généralement sour le nom de Light Railway.*" Mémoire, *op. cit.*, p. 17.

[31] Mémoire, *op. cit.*, pp. 9 and 17-19.

[32] Lovell, *The Struggle for South Africa, op. cit.*, p. 345 and Worsfold, W. Basil, *The Reconstruction of the New Colonies under Lord Milner* (London, 1913), vol. i, p. 116.

[33] Lovell, *The Struggle for South Africa, op. cit.*, p. 346.

[34] *Ibid.*, p. 344 and *Accounts and Papers*, 1890, vol. 51 [c.—5903], enclosure in No. 27, pp. 27-29 and No. 55, pp. 55-57.

[35] Weinthal, *op. cit.*, vol. i, p. 5.

[36] Walker, *History of South Africa, op. cit.*, pp. 412, 413. Walker, *Lord de Villiers and His Times, op. cit.*, p. 188.

[37] Vindex, *op. cit.*, pp. 67 and 113-114.

[38] *Ibid.*, pp. 133-136.

[39] Weinthal, *op. cit.*, vol. i, p. 5.

[40] Oom Paul Kruger to R. V. Murray, Jr. of the *Cape Times*, Major Riccarde-Seaver and Sir Charles Metcalfe " The British Sphere of Influence in South Africa," *Fortnightly Review*, March, 1889, vol. 51 (n. s.), p. 358.

[41] Walker, *De Villiers and His Times, op. cit.*, p. 188. *Accounts and Papers*, 1888, vol. 74 [c.—5390], and also C. O. 51/260 [G. 8-85], Report, Minutes and Resolution of the Customs Union and Railway Conference.

[42] *Accounts and Papers*, 1890, vol. 51 [c.—5918], No. 16.

[43] *Ibid.*, C. O. 51/259, No. 42, p. 354. Vindex, *op. cit.*, pp. 201-203. Lovell, *The Struggle for South Africa, op. cit.*, p. 130.

[44] *Accounts and Papers*, 1890, vol. 51 [c.—5903], No. 50, pp. 48-49 and No. 27, pp. 29-30.

[45] Speech of Rhodes, August, 1888, Vindex, *op. cit.*, pp. 184-186.

[46] Weinthal, *op. cit.*, vol. i, " Cecil John Rhodes. A Review of His Life and Works " by Walford Dowling (Rhodes scholar and member of the Bar of Pretoria), pp. 19-23 and also " Cecil Rhodes and his Work" by Manfred Nathan in the same volume, pp. 44-47.

[47] *Supra*, p. 87.

[48] This hope proved disappointing according to the report of the acting administrator for 1888, *Accounts and Papers*, 1889, vol. 54, no. 44 [c.—5620-e].

[49] " The chief value of this colony," wrote Sidney Shippard, administrator in 1889, "must always be the trade route to the interior." *Accounts and Papers*, 1890, vol. 48, no. 97 [c.—587].

[50] " Das Programm der englischen Heissporne von Südafrika: ' Ueber ganz Afrika, vom Tafelberge bis zum Nil, muss die britische Flagge wehen.' " Weber, Ernst von, *Vier Jahre in Afrika, 1871-1875* (Leipzig, 1878), vol. i, p. xi.

[51] Walker, *History of South Africa, op. cit.*, p. 401. Williams, *Cecil Rhodes, op. cit.*, pp. 69, 71-72.

[52] *Accounts and Papers*, 1884, vol. 57 [c.—3947], No. 19, Lord Derby to the deputation, January 25, 1884.

[53] That is, questions of native legislation, powers of the resident and the all important question of suzerainty, etc. Walker, *History of South Africa, op. cit.*, p. 404.

[54] The story of this negotiation is told in *Accounts and Papers*, 1884, vol. 57 [c.—3841] and [c.—3947].

[55] London Convention of 1884, Article i, Hertslet, *op. cit.*, vol. i, no. 28, pp. 228-232.

[56] " Bechuanaland would have passed to the Transvaal as Lord Derby was neutral on the question," Rhodes claimed. Speech of Rhodes, September 28, 1888, Vindex, *op. cit.*, p. 215. Walker, *History of South Africa, op. cit.*, pp. 403-404.

[57] Williams, *Cecil Rhodes, op. cit.*, p. 78. Lovell, *The Struggle for South Africa, op. cit.*, pp. 48 and 56-57. Mackenzie, John, *Austral Africa; Losing it or Ruling it* (London, 1887), 2 vols.

[58] Mackenzie, *Austral Africa, op. cit., passim.*

[59] *Accounts and Papers*, 1884, vol. 57 [c.—3841], No. 127, and also Rhodes' opinion of Robinson's policy in his speech, July 23, 1888. Vindex, *op. cit.*, p. 200.

[60] " His Excellency the High Commissioner, with whom I was then barely acquainted," Rhodes confessed in his speech September 28, 1888, " had grasped the fact that if Bechuanaland was lost to us, British development in Africa was at an end. He persuaded Lord Derby to deal with the Bechuanaland question, and induced Sir Thomas Scanlan, the then Prime Minister of the Cape, to share in the obligations of the undertaking." Vindex, *op. cit.*, p. 215.

[61] *Accounts and Papers*, vol. 57, 1884 [c.—3841], No. 127, Sir Hercules Robinson to the C. O., January 13, 1884.

[62] Vindex, *op. cit.*, p. 215. Walker, *History of South Africa, op. cit.*, p. 405. Williams, *Cecil Rhodes, op. cit.*, p. 73. *Accounts and Papers*, 1884, vol. 57 [c.—4194], enclosure in No. 32. The article from the *Cape Times*, July 16, 1884, gives Sir Thomas Scanlan's defense of his policy.

[63] Lovell, *The Anglo-German Estrangement of 1894-1896*, unpublished doctoral thesis.

[64] Williams, *Cecil Rhodes, op. cit.*, p. 73. Vindex, *op. cit.*, pp. 60-71 and 213-214.

[65] Williams, *Cecil Rhodes, op. cit.*, pp. 79-83.

[66] *Supra*, p. 88.

[67] *Accounts and Papers*, 1884, vol. 56 [c.—4190], No. 5. Lovell, *The Struggle for South Africa, op. cit.*, pp. 67 and 101.

[68] Lovell, *The Struggle for South Africa, op. cit.*, p. 109.

[69] Moon, Parker T., *Imperialism and World Politics* (New York, 1929), pp. 47-50.

[70] Weber, Ernest Von, *Vier Jahre in Afrika, 1871-1875* (Leipzig, 1878), vol. ii, p. 378.

[71] *Accounts and Papers*, 1884, vol. 56 [c.—4190], enclosure in No. 1. Italics supplied.

[72] Moon, *op. cit.*, pp. 50-51. Townsend, M. E., *The Rise and Fall of the German Colonial Empire* (New York, 1930), chap. ii.

[73] *Supra*, p. 89.

[74] See a discussion on this point in Lovell, *The Struggle for South Africa, op. cit.*, pp. 77-85.

[75] Vindex, *op. cit.*, pp. 114-115 and Williams, *Cecil Rhodes, op. cit.*, pp. 77-78.

[76] Williams, *Cecil Rhodes, op. cit.*, pp. 62 and 83. Vindex, *op. cit.*, p. 66.

[77] Williams, *Cecil Rhodes, op. cit.*, pp. 83-90. Cf. Lovell, *The Struggle for South Africa, op. cit.*, pp. 69-73.

[78] On September 30, 1885, the High Commissioner issued a proclamation dividing the newly acquired Bechuanaland territory into two districts. The portion bounded on the east by the South African Republic, on the south by Cape Colony, on the west by the Molopo River and on the north "by the said Molopo River to its junction with the Ramathlabam Spruit, and thence by the said Spruit to the frontier of the South African Republic", was declared to be British territory under the name of British Bechuanaland.

Over the rest of the acquired country, i. e., that "known as Bechuanaland and the Kalahari, extending over the parts of South Africa situate west of the boundary of the South African Republic, north of the Colony of the Cape of Good Hope, east of the 20° meridian of east longitude, and south of the 22nd parallel of south latitude, and not within the jurisdiction of any civilized Power," the High Commissioner proclaimed a British Protectorate. Hertslet, *op. cit.*, vol. i, no. 21, p. 190.

[79] "The affixing of the Great Seal of the United Kingdom to the charter of the British South Africa Company is an outward and visible sign of the colonizing genius of the Anglo-Saxon race . . . the charter . . . makes over to the new 'East India Company' a territory three times the size of the United Kingdom. . . . It is a fresh expansion not merely of the Anglo-Saxon race, but also of the British Empire." *Pall Mall Gazette*, November 1, 1889.

CHAPTER V

THE TRUNK LINE FROM CAPE TOWN TO CAIRO

[1] *Supra*, p. 40.

[2] "Railroads," *The South African Commercial Advertiser*, December 24, 1845, p. 1, column b.

[3] C. O. 48/342, No. 85, no. 2, Report by Charles Bell, Surveyor General of Cape Colony.

[4] C. O. 51/131, 1862, Minute No. 1, and C. O. 51/159, 1868 [A. 3], Report of a Select Committee on Railroads.

[5] Article from the *Cape Times*, July 16, 1884, *Accounts and Papers*, vol. 57, 1884 [c.—4194], enclosure 1 in No. 32.

[6] Dispatch from Sir Hercules Robinson to Lord Knutsford, November 7, 1888. *Accounts and Papers*, 1890, vol. 51 [c.—5918], No. 16.

[7] During the period of the eighties, there was much discussion of railway plans both outside and inside the colony. This general activity, in regard to railway questions, reflects the growing need for railway extension to the north. See especially C. O. 48, Nos. 500-511 and also *Accounts and Papers*, 1888, vol. 74 [c.—5390] and 1890, vol. 51 [c.—5918], No. 16.

[8] *Infra*, pp. 120-121.

[9] *Infra*, note no. 78, p. 421.

[10] Dispatch from Sir Hercules Robinson to Lord Knutsford, November 7, 1888, *op. cit.*

[11] *Supra*, p. 95.

[12] Dispatch of Sir Hercules Robinson, November 7, 1888, *op. cit.*

[13] *Ibid.*

[14] *News Telegram*, October 4, 1888 quoted in Sir Hercules Robinson's dispatch, November 7, 1888, *op. cit.*

[15] *Times* quoted in Sir Hercules Robinson's dispatch, November 7, 1888, *op. cit.*

[16] [c.—5918], *op. cit.*, no. 16, p. 28.

[17] *Ibid.*, p. 28.

[18] C. O. 51/264, Minutes of the Legislative Council, no. 1, p. 3.

[19] Sir Hercules Robinson's dispatch, November 7, 1888, *op. cit.*

[20] *Ibid.*

[21] Williams, Cecil Rhodes, *op. cit.*, p. 129.

[22] Keltie, J. Scott, *The Partition of Africa* (London, 1895), pp. 415-416.

[23] Correspondence concerning the construction of railways in Territory of Bechuanaland, C. O. 51/265 [A. 11], pp. 1228-1230. Weinthal, *op. cit.*, vol. i, "My Story of the Scheme" by Sir Charles Metcalfe, p. 97.

[24] Weinthal, *op. cit.*, vol. i, "My Story of the Scheme" by Sir Charles Metcalfe, p. 97.

[25] C. O. 51/265, 1889 [A. 11], *op. cit.*, pp. 1205-1206.

[26] They arrived in the summer of 1888. Weinthal, *op. cit.*, vol. i, p. 97. It was in the fall of the year that the Cape was informed that British Bechuanaland would remain under imperial control. *Accounts and Papers*, 1890, vol. 51 [c.—5918], No. 16.

[27] " On the eve of his departure (1899), he declared as his own personal opinion, but for all the world to hear, that there was no room for the action of the Imperial factor on a large scale in the internal affairs of South Africa." Walker, *History of South Africa, op. cit.*, p. 420.

" Remember there are three possible methods (of expansion)—direct Imperial Government, Colonial Expansion and Republicanism, and the High Commissioner has taken up and supports the second method, Colonial Expansion...." Speech of Rhodes, July 23, 1888, Vindex, *op. cit.*, p. 200.

[28] Weinthal, *op. cit.*, vol. i, p. 97.

[29] C. O. 51/265, 1889 [A.—11], *op. cit.*, pp. 1211-1212 and 1232-1233.

[30] *Ibid.*, pp. 1233-1235.

[31] *Supra*, p. 96 and Rhodes' own exposition of his railway policies in his speeches: July, 1888, Vindex, *op. cit.*, pp. 196-208; August, 1888, *ibid.*, pp. 181-187; September, 1888, *ibid.*, pp. 218-221 and in his letter to the editor of the *Cape Argus*, July 6, 1887, *ibid.*, pp. 170-174.

[32] *Infra*, pp. 122-124.

CHAPTER VI

THE CAMPAIGN FOR THE CHARTER

[1] The treaty with Umsilikazi. *Accounts and Papers*, 1885, vol. 75 [c.—5524], No. 21 and Walker, *History of South Africa, op. cit.*, p. 193.

[2] *Accounts and Papers*, 1884, vol. 57 [c.—3841], No. 127. Lovell, *The Struggle for South Africa, op. cit.*, p. 135. Weinthal, *op. cit.*, vol. i, " The Founding of Rhodesia," by E. A. Maund, p. 371. Keltie, *op. cit.*, p. 407. Williams, *Cecil Rhodes, op. cit.*, p. 129.

[3] Williams, *Cecil Rhodes, op. cit.*, p. 121.

[4] "Matabele" is the corrupted form of the name "Amandabele". Morel, *The Black Man's Burden* (London, 1920), p. 31.

[5] Sir Hercules Robinson to Sir H. T. Holland, Cape Town, March 21, 1885, *Accounts and Papers*, 1888, vol. 75 [c.—5524], No. 5.

[6] Rudd to Captain Bower, November 23, 1888, *Accounts and Papers*, 1890, vol. 51 [c.—5918], enclosure in No. 38.

[7] Williams, *op. cit.*, pp. 126-127.

[8] Weinthal, *op. cit.*, vol. i, " The Founding of Rhodesia" by E. A. Maund, pp. 371 and 373.

[9] Williams, *Cecil Rhodes, op. cit.*, pp. 129-130.

[10] Weinthal, *op. cit.*, vol. i, p. 373.

[11] *Ibid.*, p. 373. See some amusing comments on the different attitude displayed by H. M. Government towards the Maund concessions and the Rudd concession: "In one case," complained Rhodes' opponents, "Her majesty's Government refused to countenance any treaty with Lo Bengula without their sanction, and as consequence the enterprise is put a stop to. In the other case the Government declared through Sir John Gorst, *that they have no right to interfere,* and a single speculator buys for an old song the most valuable territory in South Africa." "South Africa in Parliament," *Accounts and Papers,* 1890, vol. 51 [c.—5918], enclosure in No. 80.

[12] Williams, *Cecil Rhodes, op. cit.*, pp. 128-130.

[13] Weinthal, *op. cit.*, vol. i, p. 97.

[14] *Ibid.*, pp. 97 and 99, and Metcalfe's and Seaver's article in the *Fortnightly Review*, March, 1889, vol. xiv, pp. 251-352.

[15] The Bechuanaland Exploration Company to Sir Robert G. W. Herbert, Under Secretary of State, C. O., *Accounts and Papers,* 1890, vol. 51 [c.—5918], No. 41.

[16] C. O. to The Bechuanaland Exploration Company, January 10, 1889. *Accounts and Papers,* 1890, vol. 51 [c.—5918], No. 47.

[17] Sir Hercules Robinson to Lord Knutsford, March 18, 1889, *Accounts and Papers,* 1890, vol. 51 [c.—5918], No. 77.

[18] Weinthal, *op. cit.*, vol. i, p. 99.

[19] *Accounts and Papers,* 1890, vol. 51 [c.—5918], No. 82.

[20] *Ibid.*, No. 83.

[21] The argument that Great Britain must forestall the operations of outside powers by establishing a powerful company was very much stressed in the press in 1889. See a collection of these press notices contained in a report in the Royal Empire Society's Library, entitled: *The British South Africa Company, General Information and Press Notices,* 1889.

[22] *Supra,* p. 100.

[23] Secretary at Pretoria to the High Commissioner, November 30, 1888. *Accounts and Papers,* 1890, vol. 51 [c.—5918], enclosure in No. 45.

[24] President at Pretoria to the High Commissioner, August 29, 1888. *Accounts and Papers,* 1890, vol. 51 [c.—5918], enclosure 1 in No. 4.

[25] He was killed in a conflict with the people of a native chief, Khama. *Accounts and Papers,* 1888, vol. 75 [c.—5524], Nos. 28 and 29.

[26] State Secretary at Pretoria to the High Commissioner, November 29, 1888. *Accounts and Papers,* 1890, vol. 51 [c.—5918], enclosure in No. 44.

[27] Sir Hercules Robinson to Lord Knutsford, *Accounts and Papers,* 1888, vol. 75 [c.—5524], No. 29.

[28] Groblaar's report, *Accounts and Papers,* 1890, vol. 51 [c.—5918], enclosure in No. 45.

29 Lord Knutsford to Sir Hercules Robinson, November 31, 1889, *Accounts and Papers*, 1890, vol. 51 [c.—5918], No. 56.

30 *Ibid.*, No. 84.

31 Keltie, *op. cit.*, p. 104.

32 *Ibid.*, p. 55.

33 *Ibid.*, p. 75.

34 *Ibid.*, p. 75.

35 *Ibid.*, Peace Handbook, vol. xv, *The Partition of Africa*, pp. 13-14.

36 Keltie, *op. cit.*, pp. 421 and 444-445.

37 Keltie, *op. cit.*, pp. 420-423.

38 Sir Hercules Robinson to Lord Knutsford, May 23, 1888. *Accounts and Papers*, 1888, vol. 75 [c.—5524], No. 20.

39 Keltie, *op. cit.*, p. 423.

40 *Ibid.*, p. 413.

41 Comment of the South African Committee upon a remark made by Sir John Gorst, Under Secretary of State for India, in Parliament, December 20, 1888. " Circular of the South African Committee." Section entitled "South Africa in Parliament." *Accounts and Papers*, 1890, vol. 51 [c.—5918], enclosure 1 in No. 80, p. 184.

42 *Supra*, p. 129.

43 " British Interests on the Central Zambezi ", *Times*, May 29, 1888. Cecil, Lady Gwendolen, *Life of Robert, Marquis of Salisbury* (London, 1932), vol. iv, pp. 259-263.

44 *Infra*, pp. 135 and 140.

45 Johnston, Sir Harry, *The Story of My Life* (London, 1923), pp. 211-212. Keltie, *op. cit.*, p. 444. Speech of the Under Secretary of State for Foreign Affairs, Sir James Ferguson, Hansard, series 3, vol. 323, March 2, 1888, c. 29. Speech of the Earl of Harrowby, Hansard, series 3, vol. 328, July 6, 1888, c. 543. Speech of the Marquis of Salisbury, Hansard, series 3, vol. 328, c. 548.

46 Lugard, Captain F. D., *The Rise of Our East African Empire* (London, 1893), vol. i, p. 158.

47 Weinthal, *op. cit.*, vol. i, " My Story of the Cape to Cairo Scheme " by Sir Harry Johnston, p. 76.

48 Johnston, *The Story of My Life, op. cit.*, p. 213.

49 See Lord Salisbury's statement of the Government policy in his answer to a deputation sent by the Free Church of Scotland, the Universities Missions, The African Lakes Company, etc., *Times*, May 18, 1889.

50 Johnston, *The Story of My Life, op. cit.*, pp. 201-205.

51 Weinthal, *op. cit.*, vol. i, " My Story of the Cape to Cairo Scheme " by Sir Harry Johnston, p. 77.

52 *Ibid.*, pp. 77 and 79. *Cf.* this account with Lady Cecil's, *Life of Robert Marquis of Salisbury, op. cit.*, vol. iv, pp. 242-243.

53 Johnston, *Story of My Life, op. cit.*, pp. 210 and 216.

[54] *Ibid.*, pp. 210 and 216.

[55] Weinthal, *op. cit.*, "My Story of the Cape to Cairo Scheme" by Sir Harry Johnston, vol. i, p. 79.

[56] *Ibid.*, p. 81.

[57] *Supra*, p. 125.

[58] Weinthal, *op. cit.*, "My Story of the Cape to Cairo Scheme," vol. i, pp. 82-83.

[59] Johnston, *The Story of My Life, op. cit.*, pp. 223-224.

[60] *Supra*, pp. 88-89 and 104-108.

[61] *British Documents on the Origins of the War*, 1888-1914, vol. i, Memorandum by Mr. J. A. C. Tilley, respecting the relations between Germany and Great Britain, 1892-1904, p. 323.

[62] *Infra*, pp. 251-253. *Accounts and Papers*, 1887, vol. 59 [c.—4609], No. 63 and vol. 51 [c.—6043].

[63] Weinthal, *op. cit.*, "My Story of the Scheme" by Sir Charles Metcalfe, vol. i, p. 99.

[64] *Ibid.*, p. 99. Rhodes' unpopular reputation was probably due to a speech against the "imperial factor" made July 16, 1884. See a discussion on this point in note 5, pp. 417-418.

[65] Ricarde-Seaver, F. I. and Metcalfe, Sir Charles, "The British Sphere of Influence in South Africa," *Fortnightly Review*, March, 1889, vol. 51, p. 352.

[66] C. O. to Lord Gifford, May 16, 1889, *Accounts and Papers*, 1889, vol. 51 [c.—5918], *op. cit.*, No. 87.

[67] C. O. to the F. O., May 16, 1889 [c.—5918], *op. cit.*, No. 88.

[68] F. O. to the C. O., May 27, 1889 [c.—5918], *op. cit.*, No. 92. Williams, *Cecil Rhodes, op. cit.*, p. 135.

[69] "The Nyassaland Mission," *Times*, May 18, 1889, p. 9, columns c and d.

[70] "The Royal Geographical Society," *Times*, May 28, 1889, p. 5, column f.

[71] Italics supplied.

[72] "British Interests in the Central Zambesi" from a Correspondent, *Times*, May 29, 1889, p. 6, columns a and b.

[73] *Reports of the British South Africa Company . . . & Press Notices, op. cit.*

[74] "Painting the African Map Red," *The Pall Mall Gazette*, May 29, 1889 contained in *Reports of the British South Africa Company . . . & Press Notices, op. cit.*

[75] *The Birmingham Post*, May 30, 1889 in *Reports, etc., op. cit.*

[76] C. J. Rhodes, Esq. to the C. O., June 1, 1889 [c.—5918], *op. cit.*, No. 93.

[77] C. O. to C. J. Rhodes, June 14, 1889 [c.—5918], *op. cit.*, No. 99.

[78] *The Spectator*, June 1, 1889, *Reports, etc., op. cit.*

[79] *The Scotsman*, June 8, 1889, *ibid.*

[80] *Pall Mall Gazette*, June 11, 1889, *ibid.*

[81] F. O. to C. O., July 5, 1889 [c.—5918], *op. cit.*, No. 110.

[82] Williams, *Cecil Rhodes, op. cit.*, p. 135.

[83] See especially "the Circular of the South African Committee" [c.—5918], *op. cit.*, enclosure 1 in No. 80 and the statement of Maguire, a South African agent at Lobengula's Kraal [c.—5918], *op. cit.*, No. 106.

[84] See especially, Sir John Swinburne's attacks in Parliament in Hansard, series 3, vol. 340, cc. 486, 562-565 and 568. Cawston's protest in [c.—5918], *op. cit.*, enclosure in No. 80 and Haggard's complaint [c.—5918], *op. cit.*, No. 54.

[85] [c.—5918], *op. cit.*, enclosure 1 in No. 80 and Williams, *Cecil Rhodes, op. cit.*, p. 131.

[86] "Circular of the South African Committee" [c.—5918], *op. cit.*, enclosure 1 in No. 80.

[87] MacKenzie to the C. O., April 10, 1889 [c.—5918], *op. cit.*, No. 78.

[88] Keltie, *op. cit.*, p. 407, Weinthal, *op. cit.*, vol. i, p. 371 and an article in the *Globe*, August 27, 1889, *Reports, etc., op. cit.*

[89] Hansard, series 3, vol. 340, August 26, cc. 563-564.

[90] *Ibid.*, c. 486.

[91] *Ibid.*, c. 564.

[92] *Ibid.*, c. 563.

[93] [c.—5918], *op. cit.*, enclosure in No. 128, section 20.

[94] Hansard, series 3, vol. 340, cc. 566-567.

[95] *Ibid.*, cc. 486, 567 and 569.

[96] Williams, *Cecil Rhodes, op. cit.*, p. 131.

[97] *Supra*, pp. 76-78.

[98] *Supra*, p. 136.

[99] Williams, *Cecil Rhodes, op. cit.*, p. 132.

[100] Weinthal, *op. cit.*, vol. i, pp. 82-83.

[101] In the Spring of 1888, Rhodes gave this much criticized gift to the Irish Parliamentary funds. Johnston claims that Rhodes told him cynically that "his intention at the time ... was merely to keep the Irish party in the House of Commons from opposing his Charter when he chose to apply it." Weinthal, *op. cit.*, vol. i, p. 82. Williams, on the other hand, insists that Rhodes gave the check because he was genuinely interested in Home Rule. Williams, *Cecil Rhodes, op. cit.*, pp. 113-134. In support of Williams point of view, it may be argued that Rhodes had offered to give £10,000 to the Irish party funds as early as 1887 long before the Rudd concession was concluded, or the negotiations for a charter started. He actually gave the money a whole year before the question of the charter came up in Parliament. Whether intentionally or not, however, Rhodes did secure the benevolent support of the Irish party for his African schemes. Williams, *Cecil Rhodes, op. cit.*, p. 133.

[102] *Supra*, pp. 125 and 141.

[103] Weinthal, *op. cit.*, vol. i, " The History and Finance of the Rhodesian Railway System " by Baron Émile Beaumont D'Erlanger, p. 649.

[104] Lord Gifford to the C. O., April 30, 1889 [c.—5918], *op. cit.*, No. 82.

[105] Remarks by J. S. Moffat, Assistant Commissioner of Matabeleland, July 10, 1889 [c.—5918], *op. cit.*, No. 116.

[106] [c.—5918], *op. cit.*, enclosure in No. 138.

[107] Lord Knutsford to Sir H. B. Loch, November 18, 1889 [c.—5918], *op. cit.*, No. 128.

[108] See in this connection the preamble to the charter. [c.—5918], *op. cit.*, enclosure in No. 128 and also Lord Knutsford's comment that such a company " will be able peacefully and with the consent of the native races to open up, develop, and colonize the territories to the north of British Bechuanaland with the best results both for British trade and commerce and for the interests of the native races." C. O. to the F. O., May 16, 1889 [c.—5918], *op. cit.*, No. 88 and also Lord Gifford's letter to the C. O., April 30, 1889 [c.—5918], *op. cit.*, No. 82.

[109] Article 1 of the Charter of the B. S. A. Co., Hertslet, *op. cit.*, vol. i, no. 34, p. 272.

[110] Vindex, *op. cit.*, p. 228.

[111] Articles 2, 3, 19, 20 and 24 of the Charter, Hertslet, *op. cit.*, vol. i, no. 34, pp. 272-276.

[112] The members of the board were:

The Duke of Abercorn (president of the board).

The Duke of Fife (vice-president of the board, and son-in-law of the Prince of Wales).

Albert Grey (later Earl Grey, a former opponent of Rhodes. In fact, his name is listed among the signers of the circular sent out by the South African Committee to oppose the formation of the new company). [c.—5918], *op. cit.*, enclosure 1 in No. 80.

Cecil John Rhodes and Albert Beit (directors on the board of the Gold Fields of South Africa, Ltd.).

George Cawston and Lord Gifford (directors on the board of the Bechuanaland Exploration and the Exploring Companies which were, as already noted, formerly rival companies of the Gold Fields of South Africa).

[113] *The Times*, October 15, 1889, in *Reports and Press Notices, op. cit.*

[114] *The Standard*, November 1, 1889, *ibid.*

[115] *Pall Mall Gazette*, November 1, 1889, *ibid.*

[116] *British Bechuanaland*, report of the Administrator for the year 1889. *Accounts and Papers*, 1890, vol. 48 [c.—5897].

[117] *Supra*, pp. 98 and 115.

[118] [c.—5897], *op. cit.*

[119] C. O. to the B. S. A. Co., January 24, 1890. [c.—5918], *op. cit.*, No. 139.

[120] *Ibid.*, No. 139; also Michell, *op. cit.*, vol. i, pp. 268-269 and Weinthal, *op. cit.*, vol. i, "History and Finance of the Rhodesian Railway System" by Baron Émile Beaumont d'Erlanger, p. 649.

[121] Weinthal, *op. cit.*, "The Rhodesian Railway" by Lieut. Col. H. Marshall Hole, p. 27. *Ibid.*, "My Story of the Scheme" by Sir Charles Metcalfe, vol. i, p. 101. *British Bechuanaland*, Annual Report for 1889-1890, *Accounts and Papers*, 1890-1891, vol. 51, no. 3.

CHAPTER VII

"The Forward Policy" in South Africa

[1] See especially the speech by Lord Rosebery at the 25th anniversary Banquet of the Royal Colonial Institute, March 1, 1893. *The Foreign Policy of Lord Rosebery* (London, 1901), Appendix x, p. 88 and also his speech at the Cutler's Feast, Sheffield, October 25, 1894, Coates. Thomas, F. G., *Lord Rosebery, His Life and Speeches* (New York, 1900), pp. 265-266.

[2] See the debates on supply and the votes on supplementary estimates in Hansard for the period from 1892 to 1898.

[3] Speech of Rhodes, July 18, 1899, Vindex, *op. cit.*, p. 642.

[4] *Supra*, pp. 135-136.

[5] *Infra*, p. 277.

[6] Weinthal, *op. cit.*, vol. i, "Cecil John Rhodes. A Review of His Life and Works" by Walford Dowling, p. 23.

[7] Vindex, *op. cit.*, pp. 313 and 314.

[8] *Infra*, pp. 273-279.

[9] Vindex, *op. cit.*, p. 313.

[10] *Ibid.*, pp. 315-316.

[11] *Supra*, pp. 104-105.

[12] Williams, *Cecil Rhodes, op. cit.*, p. 200.

[13] Memorandum by Mr. J. A. C. Tilley, *British Documents, op. cit.*, vol. i, p. 326.

[14] *Supra*, pp. 125, 146, 148-149.

[15] Weinthal, *op. cit.*, vol. i, "My Story of the Scheme" by Sir Charles Metcalfe, p. 101.

[16] *Ibid.*, p. 101.

[17] Baron Émile D'Erlanger estimates that the distance north between Kimberley and Rhodesia is 632 miles as opposed to a distance of 204 miles from Beira on Pungwe Bay to the eastern frontier of Mashonaland.

Weinthal, *op. cit.*, vol. i, "History and Finance of the Rhodesian Railway System" by Baron Émile Beaumont D'Erlanger, p. 641.

[18] Williams, Robert, *The Cape to Cairo Railway*, address to the African Society, April 21, 1921, p. 6.

[19] Article xiv of the Anglo-Portuguese treaty of June 11, 1891, Hertslet, *op. cit.*, vol. iii, no. 310, p. 1024.

[20] Weinthal, *op. cit.*, vol. i, p. 641.

[21] In 1895, the Beira Junction Railway Company was formed to connect the Beira Railway with the Port of Beira. The section between Fontesvilla and Beira was completed by October, 1896. Finally, the railway was extended from Umtali on the Mashonaland border to Salisbury, the capital of Southern Rhodesia, reaching the latter point in May, 1899. This last section was built on a 3 ft. 6 in. gauge where as a narrow gauge had been used between Beira and Umtali. The original narrow gauge on the Beira to Umtali section, however, was converted into the 3 ft. 6 in. gauge by August, 1900. Rhodesia was thus furnished with a direct line to the east coast on the regular gauge used throughout South Africa. *Guide to Rhodesia*, issued by authority of the Beira and Mashonaland and Rhodesia Railway, 1924, p. 60. See also Weinthal, *op. cit.*, vol. i, p. 641.

The railway from Beira to Salisbury is now connected through the Rhodesian and Congo railway systems with the Benguella to Tenge line. The Benguella to Tenge railway was completed May, 1931 according to the report of Richard C. Long, American Commercial Attaché, Lisbon (*The South and East Africa Year Book* for 1934, gives the date of opening as June, 1931). There is now, therefore, through transcontinental connection between Beira on the east coast and Benguella on the west.

[22] *Supra*, p. 92.

[23] "The History of the Delagoa Bay Railway Concession," *Accounts and Papers*, 1890, vol. 51 [c.—5903], enclosure in No. 27 and also the enclosure in No. 30. Worsfold, *op. cit.*, vol. i, pp. 115-116 and Lovell, *The Struggle for South Africa, op. cit.*, pp. 353-354.

[24] Lovell, *The Struggle for South Africa, op. cit.*, p. 354.

[25] [c.—5903], *op. cit.*, nos. 31, 47, 55, 61 and 64. Worsfold, *op. cit.*, vol. i, p. 116.

[26] *Infra*, pp. 160 and 211.

[27] *The Memoirs of Paul Kruger, op. cit.*, p. 193.

[28] Williams, *Cecil Rhodes, op. cit.*, p. 198. Worsfold, *op. cit.*, vol. i, p. 117. Rhodes' own minute regarding the negotiations. Michell, *op. cit.*, vol. ii, p. 94.

[29] At any rate, Rhodes was consulting with Lord Rothschild about the purchase. Lovell, *The Struggle for South Africa, op. cit.*, p. 342, and Worsfold, *op. cit.*, vol. i, p. 117.

[30] Michell, *op. cit.*, vol. ii, p. 93.

[31] Rhodes' minute, Michell, *op. cit.*, vol. i, p. 94. Memorandum by Mr. J. A. C. Tilley, *British Documents, op. cit.*, vol. i, p. 323. Michell, *op. cit.*, vol. ii, pp. 93-94.

[32] Lovell, *The Struggle for South Africa, op. cit.*, pp. 342-343 and Michell, *op. cit.*, vol. ii, p. 94.

[33] Memorandum by Mr. J. A. C. Tilley, *British Documents, op. cit.*, vol. i, pp. 323-324 and Michell, *op. cit.*, vol. ii, p. 95.

[34] *Supra*, pp. 82-87, 94, 96-97 and 118.

[35] Lovell, *The Struggle for South Africa, op. cit.*, pp. 297-307.

[36] *Supra*, p. 149.

[37] *Accounts and Papers*, 1893, vol. 61 [c.—7154], No. 27.

[38] *Accounts and Papers*, 1896, vol. 59 [c.—7962], especially Nos. 35 and 39. *Cf.* Lovell's account in *The Struggle for South Africa, op. cit.*, pp. 318-321.

[39] [c.—7962], *op. cit.*, No. 35.

[40] Khama had been helpful to the British in securing Bechuanaland. In 1885, he offered his dominions to the Imperial Government but the offer was rejected. Michell, *op. cit.*, vol. i, p. 203. He could be counted on as ally to the British. In 1889, he assisted the Bechuanaland Exploration Company by negotiating with it and granting it large trading rights. *Accounts and Papers*, 1890, vol. 51 [c.—5918], No. 41. In 1890 Khama supplied a native contingent to assist Rhodes' Pioneers on their march into Mashonaland. Michell, *op. cit.*, vol. i, p. 297.

[41] *Accounts and Papers*, 1896, vol. 59 [c.—7962], No. 22.

[42] [c.—7962], *op. cit.*, No. 35 and Lovell, *The Struggle for South Africa, op. cit.*, pp. 318-321.

[43] Williams, *Cecil Rhodes, op. cit.*, chapter xv, "The Raid." *Cf.* Lovell's discussion of the same subject in *The Struggle for South Africa, op. cit.*, pp. 318-321.

[44] Hansard, series 3, 1890, vol. 347, c. 978 and also *Accounts and Papers*, 1890, vol. 51 [c.—6046], enclosure in No. 1.

[45] *Accounts and Papers*, 1890, vol. 51 [c.—5918], No. 139 and 1893, vol. 61 [c.—7154].

[46] [c.—7154], *op. cit.*, Nos. 1 and 4, enclosure 2 in No. 4, Nos. 6, 19, 21, 22, 23, 24 and 27.

[47] Williams, *Cecil Rhodes, op. cit.*, p. 170.

[48] [c.—5918], *op. cit.*, enclosure in No. 101.

[49] Maguire, Rhodes' agent in Lobengula's Kraal, testified, for example, that the "Letter of April 24th purporting to be written by Lobengula . . . appears to be a portion of the organized opposition by a certain section of the white inhabitants of Matabeleland to all attempts to promote the development of that country." *Accounts and Papers*, 1890, vol. 51 [c.—5918], enclosure in No. 106 and enclosure in No. 131.

[50] [c.—5918], *op. cit.*, enclosure in No. 129.

51 *Supra*, p. 121.

52 Williams, *Cecil Rhodes*, op. cit., pp. 142-143.

53 *Ibid.*, pp. 147 and 156. Vindex, *op. cit.*, p. 255.

54 Williams, *Cecil Rhodes, op. cit.*, p. 158.

55 *Ibid.*, pp. 173-174.

56 Hansard, series 4, vol. xvi, c. 1721 and vol. xviii, c. 222 and Vindex, *op. cit.*, p. 325.

57 Speech of Rhodes at Buluwayo, December 19, 1893, Vindex, *op. cit.*, pp. 328 and 330.

58 In the words of Buxton, under Secretary of State for the Colonies, 1893: ". . . with regard to the British Africa Company . . . if that company had not undertaken at that moment the administration and opening up of Mashonaland possibly the Government was not in a position to undertake that responsibility and the territory might have been lost to the United Kingdom and absorbed into the Transvaal. That we shall admit would have been under the circumstances a great mistake. . . . " Hansard, series 4, vol. xvi, c. 680.

CHAPTER VIII

PAINTING CENTRAL AFRICA RED

1 *Supra*, pp. 152-154.

2 Weinthal, *op. cit.*, vol. i, " My Story of the Cape to Cairo Scheme " by Sir Harry Johnston, p. 73.

3 Weinthal, *op. cit.*, vol. i, " The Story of the African Lakes Corporation " by Fred L. Moir, pp. 445-446.

4 *Supra*, pp. 135-136.

5 Johnston, Sir Harry, *British Central Africa* (London, 1898), p. vii.

6 In fact, Lord Salisbury asserted that he considered the Cape-to-Cairo idea visionary and impractical. See his speech before Parliament on the Anglo-German agreement of 1890. Hansard, series 3, vol. 346, cc. 1267-1268.

7 Weinthal, *op. cit.*, vol. i, " My Story of the Cape to Cairo Scheme " by Sir Harry Johnston, pp. 77-78 and 81.

8 Williams, *Cecil Rhodes, op. cit.*, p. 56.

9 Johnston, *British Central Africa, op. cit.*, p. 83.

10 *Ibid.*, pp. 85-86.

11 *Ibid.*, pp. 86-88.

12 *Ibid.*, pp. 89-90.

13 *Ibid.*, p. 96.

[14] *Ibid.*, p. 96. For the negotiations over the Anglo-German treaty of 1890, *supra*, pp. 259-265.

[15] Johnston, *British Central Africa, op. cit.*, foot-note, p. 86.

[16] *Ibid.*, p. 80.

[17] *Supra*, p. 135.

[18] Williams, *Cecil Rhodes, op. cit.*, p. 165.

[19] *Ibid.*, p. 165 and Weinthal, *op. cit.*, vol. i, p. 446.

[20] Johnston, *British Central Africa, op. cit.*, p. 97.

[21] Williams, *Cecil Rhodes, op. cit.*, p. 166.

[22] "Conditions on extending the Field of Operations of the British South Africa Company." *Accounts and Papers*, 1895, vol. 71, Africa No. 2 [c.—7637], No. 1.

[23] *Supra*, pp. 170-171 and 172-173.

[24] Johnston, *British Central Africa, op. cit.*, p. 97.

[25] *Peace Handbook*, vol. xv, *Partition of Africa, op. cit.*, pp. 13-16 and *Accounts and Papers*, 1890, vol. 57, Africa No. 2.

[26] *Accounts and Papers*, 1890, vol. 51 [c.—6048] and [c.—6046].

[27] Keith, Arthur Berriedale, *The Belgian Congo and the Berlin Act* (Oxford, 1919) chap. vi, "The Conquest of the Katanga."

[28] Johnston, *British Central Africa, op. cit.*, p. vii and also speech of Rhodes at the second annual meeting of the B. S. A. Co., November 29, 1892, Vindex, *op. cit.*, pp. 305-306.

[29] Speech of Rhodes at the second annual meeting of the B. S. A. Co., *op. cit.*, p. 307.

[30] *Supra*, pp. 128-131.

[31] Williams, *Cecil Rhodes, op. cit.*, p. 168 and Hertslet, *op. cit.*, vol. iii, no. 308, pp. 1006-1013.

[32] Williams, *Cecil Rhodes, op. cit.*, p. 168.

[33] Lovell, *The Anglo-German Estrangement*, 1894-1896, unpublished Doctoral Dissertation, Chapter on the Portuguese difficulties, 1887-1891 and also Lovell, *The Struggle for South Africa, 1875-1889, op. cit.*, p. 175.

[34] *Supra*, pp. 81-82 and *infra*, note 5, pp. 417-418.

[35] *Supra*, p. 146 and *infra*, note 3, p. 417 and note 101, p. 427.

[36] Baron De Staal, *Correspondance Diplomatique (1884-1900)*, (Paris, 1929), vol. ii, pp. 129-130.

[37] Williams, *Cecil Rhodes, op. cit.*, pp. 80-81.

[38] *Die Grosse Politik*, vol. xi, no. 2594, pp. 22-23. Italics supplied.

[39] Lady Cecil, *Life of Lord Salisbury*, 1887-1892, *op. cit.*, vol. iv, pp. 257-276.

[40] Buckle, G. E., *Queen Victoria's Letters*, 1891-1895, third series (London, 1931), vol. ii, p. 13.

[41] *Ibid.*, pp. 454-455.

[42] Hertslet, *op. cit.*, vol. iii, no. 309, pp. 1014-1015, especially Art. iv, p. 1015.

[43] Hansard, series 3, vol. 350, c. 114 and vol. 349, c. 1284 and also *supra*, p. 130.

[44] Williams, *Cecil Rhodes, op. cit.*, p. 169.

[45] Hansard, series 3, vol. 350, cc. 1152-1153.

[46] Michell, *op. cit.*, vol. i, p. 320 and Williams, *Cecil Rhodes, op. cit.*, p. 170.

[47] Hansard, series 3, vol. 355, c. 1164.

[48] *Ibid.*, vol. 353, c. 139 and Michell, *op. cit.*, vol. i, p. 320.

[49] Articles i, iv and v of the Anglo-Portuguese agreement of July 3, 1891. Hertslet, *op. cit.*, vol. iii, no. 310, pp. 1016-1025.

[50] *Ibid.*, art. xiv and *supra*, p. 156.

[51] Article vii of the Anglo-Portuguese agreement of July 3, 1891, Hertslet, *op. cit.*, vol. iii, no. 310, p. 1020.

[52] Speech of the Prime Minister, Hansard, series 3, vol. 354, c. 138.

[53] Williams, *Cecil Rhodes, op. cit.*, p. 166.

[54] Article 2 of the Anglo-German Agreement of 1890. Hertslet, *op. cit.*, vol. iii, no. 270, p. 900.

[55] Williams, *Cecil Rhodes, op. cit.*, p. 167.

[56] Weinthal, *op. cit.*, " My Story of the Scheme " by Robert Williams, vol. i, p. 109. Hertslet, *op. cit.*, vol. ii, pp. 471, 474 and map opposite, p. 604.

[57] Williams, *Cecil Rhodes, op. cit.*, p. 180.

[58] *Ibid.*, chapter xiii.

CHAPTER IX

THE RAID AND ITS CONSEQUENCES

[1] *Supra*, p. 160.

[2] *Supra*, p. 154.

[3] *Supra*, pp. 161-164.

[4] Williams, *Cecil Rhodes, op. cit.*, p. 258. Lovell, *The Struggle for South Africa, op. cit.*, p. 288.

[5] *Supra*, p. 89. For the German attitude see *Die Grosse Politik*, vol. xi, no. 2578, p. 6.

[6] Lovell, *The Struggle for South Africa, op. cit.*, p. 347.

[7] Williams, *Cecil Rhodes, op. cit.*, pp. 253-254 and Lee, Sydney, *King Edward VII* (New York, 1925), vol. i, p. 719.

[8] *Supra*, pp. 157-158.

[9] Memorandum by Mr. J. A. C. Tilley, *British Documents, op. cit.*, vol. i, p. 326.

[10] *Supra*, pp. 159-160.

[11] Lovell, *The Struggle for South Africa, op. cit.*, p. 351.

[12] *Die Grosse Politik,* vol. xi, no. 2577, pp. 3-4.
[13] Memorandum by Mr. J. A. C. Tilley, *British Documents,* vol. i, p. 326.
[14] *Die Grosse Politik,* vol. xi, no. 2577, p. 4.
[15] *Ibid.,* vol. xi, no. 2579, pp. 9-10.
[16] *Ibid.,* vol. xi, nos. 2582-2584, pp. 13-15.
[17] *Supra,* p. 92. See also *Die Grosse Politik,* vol. xi, no. 2613, p. 33.
[18] *Supra,* pp. 162-164.
[19] Williams, *Cecil Rhodes, op. cit.,* pp. 255, 268-270.
[20] Williams, *Cecil Rhodes, op. cit.,* chapter entitled " The Raid."
[21] *Ibid.,* pp. 272-273.
[22] Hansard, series 4, vol. 57, c. 602 and the Order in Council regarding Southern Rhodesia, October 20, 1898 in *Accounts and Papers,* 1899, vol. 63 [c.—9138].
[23] Williams, *Cecil Rhodes, op. cit.,* p. 306 and Vindex, *op. cit.,* pp. 638-639.
[24] Williams, *Cecil Rhodes, op. cit.,* p. 306. Vindex, *op. cit.,* p. 306. Hansard, series 4, vol. 57, c. 603.
[25] Williams, *Cecil Rhodes, op. cit.,* p. 278.
[26] *Ibid.,* pp. 238 and 312.
[27] Speech of Cecil Rhodes, Cape Town, July 18, 1899. Vindex, *op. cit.,* p. 642.
[28] Williams, *Cecil Rhodes, op. cit.,* p. 273.
[29] *Die Grosse Politik,* vol. xi, p. 19, Marschall to Hatzfeldt, December 31, 1895.
[30] *Ibid.,* foot-note, p. 20.
[31] *Ibid.,* pp. 27-29, Marschall to Hatzfeldt, January 2, 1896, no. 2601, pp. 27-28, and Hatzfeldt to Auswärtige Amt, January 2, 1896, no. 2602, p. 28.
[32] In the original draft, the telegram read " the authority of your Government " instead of " the independence of your country against foreign aggression." The change was made by the Secretary of State, von Marschall. *Die Grosse Politik,* vol. xi, no. 2610, pp. 31-32 and the foot-note, p. 32.
[33] See in this connection: *Die Grosse Politik,* vol. xi, no. 2610, foot-note p. 32; Freiherr von Eckardstein, *Lebenserringeren und Politische Denkwürdigkeiten,* vol. 2, p. 272; Otto Hamman, *The World Policy of Germany,* 1890-1912, p. 67; Otto Hamman, " Die Entstehung der Kruger-depesche," *Archiv für Politik und Geschichte,* vol. ii, 1924, p. 203 *et seq.;* Konrad Lehmann, " Die Vorgeschichte der Krugerdepesche," *Archiv für Politik und Geschichte,* vol. iii, 1925; Arnold Askar Meyer, " Die Krugerdepesche," *Archiv für Politik und Geschichte,* vol. ii, 1924; Adolf Stein, *Wilhelm II,* p. 32; Friedrich Thimme, " Die Kruger-Depesche," *Europäische Gespräche,* vol. ii, 1924, pp. 206 *et seq.* (Thimme's account supplements the documents with evidence from the diaries of von Marschall and Admiral von Senden), Lovell, *op. cit.,* p. 362, *British Documents,* vol.

vi, no. 101, memorandum by Valentine Chirol, pp. 158-159; Lee, Sydney, *Edward VII*, vol. i, pp. 721-723.

34 Buckle, *Letters of Queen Victoria*, series 3, vol. iii, p. 21.

35 *Die Grosse Politik*, vol. xi, no. 2579, p. 10.

36 Buckle, *Letters of Queen Victoria*, series iii, vol. iii, p. 21.

37 Thimme, "Die Kruger-Depesche," *Europäische Gespräche*, vol. ii, 1924, pp. 205 *et seq*. Lovell, *The Struggle for South Africa, op. cit.*, pp. 362-363 and 370 and also *Die Grossè Politik*, vol. xi, no. 2641, pp. 70-71.

38 Lovell, *The Struggle for South Africa, op. cit.*, p. 370.

39 *Die Grosse Politik*, vol. xi, nos. 2614 and 2616, pp. 34-36.

40 Lovell, *The Struggle for South Africa, op. cit.*, p. 371.

41 *Die Grosse Politik*, vol. xi, no. 2609, p. 31 and chapter lxiv, Kontinentalliga gegen England, 1896, pp. 67-91.

42 *Die Grosse Politik*, vol. xi, no. 2615, pp. 35-36 and also no. 2628, p. 47.

43 Bourgeois et Pagès, *Les Origines et les Responsabilités de La Grande Guerre* (Paris, 1921), p. 256 and also *Die Grosse Politik*, vol. xi, no. 2641, footnote, p. 21 and pp. 69-71, 80-82.

44 Bourgeois et Pagès, *op. cit.*, pp. 256-257.

45 *Die Grosse Politik*, vol. xi, no. 2618, p. 38.

46 *Ibid.*, no. 2625, pp. 44-45 and footnote, p. 45 and no. 2627, p. 47.

47 *Ibid.*, no. 2636, p. 55.

48 Dispatch of M. de Montbello, French Ambassador at St. Petersburg to M. Berthelot, January 12, 1896. Bourgeois et Pagès, *op. cit.*, p. 257 and Lovell, *The Struggle for South Africa, op. cit.*, pp. 375-376.

49 *Die Grosse Politik*, vol. xi, no. 2622, p. 43 and no. 2623, p. 43.

50 *Ibid.*, no. 2621, p. 42.

51 *Ibid.*, no. 2628, p. 48.

52 *Ibid.*, no. 2614, p. 44.

53 *Ibid.*, no. 2642, p. 72.

54 *Ibid.*, no. 2649, pp. 77-80.

55 Memorandum by Mr. J. A. C. Tilley, *British Documents, op. cit.*, vol. i, p. 327.

56 *Die Grosse Politik*, vol. xi, no. 2649, p. 78.

57 *Ibid.*, no. 2618, pp. 38-39.

58 *Ibid.*, no. 2649, p. 79.

59 *Ibid.*, no. 2618, p. 38.

60 *Ibid.*, no. 2629, p. 49.

61 *Ibid.*, footnote, p. 20.

62 Lovell, *The Struggle for South Africa, op. cit.*, pp. 366-367.

63 Buckle, *Letters of Queen Victoria*, series 3, vol. iii, p. 13.

64 Lovell, *The Struggle for South Africa, op. cit.*, p. 366.

65 *Supra*, p. 190.

66 *Die Grosse Politik*, vol. xi, no. 2615, p. 35.

[67] *Ibid.*, no. 2619, pp. 39-40.

[68] *Ibid.*, no. 2628, p. 47 and no. 2629, p. 48.

[69] *Cambridge History of British Foreign Policy* (Cambridge, 1922-1923), vol. iii, p. 264.

[70] Hansard, series 4, vol. 37, c. 395. See also the speech by the Earl of Rosebery, February 11, *ibid.*, cc. 38-39.

[71] *Die Grosse Politik*, vol. xi, no. 2636, p. 53.

[72] Lovell, *The Struggle for South Africa, op. cit.*, p. 373.

[73] *Die Grosse Politik*, vol. xi, no. 2636, pp. 53-54.

[74] Bourgeois et Pagès, *op. cit.*, footnote, p. 258.

[75] *Supra*, pp. 103 and 107-108.

[76] General statement concerning the Raid made by Rhodes before the Select Committee in England, 1897, Vindex, *op. cit.*, p. 510.

[77] Buckle, Letters of Queen Victoria, series 3, vol. iii, p. 7.

[78] *Ibid.*, p. 8.

[79] *Ibid.*, p. 13.

[80] *Die Grosse Politik*, vol. xi, no. 2613, p. 33.

[81] *Ibid.*, no. 2613, pp. 33-34.

[82] *Ibid.*, nos. 2596 and 2597, pp. 24-25.

[83] *Ibid.*, no. 2620, p. 40.

[84] *Ibid.*, no. 2620, pp. 40-41 and no. 2632, p. 51.

[85] *Ibid.*, no. 2632, p. 51 and Lovell, *The Struggle for South Africa, op. cit.*, p. 372.

[86] *Ibid.*, footnote, p. 20 and no. 2618, pp. 37-38.

[87] Letter of Goschen to Queen Victoria. Buckle, *Letters of Queen Victoria*, series 3, *op. cit.*, vol. iii, pp. 16-17.

[88] *Die Grosse Politik*, vol. xi, no. 2618, pp. 37-38.

[89] *Ibid.*, no. 2632, p. 50; no. 2633, p. 51 and no. 2635, pp. 52-53.

[90] *Ibid.*, no. 2633, p. 51 and Michell, *op. cit.*, vol. ii, p. 150.

[91] Lee, Sydney, *King Edward VII*, vol. i, p. 726.

[92] Michell, Sir Lewis, "The Cape to Cairo Railway," *Journal of the Society of Arts*, 1906-1907, vol. iv, p. 101.

[93] Metcalfe, Sir Charles, "The Cape to Cairo Line. How the War may solve a Problem," *South Africa*, December 19, 1914. Pamphlet 4 x 4 in the Royal Empire Society.

[94] Paper read before the Royal Colonial Institute, May 8, 1917 and published in the *United Empire Journal*, 1917, vol. viii, pp. 446-462.

[95] Weinthal, *op. cit.*, "My Story of the Scheme" by Robert Williams, J. P., vol. i, p. 110.

[96] *Supra*, pp. 155-156.

[97] Weinthal, *op. cit.*, vol. i, p. 111.

[98] *Ibid.*, p. 113.

[99] *Accounts and Papers*, 1899, vol. 63 [c.—9323], no. 2.

[100] Wyndham, Member for Dover, May 6, 1898, Hansard, series 4, vol. 57, c. 571.

[101] Joseph Walton, Yorks, W. R. Barnsley, February 24, Hansard, series 4, vol. 67, cc. 510-511.

[102] Michell, Sir Lewis, "The Cape to Cairo Railway," *Journal of the Society of Arts*, 1906, vol. 55, p. 101.

[103] Speech of Rhodes to the Shareholders of the B. S. A. Co., May 2, 1899, Vindex, *op. cit.*, pp. 729-737.

[104] Gardiner, A. G., *The Life of Sir William Harcourt* (London, 1923), vol. ii, pp. 467-469.

[105] Harcourt, Sir William, May 6, 1898, Hansard, series 4, vol. 57, cc. 586-587.

[106] *Politician's Handbook*, 1900, pp. 2-5 and also *Accounts and Papers*, 1899, vol. 63 [c.—9323].

[107] *Infra*, pp. 251-253, 260-266 and 316-320.

[108] "That the Cape-to-Cairo Railway, as the plan first took form in Cecil Rhodes' mind, was to be an 'all British' route was perhaps, its principal reason for being. . . . " Freeman, Lewis R., "Rhodes' 'All Red' Cape-to-Cairo Route. The War's effect upon the Cape-to-Cairo Railway." January, 1916, Pamphlet 4 x 4 in the Royal Empire Society. And also Michell, Hon. Sir Lewis, "The Cape to Cairo Railway," *Journal of the Society of Arts*, January, 1916, vol. 55, pp. 97-107.

[109] *Infra*, p. 277.

[110] *Infra*, pp. 261-263.

[111] *Infra*, pp. 310-311.

[112] Michell, Hon. Sir Lewis, "Cape to Cairo Railway," *op. cit.*, p. 101.

[113] Weinthal, *op. cit.*, "My Story of the Scheme" by Sir Charles Metcalfe, vol. i, p. 103.

[114] *Supra*, p. 200.

[115] Weinthal, *op. cit.*, vol. i, pp. 109-113.

[116] *Infra*, pp. 218-220 and 222-223.

[117] Weinthal, *op. cit.*, vol. i, p. 114.

[118] Michell, Sir Lewis, "The Cape to Cairo Railway," *op. cit.*, p. 101.

[119] Williams in his various accounts of the Cape-to-Cairo scheme maintains that this change of route showed that Rhodes was not obsessed by the idea of an 'all red line.' In his own words:

> It has often been said that Rhodes's original plan was an "all-red" route namely, British throughout via Lake Tanganyika. I beg leave to doubt that statement. . . . Rhodes was far too practical a man to build a railway where there was no assured traffic to make it pay. The railway had followed mineral discoveries all the length of its route from Cape Town. Why, then, should it be taken to Lake Tanganyika? Simply because his attempts to get it through any other way had failed. . . . Rhodes never felt himself tied to an "all-red" route. To get the railway through some friendly state was

equally satisfactory to him, so long as the line was built. And when the Katanga mineral discoveries showed how the line could be made to pay for itself, he never hesitated, but up to his last moment was anxious for the line to be constructed up to the frontier and onwards through the Congo State.

—Weinthal, *op. cit.*, vol. i, p. 115.

I agree with Williams that Rhodes was preeminently practical. Nevertheless, I feel that Williams gives a false impression here, by implication, that the Tanganyika line would have been an "all-red-line," i. e., all-British throughout. I have just been at some pains to show that neither the Tanganyika nor the Katanga line could have been "all-red" under the conditions existing, 1899-1902. Rhodes was, therefore, *not* faced with the choice between an "all-red" or an international line. He had previously fought long and hard for an "all-red" line and had failed in the fight. I firmly believe that Rhodes was in favor of an "all-red" route but that he could not possibly have his wish. He, therefore, chose the next best, in fact, the only course open; an international railway. I do not, therefore, agree with Williams. Williams, of course, was a close friend of Rhodes. It, therefore, requires some temerity to dispute his conclusions. On the other hand, Sir Lewis Michell, Executor and Trustee of Rhodes' last will and his well-known biographer (Preface to Michell, *The Life of the Rt. Hon. Cecil J. Rhodes*, vol. i, p. viii) takes the point of view that Rhodes was ardently in favor of an "all-red" route. See also Michell, Hon. Sir Lewis, "Cape to Cairo Railway," *Journal of the Society of Arts*, Nov. 23, 1906, pp. 97-107.

[120] Weinthal, *op. cit.*, "My Story of the Scheme by Robert Williams, vol. i, p. 115.

[121] Weinthal, *op. cit.*, "The Great Zambezi Bridge. The Story of a Famous Engineering Feat" by the late G. A. Hobson, M. Inst. C. E., vol. ii, pp. 45 and 47.

[122] Michell, Sir Lewis, "The Cape to Cairo Railway," *op. cit.*, p. 101.

[123] See especially Harcourt's speech May 6, 1898, Hansard, series 4, vol. 57, c. 590 and Labouchere's attacks during 1897 and 1898.

[124] Hansard, series 4, vol. 57, c. 590.

[125] Speech of the Secretary of State for the Colonies, Hansard, series 4, vol. 57, c. 603.

[126] Hansard, series 4, vol. 57, c. 590.

[127] *Ibid.*, vol. 43, c. 828.

[128] Chamberlain, Hansard, series 4, vol. 43, c. 1450.

[129] Williams, *Cecil Rhodes, op. cit.*, p. 272.

[130] *Ibid.*, pp. 294-295.

[131] *Ibid.*, p. 276.

CHAPTER X

THE FINAL STRUGGLE FOR SOUTH AFRICA

[1] *British Documents*, vol. i, Memorandum by Mr. J. A. C. Tilley, p. 327 and also no. 65, p. 46.

[2] *Ibid.*, no. 108, p. 83.

[3] *Infra*, pp. 378-379.

[4] *Infra*, pp. 378-379 and 381-382.

[5] Sir F. Lascelles to Mr. Balfour, August 23, 1898, *British Documents*, vol. i, p. 101.

[6] *British Documents*, vol. i, no. 124, p. 104.

[7] *German Documents, 1871-1914*, translated and selected by E. T. S. Dugdale (London, 1930), vol. iii, no. 266, p. 31.

[8] *Ibid.*, no. 272, pp. 32-33.

[9] *British Documents*, vol. i, no. 62, pp. 42-43.

[10] *Ibid.*, no. 85, p. 67.

[11] *Ibid.*, vol. i, Memorandum by Mr. J. A. C. Tilley, p. 329.

[12] *Ibid.*, Memorandum by Mr. Bertie, no. 65, p. 45.

[13] *Ibid.*, vol. i, no. 108, Sir H. MacDonell to Mr. Bertie, April 20, 1898, pp. 83-84.

[14] *Supra*, p. 180.

[15] *British Documents*, vol. i, Memorandum by Mr. Bertie, June 30, 1935, no. 65, pp. 44-48 and no. 81, p. 61.

[16] *Ibid.*, no. 65, pp. 44-48 and no. 81, p. 61.

[17] *German Documents*, Dugdale trans., *op. cit.*, vol. iii, no. 261, p. 29.

[18] Bourgeois et Pagès, *op. cit.*, p. 246.

[19] *German Documents*, Dugdale trans., vol. iii, no. 266, p. 30.

[20] *Ibid.*, vol. iii, note, pp. 31-32.

[21] *British Documents*, vol. i, no. 67, p. 49.

[22] *Ibid.*, vol. i, no. 70, p. 52.

[23] *Ibid.*, vol. i, nos. 70-85, pp. 52-71.

[24] *Ibid.*, vol. i, no. 88, pp. 69-70.

[25] *Ibid.*, vol. i, enclosure in no. 90, pp. 71-72.

[26] *Ibid.*, vol. i, enclosure in no. 91, p. 73.

[27] *Ibid.*, vol. i, nos. 94 and 95, pp. 75-76 and no. 99, p. 79.

[28] *Ibid.*, vol. i, no. 109, p. 84.

[29] *Ibid.*, vol. i, no. 112, pp. 86-87 and also *German Documents*, Dugdale trans., vol. iii, p. 27.

[30] *Die Grosse Politik*, vol. xiv, part ii, no. 4074, p. 616. *Cf.* Von Bülow's comments in the same vein, *British Documents*, vol. i, no. 127, p. 108.

[31] *Die Grosse Politik*, vol. xiv, part ii, no. 4049, p. 586; no. 4056, p. 595.

[32] *Ibid.*, no. 4028, p. 567.

[33] *British Documents*, vol. i, footnote, pp. 108-109 and no. 147, p. 123. *The Politician's Handbook, 1900* (London, 1900), p. 184.

[34] *British Documents*, vol. i, no. 130, p. 110 and also *Die Grosse Politik*, vol. xiv, part ii, no. 4040, p. 576.

[35] See Baron von Richthofen's statement that ". . . the whole of Samoa was not worth the money spent upon telegrams to and from Apia." *British Documents*, vol. i, no. 128, p. 109.

Baron von Bülow, on the other hand, claimed that: "It was towards Samoa that Germany had first looked when she began colonizing, and since then the loss of German ships and lives had excited interest in the minds of the German public. These might be sentimental grievances but they had none the less to be taken into account." *British Documents*, vol. i, no. 133, p. 111.

[36] Baron von Eckardstein, *Ten Years at the Court of St. James* (London, 1921), p. 112.

[37] *Die Grosse Politik*, vol. xiv, part ii, no. 4039, p. 575; no. 4040, p. 576; no. 4048, p. 584; no. 4049, pp. 585-587 and *British Documents*, vol. i, no. 132, pp. 110-111.

[38] *Die Grosse Politik*, vol. xiv, part ii, no. 4044, p. 579; no. 4056, p. 595, and no. 4060, pp. 600-601. Gooch, *History of Modern Europe* (New York, 1923), p. 305. Baron von Eckardstein, *Ten Years at the Court of St. James, op. cit.*, pp. 105-107.

[39] *Ibid.*, no. 4064, pp. 603-604 and no. 4067, p. 606.

[40] Eckardstein, *op. cit.*, p. 106.

[41] *Die Grosse Politik*, vol. xiv, part ii, no. 4046, p. 582.

[42] *Ibid.*, no. 4064, p. 603. Hatzfeldt to Baron von Holstein, April 12, 1899.

[43] Eckardstein, *op. cit.*, p. 102.

[44] *Supra*, pp. 152-154 and 198-205.

[45] *Die Grosse Politik*, vol. xiv, part ii, no. 4045, p. 581 and no. 4046, pp. 582-583.

[46] *Ibid.*, vol. xiv, part ii, footnote, p. 581.

[47] *Ibid.*, vol. xiv, part ii, no. 4045, p. 581.

[48] *Ibid.*, vol. xiv, part ii, no. 4046, pp. 582-583.

[49] The dates here are somewhat confusing. The footnote on p. 581 in *Die Grosse Politik*, vol. xiv, part ii, indicates that Rhodes' interview with Leopold took place sometime before February 5, 1899. Sir Lewis Michell in his life of Rhodes mentions the interview but gives no date. Michell, *op. cit.*, vol. ii, p. 252. Basil Williams, however, says that Rhodes visited both Leopold and the Kaiser in March, 1899, on his way back to England from Egypt. Williams, *Cecil Rhodes, op. cit.*, p. 310. Whether, therefore, Rhodes went to Brussels in the winter or in the spring is a debatable question. It is sure, however, that the interview with Leopold preceded those with the Kaiser. See especially, in this

connection, Rhodes' own letter to the Prince of Wales in Buckle, *Letters of Queen Victoria*, series 3, vol. iii, p. 350.

[50] Buckle, *Letters of Queen Victoria*, series 3, vol. iii, pp. 349-350.

[51] Williams, *Cecil Rhodes, op. cit.*, p. 310.

[52] Weinthal, *op. cit.*, vol. i, p. 114.

[53] Buckle, *op. cit.*, series 3, vol. iii, p. 350.

[54] *Die Grosse Politik*, vol. xiv, part ii, footnote, p. 581. According to Eckardstein's version of the story, the visit was arranged in March through the instrumentality of Herr von Buchka, Director of the Colonial Section and Davis, a business associate of Cecil Rhodes. Von Buchka met Davis in the early part of March and discussed with him the prospects of Rhodes' Cape-to-Cairo schemes. Davis, in turn, invited Rhodes to Berlin and Herr von Buchka saw to it that Rhodes was personally received by the Kaiser and other leading personages. Rhodes "accordingly came to Berlin at the end of March, 1899," Eckardstein asserts. Freiherr von Eckwardstein, *Lebenserinnerungen u. Politisch Denkwürdigkeiten* (Leipzig, 1919), vol. i, pp. 314-315.

In *Die Grosse Politik*, however, the date of Rhodes' interview with the Kaiser is given as March 11. This does not tally with Eckardstein's account because March 11 is hardly, as he said, "the end of March." Too much importance, however, should not be attached to this discrepancy. The significant point is that Rhodes did have a personal interview with the Kaiser sometime in March, 1899.

[55] Hansard, series 4, vol. 69, c. 784.

[56] Williams, *Cecil Rhodes, op. cit.*, p. 310.

[57] Wilhelm II, *The Kaiser's Memoirs* (New York, 1922), p. 88.

[58] Plomer, *op. cit.*, p. 99.

[59] *The Kaiser's Memoirs, op. cit.*, p. 88.

[60] *Ibid.*, p. 88.

[61] *Ibid.*, p. 88. Sir Edward Grey in a later account of the interview remarks that Rhodes made his suggestion about the Bagdad railway "spontaneously to the Emperor at the very moment the latter had conceived the idea of the Bagdad Railway, and when there were only four persons—himself, the Sultan, the German Chancellor, and the German Ambassador at Constantinople—who knew of the project." Memorandum by Sir Edward Grey, November 13, 1907. *British Documents*, vol. vi, no. 60, p. 93.

[62] *Die Grosse Politik*, vol. xiv, part ii, no. 4047, p. 583.

[63] *Ibid.*, no. 4050, p. 588 and also Cecil Rhodes' letter to the Prince of Wales, March, 1899. Buckle, *op. cit.*, series 3, vol. iii, p. 350.

[64] *The Kaiser's Memoirs, op. cit.*, p. 88.

[65] Vindex, *op. cit.*, p. 640.

[66] *Supra*, pp. 107-108.

[67] *British Documents*, vol. vi, no. 60, p. 93.

[68] Stead, W. T., *The Last Will and Testament of Cecil John Rhodes* (London, 1902).

[69] Eckardstein, *Ten Years at the Court of St. James, op. cit.,* p. 103.

[70] Krause, Gustav, "Gespräche mit Cecil Rhodes," *Deutsche Revue,* 1899, vol. xxiv, p. 115.

[71] Buckle, *op. cit.,* series 3, vol. iii, pp. 350-351.

[72] *Die Grosse Politik,* vol. xiv, part ii, no. 4050, p. 588 and no. 4068, pp. 609-610.

[73] *British Documents,* vol. i, no. 150, pp. 126-127 and no. 154, pp. 129-130.

[74] *Die Grosse Politik,* vol. xiv, part ii, no. 4068, pp. 609-610.

[75] There were possibly two agreements: one the preliminary and then the final one. Rhodes told a Cape Town audience that he signed the telegraph agreement with the Kaiser's Minister three days after his interview. Williams, on the other hand, maintains that,

> . . . the final agreement was not signed till the end of the year, after the despatch of a cable signed "C. J. Rhodes": "What about my telegraph? I am close to the German border and should not like to enter German territory without authority. The only alternative dismissing the whole staff"; the cable happily arrived when the Kaiser was about to visit England and wanted to improve English feeling by publishing the fact of the agreement.

—Williams, *Cecil Rhodes, op. cit.,* pp. 310-311.

[76] Michell, *op. cit.,* vol. ii, pp. 253-254.

[77] Williams, *Cecil Rhodes, op. cit.,* p. 311.

[78] *Die Grosse Politik,* vol. xiv, part ii, no. 4050, p. 588.

[79] Michell, *op. cit.,* vol. ii, p. 253.

[80] Williams, *Cecil Rhodes, op. cit.,* p. 311.

[81] Weinthal, *op. cit.,* vol. i, p. 114.

[82] *The Kaiser's Memoirs, op. cit.,* p. 88.

[83] *Ibid.,* p. 88 and *British Documents,* vol. vi, no. 60, p. 93.

[84] Cammaerts, "Le Cap au Caire. La Situation Actuelle." *Bulletin de Colonisation Comparée,* August 20, 1912, p. 347.

[85] *Die Grosse Politik,* vol. xiv, part ii, footnote, p. 581.

[86] Metcalfe, Sir Charles, *The Cape to Cairo Line, How the War May Solve a Problem,* pamphlet, South Africa, December 19, 1914, 4 x 4, Royal Empire Society.

[87] Cammaerts, "Le Cap au Caire," *op. cit.,* pp. 347-348.

[88] Renty, E. de, "Deux Transafricains Anglais," *Quest. Dipl.,* vol. xiv, 1910, p. 477.

[89] Metcalfe, Sir Charles, *The Cape-to-Cairo Line. How the War May Solve a Problem, op. cit.*

[90] Krause, *op. cit.,* p. 114.

[91] Bourgeois et Pagès, *op. cit.,* p. 282.

[92] *German Documents,* Dugdale Trans., *op. cit.,* vol. iii, no. 412, p. 107.

[93] *Ibid.,* vol. iii, no. 412, pp. 107-108 and no. 413, p. 109.

94 *Ibid.*, vol. iii, no. 413, p. 108 and also Bourgeois et Pagès, *op. cit.*, p. 284.

95 *German Documents*, Dugdale trans., vol. iii, note p. 113.

96 Williams, *Cecil Rhodes*, *op. cit.*, p. 316.

97 Vindex, *op. cit.*, p. 513.

98 Lovell, *The Struggle for South Africa*, *op. cit.*, pp. 297-300.

99 See especially Kruger's reply to Germany's offer of help at the time of the Raid: "With the help of God, he and his people hoped to do everything further that is possible for the holding of our dearly-bought independence and the stability of our beloved Republic." Whates, *The Third Administration of Lord Salisbury, 1895-1900* (London, 1900), pp. 279-280. See also *German Documents*, Dugdale translation, vol. iii, no. 385, Count Hatzfeldt to Emperor William, August 27, 1899, pp. 95-96.

100 *German Documents, Dugdale translation*, vol. iii, no. 385, pp. 95-96.

101 Bourgeois et Pagès, *op. cit.*, p. 285.

102 *Cambridge History of British Foreign Policy*, *op. cit.*, vol. iii, p. 276.

103 *Ibid.*, p. 284.

104 *German Documents*, Dugdale trans., vol. iii, no. 370, Bernard von Bülow to Count Hatzfeldt, July 4, 1899.

105 *Ibid.*, no. 372, pp. 85-86.

106 *Ibid.*, nos. 375 and 377, pp. 87-88.

107 *Ibid.*, no. 381, p. 92.

108 *Ibid.*, no. 382, p. 93.

109 *Ibid.*, no. 395, p. 102.

110 *Ibid.*, no. 655, p. 105.

111 *Ibid.*, no. 405, p. 106.

112 *Ibid.*, no. 504, p. 120.

113 *Supra*, p. 224.

114 *German Documents*, Dugdale trans. vol. iii, no. 426, pp. 115-116.

115 *Ibid.*, no. 518, pp. 122-123 and notes p. 123.

116 *Ibid.*, note, p. 124.

117 *Ibid.*, no. 549, p. 126.

118 *The Daily Telegraph* attributed the article to the work of a retired diplomatist. The *Norddeutsche Allegemeine* maintained that it was collated from a series of conversations with various personages at various times and presented to the Emperor by an Englishman. The Kaiser, says Gooch, read the account and made some corrections. It was sent by the Kaiser to von Bülow and by the latter to the German Foreign Office. It received the approval of that Office and was then published. *Cambridge History of British Foreign Policy, op. cit.*, vol. iii, p. 391 and footnote on p. 392.

119 *Ibid.*, p. 392.

120 *British Documents*, vol. vi, no. 35, pp. 56-57.

121 *Ibid.*, no. 137, p. 219.

[122] *Ibid.*, no. 129, Memorandum as to the attitude of Germany in regard to intervention during the Boer War, pp. 204-206.

[123] *Cambridge History of British Foreign Policy, op. cit.*, vol. iii, pp. 280-282.

[124] *German Documents*, Dugdale trans., *op. cit.*, vol. iii, note pp. 117 and 118.

[125] *Cambridge History of British Foreign Policy, op. cit.*, vol. iii, pp. 280-282.

[126] *British Documents*, vol. vi, no. 137, p. 219.

[127] *German Documents*, Dugdale trans., *op. cit.*, vol. iii, no. 544 and note p. 125.

[128] *British Documents*, vol. i, no. 118, pp. 93-94.

[129] *Ibid.*, vol. vi, no. 133, p. 212.

[130] Whates, *op. cit.*, p. 259.

CHAPTER XI

INTO THE HEART OF THE DARK CONTINENT

[1] As stated in the preface, this book has been arranged geographically and topically rather than chronologically. The writer, in this chapter, has skipped back from the Boer War, 1899-1902, to the period of exploration in the sixties. This jump backwards is justified by the fact that chapter xi begins an entirely new section. Chapters ii through x dealt with the development of Cape-to-Cairo projects and the spread of British influence throughout South Africa up to the Lake regions. The following chapters sketch the story of the growth of British influence between Egypt and the Lake region in East Africa and the Sudan. In order to fill in the background for this history, it was necessary to go back to the earlier period.

[2] Weinthal, *op. cit.*, vol. i, " Burton, Speke and Grant," pp. 134-136.

[3] *Supra*, pp. 51 and 53.

[4] Weinthal, *op. cit.*, vol. i, p. 136.

[5] *Ibid.*, vol. i, " Sir Samuel White Baker," pp. 137-138 and Baker's own account in *The Albert N'yanza, Great Basin of the Nile and the Explorations of the Nile Sources* (London and N. Y., Macmillan & Co., 1898).

[6] *Encyclopedia Britannica*, " Nile River."

[7] Baker, Sir Samuel White, *In the Heart of Africa* (New York, 1884), firman granted by Ismail to Baker, p. 6.

[8] Weinthal, *op. cit.*, vol. i, p. 138 and Baker, *In the Heart of Africa, op. cit.*, p. 506.

[9] Baker, *In the Heart of Africa, op. cit.*, p. 506.

[10] *Ibid.*, p. 509.

[11] *Supra*, chap. ii, pp. 47-48.

[12] Hill, G. B., *Colonel Gordon in Central Africa* (London, 1881), p. xxx and Weinthal, *op. cit.*, vol. i, " Gordon, Cromer and Kitchener," p. 159.

[13] Hill, G. B., *op. cit.*, pp. xl-xli, 65-68 and 203, 322 and 349. Weinthal, *op. cit.*, vol. i, p. 159.

[14] *Ibid.*, p. 322.

[15] *Ibid.*, p. 68.

[16] *Ibid.*, pp. 65-67.

[17] *Ibid.*, p. 349.

[18] Achmed Abdullah, *Dreamers of Empire* (New York, 1929), p. 333. Hill, *op. cit.*, pp. 65, 68, 146 and 150. Biovès, Achille, *Un Grand Aventurier du XIX⁰ siècle, Gordon Pacha* (Paris, 1907), p. 151. Lugard, F. J. D., *The Rise of Our East African Empire* (Edinburgh and London, 1893), vol. i, p. 3.

[19] *Supra*, pp. 37-38.

[20] *The Autobiography of Henry M. Stanley* (New York, 1909), pp. 333-334.

[21] Lugard, *op. cit.*, vol. i, p. 3.

[22] McDermott, *British East Africa or IBEA* (London, 1893), p. 121.

[23] Lugard, *op. cit.*, vol. i, pp. 3-4. Weinthal, *op. cit.*, vol. i, " Sir Henry Morton Stanley," p. 143.

[24] Lugard, *op. cit.*, vol. i, pp. 3-4.

[25] Keith, A. B., *The Belgian Congo and the Berlin Act* (Oxford, 1919), pp. 31-33 and *The Proceedings of the Royal Geographical Society*, July, 1877, vol. xxii (o. s.), p. 11.

[26] Keith, *op cit.*, pp. 34-36.

[27] *Ibid.*, p. 37, quotation from the *Daily Telegraph* of November 12, 1877.

[28] Keith, *op. cit.*, pp. 37-38.

[29] *Ibid.*, pp. 38-41.

[30] De Brazza was a naturalized Frenchman of Italian ancestry. Ironically enough, his expedition was financed by the French committee of the International Association founded by Leopold. Keith, *op. cit.*, pp. 42-43.

[31] *Ibid.*, pp. 42-43.

[32] *Ibid.*, pp. 49-50. Keith remarks, " It is a minor point that the treaties published show a distressing confusion between the International African Association and the International Congo Association."

[33] Keith, *op. cit.*, p. 53.

[34] *Ibid.*, p. 52.

[35] *Ibid.*, pp. 53-54 and Hertslet, *op. cit.*, vol. ii, no. 176, pp. 602-603.

[36] Keith, *op. cit.*, p. 54 and Hertslet, *op. cit.*, vol. ii, no. 151, p. 562.

[37] Keith, *op. cit.*, p. 55.

[38] The Berlin Act, Hertslet, *op. cit.*, vol. ii, no. 128.

[39] *Ibid.*, article i, pp. 471-472.

[40] *Ibid.*, article x, pp. 474-475.

[41] *Ibid.*, article viii, p. 474.

[42] *Ibid.*, preamble, pp. 468-470.

[43] *Ibid.*, article xxxiv, pp. 484-485.

[44] *Ibid.*, article xxxv, p. 485.

[45] *Infra*, pp. 258-259, 261, 313, 315-316, 337-341, 368, 370-371.

CHAPTER XII

The German Barrier Across the Cape-to-Cairo Route

[1] Johnston, Sir Harry H., *The Story of My Life* (New York, 1923), p. 134.

[2] *Ibid.*, pp. 134-135.

[3] *Supra*, pp. 29, 133-135 and 170-171.

[4] Weinthal, *op. cit.*, vol. i, "My Story of the Cape to Cairo Scheme" by Sir Harry Johnston, pp. 70-71.

[5] Johnston, *The Story of My Life, op. cit.*, pp. 133-134.

[6] *Accounts and Papers*, 1887, vol. 59 [c.—4609], no. 35.

[7] *Ibid.*, no. 35 and Weinthal, *op. cit.*, vol. i, "Dr. Carl Peters," p. 154.

[8] McDermott, *British East Africa or IBEA* (London, 1893), p. 5.

[9] Hertslet, *op. cit.*, vol. iii, no. 264, pp. 882-888.

[10] Schweitzer, George, *Emin Pasha* (London, 1898), vol. i, pp. xxix, 27-29 and 210.

[11] *Ibid.*, vol. i, p. 27.

[12] *Ibid.*, vol. i, p. 210.

[13] *Ibid.*, vol. i, p. 32.

[14] *Ibid.*, vol. i, p. 210.

[15] *Ibid.*, vol. i, pp. xxix-xxx.

[16] *Ibid.*, vol. i, pp. 216-217.

[17] *Ibid.*, vol. i, p. 34.

[18] *Ibid.*, vol. i, pp. xxiv-xxv.

[19] *Ibid.*, vol. i, pp. 261 and 274.

[20] *Ibid.*, vol. i, pp. 261, 274 and 276.

[21] *Ibid.*, vol. i, p. 29.

[22] Hertslet, *op. cit.*, vol. iii, p. 889. Stanley, *In Darkest Africa* (New York, 1890), vol. i, p. 58.

[23] The Marquis of Salisbury to Sir E. Malet, F.O., July 2, 1887, Hertslet, *op. cit.*, vol. iii, no. 267 (i), pp. 888-889.

[24] *Ibid.*

[25] *Ibid.*, and also Mr. Scott to the Marquis of Salisbury, Berlin, July 8, 1887, Hertslet, *op. cit.*, vol. iii, no. 267, (2), pp. 889-890.

[26] *Supra*, pp. 138, 140-142.

[27] Hansard, series 3, vol. 346, c. 1268.

[28] See in this connection, Weinthal, *op. cit.*, vol. i, "My Story of the Cape to Cairo Scheme" by Sir Harry Johnston, pp. 76-77, 81 and 83 and also Whates, *The Third Salisbury Administration* (Westminster, 1900), pp. 238-239.

[29] *Accounts and Papers*, 1890, vol. 51 [c.—6043], Africa No. 5 (1890).

[30] *Infra*, pp. 261-263.

[31] Schweitzer, *op. cit.*, vol. i, pp. 263 and 317.

[32] *Ibid.*, vol. i, pp. 322-323.

[33] Stanley, *In Darkest Africa, op. cit.*, vol. ii, pp. 416-417.

[34] *Ibid.*, vol. ii, pp. 199-227.

[35] Schweitzer, *op. cit.*, vol. i, pp. 316-319 and vol. ii, pp. 1-9, 12, 27 and 37.

[36] *Ibid.*, vol. ii, p. 41.

[37] *Ibid.*, vol. i, p. 324.

[38] Lugard, *The Rise of Our East African Empire* (Edinburgh and London, 1893), vol. ii, pp. 11-13 and Fraisse, *Situation Internationale des Pays Tributaires du Bassin du Congo* (Carcassone, 1904), p. 289.

[39] McDermitt, *op. cit.*, pp. 8-11 and 16.

[40] *Ibid.*, pp. 10-11.

[41] *Ibid.*, p. 119.

[42] *Supra*, pp. 237-238.

[43] See in this connection, Lady Cecil, *Life of Robert Marquis of Salisbury* (London, 1921-1932), vol. iv, pp. 277-278 and McDermott, *op. cit.*, pp. 143-144.

[44] Hansard, series 3, vol. 346, cc. 1263-1264.

[45] McDermott, *op. cit.*, pp. 33-34, 36-38, 41-44 and 61-63.

[46] *Supra*, pp. 170-171.

[47] *Accounts and Papers*, 1890, vol. 51 [c.—6043], Africa No. 5 (1890).

[48] Hansard, series 3, vol. 346, c. 1267.

[49] *Die Grosse Politik*, vol. iv, no. 738, p. 51.

[50] The Kiel Canal between the North Sea and the Baltic was begun in 1887 and finished in 1895. Gooch, *History of Modern Europe* (New York, 1923), pp. 104, 201 and 208.

[51] *Die Grosse Politik*, vol. iv, no. 738, pp. 51 and 56.

[52] Gooch, *op. cit.*, p. 105. *Cf.* the storm of protest against the cession in the Parliamentary Debates in 1890.

[53] *Die Grosse Politik*, vol. viii, no. 1672, pp. 3-4 and no. 1674, pp. 6-8.

[54] *Die Auswärtige Politik des Deutschen Reiches, 1871-1914* (Hamburg, 1928), vol. i, p. 490 and also Lady Cecil, *op. cit.*, vol. iv, p. 280.

[55] *Accounts and Papers*, 1890, vol. 51 [c.—6046], Africa No. 6, enclosure in No. 1, Sir P. Anderson to Sir E. Malet, June 28, 1890 and also *Die Grosse Politik*, vol. viii, no. 1675, pp. 8-11.

[56] *Supra*, p. 253.

[57] "Germany and England in East Africa," *Times*, May 30, 1890, p. 7, c. a.

[58] *Die Grosse Politik*, vol. viii, no. 1677, p. 14.

[59] *Supra*, pp. 246-247.

[60] Cabinet memorandum, June 2, 1890. Lady Cecil, *op. cit.*, vol. iv, pp. 283-284.

[61] Lady Cecil, *op. cit.*, vol. iv, p. 294 and *Die Grosse Politik*, vol. viii, no. 1676, p. 13.

[62] Lady Cecil, *op. cit.*, vol. iv, pp. 284-285 and Williams, *Cecil Rhodes, op. cit.*, pp. 166-167.

[63] Lady Cecil, *op. cit.*, vol. iv, p. 285.

[64] *Die Grosse Politik*, vol. viii, no. 1678, p. 15.

[65] Lady Cecil, *op. cit.*, vol. iv, pp. 284-285.

[66] *Die Grosse Politik*, vol. viii, no. 1682, p. 19.

[67] *Accounts and Papers*, 1890, vol. 51 [c.—6043], Africa No. 5 (1890), p. 21.

[68] It is a debatable question, to be sure, whether this demand for a passageway between the lakes was definitely presented as part of the British program during the negotiations. According to the German account, the British would appear to have demanded this corridor in May. *Die Grosse Politik*, vol. viii, no. 2042, pp. 440-441. The Earl of Kimberley, however, denied that an official proposal for this strip had ever been made to Germany. Kimberley wrote to Sir E. Malet, July 2, 1894, "I cannot find any record that a proposal for the acquisition of a narrow strip of this kind was actually made on behalf of Great Britain, or rejected on behalf of Germany, although it may undoubtedly be inferred from the general tenor of the negotiations, and from observations made by Lord Salisbury in the House of Lords after their conclusion and that if made it would not have been accepted." The Earl of Kimberley to Sir E. Malet, F. O., July 2, 1894, *Accounts and Papers*, 1894, vol. 96 [c.—7390], no. 8. On the other hand, the German Secretary of Foreign Affairs, von Marschall, insisted that Sir Percy Anderson, in 1890, in the presence of Sir Edward, made such a demand and that it was flatly refused for the reason that such a strip in British hands would put an English belt around Germany's East African possessions. *Die Grosse Politik*, vol. viii, no. 2042, pp. 440-441. *Cf.* nos. 1676, 1677 and 1678, pp. 11-15.

[69] "Germany and England in East Africa," *Times*, May 30, 1890, p. 7, c. a.

[70] Hansard, series 3, vol. 346, c. 1268. Lady Cecil, on the other hand, hints that the Germans would have yielded on this point also if Lord Salisbury insisted. *Life of Robert Marquis of Salisbury*, vol. iv, pp. 295-296.

[71] Sir E. Malet to the Marquis of Salisbury, June 14, 1890, *Accounts and Papers*, 1890, vol. 51 [c.—6043].

[72] *Supra*, pp. 251-253.

[73] Michell, "The Cape to Cairo Railway," *Journal of the Society of Arts*, 1906, vol. lv, p. 101.

[74] *Die Grosse Politik*, vol. viii, no. 1680, pp. 16-17.

[75] *Ibid.*, no. 1681, pp. 17-18.

[76] *Ibid.*, vol. viii, no. 1683, p. 20.

[77] Lady Cecil, *op. cit.*, vol. iv, pp. 295-296.

[78] *Supra*, pp. 252-253.

[79] Agreement between the British and German Governments, respecting Africa and Heligoland, Berlin, July 1, 1890, Hertslet, *op. cit.*, vol. iii, no. 270, pp. 899-906.

[80] *Ibid.*, article iii.

[81] *Ibid.*, article viii.

[82] Gooch, *op. cit.*, pp. 202-203.

[83] Hansard, series 3, vol. 346, *passim*.

[84] Hansard, series 3, vol. 346, c. 1269.

[85] *Accounts and Papers*, 1890, vol. 51, Africa No. 6 (1890) [c.—6046], enclosure in No. 1.

[86] Stevenson, F. S., Hansard, series 3, vol. 347, c. 920.

[87] Hansard, series 3, no. 347, c. 978.

[88] Sir R. Temple, Hansard, series 3, vol. 347, cc. 930-931.

[89] Buckle, *Letters of Queen Victoria, op. cit.*, series 3, vol. i, pp. 613-614.

[90] Hansard, series 4, vol. xxv, c. 150.

[91] Hertslet, *op. cit.*, vol. iii, no. 270, article xi, p. 906.

[92] Fraisse, *op. cit.*, p. 291.

[93] *Infra*, p. 348.

[94] Lugard, *op. cit.*, vol. ii, p. 566. *Cf.* Fraisse, *op. cit.*, p. 246.

CHAPTER XIII

UGANDA, THE KEY TO AFRICA

[1] Hansard, series 4, vol. 1, cc. 1842-1845.

[2] Hertslet, *op. cit.*, vol. ii, no. 130; art. i, p. 490; art. iii, p. 492 and art. iv, p. 492.

[3] *Supra*, p. 270.

[4] *Cf.* Lugard, op. cit., vol. ii, pp. 566-567 and the discussion over this point in Parliament. Hansard, series 4, vol. 1, Speech of Bryce, cc. 1861-1862; *ibid.*, Speech of Sir William Hartcourt, cc. 70-71 and *ibid.*, vol. x, Speech of J. W. Lowther, c. 778.

[5] Speech of Sir Edward Grey, Hansard, series 4, vol. 10, c. 727.

[6] Speech of Joseph Chamberlain, Hansard, series 4, vol. 10, c. 597.

[7] Lugard, *op. cit.*, vol. ii, p. 11.

[8] Fraisse, *op. cit.*, p. 126 and Lugard, *op. cit.*, vol. ii, p. 14.

[9] McDermott, *op. cit.*, pp. 126-127; Lugard, *op. cit.*, vol. ii, p. 67.

[10] Lugard, *op. cit.*, vol. ii, p. 126.

[11] *Supra*, p. 256.

[12] McDermott, *op. cit.*, pp. 124-125 and 134.

[13] *Supra*, pp. 255-256.

[14] McDermott, *op. cit.*, p. 113.

[15] *Ibid.*, p. 115.

[16] Hansard, series 4, vol. 8, c. 579.

[17] Lugard, *op. cit.*, vol. i, p. viii and vol. ii, pp. 16 and 19-20.

[18] *Ibid.*, vol. ii, pp. 29-31.

[19] *Ibid.*, vol. ii, p. 435.

[20] *Ibid.*, vol. ii, pp. 289-290; McDermott, *op. cit.*, pp. 179-202.

[21] Hansard, series 4, vol. 4, c. 829.

[22] McDermott, *op. cit.*, pp. 192-193 and 202-203.

[23] *The Outlook*, London, January 21, 1899, vol. ii, p. 780. *Cf.* also Speech of Rhodes at Good Hope Hall, Cape Town, October 25, 1898. Quoting Gladstone: " Our burden is too great, as it is, I cannot find the people to govern all our dependencies. We have too much, Mr. Rhodes to do. . . . We have too much of the world and now these wretched missionaries are dragging me into Uganda." Vindex, *op. cit.*, pp. 622-623.

[24] The votes on African questions recorded in Hansard for the years 1892-1900 corroborate this statement.

For the radical Anti-Jingo point of view, read Labouchere's long but spicy dissertations in the House during this period.

[25] Speech of Lord Rosebery, June 23, 1892, in support of the Liberal candidate for St. George's-in-the-East, *The Foreign Policy of Lord Rosebery* (London, 1901), p. 74.

[26] Hansard, series 4, vol. 8, c. 572.

[27] *Ibid.*, cc. 588 and 469.

[28] *Ibid.*, cc. 562, 564-565 and 574.

[29] *Ibid.*, c. 574 and vol. 10, speech by Joseph Chamberlain, cc. 594-596.

[30] Speech of Sir E. Grey, Under Secretary of State for Foreign Affairs. Hansard, series 4, vol. 8, c. 588 and speech of Sir E. Ashmead-Bartlett, Hansard, series 4, vol. 22, c. 399.

[31] Speech of R. C. Jebb of Cambridge University, Hansard, series 4, vol. 8, c. 587.

[32] Lugard, *op. cit.*, vol. ii, p. 591.

[33] Speech of Labouchere, Hansard, series 4, vol. 3, c. 468.

[34] Speech of Lord Rosebery, Hansard, series 4, vol. 10, c. 577.

[35] *Supra*, p. 153.

[36] Speech to the shareholders of the B. S. A. Co., November 29, 1892, Vindex, *op. cit.*, p. 313.

[37] Williams, *Cecil Rhodes, op. cit.*, pp. 236-237.

[38] *Ibid.*, p. 237 and Lugard, *op. cit.*, vol. ii, p. 608.

[39] Williams, *Cecil Rhodes, op. cit.*, p. 237. "Mr. Rhodes, Lord Rosebery and Mr. Gladstone. A Page of Unwritten History," *The Outlook*, London, vol. ii, p. 780.

Dispatch from the F. O. to the Ibea, September 30, 1892 in McDermott, *op. cit.*, p. 342.

[40] Hansard, series 4, vol. 5, cc. 115 and 479-488.

[41] Hansard, series 4, vol. 8, c. 469.

[42] McDermott, *op. cit.*, p. 346 and Williams, Cecil Rhodes, *op. cit.*, p .237.

[43] The Earl of Rosebery to Sir G. Portal, December 10, 1892. McDermott, *op. cit.*, p. 345.

[44] Lugard, *op. cit.*, vol. ii, pp. 549 and 564.

[45] Instructions of the Earl of Rosebery, McDermott, *op. cit.*, p. 345. The Letter from King Mwanga, June 17, 1892, reads as follows: " Now, I earnestly beseech you to help me; do not recall the Company from my country. I and my chiefs are under the English flag, as the people of India are under your flag; we desire very very much that the English should arrange this country; should you recall these agents of the company, my friend, my country is sure to be ruined, war is sure to come." Hansard, series 4, 1893, vol. 10, c. 564.

[46] Speech of the Earl of Rosebery, Hansard, series 4, vol. 23, c. 181.

[47] Speech of Lord Stanmore, Hansard, series 4, vol. 24, c. 134.

CHAPTER XIV

The Southward March from Egypt

[1] Cromer, *Modern Egypt* (New York, 1908), vol. i, pp. 12 and 14-15.

[2] Hallberg, C. W., *The Suez Canal* (New York, 1931), p. 268 and chapter xvi, " The Protection of the Canal."

[3] Dicey, " The Future of Egypt," *The Nineteenth Century*, August, 1877, vol. i, p. 2.

[4] Cromer, *op. cit.*, vol. i, chap. xvi, " The Bombardment of Alexandria."

[5] *Ibid.*, vol. i, p. 301.

[6] Milner, *England in Egypt* (London, 1904), p. 18.

[7] Gladstone, W. E., "Aggression on Egypt and Freedom in the East," *The Nineteenth Century*, August, 1877, vol. i, pp. 158-159.

[8] Cromer, *op. cit.*, vol. i, chapters xxix-xlii.

[9] *Ibid.*, vol. ii, p. 29 and chapter xl, " The British Officials " and chapter xliii, " The Workers." Also Milner, *op. cit.*, chapter iii, " The Veiled Protectorate."

[10] Famous Grey Declaration of March 28, 1895, Hansard, series 4, vol. 32, c. 405.

[11] Hansard, series 4, vol. 41, c. 934.

[12] Arthur, Sir George, *Life of Lord Kitchener* (London, 1920), vol i, p. 191.

[13] Giffen, M. B., *Fashoda* (Chicago, 1930), pp. 25-26.

[14] Cromer, *op. cit.*, vol. i, p. 364.

[15] *Ibid.*, vol. i, p. 365.

[16] *Ibid.*, vol. i, p. 367.

[17] Cromer, *op. cit.*, vol. i, p. 355 and Gladstone, W. E., "Aggression on Egypt and Freedom in the East," *op. cit.*, pp. 149-166.

[18] Cromer, *op. cit.*, vol. i, pp. 379-380.

[19] Cromer, *op. cit.*, vol. i, p. 383 and pp. 380-384.

[20] *Supra*, pp. 235-237.

[21] Cromer, *op. cit.*, vol. i, pp. 443-444.

[22] " ... the strange and striking personality of General Gordon had obtained a well-marked place in the affections of his countrymen, and had struck the popular imagination. His exploits at Sebastopol and in China, his achievements in the Soudan were legendary." Fitzmaurice, *The Life of Lord Granville* (London, 1906), vol. i, pp. 339-400.

[23] *Ibid.*, vol. i, pp. 480-488.

[24] *Ibid.*, vol. i, pp. 496, 507 and 542 and also Fitzmaurice, *The Life of Lord Granville, op. cit.*, vol. i, p. 390.

[25] Cromer, *op. cit.*, vol. i, p. 582.

[26] *Ibid.*, p. 429.

[27] Fitzmaurice, *The Life of Lord Granville, op. cit.*, vol. i, p. 400 and vol. ii, pp. 380-381.

[28] Cromer, *op. cit.*, vol. ii, p. 19 and Giffen, *op. cit.*, p. 27.

[29] Cromer, *op. cit.*, vol. ii, chapter xxix " The Evacuation."

[30] *Ibid.*, vol. ii, pp. 45, 62-63, 66-67, 81, 355 and 404.

[31] *Ibid.*, vol. i, p. 355 and vol. ii, p. 445.

[32] Milner, *op. cit.*, p. 156 and Hansard, series 4, vol. 42, c. 1581.

[33] *Ibid.*, vol. 37, c. 1027.

[34] *Ibid.*, series 3, vol. 350, c. 1442.

[35] *Ibid.*, c. 1439.

[36] *Ibid.*, vol. 450, cc. 1439 and 1453.

[37] *Ibid.*, series 4, vol. 17, c. 1495.

[38] *Ibid.*, c. 511.

[39] *Ibid.*, vol. 38, cc. 1029 and 1042.

[40] *Supra*, pp. 249-250.

[41] Cromer, *op. cit.*, vol. ii, p. 74.

[42] *Ibid.*, vol. ii, pp. 76-77 and Hansard, series 3, vol. 349, cc. 1379-1380 and vol. 351, c. 1137.

[43] *Supra*, p. 286 and also Hansard, series 3, vol. 349, cc. 1937-1939.

[44] Hansard, series 3, vol. 350, cc. 1379, 1439, 1453 and 1695.

[45] *Ibid.*, vol. 351, c. 132 and vol. 350, c. 1937.

[46] *Supra*, p. 286. The italics are supplied.

[47] Cromer, *op. cit.*, vol. i, p. 552. The italics are supplied.

[48] Hansard, series 3, vol. 351, cc. 233-234 and 1137.

[49] *Ibid.*, cc. 1136-1137.

[50] *Ibid.*, cc. 132-133.

[51] *Ibid.*, vol. 350, c. 1453.

CHAPTER XV

GUARDING THE NILE VALLEY

[1] Hansard, series 4, vol. 32, c. 391.

[2] British engineer engaged in reclaiming land and river control in Egypt. Fitzmaurice, *Life of Lord Granville, op. cit.*, vol. ii, p. 310.

[3] Hansard, series 4, vol. 32, c. 391. Giffen in his book entitled the *Fashoda Incident and Its Diplomatic Setting*, does not agree with this point of view. He thinks the British argument that the Power holding Egypt must hold the Nile sources, is overrated as far as the White Nile was concerned. "Sir William Garstin's *Reports* of 1901 and 1904," he says, "show that the flood discharges which are so vitally important to Egypt are drawn principally from the Atbara, the Blue Nile, and the Sobat, and not from the White Nile or Bahr-el-Ghazelle; that even when the White Nile is free from *sudd* ' some fifty per cent of its summer volume is lost in the Marshes between Bor and Lake No '; and that the Bahr-el-Ghazelle, beyond acting as a reservoir and thus assisting the constancy of the supply, plays a very small part in the summer discharge of the White Nile, and even its flood discharge is comparatively insignificant.'" Giffen, Morrison, Beall, *Fashoda. The Incident and Its Diplomatic Setting*, pp. 55-56.

See also a further discussion of this point in Langer, Wm. L., "The Struggle for the Nile," *Foreign Affairs*, January, 1936, vol. no. 2, pp. 260-267.

While, however, it is interesting to note these modern points of view, it is more pertinent in this book to understand the current belief in the nineties.

Whether or not the White Nile is really vital to the life of Egypt, the fact still remains that the British people from 1887 to 1902 believed that it was essential to keep the White Nile sources in British hands. It **was** a potent, even if an erroneous argument.

[4] Sir E. Grey, Hansard, series 4, vol. 67, cc. 493-494.

[5] *Supra*, p. 236 and Lugard, *op. cit.*, vol. ii, pp. 610-611.

[6] McDermott, *op. cit.*, pp. 141-142.

[7] *Supra*, pp. 289-293.

[8] *Supra*, pp. 29, 66-70, 81-82, 133-135, 170-171, 172-175 and 273.

[9] Hansard, series 3, vol. 347, c. 940.

[10] *Ibid.*, series 4, vol. 2, c. 399.

[11] Williams, *Cecil Rhodes, op. cit.*, pp. 132-133.

[12] *Supra*, pp. 78-79, 159 and Weinthal, *op. cit.*, vol. i, " The House of Rothschild and the Cape to Caire Route," pp. 633-637.

[13] *Supra*, pp. 266-267 and *infra*, pp. 337-338, 351-353 and Hansard, series 4, vol. 66, c. 28.

[14] See the votes taken on various colonial questions. See especially the enthusiastic reception in the House of the announcement that the government had decided to dispatch a military expedition to Dongola, Hansard, series 4, vol. 41, cc. 516-538. See again the marks of national approval over the establishment of a Protectorate over Uganda, Hansard, series 4, vol. 25, c. 134.

[15] *Supra*, p. 264.

[16] Keith, *op. cit.*, p. 101. Beyens, in *La Question africaine*, p. 38 "... il a revé d'un empire central qui, s'appuyant à la fois sur le Congo et sur le Nil, serait maître du cours des deux fleuves géants, ... Empereur du Congo et du Nil—comme sa cousine Victoria était impératrice des Indes."

[17] Wauters, A. J., *L'État Indépendant du Congo* (Brussels, 1899), p. 428 and Cromer, *op. cit.*, vol. i, pp. 464-467.

[18] Stanley, *In Darkest Africa, op. cit.*, vol. i, pp. 43-44.

[19] *Supra*, pp. 250 and 254.

[20] Fraisse, *op. cit.*, p. 301.

[21] *Supra*, p. 253. Also, see the provisions assigning the region as a British sphere of influence in the Anglo-German treaty of 1890. Hertslet, *op. cit.*, vol. ii, no. 270, p. 899 and map p. 604: Also Hertslet, *op. cit.*, vol. ii, p. 582 and Keith, *op. cit.*, p. 102.

[22] It is hard to determine dates precisely but apparently the interview was in the winter of 1890.

[23] *The Autobiography of H. M. Stanley, op. cit.*, pp. 413 and 417-418 and Keith, *op. cit.*, p. 102.

[24] *Ibid.*, p. 418.

[25] Explanatory dispatch relating to the Anglo-Congolese Agreement of 1894 from the Earl of Kimberley to Hardinge, F. O., May 23, 1894, Hertslet, *op. cit.*, vol. ii, no. 163, p. 582.

[26] *Supra*, p. 264.

[27] Hertslet, *op. cit.*, vol. ii, no. 270, art. i, p. 899.

[28] *Ibid.*, no. 163, p. 582.

[29] *Supra*, pp. 307-311.

[30] Hansard, series 4, vol. 25, c. 143.

[31] *Ibid.*, c. 149.

[32] Hanotaux, Gabriel, *Fachoda* (Paris, 1909), pp. 60-63.

[33] Milner, *op. cit.*, p. 26.

[34] Darcy, *Cent Années, op. cit.*, p. 349.

[35] Hansard, series 4, vol. 32, c. 394.

[36] Fraisse, *op. cit.*, p. 294 and Bourdarie, Paul, *Fachoda—La Mission Marchande* (Paris, 1899), p. 10.

[37] Darcy, *op. cit.*, pp. 358, 364 and 366 and Work Ernest, *Ethiopia, A Pawn in European Diplomacy* (New York, 1935), pp. 114-115, 243-247 and 298-299.

[38] Hanotaux, *Fachoda, op. cit.*, p. 155.

[39] Fraisse, *op. cit.*, p. 301.

[40] Hanotaux, *Fachoda, op. cit.*, pp. 71-72.

[41] *Supra*, pp. 302-303.

[42] Darcy, *op. cit.*, pp. 283-284 and Bourgeois, *Manuel Historique du Politique Étrangère* (Paris, 1926), p. 350.

[43] *Supra*, pp. 300-301.

[44] Hertslet, *op. cit.*, vol. ii, no. 160, art. vi, p. 573.

[45] *Ibid.*, no. 152, art. v, p. 563.

[46] *Ibid.*, no. 169, art. v, p. 592.

[47] *Ibid.*, no. 139, art. ii, p. 544.

[48] *Ibid.*, map, p. 604.

[49] *Ibid.*, no. 145, articles i and ii, p. 552.

[50] Fraisse, *op. cit.*, p. 302.

[51] *Ibid.*, p. 302.

[52] *Ibid.*, p. 302 and Hertslet, *op. cit.*, vol. ii, no. 152, art. v, p. 565 and vol. ii, paragraph 2, p. 568.

[53] Fraisse, *op. cit.*, pp. 300-303.

[54] *Ibid.*, pp. 303-305.

[55] The Marquis of Salisbury, Hansard, series 4, vol. 25, c. 149.

[56] Sir E. Ashmead-Bartlett, Hansard, series 4, vol. 28, c. 1476.

CHAPTER XVI

THE SURRENDER OF THE CAPE-TO-CAIRO CORRIDOR

[1] *Supra*, p. 306.

[2] The Anglo-Congolese Agreement, May 12, 1894, Hertslet, *op. cit.*, vol. ii, no. 163.

[3] *Ibid.*, Preamble, p. 578.

[4] *Ibid.*, art. ii, p. 579.

[5] *Ibid.*, p. 579.

[6] *Supra*, p. 301.

[7] *Supra*, p. 305.

Circular of the Administrator—General of the Department of Foreign Affairs of the Independent State of the Congo, declaring the neutrality of that State, within its limits as defined by Treaties. Brussels, August 1, 1885. Hertslet, *op. cit.*, vol. ii, no. 145, pp. 552-553.

[8] Hertslet, *op. cit.*, vol. ii, no. 163, art. iii, pp. 579-580.

[9] *Ibid.*, art. v, p. 580.

[10] *Supra*, pp. 275 and 277.

[11] Sir E. Grey, Hansard, series 4, vol. 25, c. 183.

[12] Hansard, series 4, vol. 25, c. 143.

[13] *Ibid.*, c. 149.

[14] Hanotaux, *Fachoda, op. cit.*, p. 74.

[15] *Ibid.*, p. 49 and Bourgeois et Pagès, *op. cit.*, p. 246. See also speech of Sir E. Grey. Hansard, series 4, vol. 25, cc. 178 and 805.

[16] Hanotaux, *Fachoda, op. cit.*, pp. 75-76 and also *Accounts and Papers,* 1899, vol. 112 [c.—9054], appendix i. In regard to the firmans see Freycinet, *La Question d'Égypte* (Paris, 1905), pp. 82-97, 123-133 and 140-142.

[17] [c.—9054], *op. cit.*, appendix no. 1.

[18] *Ibid.*, and also *supra*.

[19] [c.—9054], *op. cit.*, appendix no. 1.

[20] *Ibid.*, appendix no. 1.

[21] [c.—9054], *op. cit.*, appendix no. 1. See also exchanges of notes between the Congo State and France respecting the right of preemption of France over the territory of the Congo State, April and May, 1884 and April 22 and 29, 1887. Hertslet, *op. cit.*, vol. ii, no. 151, pp. 562-563 and no. 155, p. 567.

[22] [c.—9054], appendix 1.

[23] [c.—9054], *op. cit.*, appendix no. 2, memorandum of August 7, the Earl of Kimberley to the Marquis of Dufferin, F. O., August 14, 1894.

[24] Hertslet, *op. cit.*, vol. ii, no. 163, (1) and (2), pp. 580-581.

[25] [c.—9054], *op. cit.*, appendix no. 2.

[26] *Ibid.*

[27] *Ibid.*

[28] *Ibid.*

[29] *Ibid.*

[30] *Supra*, pp. 264-265.

[31] *Infra*, p. 332.

[32] [c.—9054], *op. cit.*, appendix no. 2.

[33] *Ibid.*

[34] *Ibid.*

[35] Die Grosse Politik, vol. viii, no. 2048.
[36] Hertslet, op. cit., vol. ii, no. 160, pp. 572-573.
[37] Die Grosse Politik, vol. viii, no. 2042, p. 441.
[38] See a further discussion of this subject in the notes for chapter xii, note 68.
[39] Die Grosse Politik, vol. viii, no. 2043, p. 443.
[40] Die Grosse Politik, vol. viii, no. 2042, pp. 440-441, and no. 2048, p. 448.
[41] Bourgeois et Pagès, op. cit., pp. 246-247.
[42] Die Grosse Politik, vol. viii, no. 2061, appendix 461.
[43] Ibid., no. 2032, p. 429.
[44] Ibid., no. 2042, n. 442 and no. 2047, p. 447.
[45] Ibid., no. 2042, p. 442. Cf. no. 2053, p. 454.
[46] Ibid., no. 2048, pp. 449-450 and no. 2052, pp. 453-454.
[47] Ibid., no. 2047, pp. 447-448.
[48] Ibid., no. 2050, p. 451. Cf. no. 2057 and footnote, p. 457.
[49] Ibid., no. 2048, p. 449.
[50] Hanotaux, Fachoda, op. cit., p. 77.
[51] Supra, p. 314.
[52] Accounts and Papers, 1894, vol. 96, Africa No. 5 [c.—7390], no. 8.
[53] [c.—7390], no. 2.
[54] Ibid., no. 5.
[55] Ibid., nos. 2 and 5.

The case for Great Britain is strongly supported by William Edward Hall in his *A Treatise on International Law* (Oxford, 1917), footnote, p. 91. Hall maintains: (1) " That the direct trade communications between the German protectorate and the Congo State would in a geographical sense be interrupted ... " but that that fact was immaterial. After all, Great Britain " could only receive a lease of the territory subject to the provisions of antecedent treaties made between the Congo State and Germany; and notwithstanding a slight ambiguity in the language of the treaty made in 1884 between the two states, there can be no doubt that she would have been precluded from levying duties upon goods imported from German sources." In other words, Germany could not be injured commercially by the Anglo-Congolese Agreement.

(2) "As regards the general ' political positions ', the Congo State was neutral, and the treaty provides that in the event of cession of any part of its territory ' the obligations contracted by the Assoctiaion ' [i. e., the Congo State] ' towards the German Empire shall be transferred to the occupier '." Assuming then for a moment that a lease of indefinite duration is equivalent to a cession, the territory leased to Great Britain would have remained affected by the duties of neutrality, and could not have been used to prejudice the position of Germany. The treaty, it should be added, contains no stipulation, express or implied, that transfer of territory in any form should be dependent on German consent.

(3) " The Congo State had all rights of a neutral state, of which it has not been deprived by express compact. Those rights beyond question included the right to do all state acts which neither compromised or tended to compromise neutrality. In the particular case the Congo state was clearly competent to grant a lease, because the lease carried with it of necessity the obligations of neutrality. Although a lease for an indefinite time may in certain aspects be the equivalent of a cession, in law it is not so; a state may be able to make a cession of territory freed from its own obligations, but in granting a lease it cannot give wider powers than it possesses itself, and consequently altogether apart from the treaty with Germany, the Congo State could not disengage territory from neutral obligations by letting it out upon a subordinate title."

56 [c.—7390], no. 1.

57 *Ibid.*, enclosure 1 in no. 1.

58 *Die Grosse Politik*, vol. viii, nos. 2057-2058, pp. 457-458 and *cf.* footnote, p. 463.

59 *Ibid.*, no. 2059, pp. 458-459 and nos. 2064-2071, pp. 464-473. *Cf.* also *Accounts and Papers*, 1894, vol. 96, Africa No. 5 [c.—7390], no. 5.

60 Hertslet, *op. cit.*, vol. ii, no. 164, p. 584.

61 Bourgeois et Pagès, *op. cit.*, p. 248. *Die Grosse Politik*, vol. viii, nos. 2061, 2066, 2069, pp. 459-462, 465-466 and 469-470. *Cf.* the previous agreement of the two countries to work together and not to give in until both were satisfied. *Supra*, pp. 317-318.

62 Speech of Sir E. Grey, Hansard, series 4, vol. 28, c. 1252.

63 Boundary Agreement between France and the Congo State, August 14, 1894. Hertslet, *op. cit.*, vol. ii, no. 157, pp. 569-570.

64 *The Foreign Policy of Lord Rosebery* (London, 1901), p. 37. *Cf.* Speech of J. W. Lowther, Hansard, series 4, vol. 28, c. 1468.

65 Hertslet, *op. cit.*, vol. ii, no. 165, pp. 584-586.

66 Speech of Commander Bethell, Hansard, series 4, vol. 27, c. 1311.

67 Speech of Sir E. Grey, Hansard, series 4, vol. 27, c. 1320.

68 *Ibid.*

69 Speech of Sir E. Ashmead-Bartlett, Hansard, series 4, vol. 28, cc. 1475-1476 and also speech of Major Darwin, Hansard, series 4, vol. 32, c. 396.

70 *Die Grosse Politik*, vol. viii, no. 2061, p. 461.

71 [c.—7390], *op. cit.*, nos. 5 and 8.

72 Speech of Sir E. Grey, Hansard, series 4, vol. 32, c. 404.

73 [c.—7390], *op. cit.*, no. 5.

74 Speech of Burdett—Coutts, Hansard, series 4, vol. 43, c. 722.

CHAPTER XVII

Plots Laid in Ethiopia

[1] *Garstin's Report, Blue Book, Egypt*, no. 2, 1904 and Langer, Wm. L., "The Struggle for the Nile," *Foreign Affairs*, January, 1936, vol. 14, pp. 259-273.

[2] Work, Ernest, *Ethiopia: A Pawn in European Diplomacy* (New York, 1935), pp. 20-21.

[3] *Ibid.*, pp. 21 and 223-227.

[4] *Ibid.*, p. 237.

[5] *Ibid.*, p. 237.

[6] *Ibid.*, pp. 237-239.

[7] Bourgeois, *Manuel Historique du Politique Étrangère, op. cit.*, p. 366 and Work, *op. cit.*, pp. 143 and 237.

[8] Darcy, *op. cit.*, pp. 358, 364-366 and 369 and Work, *op. cit.*, pp. 243-244.

[9] See the map printed for distribution among the French Chamber of Deputies, January, 1895, showing French possessions and territories to be possessed from the Equator to the Mediterranean mentioned by Work in his book, p. 245.

[10] *Supra*, pp. 302-304.

[11] Work, *op. cit.*, pp. 250-251.

[12] *Ibid.*, p. 239.

[13] *Ibid.*, p. 246.

[14] Work, *op. cit.*, pp. 21-22 and 53-54.

[15] Handbook, no. 97, *British Somaliland and Sokotra*, prepared under the direction of the Historical Section of the British Foreign Office (1920).

[16] *Supra*, pp. 286 and 291.

[17] Bourgeois, *op. cit.*, pp. 366-367 and Work, *op. cit.*, p. 25.

[18] *Supra*, p. 326.

[19] Darcy, *op. cit.*, pp. 370-373, Fitzmaurice, *Life of Lord Granville, op. cit.*, vol. ii, pp. 436-439 and Work, *op. cit.*, chapter ii, "The Treaty of Uccialli," pp. 51-96.

[20] Work, *op. cit.*, p. 86 and also art. xvii of the treaty as recorded in Hertslet, *op. cit.*, vol. ii, no. 120, p. 455.

[21] Work, *op. cit.*, pp. 118-121. For a discussion on this point read Work, *op. cit.*, pp. 83-91 and 106-125 and also Rodd, James Rennell, *Diplomatic Memories* (second series), (London, 1923), vol. ii, pp. 111-112, 164 and 168.

[22] Work, *op. cit.*, p. 86.

[23] *Supra*, pp. 304, 306 and 307.

[24] Whates, *The Third Salisbury Administration, op. cit.*, pp. 10-11.

[25] Work, *op. cit.*, p. 127.

[26] Hertslet, *op. cit.*, vol. iii, no. 288, art. i, p. 948.
[27] *Ibid.*, no. 289, art. i, p. 949.
[28] *Ibid.*, art. ii, pp. 949-950.
[29] Speech of Sir E. Ashmead-Bartlett, Hansard, series 4, vol. 32, c. 395.
[30] Work, *op. cit.*, p. 132.
[31] *Ibid.*, p. 138.
[32] *Ibid.*, p. 232.
[33] *Ibid.*, pp. 229-230.
[34] *Ibid.*, p. 229 and *supra*, p. 326.
[35] *Ibid.*, pp. 229-230 and 232-233.
[36] *Ibid.*, pp. 232-235.
[37] *Ibid.*, p. 138.
[38] *Ibid.*, pp. 101-127.
[39] *Ibid.*, pp. 134-135.
[40] *Ibid.*, p. 135.
[41] *Ibid.*, pp. 239-240.
[42] *Ibid.*, pp. 135-145.
[43] *Ibid.*, p. 145.
[44] *Ibid.*, pp. 145-152.
[45] *Ibid.*, p. 242.

CHAPTER XVIII

The Reconquest of the Sudan

[1] The Marquis of Salisbury, June 1, 1894, Hansard, series 4, vol. 25, cc. 150-152.
[2] The Earl of Rosebery, June 1, 1894, Hansard, series 4, vol. 25, c. 154.
[3] Sir E. Grey, Hansard, series 4, vol. 24, cc. 559 and 599.
[4] *Supra*, pp. 307-308 and 321-322.
[5] Hanotaux, *Fachoda* (Paris, 1909), pp. 80 and 84.
[6] *Ibid.*, pp. 78, 79 and 109.
[7] *Ibid.*, pp. 89-91.
[8] Sir Ashmead-Bartlett, March 28, Hansard, series 4, vol. 32, cc. 390-392.
[9] Hanotaux, *op. cit.*, pp. 98 and 100-107.
[10] *Ibid.*, pp. 106-107.
[11] *Ibid.*, pp. 108-109.
[12] *Ibid.*, p. 143.
[13] Work, *op. cit.*, p. 184.
[14] *Accounts and Papers*, 1899, vol. 112 [c.—9054], appendix 4.
[15] *Supra*, pp. 302-303.
[16] Hanotaux, *op. cit.*, pp. 88-89.
[17] Gooch, *op. cit.*, pp. 183-184.

[18] *Supra*, p. 327 and Rodd, Sir James Rennell, *Social and Diplomatic Memories*, second series (London, 1923), vol. ii, p. 113.

[19] Sir H. Rumbold to the Marquis of Salisbury, December 5, 1898, *British Documents*, vol. i, no. 123, p. 102 and also Sir F. Lascelles to the Marquis of Salisbury, December 21, 1898, *ibid.*, no. 125, pp. 104-105.

[20] Sir E. Ashmead-Bartlett, March 28, 1895, Hansard, series 4, vol. 32, c. 395.

[21] *Ibid.*, cc. 390-392.

[22] *Ibid.*, c. 392.

[23] Major Darwin, March 28, 1895, Hansard, series 4, vol. 32, cc. 397-398.

[24] Famous Grey declaration, March 28, 1895, Hansard, series 4, vol. 32, cc. 404-406.

[25] Viscount Grey, *Twenty-Five Years, 1892-1916* (New York, 1923), vol. i, pp. 18-19.

[26] Lord Rosebery's Speech, "England, Egypt and the Soudan," at the annual dinner of the Surrey Agricultural Association at Epsom, October 12, 1898, *The Foreign Policy of Lord Rosebery* (London, 1901), appendix ix, p. 84.

[27] Sir E. Monson to M. Hanotaux, Paris, December 10, 1897, *Accounts and Papers*, 1899, vol. 112, Egypt No. 2 (1898) [c.—9054], enclosure in No. 1 and also Sir E. Monson to the Marquis of Salisbury, September 18, 1889, *ibid.*, no. 9.

[28] Whates, *The Third Salisbury Administration, op. cit.*, p. 180.

[29] Vindex, *op. cit.*, pp. 621-623. *Cf. Lord Rosebery's Foreign Policy, op. cit.*, p. 31.

[30] Rosebery's speech, "England, Egypt and the Soudan," *op. cit.*, p. 85.

[31] Hanotaux' speech to the Senate, April 5, 1895, *Accounts and Papers*, 1899, vol. 112 [c.—9054], no. 5.

[32] *Supra*, pp. 267-268.

[33] Hanotaux' speech, *op. cit.*

[34] *Supra*, p. 339.

[35] Hanotaux, *Fachoda, op. cit.*, p. 99 and also Hanotaux' speech.

[36] Hanotaux' speech, *op. cit.*

[37] Viscount Grey of Falloden, *op. cit.*, vol. i, pp. 19-20.

[38] Sir E. Grey, "The Nile Waterway," the *Times*, April 1, 1895, p. 8, column d.

[39] The Earl of Kimberley to the Marquis of Dufferin, F. O., April 1, 1894, *Accounts and Papers*, 1899, vol. 112 [c.—9054], appendix no. 4.

[40] Hanotaux, *Fachoda, op. cit.*, p. 93.

[41] *Ibid.*, p. 93. *Cf.* the version which Hanotaux gives of the conversations between de Courcel and Kimberley, *ibid.*, pp. 82-95, with the rather different version of these same conversations given by the Earl of Kimberley to the Marquis of Dufferin, April 1894 [c.—9054], *op. cit.*,

appendix no. 4 and *cf.* also, the account in Darcy, *Cent Années, op. cit.,* p. 398.

[42] Lowther, Hansard, series 4, vol. 28, c. 1469.

[43] Rose, J. Holland, *The Development of the European Nations* (New York and London, 1905), vol. ii, p. 223.

[44] See, for example, Chamberlain's attitude towards the Egyptian question in 1885, Gardiner, *The Life of Sir William Harcourt* (London, 1923), vol. i, pp. 514-515.

[45] Williams, Cecil Rhodes, *op. cit.,* pp. 240 and 258-260.

[46] See, for example, his speech in the House on the Grey Declaration, March 28, 1895, Hansard, series 4, vol. 32, cc. 407-408.

[47] Gardiner, *op. cit.,* vol. ii, p. 367 and also Giffen, *op. cit.,* p. 107.

[48] Whates, *The Third Salisbury Administration, op. cit.,* p. 165.

[49] Giffen, *op. cit.,* p. 25 and Hanotaux, *Fachoda, op. cit.,* p. 101.

[50] Hanotaux, *Fachoda, op. cit.,* pp. 101-102.

[51] Darcy, *Cent Années, op. cit.,* pp. 400-402.

[52] *Supra,* p. 321.

[53] Buckle, *Letters of Queen Victoria,* series 3, vol. iii, *op. cit.,* pp. 24-25.

[54] Extract from the Queen's Journal, April 16, 1896, Buckle, *op. cit.,* p. 39.

[55] The Marquis of Salisbury, June 12, 1896, Hansard, series 4, vol. 41, c. 938.

[56] Broderick, February 24, 1899, Hansard, series 4, vol. 67, c. 481.

[57] Hansard, series 4, vol. 67, February 24, 1899, c. 466.

[58] Arthur, *Life of Lord Kitchener, op. cit.,* vol. i, p. 191.

[59] *Supra,* p. 336.

[60] The Marquis of Salisbury, June 23, 1896, Hansard, series 4, vol. 41, c. 935.

[61] Rodd, *Diplomatic Memories,* second series, vol. ii, *op. cit.,* pp. 85-86.

[62] Curzon, Under Secretary of Foreign Affairs, March 23, 1896, Hansard, series 4, vol. 38, c. 1027.

[63] Rodd, *Diplomatic Memories,* second series, vol. ii, *op. cit.,* pp. 87-88.

[64] The First Lord of the Treasury, June 23, 1896, Hansard, series 4, vol. 41, c. 537. In fact, there is some evidence to show that although the Italians were grateful for the British diversion, they were on the point of embarking on a policy of colonial retrenchment. They were tired of their disastrous campaign. Indeed, they were contemplating retiring from their dangerous position at Kassala and to evacuate the post. General Baldisera was only persuaded to remain on the urgent plea of the British Government that the occupation be sustained. Labouchere, June 23, Hansard, series 4, vol. 40, cc. 522-526.

[65] Giffen, *op. cit.,* p. 29.

[66] Cromer, *op. cit.,* vol. ii, pp. 83-85 and 109 and, also Milner, *op. cit.,* pp. 159-160.

[67] The Marquis of Salisbury, June 12, Hansard, series 4, vol. 41, c. 936.
[68] See, for example, the attitude of the Egyptian Government towards the dispatch of the Hicks expedition. Cromer, *op. cit.*, vol. i, ch. xix and again in 1891, the attitude of the military party at Cairo towards the Tokar campaign. Hansard, series 3, vol. 350, c. 1442. There is some evidence that the British and Egyptian authorities in Egypt were eager for an aggressive Sudanese campaign long before H. M. Government at home approved it. In fact, the policy of abandoning the Sudan in 1884 was strongly resisted by the Egyptian Government and it was only after the resignation of the Chérif Pasha Ministry that the Khedive was obliged to accept the British policy. Cromer, *op. cit.*, vol. i, pp. 381-384.

[69] The Marquis of Salisbury, June 23, 1896, Hansard, series 4, vol. 41, c. 934.

[70] Sir E. Grey, February 24, 1899, Hansard, series 4, vol. 67, cc. 493-494.
[71] *Ibid.*, c. 493.

[72] Grew, Edwin S., *Kitchener* (London, 1916), vol. i, p. 46.

[73] Williams, *Cecil Rhodes, op. cit.*, pp. 285, 309 and footnote p. 309 and 233; McDonald, *Rhodes, A Life, op. cit.*, p. 151.

[74] Williams, *Cecil Rhodes, op. cit.*, p. 313 and Vindex, *op. cit.*, pp. 635 and 655.

[75] Cromer, *op. cit.*, vol. ii, p. 89.

[76] Rodd, *Diplomatic Memories*, second series, vol. ii, *op. cit.*, pp. 157-160 and 187-188; Arthur, *Life of Lord Kitchener, op. cit.*, vol. i, p. 209.

[77] Weinthal, *op. cit.*, vol. ii, "The Sudan Military Railways in 1896-1898" by Col. Sir Edouard Percy Girouard, Director of the Sudan Railway during this period, p. 327.

[78] *Supra*, p. 33.

[79] Weinthal, *op. cit.*, vol. ii, "The Railway System of the Sudan" by Lieut-Col. W. E. Longfield, Deputy General Manager of the Sudan Government Railways and Steamers, pp. 309-311.

[80] Weinthal, *op. cit.*, vol. ii, "The Sudan Military Railways," *op. cit.*, p. 327. After the completion of the line from Wadi Halfa to Abu Hamed, the Wadi Halfa to Kerma line had no further value. "It was therefore decided to pull up the old track between Kerma and Koshi—a distance of some 200 miles—and to utilize the rails for building the new branch line to Kareima. The construction of this line was carried on simultaneously with that of the Nile-Red Sea railway, and the line was opened to traffic in March, 1906." Weinthal, *op. cit.*, vol. ii, "The Railway System of the Sudan," *op. cit.*, p. 321.

[81] Hanotaux, *Fachoda*, op. cit., p. 109 and Giffen, *op. cit.*, p. 23.

[82] Sir E. Monson to Hanotaux, Paris, December 10, 1897, *Accounts and Papers*, 1899, vol. 112, Egypt No. 2 (1898) and [c.—9054], no. 1.

[83] *Supra*, pp. 346 and 350 and also Hanotaux, *Fachoda, op. cit.*, pp. 92-93.

[84] Hanotaux à Sir Edmund Monson, Paris, December 24, 1897, *Documents Diplomatiques, Affaires du Haut Nil et du Bahr-El-Ghazal, 1897-1898*, No. 2, p. 3. See also, Hauser, Henri, *Manuel de politique européene, Histoire diplomatique de l'Europe (1871-1914)*, (Paris, 1920), vol. i, p. 367.

[85] *Doc'ts Dipl., op. cit.*, no. 2, p. 3.

[86] Weinthal, *op. cit.*, vol. ii, pp. 329 and 331.

[87] Arthur, *op. cit.*, vol. i, p. 211.

[88] Grew, *op. cit.*, vol. i, p. 168.

[89] Arthur, *op. cit.*, vol. i, pp. 209 and 211.

[90] Weinthal, *op. cit.*, vol. ii, p. 333.

[91] Grew, *op. cit.*, vol. i, p. 170.

[92] Weinthal, *op. cit.*, vol. ii, p. 333 and Cromer, *op. cit.*, vol. ii, pp. 102-103.

[93] Grew, *op. cit.*, vol. i, p. 172.

[94] Cromer, *op. cit.*, vol. ii, pp. 104-105.

[95] Weinthal, *op. cit.*, vol. ii, p. 313.

[96] Grew, *op. cit.*, pp. 22-23 and 163.

[97] Michell, *op. cit.*, vol. ii, p. 232.

[98] Speech of Cecil Rhodes, Port Elizabeth, September 17, 1898, Vindex, *op. cit.*, p. 609.

[99] Williams, *Cecil Rhodes, op. cit.*, pp. 312-313 and Vindex, *op. cit.*, pp. 635 and 641-642.

[100] The Marquis of Salisbury to Sir E. Monson, September 9, 1898, *Accounts and Papers*, 1899, vol. 112 [c.—9045], no. 6.

[101] Decle, Lionel, "The Fashoda Question," *The Fortnightly Review*, November 1, 1898, vol. 70, p. 665.

CHAPTER XIX

THE FASHODA CRISIS

[1] The Marquis of Salisbury, Hansard, series 4, vol. 66, cc. 27-28.

[2] Giffen, *op. cit.*, pp. 4-6.

[3] Giffen, *op. cit.*, pp. 4-5 and *infra*, pp. 328, 363-366.

[4] *Supra*, pp. 328-329.

[5] Giffen, *op. cit.*, p. 18.

[6] Work, *op. cit.*, p. 2.

[7] Giffen, *op. cit.*, p. 18.

[8] Work, *op. cit.*, pp. 251-253 and Darcy, *op. cit.*, pp. 390-391 footnote.

[9] *Ibid.*, p. 252.

[10] *Ibid.*, p. 253.

[11] *Ibid.*, pp. 254-255.

[12] *Ibid.*, pp. 261-262.

[13] *Ibid.*, pp. 266-267.

[14] *Supra*, pp. 342-345.

[15] Rodd, Sir J. Rennell, *Social and Diplomatic Memories, 1894-1901* (second series), vol. ii (London, 1923), pp. 112-114.

[16] *Ibid.*, pp. 158, 159, 167, 168 and 177.

[17] *Ibid.*, pp. 186 and 195-196.

[18] Sir E. Grey, February 24, 1898, Hansard, series 4, vol. 53, c. 1602.

[19] Sir E. Durning – Lawrence, February 24, 1899, Hansard, series 4, vol. 67, c. 489.

[20] Buckle, *Letters of Queen Victoria, op. cit.*, series 3, vol. iii, p. 73.

[21] *British Documents*, vol. i, p. 163.

[22] Whates, *op. cit.*, p. 198.

[23] *Ibid.*, pp. 197-198.

[24] Hanotaux, *Fachoda, op. cit.*, p. 108.

[25] Balfour, First Lord of the Treasury, February 8, 1898, Hansard, series 4, vol. 53, c. 93.

[26] Sir Charles Dilke, March 3, 1898, Hansard, series 4, vol. 54, cc. 546-548.

[27] Whates, *op. cit.*, p. 197 and Balfour, Hansard, series 4, vol. 53, c. 93.

[28] Whates, *op. cit.*, pp. 197-198 and the Marquis of Salisbury, March 20, 1899.

[29] Giffen, *op. cit.*, pp. 4-6.

[30] Bourdarie, Paul, *Fachoda—La Mission Marchand* (Paris, 1899), p. 19.

[31] *Ibid.*, p. 19 and Giffen, *op. cit.*, p. 16.

[32] Telegram from the British Agent at Cairo communicated by the British Ambassador at Paris, September 30, 1898, *Doc'ts Dipl., op. cit.*, no. 18.

[33] Delcassé au baron de Courcel, Paris, October 11, 1898, *Doc'ts Dipl., op. cit.*, no. 29.

[34] Giffen, *op. cit.*, p. 45.

[35] Rodd to the Marquis of Salisbury, September 22, 1898, *Accounts and Papers*, 1899, vol. 112 [c.—9054], no. 11.

[36] Telegram from the British diplomatic agent at Cairo, *Doc'ts Dipl., op. cit.*, no. 18 and Rodd to the Marquis of Salisbury, September 25, 1898, *Accounts and Papers*, 1899, vol. 112 [c.—9045], no. 13.

[37] Rodd to the Marquis of Salisbury, *op. cit.*

[38] Giffen, *op. cit.*, p. 45.

[39] Sir E. Monson to the Marquis of Salisbury, September 8, 1898, *British Documents, op. cit.*, vol. i, no. 188, p. 163.

[40] The Marquis of Salisbury to Sir E. Monson, September 9, 1898 [c.—9045], *op. cit.*, no. 6. See also his speech in the House, Hansard, series 4, vol. 66, cc. 27-28.

[41] Sir E. Monson to the Marquis of Salisbury, September 18, 1898, *British Documents*, vol. i, no. 191, pp. 165-166.

[42] Giffen, *op. cit.*, p. 9.

[43] Kitchener to Lord Cromer, Dal, White Nile, September 21, 1898, *Accounts and Papers*, 1899, vol. 112, Egypt No. 3 (1898) [c.—9055], enclosure 1 in No. 2 and Rye, James, B., *Kitchener in His Own Words* (London, F. Fisher Unwin Ltd., undated, written sometime after Kitchener's death), pp. 134-135.

[44] *Ibid.*

[45] [c.—9055], *op. cit.*, enclosure 4 in No. 2.

[46] *Ibid.*, enclosure 1 in No. 2.

[47] Giffen, *op. cit.*, pp. 9-10.

[48] See, especially, reaction to the speech of the Chancellor of the Exchequer, Sir Michael Hicks Beach, concerning the advance beyond Khartoum, Hansard, series 4, vol. 45, cc. 1445-1446.

[49] *Supra*, pp. 347-351.

[50] Sir E. Monson to the Marquis of Salisbury, Secret; Oct. 21, 1898, *British Documents*, vol. i, no. 214, p. 182.

[51] Lord Rosebery, "England, Egypt and The Soudan", Speech at the Annual Dinner of the Surrey Agricultural Association at Epsom, Oct. 12, 1898, *The Foreign Policy of Lord Rosebery, op. cit.*, appendix ix, pp. 85 and 87.

[52] Whates, *op. cit.*, pp. 186-187. "Even the Council of the British and Foreign Arbitration Association resolved that M. Marchand's invasion of the Nile Valley 'was a trespass upon and infringement of the territorial rights of a friendly and neighbouring State and cannot therefore be the subject of arbitration'".

[53] Giffen, *op. cit.*, pp. 68 and 83.

[54] Sir E. Monson to the Marquis of Salisbury, Sept. 28, 1898, *British Documents*, vol. i, no. 200, p. 172.

[55] The Marquis of Salisbury to Rodd, October 1, 1898, *ibid.*, no. 201, p. 173.

[56] *Ibid.*, no. 196, p. 170.

[57] Sir E. Monson to the Marquis of Salisbury, Oct. 7, 1898, *ibid.*, no. 204, p. 175.

[58] Sir E. Monson to the Marquis of Salisbury, September 30, 1898, *British Documents*, vol. i, no. 200, p. 172.

[59] Giffen, *op. cit.*, p. 68.

[60] Sir E. Monson to Lord Salisbury, October 7, 1898, *British Documents, op. cit.*, vol. i, no. 204, p. 176.

[61] Giffen, *op. cit.*, pp. 109-110.

[62] Sir E. Monson to the Marquis of Salisbury, October 7, 1898, *British Documents*, vol. i, no. 204, p. 176.

[63] *Supra*, pp. 327 and 365-366.

[64] Sir E. Monson to the Marquis of Salisbury, October 7, 1898, *British Documents*, vol. i, no. 204, p. 163, and Sir F. Lascelles to the Marquis of Salisbury, December 21, 1898, *British Documents*, vol. i, no. 125, p. 105.

[65] Sir E. Monson to the Marquis of Salisbury, Oct. 21, 1898, *British Documents*, vol. i, no. 213, p. 181.

[66] *Ibid.*, no. 215, p. 182 and also Buckle, *Letters of Queen Victoria, op. cit.*, series 3, vol. iii, p. 299.

[67] Buckle, *op. cit.*, vol. iii, p. 303, The Marquis of Salisbury to Queen Victoria, October 29, 1898.

[68] *Ibid.*, p. 312, Sir Charles Scott, British Ambassador to Russia to the Marquis of Salisbury, and also Sir H. Rumbold to the Marquis of Salisbury, December 5, 1898, *British Documents*, vol. i, no. 123, p. 102.

[69] Sir P. Currie to the Marquis of Salisbury, October 26, 1898, *British Documents*, vol. i, no. 217, p. 183.

[70] *Supra*, pp. 207-208, 212-214, 221, 224, 227-229.

[71] Milner, *op. cit.*, p. 335 and Bourgeois et Pagès, *op. cit.*, p. 259.

[72] Buckle, *Letters of Queen Victoria, op. cit.*, series 3, vol. iii, p. 242.

[73] Rodd, *Social and Diplomatic Memories, op. cit.*, vol. ii, p. 210.

[74] *Supra*, pp. 212-214.

[75] Bourgeois et Pagès, *op. cit.*, pp. 275-276.

[76] Giffen, *op. cit.*, pp. 98, 142 and 157.

[77] *Supra*, p. 371.

[78] Geoffray to Delcassé, *Doc't. Dipl., op. cit.*, no. 11.

[79] Delcassé to Geoffray, October 3, 1898, *ibid.*, no. 22.

[80] Delcassé to Geoffray, Sept. 28, 1898, *ibid.*, no. 13.

[81] Telegram from Salisbury, September 28, and telegram from Delcassé to M. P. Lefèvre-Pontalis, French agent and consul general at Cairo, *ibid.*, nos. 15 and 17.

[82] Delcassé to Baron de Courcel, October 4, 1898, *ibid., op. cit.*, no. 24.

[83] Baron de Courcel to Delcassé, October 5, 1898, *ibid.*, no. 25.

[84] *Ibid.*, no. 25, Hanotaux, *op. cit.*, pp. 142-146 and Giffen, *op. cit.*, pp. 73-74.

[85] Hanotaux, *op. cit.*, pp. 146-147.

[86] *Ibid.*, pp. 142 and 147.

[87] *Ibid.*, p. 147; Giffen, *op. cit.*, pp. 67-68 and Whates, *The Politician's Handbook*, 1900, pp. xxviii-xxix.

[88] Hanotaux, *op. cit.*, p. 148 and Baron de Courcel to Delcassé, *Doc'ts. Dipl., op. cit.*, no. 30.

[89] Hanotaux, *op. cit.*, p. 151 and Giffen, *op. cit.*, pp. 76-77.

[90] Giffen, *op. cit.*, pp. 82-83, 78 and 87-89.

[91] Sir F. Lascelles to the Marquis of Salisbury, December 21, 1898, *British Documents*, vol. i, no. 124, p. 103.

[92] Giffen, *op. cit.*, pp. 87-89.

[93] *Supra*, pp. 339, 348-349 and 359.

[94] Hertslet, *op. cit.*, vol. ii, no. 244, articles 2 and 3, pp. 796-797.
[95] *Ibid.*, art. 4, p. 797.
[96] Giffen, *op. cit.*, pp. 185-186.
[97] Hanotaux, *Fachoda, op. cit.*, p. 155.
[98] See the speech of M. Étienne, June 7, 1894, in the Chamber of Deputies, Darcy, *op. cit.*, p. 377.
[99] Darcy, *op. cit.*, p. 357.
[100] Whates, *op. cit.*, pp. 194-195.

CHAPTER XX

Epilogue

[1] *Supra*, pp. 251-253.
[2] *Supra*, pp. 260-266.
[3] *Supra*, p. 320.
[4] *Supra*, pp. 311-312 and 353-354.
[5] *Supra*, p. 26.
[6] *Supra*, p. 106.
[7] *Supra*, pp. 316-317.
[8] *Supra*, p. 223.
[9] Renty, E. de, "Deux Transafricain Anglais", *Quest. Dipl.*, vol. xiv, 1910, p. 476.
[10] *Supra*, p. 383.
[11] Hanotaux, *op. cit.*, p. 84.
[12] Darcy, *op. cit.*, pp. 360, 361-362 and 376.
[13] *Ibid.*, p. 366 and *supra*, p. 383.
[14] Renty, E. de, "Deux Transafricains Anglais", *op. cit.*, p. 477.
[15] Cammaerts, M. E., "Le Cap au Caire. Sa Situation Actuelle." *Bulletin de Colonisation Comparée*, August 20, 1912, p. 343.
[16] Sir Edward Grey to Sir E. Goschen, F. O., December 20, 1911, *British Documents*, vol. vi, no. 480, p. 651.
[17] *Ibid.*, p. 651.
[18] Report of Sir H. H. Johnston, April 27, 1900, *The Politician's Handbook*, 1901, pp. 96-97.
[19] Weinthal, *op. cit.*, vol. ii, "Fighting Floating Islands on the Nile", by A. D. Milne, who was in charge of the expedition for clearing a passage through the sudd in 1899, p. 218.
[20] *Supra*, p. 370.
[21] Schweitzer, *op. cit.*, vol. i, pp. xx-xxi.
[22] Weinthal, vol. ii, *op. cit.*, article by A. D. Milne, p. 223.

[23] Weinthal, vol. ii, *op. cit.*, chapter entitled " The Upper Nile Valley," p. 226.

[24] Darcy, *Cent Années, op. cit.*, p. 353.

[25] *Ibid.*, p. 353.

[26] Hertslet, *op. cit.*, vol. ii, no. 100, art. v, p. 432.

[27] Darcy, *op. cit.*, p. 469. See also article by E. de Renty, " Deux Transafricains Anglais," *op. cit.*, p. 475.

[28] Williams, Sir Robert, " The Milestones of African Civilization", *United Empire Journal*, vol. viii (new series), 1917, p. 453.

[29] *Infra*, p. 396.

[30] *Supra*, p. 333.

[31] Work, *op. cit.*, p. 132.

[32] *Ibid.*, p. 269.

[33] *Ibid.*, p. 271.

[34] *Supra*, pp. 308 and 322.

[35] Agreement between Great Britain and the Independent State of the Congo, modifying the agreement signed at Brussels, May 12, 1894. Signed at London, May 9, 1906, Hertslet, *op. cit.*, vol. ii, no. 165, art. i and ii, pp. 584-585.

[36] Hertslet, *op. cit.*, vol. ii, no. 165, art. iv and v, pp. 585-586.

[37] Freeman, Lewis R., " Rhodes's 'All Red' Route. The War's Effect upon the Cape to Cairo Railway." *World's Work*, London, 1915-1916, vol. xxvii, p. 169.

[38] Witness the student riots in Egypt during the recent Italian campaign in Ethiopia.

[39] *Supra*, p. 203.

[40] See in this connection the article by Williams in Weinthal, *op. cit.*, vol. i, " My Story of the Scheme" and his addresses:

The Story of the Cape to Cairo Railway made April 21, 1921, before the African Society, Macmillan & Co., Ltd., London.

" The Cape to Cairo Railway from the Point of View of African Development" made before the Central Asian Society, April 5, 1922 and contained in the *Journal, Central Asian Society*, vol. ix, 1922, pp. 147-166.

" The Milestones of African Civilization," read before a meeting of the Royal Colonial Institute, May 8, 1917 and printed in *United Empire Journal*, vol. viii, new series, 1917, pp. 446-462.

[41] *Supra*, pp. 204-205.

[42] *Supra*, p. 218.

[43] Williams, " The Milestones of African Civilization." It will be recalled, also, that this concession led to Williams sending out several prospecting expeditions between 1899 and 1904. As a result of these expeditions under the leadership of George Grey, the Kansanshi Copper Mine in Rhodesia and the whole extent of the great Katanga copper belt,

besides important gold, tin and diamond deposits were revealed. *Supra,* pp. 202 and 204 and Williams, "The Cape to Cairo Railway," p. 8.

[44] Williams, Sir Robert, "The Cape to Cairo Railway," *op. cit.,* p. 10.

[45] Williams, Sir Robert, "The Milestones of African Civilization," *op. cit.,* p. 6.

[46] *Ibid.,* p. 6.

[47] Williams, "The Milestones of African Civilization," p. 6.

[48] *Ibid.,* pp. 8-10.

[49] *Ibid.,* pp. 9-10.

[50] Weinthal, *op. cit.,* vol. i, pp. 114-115.

[51] *Supra,* note 21, p. 430.

[52] *The Benguella Railway,* reprint of a paper read before the Liverpool Engineering Society (Liverpool, 1929), p. 2.

[53] Williams gives no date except that his conversation with King Leopold took place after the Roger Casement report on the Congo, i. e., about 1903.

[54] Williams, "The Cape to Cairo Railway," p. 12.

[55] Williams, "The Milestones of African Civilization," p. 8.

[56] *Ibid.,* p. 8.

[57] *Ibid.,* p. 8.

[58] Williams, *The Cape to Cairo Railway,* p. 12.

[59] Williams, "The Milestones of African Civilization," p. 8.

[60] Williams, *The Story of the Cape to Cairo Railway,* pp. 12-13 and also "The Milestones of African Civilization," pp. 9-13.

[61] Williams, *The Story of the Cape to Cairo Railway,* p. 13.

[62] Weinthal, *op. cit.,* vol. i, p. 119.

[63] Weinthal, *op. cit.,* vol. i, p. 119 and Williams, "The Milestones of African Civilization," *passim.*

[64] Weinthal, *op. cit.,* vol. iii, "The Nile-Congo Divide" by Major Cuthbert Christy, pp. 79 and 119; Williams, *The Story of the Cape to Cairo Railway, op. cit.,* pp. 14-15.

[65] Christy, Dr. Cuthbert, "The Cape-to-Cairo Railway," *The Scottish Geographical Magazine,* vol. 40, December 15, 1924, p. 333 and also chapter by Dr. Christy entitled "The Nile-Congo Divide," Weinthal, *op. cit.,* vol. iii, pp. 79-83.

[66] *Official Steamship and Airways Guide. International,* published by the Transportation Guides, Inc., 420 Lexington Ave., New York, vol. v, June, 1936, table 982, p. 253.

[67] For example, Tommy Rose, a British flying officer flew, from Lympne, England to Cape Town, in three days, seventeen hours and thirty-eight minutes. This record flight was made within the past year, from February sixth to the ninth. He bettered by more than thirteen hours the record set by Mrs. Amy Johnson Mollison in 1932.

[68] Treatt, Stella Court, *Cape to Cairo* (London, 1927), pp. 29 and 244.

[69] Shay, Felix, "Cairo to Cape Town Overland," *National Geographic Magazine*, vol. xlvii, no. 2, February, 1925, pp. 124-260.

[70] *The South and East African Year Book for 1935*, pp. 432-433.

[71] *Ibid.*, pp. 432-433.

[72] Discussion over a paper by Sir A. Sharpe entitled "The Back-bone of Africa," *Journal of the Royal Geographical Society*, vol. 52, p. 157.

[73] Prout, Colonel H. G., "The Cape to Cairo Railway," *Munsey's Magazine*, vol. xxi, April 1899, p. 113.

[74] *Ibid.*, p. 113.

[75] *Ibid.*, p. 113.

[76] Discussion over a paper presented by Sir A. Sharpe entitled "The Back-bone of Africa," *op. cit.*

[77] Demangeon, A., "The Cape to Cairo Dream," *The Living Age*, vol. 335, January, 1929, pp. 364-368 and 398.

[78] Shepstone, J. H., "The Cape to Cairo Railroad," *The Westminster*, vol. xxi, no. 2, August 1912, p. 83.

[79] Rt. Hon. Viscount Milner, Chairman of meeting of the Society of Arts, November 23, 1906, *Journal of the Society of Arts*, vol. 55, December 21, 1906, p. 106.

[80] Williams, Robert, *The Cape to Cairo Railway*, address, April 21, 1921, before the African Society, p. 16.

[81] Vernon, S. P., "The Cape to Cairo Railway," *Liberia Bulletin*, No. 15, November 1899, pp. 33-34.

[82] Michell, Sir Lewis, "The Cape to Cairo Railway," *Journal of the Society of Arts*, vol. 55, December 21, 1906, pp. 102-103.

[83] Christy, Dr. Cuthbert, "The Cape-to-Cairo Railway," *The Scottish Geographical Magazine*, vol. 40, November 15, 1924, p. 333.

[84] Demangeon, A., "The Cape to Cairo Dream," *The Living Age*, vol. 335, January 1929, p. 368 and map on p. 364 and also the new map of Africa in *The National Geographic Magazine*, vol. lxviii, July, 1935.

[85] Christy, *op. cit.*, p. 334.

[86] *Journal of the Royal Geographical Society*, vol. 52, Sept. 1918, p. 157.

BIBLIOGRAPHY

BIBLIOGRAPHY

Sources

Belgium

A. *Ministère des Colonies.*
Exposé de la Question des Chemins de Fer, Brussels, 1911.
Notes et Documents rélatif à la Politique des Chemins de Fer, Brussels, 1914.
B. *Administration de Fonds Spécial. Notes sur la Question des Transports en Afrique.* Précedées d'un Rapport au Roi par le Briey, administrateur du Fonds spécial, Brussels, 1918.

France

Documents Diplomatiques.
Affaires du Haut-Nil et du Bahr-El-Ghazal 1897-1898.

Germany

Die Grosse Politik der Europäischen Kabinette, 1871-1914.

Great Britain

A. *British Documents on the Origins of the War*, edited by G. P. Gooch and H. Temperley, H. M. Stationery Office, 1926-1934.
B. *Parliamentary Debates.* Hansard, 1885-1901.
   Series 3, vols. 291-355.
   Series 4, vols. 1-97.
C. *Parliamentary Papers*, 1865-1906 (given in the footnotes as *Accounts and Papers*).
D. *Reports.*
   (1) *Records of the British South African Company*, C. O. 468 covering the period 1889-1898.
   (2) *Reports on African Railways*, Rhodesia. Acworth, Commissioner; *Report of William Acworth on the subject of Railway Questions in Southern Rhodesia*, Bulawayo, Argus Printing and Publishing Co., Ltd., 1918; Hammond, Frederick Dawson, Brigadier-General, *Railroad System of Southern Rhodesia*, Salisbury, Rhodesia, Government Printer, 1926.
E. Hertslet, Sir E., *The Map of Africa by Treaty*, revised and completed to the end of 1908 by R. W. Brant, Librarian and

475

Keeper of the Papers and H. L. Sherwood of the Foreign Office, vols. i, ii and iii and collection of maps, London, H. M. Stationery Office, 1909.

F. *Peace Handbooks* prepared under the direction of the Historical Section of the Foreign Office, 1920.
Vol. 15, *The Partition of Africa.*
Vol. 97, *British Somaliland and Sokotra.*
Vol. 98, *The Anglo-Egyptian Soudan.*

Cape Colony

A. *Colonial Dispatches*; C. O. 48 series, nos. 250-511 covering the years 1845-1885.

B. *Entry Books*, C. O. 49 series, nos. 41-53 covering the years 1848-1857.

C. *The Records of the Cape Legislature*, C. O. 51 series, nos. 93-265 covering the years 1854-1889 includes:
(1) Minutes of the Legislative Council.
(2) Votes and proceedings of the House of Assembly.
(3) Appendices to the proceedings of Parliament.
These appendices often contain valuable material for the history of railway development in the Colony. They include reports of select committees, the reports of railway managers, reports of surveys, etc.

D. *The Cape Hansard*, 1890-1898.

SECONDARY AUTHORITIES

I. GENERAL

Baker, Sir Samuel White, *The Albert N'yanza, Great Basin of the Nile*, Philadelphia, J. B. Lippincott & Co., 1870.

——, *In the Heart of Africa*, New York, Funk & Wagnalls, 1884.

——, *Ismailia*, 2 vols. A narrative of the expedition to Central Africa for the Suppression of the Slave Trade, Macmillan Co., London, 1874.

Barré, Paul, *Fachoda et Le Bahr-el-Ghazal*, Paris, Librairie Plon, 1898.

Beer, George Louis, *African Questions at the Paris Peace Conference*, Macmillan Co., 1923.

Beyens, Le Baron, ancien ministre de Belgique à Berlin, *La Question Africaine*, Brussels and Paris, Van Oest et Cie, 1918.

Bourdairie, Paul, *Fachoda — La Mission Marchand*, Imprimerie, Paris, F. Leve, 1899.

Bourgeois, Émile, *Manuel Historique de Politique Étrangère, 1878-1919.* Vol. 4, Librairie Classique Eugène Belin, Paris, Belin Frères, 1926.

Bourgeois et Pagès, *Les Origines et les Responsibilités de la Guerre*, Paris, Librairie Hachette, 1921.

Buckle, George Earle, *The Letters of Queen Victoria* (series 2), vol. iii, 1879-1885, Longmans Green & Co., New York, 1928; (series 3), vol. i, 1886-1890, John Murray, London, 1930; vol. ii, 1891-1895, John Murray, London, 1931; and vol. iii, 1895-1901, John Murray, London, 1930.

Cambridge History of British Foreign Policy, 1866-1919, vol. iii, edited by Sir Adolphus W. Ward and G. P. Gooch, The Cambridge University Press, 1922-1923.

Commerce and Industry. A historical review of the economic conditions of the British Empire from the Peace of Paris in 1815 to the declaration of war in 1914, based on Parliamentary Debates, edited by William Page, London, Constable and Co., Ltd., 1919.

Crabitès, Pierre, *The Winning of the Sudan,* London, George Routledge and Sons, Ltd., 1934.

Cromer, Earl of, *Modern Egypt,* vols. i and ii, Macmillan Co., 1908.

Cunningham, William, *The Rise and Decline of the Free Trade Movement,* London, C. J. Clay and Sons, 1904.

Darcy, Jean, *France et l'Angleterre, Cent Années de Rivalité Coloniale,* Librairie Academique Didier, Perrin et Cie, Paris, 1904.

Earle, Edward Mead, *Turkey, The Great Powers, and the Bagdad Railway,* New York, Macmillan & Co., 1923.

Egerton, H. E., *A Short History of British Colonial Policy,* London, Methuen & Co., 1897.

Eliot, Sir Charles, N. E., *The East Africa Protectorate,* Edward Arnold, publisher to H. M. India Office, London, 1905.

Fraisse, Gustave, *Situation Internationale des Pays Tributaires de Bassin du Congo.* Thèse pour le Doctorat. Imprimerie André Gabelle, Carcassone, 1904.

Freycinet, Charles Louis de Saulces de, *La Question d'Égypte,* Paris, Calmann-Lévy, 1905.

Friedjung, Heinrich, *Das Zeitalter des Imperialismus,* 3 vols., Berlin, Verlag Neufeld und Henius, 1919.

Giffen, Morrison Beall, *Fashoda. The Incident and Its Diplomatic Setting,* The University of Chicago Press, 1930.

Gibbons, *The New Map of Africa,* New York, The Century Co., 1918.

Gooch, G. P., *History of Modern Europe, 1878-1919,* New York, Henry Holt & Co., 1923.

Grey, Viscount, *Twenty-Five Years,* vol. i, New York, Frederick Stokes & Co., 1935.

Hall, William E., *A Treatise on International Law,* edited by Pearce Higgins, Oxford, The Clarendon Press, 1917.

Hallberg, Charles W., *The Suez Canal, Its History and Diplomatic Importance,* Columbia University Press, 1931.

Hanotaux, Gabriel, *Le Partage de l'Afrique, Fachoda*, Ernest Flammerion, Paris, 1909.

Hauser, Henri, *Histoire Diplomatique de l'Europe, 1871-1914*, 2 vols., Les Presses Universitaires, Paris, 1929.

Hobson, Charles Kenneth, *Export of Capital*, London, Constable and Co., Ltd., 1914.

Jessett, Montague G., *The Key to South Africa, Delagoa Bay*, London, T. Fisher Unwin, 1899.

Johnston, Sir Harry H., *British Central Africa*, London, Methuen & Co., 1898.

——, *History of the Colonization of Africa by Alien Races*, in Cambridge Historical Studies edited by G. W. Prothero, Cambridge University Press, 1913.

Keith, Arthur Berriedale, *The Belgian Congo and the Berlin Act*, Oxford, Clarendon Press, 1919.

Keltie, J. Scott, *The Partition of Africa*, London, Edward Stanford, 1893.

Kiewiet, Cornelius Willem de, *British Colonial Policy and the South African Republics, 1848-1872*, published as no. 3 in *Imperial Studies*, London, Longmans, Green & Co., 1929.

Knowles, L. C. A., *The Economic Development of the British Overseas Empire*, London, George Routledge & Sons, Ltd., 1924.

Langer, W. L., *European Alliance and Alignments*, A. A. Knopf, New York, 1931.

Lacerda e Almedia, Francisco José Maria de, *The Lands of Cazembe, Lacerda's Journey to Cazembe in 1798.* Tr. and annotated by Captain R. F. Burton. Published by the Royal Geographical Society, J. Murray, London, 1873.

Livingstone, David, *Missionary Travels and Researches*, J. Murray, London, 1899.

Lovell, Reginald Ivan, *The Anglo-German Estrangement, 1894-1895.* Unpublished doctoral thesis, Harvard University.

——, *The Struggle for South Africa, 1875-1899*, New York, Macmillan Co., 1934.

Lugard, Captain F. D., *The Rise of Our East African Empire*, 2 vols., Edinburgh and London, William Blackwood & Sons, 1893.

McDermott, P. L., assistant Secretary of the Imperial British East Africa Company, *British East Africa or Ibea*. A history of the formation and work of the Imperial British East Africa Company, London, Chapman and Hall, Ltd., 1893.

Milner, Viscount, *England in Egypt*, Edward Arnold, publisher to H. M. India Office, London, 1904.

Moon, Parker T., *Imperialism and World Politics*, New York, Macmillan Co., 1930.

Neuman, W. A., Dean of Cape Town, *Biographical Memoir of John Montague* during his administration as Colonial Secretary, 1843-1853. Cape Town, Harrison, London and Robertson, 1855.

Newton, A. P. and Ewing, J., *The British Empire since 1783*, London, Methuen & Co., 1929.

Nys, Ernest, *The Independent State of the Congo and International Law*, J. Lebègue & Cie, Brussels, 1904.

Politician's Handbook. A Review and Digest of the State Papers,— Diplomatic Correspondence, Reports of Royal Commissions, Select Committees, Treaties, Consular Reports, Sessions 1900 and 1901, etc. by H. Whates, Vacher & Sons, Westminster, London.

Prout, Major H. G., *Province of Kordofan*, General Report, published by the Egyptian General Staff, Cairo, 1877.

Rose, J. Holland, *Development of the European Nations, 1870-1900*, 2 vols., G. P. Putnam's Sons, New York and London, Knickerbocker Press, 1905.

Rodd, Sir J. Rennell, *Social and Diplomatic Memoirs, 1894-1901* (second series), vol. ii, London, Edward Arnold & Co., 1923.

Sanderson, *Great Britain in Modern Africa*, London, Seeley & Co., 1907.

Smuts, General J. C., *Africa and Some World Problems*, including the Rhodes Memorial Lectures delivered in Michaelmas Term, 1929, Oxford, the Clarendon Press, 1930.

Stanley, Henry Morton, *In Darkest Africa or the Quest, Rescue and Retreat of Emin Governor of Equatoria*, 2 vols., New York, Charles Scribner's Sons, 1890.

Stanley, H. M., W. T. Stead, F. D. Lugard, J. Scott Keltie, Henry Norman, *Africa. Its Partition and Its Future*, New York, Dodd, Mead & Co., 1898.

Tucker, Alfred R., Bishop of Uganda, *Eighteen Years in Uganda and East Africa*, Edward Arnold, publisher to the India Office, 1911.

Walker, Eric A., *History of South Africa*, Longmans, Green & Co., Ltd., 1928.

——, *Lord De Villiers and His Times. South Africa, 1842-1914*, London, Constable & Co., Ltd., 1925.

Wauters, A. J., *L'État Indépendent du Congo*, Brussels, Librairie Falk Fils, 1899.

Williams, Gardner F., *The Diamond Mines of South Africa*, 2 vols., New York, B. F. Buck & Co., 1905.

Woolf, Leonard, *Commerce and Empire in Africa*, London, G. Allen and Unwin, Ltd., 1919.

Work, Ernest, *Ethiopia: A Pawn in European Diplomacy*, New York, The Macmillan Co., 1935.

Worsfold, Basil, *Lord Milner's Work in South Africa*, Kegan Paul, Trench, Trubner & Co., Ltd., London, E. P. Dutton & Co., New York, 1913.

Zimmermann, *The German Empire of Central Africa*, New York, George H. Doran & Co., 1918.

II. HISTORY OF RAILWAYS IN AFRICA

Baltzer, Franz Adolph Wilhelm, *Die Erschliessung Afrikas durch Eisenbahnen*, Dietrich Reimer, Berlin, 1913.

——, *Die Kolonialbahnen mit besonderer Berucksichtigung-Afrikas*, G. J. Goschen Verlagshandlung, Berlin, 1916.

Berge, J., *Le Chemin de Fer Transafricain de l'Algérie au Cap*, Extrait du correspondent avec quelques notes supplémentaires, Louis de Soyle, Imprimeur, Paris, 1912.

Bourrat, Charles, *Les Chemins de fer en Afrique et Leur rôle dans l'expansion Coloniale*, Perpignan, J. Martz, 1910.

Meyer, H. de, *Die Eisenbahnen in tropischen Afrika*, Leipzig, 1902.

Renty, E. A. de, *Les Chemins de fer Coloniaux en Afrique*, Paris, 1904.

Roumens, *L'Imperialisme français et les Chemins de fer trans-Africains*, Plon-Nourrit et Cie., Paris, 1914.

Van der Poel, Jean, *The Railway and Customs Policy of the South African States and Colonies, 1885-1910*, Imperial Studies Series, Longmans, Green & Co., London.

Talbot, Frederick A., *The Railway Conquest of the World*, W. Heinemann, London, 1911.

Weinthal, Leo, editor of *The Story of the Cape to Cairo Railway and River Route, 1887-1922*, 4 vols., with a collection of maps. Contains accounts of railway, telegraph and commercial development in Africa by men who were, and some of whom still are, active in promoting such undertaking in Africa, The Pioneer Publishing Company, London, 1923.

Williams, Sir Robert, addresses:

(1) *Milestones of African Civilization* read at the meeting of the Royal Colonial Institute, May 8, 1917, printed in *United Empire Magazine*, 1917, vol. viii, pp. 446-463 and in pamphlet form.

(2) *The Cape to Cairo Ralway*, address to the African Society, April 21, 1921. Pamphlet 4x in the Royal Empire Society.

(3) *An African-Romance and Development*. Story of the Cape to Cairo Railway. *South Africa*, Sept. 7, 1918, pp. 370-373.

(4) *The Cape to Cairo Railway from the Point of View of African Development*. Address at a meeting of the Central Asian Society, April 5, 1922, printed in *Journal of the Central Asian Society*, vol. ix, 1922, pp. 147-166.

Michell, Hon. Sir Lewis, *The Cape to Cairo Railway*, Paper read before the Society of Arts, December 4 and printed in *Journal of the Society of Arts*, vol. lv, November, 1906, pp. 97-109.

III. BIOGRAPHIES

A. *Alfred Beit*

Seymour, Fort G., *Alfred Beit, A Study of the Man and His Works*, London, Ivor, Nicholson and Watson, 1932.

B. *Joseph Chamberlain*

Garvin, J. L., *The Life of Joseph Chamberlain*, 2 vols., London, Macmillan & Co., Ltd., 1932.

C. *Emin Pasha*

Schweitzer, Georg, *Emin Pasha. His Life and Works*, compiled from his journals, letters, scientific notes and from official documents, 2 vols., Westminster, London, Archibald Constable & Co., 1898.

D. *Gordon, Colonel Charles*

Achille Biovès, *Gordon Pacha*, Albert Fontenoing Éditeur, Paris, 1907.

Abdullah, Achmed, *Dreamers of Empire*, New York, Frederick A. Stokes Co., 1929.

Briefe und Tagebuchblätter des Generals Charles of Khartoum ausgewählt und übersetzt von Dr. Max Goos, Hamburg, Gutenberg-Verlag, 1908.

Hill, George Birkbeck, *Colonel Gordon in Central Africa* from original letters and documents, Thos. de La Rue & Co., London, 1881.

E. *The Second Earl Granville.*

Fitzmaurice, Lord Edmund G. P., *The Life of Granville Leveson Gower, Second Earl Granville, K. G., 1815-1891*, 2 vols., London, Longmans, Green & Co., 1906.

F. *Sir William Harcourt*

Gardiner, A. G., *The Life of Sir William Harcourt*, 2 vols., London, Constable & Co., Ltd., 1923.

G. *Jan Hofmeyer*

Hofmeyer, J. H., *The Life of Jan Hendrik Hofmeyer, " Onze Jan,"* Cape Town, Van de Sandt–de Villiers Printing Co., Ltd., 1913.

H. *Sir Harry Hamilton Johnston*

Johnston, Alexander, *Life and Letters of Sir Harry Johnston*, London, J. Cape, 1929.

Johnston, Sir H. H., *The Story of My Life*, London, Chatto and Windus and also Bobbs-Merrill Co., Ltd., 1923.

I. *Kitchener*

Arthur, Sir George, *Life of Lord Kitchener*, 3 vols., The Macmillan Co., 1920.

Ballard, Brigadier-General Colon Robert, *Kitchener*, London, Faber & Faber, Ltd., 1930.

Davray, Henry D., *L'Oeuvre et le Prestige de Lord Kitchener*, Paris, Plon-Nourrit et Cie, 1917.

Grew, Edwin S., *Kitchener*, 2 vols., London, Gresham Publishing Co., 1916.

Rye, James B., *Kitchener in His Own Words*, London, F. Fisher, Unwin, Ltd. (undated but written sometime after Kitchener's death).

J. *Paul Kruger*

The Memoirs of Paul Kruger, 2 vols., London, F. Fisher Unwin, Ltd., 1902.

K. *David Livingstone*

Blaikie, William Garden, *The Personal Life of David Livingstone*, New York, Harper & Bros., 1881.

L. *Cecil John Rhodes*

I have cited both monographs and periodical articles in this list in order to keep the Rhodes material together.

Abdullah, Achmed, *Dreamers of Empire*, New York, Frederick A. Stokes Co., 1929.

Baker, Herbert, *Cecil Rhodes* by his Architect, London, Oxford University Press, 1934.

——, " Reminiscences of Cecil Rhodes," *The Nineteenth Century and After*, vol. 87, 1920, pp. 88-102.

Bourelly, Général, " Cecil Rhodes," *Le Correspondent*, n. s. 162, 190, pp. 572-599.

Cust, H., " Cecil Rhodes," *North American Review*, vol. 175, Jl.–Dec., 1902, pp. 99-114.

Decle, Lionel, " The Fashoda Question," *Fortnightly Review*, n. s., vol. 64, 1898.

Dicey, Edward, " Cecil Rhodes in Egypt," *Fortnightly Review*, vol. 77, 1902.

——, " Rhodes Redivivus," *Fortnightly Review*, n. s., vol. 64, 1898.

Fuller, Sir Thomas E., *The Right Honourable Cecil John Rhodes*, Longmans, Green & Co., London, 1910.

Garrett, F. Edmund, an editor of the *Cape Times*, " The Character of Cecil Rhodes," *Contemporary Review*, vol. 81, Jan.–June, 1902, pp. 761-779.

Grogan, Ewart Scott, "Cecil Rhodes," *World's Work*, vol. i, Nov., 1900–April, 1901, pp. 367-371.

Hensman, Howard, *Cecil Rhodes*, William Blackwood & Sons, Edinburgh and London, 1901.

Imperialist, *Cecil Rhodes*. A Biography and Appreciation by Imperialist with Personal Reminiscences by Dr. Jameson, Chapman & Hall, Ltd., London, 1897.

Ivan-Müller, E. B., "Cecil John Rhodes," *The Fortnightly Review*, vol. 77, May, 1902, pp. 741-761.

Jadot, Louis, "Cecil Rhodes," *La Nouvelle Revue, n. s.* 15, March–April, 1902, pp. 457-470.

Jourdan, Phillip, Cecil Rhodes, *His Private Life by His Private Secretary*, John Lane Co., London and New York, 1911.

Krause, Gustav, "Gespräche mit Cecil Rhodes," *Deutsche Revue*, Jahrig, 24, July–December, 1899, pp. 112-119.

Lockhart, John Gilbert, *Cecil Rhodes*, London, Duckworth, 1933.

Low, Sidney, "Personal Recollections of Cecil Rhodes," *The Living Age*, vol. xv, April–June, 1902, pp. 577-587.

Le Sueur, Gordon, *Cecil Rhodes. The Man and His Work*, John Murray, London, 1913.

Macdonald, J. G., *Rhodes, A Life*, Phillip Allen & Co., Ltd., London, 1927.

Michell, Sir Lewis, *The Life of the Right Honourable Cecil John Rhodes, 1853-1902*, 2 vols., Edward Arnold, London, 1910.

Millin, Sarah Gertrude, *Cecil Rhodes*, Chatto & Windus, London, 1933

"Mr. Rhodes, Lord Rosebery and Mr. Gladstone. A Page of Unwritten History," *The Outlook*, London, vol. ii, January, 1899, p. 780.

Plomer, William C. F., *Cecil Rhodes*, D. Appleton and Co., New York, 1933.

Stead, W. T., "Cecil John Rhodes," *American Monthly Review*, vol. xxv, Jan.–June, 1902, pp. 548-560.

——, "Character Sketch. Cecil Rhodes of Africa," *Review of Reviews*, vol. xx, Jl.–Dec., 1899, pp. 451-462.

——, *The Last Will and Testament of Cecil John Rhodes* with elucidatory notes, edited by W. T. Stead, *Review of Reviews* Office, London, 1902.

Sauer, Hans, "Cecil Rhodes," *Empire Review*, May, 1902, pp. 363-378.

Warren, Charles, "Cecil Rhodes' Early Days in South Africa," *Contemporary Review*, vol. 81, Jan. to June, 1902, pp. 643-654.

Weinthal, Leo, *The Story of the Cape to Cairo Railway and River Route, 1887-1922*, vol. i, Sketches about Cecil Rhodes by Walford

Dowling, Manfred Nathan, Sir Percy Fitzpatrick and General Smuts.

Williams, Basil, *Cecil Rhodes,* Henry Holt & Co., New York, 1921.

Verschoyle, F., under the pseudonym Vindex, *Cecil Rhodes. His Political Life and Speeches, 1881-1900,* Chapman and Hall, London, 1900.

Viallete, Achille, " Cecil Rhodes," *Revue de Paris,* vol. ii, 1900, pp. 47-71.

M. *Lord Rosebery*

Coates, Thomas, F. G., *Lord Rosebery. His Life and Speeches,* 2 vols., E. P. Dutton & Co., New York, 1900.

Crewe, K. G., Marquess of, *Lord Rosebery,* New York, Harper Bros., 1931.

The Foreign Policy of Lord Rosebery. Two Chapters in Recent Politics 1886 and 1892-1895. With extracts from Lord Rosebery's Speeches, Arthur L. Humphreys, Piccadilly, London, 1901.

N. *The Marquis of Salisbury*

Cecil, Lady Gwendolyn, *Life of Robert, Marquis of Salisbury* by his daughter, vols. i-iv, Hodder and Stoughton, Ltd., London, 1921-1932.

Whates, H., *The Third Salisbury Administration, 1895-1900,* with maps, treaties and other diplomatic papers, Vacher & Sons, Westminster, London, 1900.

O. *Stanley, Henry Morton*

The Autobiography of Henry M. Stanley, edited by his wife, Dorothy Stanley, Houghton Mifflin Co., The Riverside Press, Cambridge, 1909.

IV. NEWSPAPERS

A. South Africa

The South African Commercial Advertiser, 1845-1856.
The Government Gazette.
The Cape Argus.

B. England

The London Times.
The Economist.
Herapath's Railway and Commercial Journals.

V. PERIODICALS

Black, J. Boisse de, " Statistique Concernant Les Trafics des Réseaux Africains. Leurs Possibilités D'Avenir," *Journal de la Société de Statistique de Paris,* vol. 61, May, 1920, pp. 123-134.

British South Africa. Information of the Country and Press Notices, a convenient collection of press extracts about the Chartered Company, 1889. Collection kept in the Royal Empire Society library.

Cammaerts, N. E., " Le Cap au Caire. Sa Situation Actuelle," Bulletin de Colonisation Comparée, no. 8, August 20, 1912, pp. 338-342.

Caix, Robert de, " Les Allemands et le Cap au Caire," Bulletin Mensuel du Comité de l'Afrique Françoise et du Comité du Maroc, fondé par Harry Alis, vol. 23, September, 1913, pp. 317-319.

Christy, C., " The Cape to Cairo Railway," Scottish Geographical Magazine, vol. 40, November, 1924, pp. 331-334.

Demangeon, A., " The Cape to Cairo Dream," The Living Age, vol. 335, January, 1929, pp. 365-368 and 398.

Dicey, Edward, " The Future of Egypt," Nineteenth Century, vol. ii, August, 1877, pp. 1-14.

Diplomaticus, " The Anglo-German Agreement," Fortnightly Review, vol. 64, London, 1898, pp. 627-634.

Earle, E. M., " Egyptian Cotton and the American Civil War," Political Science Quarterly, 1926, vol. xli, pp. 520-545.

Freeman, Lewis R., " Rhodes' 'All Red' Route. The War's Effect upon the Cape-to-Cairo Railway," The World's Work, vol. 27, London, 1916, pp. 159-177.

Gladstone, W. E., " Aggression on Egypt and Freedom in the East," Nineteenth Century, vol ii, August, 1877, pp. 149-166.

Johnston, Sir H. H., " Railway Projects in Africa and the Near East," The Nineteenth Century and After, vol. 72, London, 1912, pp. 558-569.

Johnston, Alex., " Fresh Fields for African Railways," Journal of the African Society, April, 1903, pp. 271-280.

Langer, William L., " The Struggle for the Nile," Foreign Affairs, January, 1936, vol. xiv, pp. 259-273.

Lewin, P. E., " Cape to Cairo Railway," African World, vol. xxiv, London, 1911, pp. 863-864.

McIlwraith, Malcolm, " The Delagoa Bay Arbitration," Fortnightly Review, vol. 74, London, 1900, pp. 410-429.

Metcalfe, Sir Charles, H. F., " Railway Development of Africa, Present and Future," Geographical Journal, vol. 27, London, 1916, pp. 3-20.

Renty, E. de., " Deux Transafricains Anglais," Questions Diplomatiques, vol. xiv, 1910, pp. 471-473.

Ricarde-Seaver, Major F. J. and Metcalfe, Sir Charles, " The British Sphere of Influence in South Africa," Fortnightly Review, vol. 51, n. s., March, 1889, pp. 351-352.

Sivewright, James, " South African Telegraphs," Journal of the Society of Telegraph Engineers, vol. viii, 1879, pp. 177-212. Paper read at the seventy-sixth ordinary general meeting of the society, March, 26, 1879.

Sharpe, Sir A., "Back-bone of Africa," *Geographical Journal*, vol. 52, 1918, pp. 141-157.

Shepstone, H. J., "Cape to Cairo Railroad," *Westminster*, vol. 21, August, 1912, pp. 83-91.

Stern, W. B., "The Treaty Background of the Italo-Ethiopian Dispute," *The American Journal of International Law*, vol. 30, no. 2, April, 1936, pp. 189-203.

Streit, Clarence K., "Britain Gave Italy Rights Under Secret Pact in 1891 to Rule Most of Ethiopia," *N. Y. Times*, July 22, 1935, p. 1 columns g and p. 9, columns b, c, d, e and f.

Vernon, S. P., "Cape to Cairo Railway," *Liberia Bulletin*, no. 16, 1899, pp. 30-40.

Williams, Judith B., "The Development of British Trade with West Africa," *Political Science Quarterly*, vol. l, June, 1935, pp. 194-213.

Woolbert, Robert Gale, "Italy in Abyssinia," *Foreign Affairs*, vol. xiii, no. 3, April, 1935, pp. 499-508.

VI. PROCEEDINGS OF THE ROYAL GEOGRAPHICAL SOCIETY

Old Series, vol. 21, 1877, pp. 16-19. Address of Sir Rutherford Alcock, president of the society, at the opening of the forty-seventh session. Mentions prospects of a telegraph line from Khartoum to the Diamond Fields.

Old Series, vol. 21, 1877, pp. 388-396. African Exploration Fund. Remarks about the International Conference at Brussels, September, 1876.

Old Series, vol. 21, 1877, p. 601. Meeting of the African Exploration Fund Committee, July 19.

Old Series, vol. 21, 1877, p. 606. Remarks by Sir Rutherford Alcock on the prospective Overland Telegraph.

Old Series, vol. 21, 1877, pp. 613-615. Proposals of Sir H. Barkly concerning the opening of Central Africa and remarks by Kerry Nichols concerning the proposed Overland Telegraph.

Old Series, vol. 21, 1877, pp. 616-632, Minute of a Conference concerning the feasibility of a line of Overland Telegraph through Africa to connect the lines in South Africa with those of Egypt.

Old Series, vol. 22, 1878, pp. 7-28. Address of the president at the opening of the session, November 12, 1877. Remarks on the International Conference at Brussels and on the prospects of an Overland Telegraph through Africa.

Old Series, vol. 22, 1878, pp. 224-225. Remarks by R. Frewen, Esq., on "spanning the as yet unconnected link between the Cape of Good Hope and the Mediterranean Sea," and Remarks by St. Vincent Erskine.

Old Series, vol. 22, 1878, p. 254. Remarks of Stanley on penetration into the heart of Africa.

Old Series, vol. 22, 1878, pp. 473-475. Remarks of Colonel Grant, Sir Harry Verney and Frewen on the Overland Telegraph.

New Series, vol. 1, 1879, p. 63. Keith Johnston's East African Expedition. Relationship of that expedition to plans for the proposed Overland Telegraph.

New Series, vol. 1, 1879, pp. 123-124. "Overland Telegraph through Africa." History of the part taken by the Royal Geographical Society in promoting the project.

New Series, vol. 1, 1879, pp. 217-218. Correspondence concerning the Overland Telegraph.

New Series, vol. 1, 1879, pp. 264-271. Report of a conference "to consider the feasibility of a line of Overland Telegraph through Africa, to connect the lines in South Africa with those of Egypt."

VII. PAMPHLETS

Nicholls, pamphlet listed under the name Nicholls in the library of the Royal Geographical Society. Contains memoranda by Edwin Arnold, Kerry Nicolls and Colonel J. A. Grant on the Overland Telegraph.

Metcalfe, Sir Charles, *The Cape-to-Cairo Line. How the War may solve a Problem. South Africa*, Dec. 19, 1914. Pamphlet 4 x 4 in the Library of the Royal Empire Society.

Pamphlet Z. 68., 13 in the library of the Royal Geographical Society. Contains reports and correspondence concerning the Overland Telegraph project.

INDEX

Abbas Pasha I, Suez railway proposal, 32

Abercorn, Fort, *see* Abercorn, Duke of

Abercorn, James Hamilton, 2d Duke of, 148, 180, 148, n112, 428

Aborigines Protection Society, 101, 143

Abu Hamed, railway to, 360, 361

Abyssinia, *see* Ethiopia

Addis Ababa, Captain Clochette at, 328, 329, 363, 364; Rodd Mission to, 366, 367; Russian Missions to, 327

Aden, Red Sea port, 31, 60, 64, 61

Adowa, Italian defeat at, 336, 354; Italian occupation of, 335

Aeroplane flights, *Daily Telegraph*, n20, 413, n67, 471

Africa: anglicizing, dreams of, 23, 66-70, 201-202; awakening interest in, 34-44, 47-48, 51-52, 54-55, 104-107, 129, 237-238, 253-254; British expansion in, 21, 25-34, 40-41, 67-68, 70-71, 89, 100, 109-112, 115, 120-122, 126-128, 130-136, 149, 165-169, 170-182, 232-238, 244-268, 269-279, 280-286, 288-298, 307-312, 323, 329-333, 337-338, 351-362, 363, 366-383, 390-393; communications with, 44-46, 58-60, n1, 412; explorations in, 29, 34-38, 51-56, 129, 131, 170, 171-173, 181, 199, 200, 233-241, 244-246, 250-256, 259, 280-283, 298, 301-304, 325, 328, 338-339, 340-341, 363-366, 368-371, 397-398; indifference to, 25, 377-378

African International Association, 238-239

African Lakes Company, 170, 173-174

Afrikander Bond, effect of raid on, 206; influence of, 82, 83; Rhodes' cooperation with, 84-85, 206

Ahmed, Mohammed, *see* Mahdists

Akasheh, railway to, 358

Albert, Lake, *see* Albert Nyanza

Albert Nyanza, Lake Albert: agreement of 1890, 299-300; exploration of, 37, 234

(Albert) Edward, Lake, *see* Edward, Lake

Albuquerque, Major Mousinho da, Portuguese loan, 210

Alcock, Sir Rutherford, Overland Telegraph scheme, 55; transportation in Africa, 45

Alexandria, bombardment of, 281; railway from, 31-32; Telegraph to, *see* Overland Telegraph

Amandebele tribe, *see* Matabeleland

Amatongaland, annexation of, 89, 184

Amba Allagi, Italian defeat at, 354

Ambabo, French foothold at, 325

America, *see* United States of America

Amiens, Treaty of, *see* Treaties and Agreements

Anderson, Sir Percy, Africa, interest in, 133; Anglo-German treaty of 1890, 259, 260, 265, 317; Cape-to-Cairo corridor, 316, 317, n68, 449

Anglo-Boer relations, *see* Transvaal

Anglo-Congolese Agreement of 1894, *see also*, Treaties and Agreements: Agreement of 1890, relation to, 299-301; Bahr-el-Ghazal, lease of, Article II, 308, 312-315, 320-322; British defense of, 311, 312, 314-315, 319-320; British sphere of influence in, 307, 308, 310, 323; Cape-to-Cairo Corridor in, Article III, 23, 309-311, 313-317, 319-320, 323, n55, 458; French opposition to, 312-315, 338; German opposition to, 312, 316-320; Telegraph clause in, Article V, 310, 324

489